Emily Dickinson's

Music Book

and the

Musical Life

of an

American Poet

Emily Dickinson's MUSIC BOOK and the MUSICAL LIFE of an AMERICAN POET

George Boziwick

University of Massachusetts Press
Amherst and Boston

Copyright © 2022 by University of Massachusetts Press
All rights reserved
Printed in the United States of America

ISBN 978-1-62534-659-9 (paper); 660-5 (hardcover)

Designed by Sally Nichols
Set in Baskerville
Printed and bound by Books International, Inc.

Cover design by Kristina Kachele Design, llc
Cover art: William Morris pattern.
Matthew Carrigan / Alamy Stock Photo.

Library of Congress Cataloging-in-Publication Data
Names: Boziwick, George, 1954– author.
Title: Emily Dickinson's music book and the musical life of an American poet / George Boziwick.
Description: Amherst : University of Massachusetts Press, [2022] | Includes bibliographical references and index.
Identifiers: LCCN 2021054480 (print) | LCCN 2021054481 (ebook) | ISBN 9781625346599 (paperback) | ISBN 9781625346605 (hardcover) | ISBN 9781613769379 (ebook) | ISBN 9781613769386 (ebook)
Subjects: LCSH: Dickinson, Emily, 1830–1886—Knowledge and learning. | Music appreciation. | Dickinson, Emily, 1830–1886—Criticism and interpretation. | Music and literature—History—19th century. | LCGFT: Literary criticism.
Classification: LCC PS1541.Z5 B556 2022 (print) | LCC PS1541.Z5 (ebook) | DDC 811/.4—dc23/eng/20220324
LC record available at https://lccn.loc.gov/2021054480
LC ebook record available at https://lccn.loc.gov/2021054481

British Library Cataloguing-in-Publication Data
A catalog record for this book is available from the British Library.

Portions of chapters 1, 4, 5, 7, 8, 9, 10, and 11 were adapted with permission from a series of eight public musicology performance programs co-authored by George Boziwick and Trudy Williams, 2012–2018: "The Musical Parlor of Emily Dickinson," 2012, revised 2013; "'My Business is to Sing': Emily Dickinson, Musician and Poet," 2015; "'My Wars are laid away in Books — ': Emily Dickinson's Music Book: A Prelude to the Civil War," 2015; "Emily Dickinson in Her Elements: Accomplished Musician, Emerging Poet," 2015; "Musicians Wrestle Everywhere — ': Music, Nature, Hymnody, and the Poetic Conversion of Emily Dickinson," 2017; "Dickinson's Musical Eden. Emily and Lavinia: Music Making at the Homestead," 2017; "Emily and Lavinia: Music Making and Dickinson's Eden," 2018. Copyright © 2012–2018 George Boziwick and Trudy Williams. All rights reserved.

Earlier versions of portions of chapters 1, 4, 5, 7, 9, 10, 11, and 12 were previously published in the following "'My Business is to Sing': Emily Dickinson's Musical Borrowings," *Journal of the Society for American Music* 8, no. 2 (2014): 130–66. Copyright © The Society for American Music, published by Cambridge University Press. Reproduced with permission of the Licensor through PLSclear; "Emily Dickinson's Music Book: A Performative Exploration," *Emily Dickinson Journal* 25, no. 1 (2016): 83–105. Copyright © 2016 Johns Hopkins University Press. Reproduced with permission by Johns Hopkins University Press.

The Poems of Emily Dickinson: Reading Edition, edited by Ralph W. Franklin. Cambridge, MA: The Belknap Press of Harvard University Press, Copyright © 1998, 1999 by the President and Fellows of Harvard College. Copyright © 1951, 1955 by the President and Fellows of Harvard College. Copyright © renewed 1979, 1983 by the President and Fellows of Harvard College. Copyright © 1914, 1918, 1919, 1924, 1929, 1930, 1932, 1935, 1937, 1942 by Martha Dickinson Bianchi. Copyright © 1952, 1957, 1958, 1963, 1965 by Mary L. Hampson. Used by permission. All rights reserved.

The Letters of Emily Dickinson, edited by Thomas H. Johnson, Associate Editor, Theodora Ward. Cambridge, MA: The Belknap Press of Harvard University Press, Copyright © 1958 by the President and Fellows of Harvard College. Copyright © renewed 1986 by the President and Fellows of Harvard College. Copyright © 1914, 1924, 1932, 1942 by Martha Dickinson Bianchi. Copyright © 1952 by Alfred Leete Hampson. Copyright © 1960 by Mary L. Hampson. Used by permission. All rights reserved.

to Stephanie, Anna, and Emily

Contents

Preface ix
Acknowledgments xi

Prelude
1

CHAPTER 1
Childhood
"I attend singing school"
19

CHAPTER 2
School Days
"You know what it is to 'love school'"
26

CHAPTER 3
The Avid Music Collector
"Home as a Waltz"
46

CHAPTER 4
The Age of the Virtuosi
"I never heard sounds before"
65

CHAPTER 5
Home Music-Making
"Sounds From Home"
84

CHAPTER 6
Edward Dickinson
"Hail to the Chief"
94

CHAPTER 7
Music-Making and the Dickinson Family Correspondence
"Vinnie is at the instrument"
104

CHAPTER 8
The American Political Struggle
"Decades of Arrogance"
115

CHAPTER 9
Fiddle Tunes, Minstrel Music, and Musical Borrowing
"No Black bird bates His Banjo — "
131

CHAPTER 10
The Poetry Takes Hold
" — and the noise in the Pool, at Noon — excels my Piano"
145

CHAPTER 11
Hymns and Ballads: More Musical Borrowings
"Let Emily sing for you because she cannot pray."
154

CHAPTER 12
The White Dress
"Ossian's Serenade"
162

POSTLUDE
"Musicians wrestle everywhere"
168

Appendix A   175
Contents Listing of Emily Dickinson's
Bound Volume of Sheet Music

Notes   185

Index   227

An annotated bibliography of Emily Dickinson's bound volume of sheet music in the Emily Dickinson Collection, Houghton Library, Harvard University (Appendix B); a checklist of music titles cited in the Dickinson family correspondence not included in Emily Dickinson's bound volume of sheet music (Appendix C); and audio recordings of selections from Emily Dickinson's bound music book are available online at http://umpressopen.library.umass.edu/projects/emily-dickinsons-music-book.

Preface

Who knew that before there was poetry in the life of Emily Dickinson, there was music? As a young woman, Dickinson was an ambitious student of voice and piano. She attended concerts with her family and collected a large amount of published sheet music to perform at home.

While many women of Dickinson's time and social class played the piano and collected sheet music, this biographical and musical detail from Emily Dickinson's life had its own particular musical reverberations for me. My first encounter with Dickinson's poetry was as a twenty-one-year-old composer. Armed with my first commission to set three of her poems, I found that "the music seemed to write itself."[1] Why was that? I would come to learn that I was not the first composer to experience that musical magic about her poetry; and it wasn't until reading Richard Sewall's 1974 biography of Dickinson that I learned that Emily Dickinson was a musician before she was a poet.

Indeed, Dickinson was very musical, and while this musicality has been widely discussed in relation to her poetry and correspondence, there was yet to emerge a full consideration of Emily Dickinson's daily musical life. That vision was brought to life when Trudy Williams and I co-authored a series of programs animating the life of Emily Dickinson, performed by our Red Skies Music Ensemble, which we co-founded in 2010. Those programs explored the many facets of Dickinson's early musical life and the music Dickinson, knew, performed, and collected. This book continues and enlarges those explorations, examining Dickinson the musician/poet through the lens of music history, situating her as a fully engaged and ambitious musician from the years of her first piano, acquired in 1845, until her poetry emerges in the 1850s.

During those formative musical years, Emily Dickinson, like other women of her time, collected a great deal of published sheet music. At the conclusion of her music studies, as was the custom, this music was bound into a keepsake book. Emily Dickinson's large bound volume of sheet music, which is in the Dickinson Collection in the Houghton Library at Harvard University, guides the historical narrative of this book. Discovering the stories behind the music Dickinson collected animates both her daily musical life and the historical and cultural events of her time that affected the Dickinson family and Emily herself.

While she was deeply engaged with music, there was another gravitational pull arising in the young Emily Dickinson, and according to her biographer Sewall, "as her practical interest in music declined, her metaphorical interest increased."[2] That aspect of Dickinson's musical life resonated with my own story of being a composer and, later, a music librarian. The fact that Dickinson may have made a conscious transition from musician to poet, according to Sewall, fascinated me and is given thoughtful consideration in a chapter later in the book.

This book covers virtually everything musical about Dickinson. Most importantly, it is the first time that each one of the 107 pieces of music in Dickinson's bound volume of published sheet music is thoroughly examined, animating and positioning Dickinson as a keen observer of her culture and her world, well beyond her town of Amherst, Massachusetts. Contextualizing all of this music into the historical setting and chronology of Dickinson's time and place is a hefty task. Guiding me in this endeavor is my passion since childhood for US history and my many years as a music librarian (particularly as Curator of American Music) at The New York Public Library for the Performing Arts, located at Lincoln Center. The sheet music holdings of the Performing Arts Library are some of the finest in the world, and my intimate daily experiences with these and other collections both behind the scenes and in assisting scholars and the general reader across the reference desk have been an enormous and fortunate asset to the writing of this book. For that I am very grateful.

Acknowledgments

Very special thanks go first to Trudy Williams. Much of my research for this book began in preparation for our co-authored programs on Emily Dickinson and music (2012–2018) performed by The Red Skies Music Ensemble, which Trudy and I co-founded in 2010 with the mission of making archives and special collections come alive through research and performance. Trudy's public musicology model proved to be enormously successful, and indeed these programs were great fun to produce and share with a wide and appreciative audience. I'm not sure this book would have come to exist without Trudy's critical interpretations and contributions during our fruitful collaboration over many years.

I am additionally grateful for Trudy's theatrical expertise, which brought our programs to life onstage, and to The Red Skies Music Ensemble performers and technical staff for our Dickinson programs, whose performances and skills helped turn Emily Dickinson's life into engaging musical and theatrical events: Will Armstrong, Sara Banleigh, Brendan Dolan, the late great Phil Forbes, Laura Hankin, Jeaninne Intriago, Suzanne Lenz, Jared Libby, George Marshall, Don Meade, Rob Meador, Catherine Miller, Mark Russo, and Elise Toscano, joined by Trudy as bass player and myself as harmonica player and in the role of narrator.

My professional career as a music librarian gave me multiple opportunities to research and present programs and papers on a variety of musical subjects. These activities were supported by Jacqueline Z. Davis, former Executive Director of The New York Public Library for the Performing Arts (LPA), who also provided constant support throughout my eleven-year tenure as Chief of the library's Music Division. I owe a great deal to so many at LPA, especially Tema Hecht, who was often my right hand, for which I am very grateful. Assistant Curator of Music and Recorded Sound Jessica Wood; Music Librarian, Rare Books and Manuscripts, Bob Kosovsky; Reference Librarian Dave McMullen; and Managing Librarian of Music and Recorded Sound Rebecca Littman have all been enormously helpful. Linda Murray, Curator of the Jerome Robbins Dance Division, has been a wonderful and supportive colleague. Thanks also to Tanisha Jones of the Dance Division for her kind and enthusiastic assistance. Indeed, all of the staff at LPA have encouraged me in one way or another, many of them waiting in great anticipation for me to inevitably find an opportunity to drop a relevant anecdote about Emily Dickinson into our staff meetings. Last but not least, the former LPA Public Programs staff—Alan Pally, Cheryl Raymond, Betsey Perlmutter, and Evan Leslie—all have my praise and complete gratitude. A number of my former colleagues at the Forty-second Street Library have also been very helpful; in particular I would like to thank Tal Nadan of the Archives and Manuscripts Division; Ruth Carr (retired) of the Milstein Division of United States History, Local History and Genealogy; and Thomas Lisanti, (retired) Manager, Permissions and Reproduction Services.

To the staff of the Houghton Library at Harvard University, my sincere thanks go to Leslie Morris, the Gore Vidal Curator of Modern Books and Manuscripts, for her assistance with the Dickinson Collection and for invaluable discussions about Dickinson and her music book, and the Dickinson piano. Thanks also to Assistant Curator, Christine Jacobson. Thanks to John Overholt, Curator of The Donald and Mary Hyde Collection of Dr. Samuel Johnson/Early Books & Manuscripts, for his expertise and advice on issues concerning descriptive bibliography. Thanks also to Heather Cole, formerly at Houghton, for her assistance early on with Dickinson's music book, and thanks to Mary Haegert for assisting me with digital reproductions from Dickinson's music book. To Katie Callam, former Houghton Library Bibliographic Assistant and PhD in historical musicology, I owe a great deal of thanks for her close reading of the book manuscript and annotated bibliography, and her superb work in producing the updated and detailed catalog record of the Dickinson music book for the Houghton Library, which I relied on a great deal in compiling my annotated online bibliography of

Dickinson's music book. I can never say enough about my former New York Public Library colleague and friend Andrea Cawelti, the Ward Music Cataloger at the Houghton Library, for her tremendous enthusiasm and advice on descriptive bibliography and other matters, particularly her close reading of the annotated bibliography, and her research assistance on some very difficult and obscure identities within the pages of Dickinson's bound music book.

I wish to thank the Special Collections staff at the Mount Holyoke College Archives: Deborah Richards, the College Archivist; and Leslie Fields, Head of Archives and Special Collections. At Yale University, the public services staff, and in particular Michael Frost of Manuscripts and Archives in the Sterling Memorial Library have been very helpful. I am also grateful to my Yale University colleagues Suzanne Eggleston Lovejoy, Music Librarian for Access and Research Services, and Ruthann McTyre, Director of the Irving S. Gilmore Music Library, for their expertise, support, and years of friendship. That same friendship and camaraderie extends to my colleagues Gerry Szymanski and Jim Farrington at the Eastman School of Music in Rochester, New York, for their assistance with Jenny Lind research and for sharing with me information about the Sibley Music Library's "Home, Sweet Home" Collection. At the Rochester Public Library, my thanks go to Michelle Finn, Deputy Historian, City of Rochester, and Senior Historical Researcher, Rochester Public Library; Brandon Fess, Librarian, Local History & Genealogy Division; and Library Assistant Jordan Wallance of the Rochester Public Library.

Thanks to Ray Heigemeir, Public Services Librarian at the Stanford University Music Library, for additional assistance with Jenny Lind research. Thanks also to the reference staff at Brown University, and particularly my now retired library colleague Ned Quist, former Associate University Librarian for Research and Outreach Services. Grateful thanks to Karen Morse of the University of Rhode Island Archives in Kingston, Rhode Island, for historical documentation on the St. John's Episcopal Church in Providence.

In Amherst, Massachusetts, thanks to Tevis Kimball and Kate Boyle, formerly of the Jones Library; and a big note of thanks to Mike Kelly, Head, Archives and Special Collections in the Frost Library at Amherst College. Thanks to Jane Wald, Executive Director of the Emily

Dickinson Museum; and much thanks to Marta McDowell, Gardener in Residence of the Emily Dickinson Museum, for her explanations on japonicas, tulips, and other plant life at the Homestead that is reflected in some of the sheet music in Dickinson's bound volume.

I would like to thank the staff of the American Antiquarian Society, particularly Nan Wolverton, Director of the Center for Historic American Visual Culture, and Dan Boudreau, Assistant Head of Reader Services, both of whom have been so very helpful and generous with their time and resources. Thanks to Betsy Strauss of the Amenia Historical Society, Amenia, New York, for help with the history of the Amenia Seminary and the "Home Quick Step" written by former student William Smith and dedicated to Amenia Seminary trustee Dr. Luke W. Stanton. At the Historical Society in Cherry Valley, New York, my thanks go to Susan Murray-Miller, who was very helpful in identifying and sharing material relating to composer/teacher Jonathan Fowler of the Cherry Valley Female Academy. Thanks also to the staff of the Oneida County History Center in Utica, New York: Executive Director Rebecca McLain; Research Librarian Mary Pat Connors; and Director of Public Programs Patrick Reynolds. Thanks to Paula Lemire, Director of Historical Development at the Friends of Albany Rural Cemetery, and to Becky Chapin, Archivist at Historic Geneva in Geneva, New York.

There are a number of longtime colleagues from the Society for American Music who deserve my warm thanks for both their scholarship and support: Douglas Bomberger, Michael Broyles, Raoul Camus, Dale Cockrell, Richard Crawford, R. Allen Lott, Katherine Preston, Deane Root, Douglas Shadle, Denise Von Glahn, and especially Paul Wells for his expertise and assistance with the traditional fiddle repertoire in Dickinson's bound volume. Thanks also to Mark Katz, who as editor of the *Journal of the Society for American Music* in 2014 published my first article on Dickinson and her music book.

Others whose scholarship and support have meant a great deal to me include Emma Duncan, Chris Goertzen, Philip F. Gura, Wendy Tronrud, and R. H. Winnick. Thank you to musicologist and author Andrea Olmstead for her encouragement and advice; and thanks to pianist/composer Kit Young for sharing her invaluable musical insights into Dickinson's music book.

There are so many Emily Dickinson scholars to whom I owe much thanks. Many of them are my newest friends, and every one of them has been so supportive. Much of their fine scholarship fills the pages of this book. Thanks to Richard Brantley, Adeline Chevrier-Bosseau, Paul Crumbley, Jane Donahue Eberwein, Páraic Finnerty, Jonnie Guerra, Eleanor Heginbotham, Gerald Holmes, Samantha Landau, Daniel Manheim, Cristanne Miller, Eliza Richards, Martha Nell Smith, and Marta Werner. Thanks to Georgiana Strickland for reading an early version of my book and for bringing some important details about Dickinson and her family to my attention.

Thanks to Dickinson scholars Cristanne Miller and James Guthrie for shepherding, editing, and publishing my 2016 article on Dickinson's music book for the *Emily Dickinson Journal*, and especially to Cris Miller for suggesting that I show my book on Dickinson and music to the University of Massachusetts Press.

At the University of Massachusetts Press, thank you to Senior Editor Brian Halley; to the two anonymous readers whose reports were not only insightful but also a great read; to the UMass Faculty Board for their unanimous vote of confidence; and to Production Editor Rachael DeShano and Marketing and Sales Director Courtney Andree.

Finally, I thank my family—my wife, Stephanie Doba, and our daughters, Anna and Emily Boziwick—for their encouragement and support. This book is for them. It was providential that our daughter Anna attended the University of Massachusetts in Dickinson's hometown. Our many trips to Amherst during Anna's undergraduate years included my first visit to the Emily Dickinson Museum. And while our daughter Emily was named for my great-uncle Emil (which is also my middle name), and not for the subject of this book, having an Emily in our family is a blessing. Most of all, I owe thanks to Stephanie for her practical and emotional support over the years of this project, from taking research trips with me around the Northeast to lending her welcomed skills as my sounding board, first reader, and editor. Whether her prodding was on topic sentences or insisting that I not shy away from making that necessary phone call, her time and attention helped see me through.

Emily Dickinson's

Music Book

Musical Life

American Poet

PRELUDE

MANY HAVE BEEN DRAWN TO the American poet Emily Dickinson (1830–1886), but few who love her poetry also know that in Dickinson's early years, music occupied a significant place in her daily life. The Dickinson parlor in Amherst, Massachusetts, was a nexus of lively musical activity in which all of the family participated.[1]

Much of this musical activity finds expression in an important artifact of Emily Dickinson's early life: her bound volume of published sheet music, comprising a large selection of instrumental piano music and vocal music of her time. Like most young women of her era and class, Emily Dickinson took lessons in piano and voice, attended concerts, acquired sheet music, and engaged in home music-making. At the conclusion of those years of study, her music was bound into a book. This bound volume is part of the Emily Dickinson Collection in the Houghton Library of Harvard University.[2]

Exploring the 107 pieces in Dickinson's bound music volume provides the framework for this book. The stories behind the music, the composers who created these pieces, and Dickinson's encounters with the famous touring groups that performed them animate the trends and events in the cultural and political life of the young republic, affecting the Dickinson family and Emily herself. The backstories and cultural context of the music Dickinson heard, played, sang, and collected provide insight into the multiple layers of meaning that music held for her. As I explore the musical world of Emily Dickinson, the guiding principle of the story is in the music itself—the music with which Dickinson was fully engaged both inside and outside her bound music book: the hymns from her youth which she knew intimately, the vernacular music of the Dickinson servants, the concerts she attended, and the musical personalities she witnessed firsthand. All of these experiences will play a role in the overarching story of Emily Dickinson the musician, and the poet that she would become.

Emily Dickinson and Music

Emily Dickinson's poetry has long been acknowledged to have a musicality of expression. Judy Jo Small's *Positive as Sound: Emily Dickinson's Rhyme* (1990) examines in full detail the "prominence in her poetry of sound and music."[3] Dickinson's early familiarity with and poetic connection to the tradition of New England hymnody is another musical topic with a long and argued history, chiefly concerning Dickinson's borrowing from the meters of the hymnist Isaac Watts. This was first elucidated by Thomas Johnson in his 1955 *Interpretive Biography* of Dickinson.[4] Also significant for this discussion is Martha Winburn England's essay "Emily Dickinson and Isaac Watts" (1965).[5] The most in-depth and comprehensive exploration of Dickinson and the sacred music tradition of her time to date is Victoria Morgan's *Emily Dickinson and Hymn Culture*, published in 2010.[6] Morgan goes into and beyond the argument of metrical borrowing from Watts, delving deeply into Watts's imagery, parody, and tropes, a great deal of which was appropriated by Dickinson—the best known being Dickinson's poetic "busy bee."[7] Morgan also discusses Dickinson in relation to the leading female hymn writers of her day, a topic that will be an important element in our story of Dickinson the musician/poet.

Important studies centering on Dickinson's poetry and nineteenth-century culture include Barton Levi St. Armand's *Emily Dickinson and Her Culture: The Soul's Society* (1984).[8] Among studies of nineteenth-century culture that specifically discuss music is Cristanne Miller's *Reading in Time: Emily Dickinson in the Nineteenth Century* (2012). In her chapter "Hymn, the 'Ballad Wild,' and Free Verse," Miller explores and contextualizes Dickinson's engagements with nineteenth-century ballads and hymns as popular forms "for imitation and experiment."[9] Sandra Runzo's *"Theatricals of Day": Emily Dickinson and Nineteenth-Century American Popular Culture* (2019) is another important contribution to Dickinson musical scholarship, offering an engaging in-depth look into several aspects of nineteenth-century popular musical culture, in which Dickinson was an active participant.[10]

Runzo devotes one of her chapters to the music of the famous Hutchinson Family Singers as both a social-political as well as a musical model for Dickinson's verse. Four songs associated with the Hutchinson Family were collected by Dickinson and are in her bound volume of sheet music.[11]

In Runzo's chapter on minstrel music, she discusses the song "Old Dan Tucker," which Dickinson collected in her music book. Runzo's take on the character of "Old Dan Tucker" as being rebellious and "energizingly subversive" fits well with Dickinson as an aspect of her playful musical and poetic personality within the context of how minstrel music was perceived, understood, and utilized in the nineteenth century.[12] In the twenty-first century, however, the specter of minstrelsy remains a painful subject from our American musical past. This aspect of Dickinson's musical world and her role in it will be given an appropriate historical assessment in the pages of this book.

The musical historiography of Dickinson's young years as noted by family members and early biographers is scant and opinionated, and in some cases misinterprets the music of the period and Dickinson's interactions with it. In her 1924 book *The Life and Letters of Emily Dickinson*, Emily Dickinson's niece Martha Dickinson Bianchi gives some brief examples of Emily's engagements with music and the piano. Importantly, she mentions that Dickinson "improvised brilliantly upon the piano all sorts of dramatic performances of her own."[13] Genevieve Taggard's 1930 biography contextualizes the "music lessons at the piano, and Sunday-school singing to improve her voice [that] went with young-ladyhood, poised for flight."[14] With George Frisbie Whicher's 1939 biography, the musical portrait of Dickinson becomes skewed. Whicher states flatly that "her nearest approach to a merely ornamental accomplishment was the piano playing of her girlhood. It was no more than that, and in later life was discontinued." He notes that she quickly learned to play simple popular songs of the day, but "beyond this there was no one to guide her."[15] Whicher's twentieth-century vantage point makes him quick to assess the music that Dickinson knew as merely "popular."[16] In Dickinson's day, however, such a musical distinction between popular and art music did not exist and would not evolve until later in the nineteenth century, becoming more firmly entrenched in the next.[17] Whicher observes that "it is hard to realize how untrained the musical taste of most Americans was a century ago."[18] While there is certainly truth to his statement, Whicher aims his proclamation directly at Dickinson, characterizing her observations that have come down to us regarding the concerts she attended as being those of a "plain Yankee."[19] To the contrary, we shall see that Dickinson's concert-going and other musical experiences assisted her in creating a musical persona that allowed her to both express and transcend her Yankee "listening ear."[20] These experiences would serve as early informants to her correspondence and, later, her poetry.

In her 1955 book *Emily Dickinson's Home*, Millicent Todd Bingham states that "both Emily and Vinnie [Emily's sister, Lavinia] dabbled in music for a time," but "whether or not Emily Dickinson was really musical is hard to say," and that Dickinson's comments about the important concerts she witnessed had "more to do with histrionics than with music."[21] By the 1970s such uninformed claims about Dickinson and music were about to become undone.

In her 1971 master's thesis, "Music in the Life and Poetry of Emily Dickinson," Louise W. Reglin comprehensively enumerates Dickinson's musical activities as drawn from her correspondence, bringing together the first solid evidence regarding the importance of music in her early life and in her poems. Reglin observes that "from her experiences in music, Emily Dickinson gained a music vocabulary extensive enough to justify the inclusion of music along with other special sources from which she drew her poetic vocabulary." Reglin seems to agree with earlier assessments of Dickinson's piano playing, noting that "though she never achieved a high degree of proficiency, she continued for a number of years into adulthood to play the piano and often improvised melodies of her own."[22]

Not until Richard Sewall's 1974 biography of Dickinson, which leaves no musical stone unturned, did a more thorough assessment of Dickinson's musical activities begin to emerge. For Sewall, Dickinson's engagements with music, and in particular her improvisations at the keyboard, were "of no little significance in what they tell us about her music and the part it played in her developing poetic career."[23] By the 1980s, the idea that Dickinson was actually "a gifted musician" was coming more clearly into view.[24]

In her book *The Music of Emily Dickinson's Poems and Letters: A Study of Imagery and Form* (2003), Carolyn Lindley Cooley follows Sewall's lead in taking us through these same findings, offering an overview of Dickinson's musical activities. In citing a few examples from Dickinson's bound music volume of the more challenging repertoire with which Dickinson was engaged, Cooley presents some evidence of Dickinson's proficiency at the keyboard. Expanding on Sewall's hypothesis on how music shaped Dickinson's poetic career, Cooley notes that "from the disciplined study of music to the creative development of her musical talent, it was but a short, metaphoric leap into the combined disciplines of music and poetry in her creative verse."[25] Cooley concludes her book with a study of selected musical settings of Dickinson's poems.

Even as interest in Dickinson and music began to grow, Dickinson's bound volume of sheet music still awaited its formal debut. An early handlist of its contents resides in the Millicent Todd Bingham Papers at Yale University.[26] Bingham was the daughter of Mabel Loomis Todd, who, along with Thomas Wentworth Higginson, edited the first collections of Emily Dickinson's poems in 1890 and 1891. The handlist is part of several folders of notes created by Dickinson chronicler Jay Leyda for his book *The Years and Hours of Emily Dickinson,* published in two volumes by Yale University Press in 1960.

But it was Carlton Lowenberg who first introduced us to the whole of Emily Dickinson's bound music volume. The main focus of Lowenberg's book, *Musicians Wrestle Everywhere,* was to document as many composers' settings of Dickinson's poems as were available to him. To achieve this documentation, he communicated not only with libraries and archives but also with music service organizations, putting him in touch with as many composers as possible (including myself) in an attempt to compile the broadest possible annotated bibliography of primarily twentieth-century published and unpublished Dickinson settings.[27] His book, which documents 1,615 settings, is a tribute to the sheer musical magnetism of Dickinson's poetry. Since the publication of Lowenberg's book in 1992, the number of Dickinson settings has nearly doubled, making it abundantly clear that the musicality of Dickinson's verse continues to attract composers of all generations and styles.[28] It is, however, the appendices of his book that concern us here. In those back pages, besides the listing of the "contents of Emily Dickinson's personal album of sheet music," Lowenberg also compiled a selected listing of the music books in the Dickinson Homestead library.[29] He also gathered into a concordance all of the music-related terms mentioned in Dickinson's poems and letters.

Over the years, nearly all of Dickinson's references to music have been cited but never fully contextualized and brought to life. A vision for achieving this goal led to a series of eight Dickinson performance programs co-authored by Trudy Williams and myself from 2012 to 2018. These programs were performed live by The Red Skies Music Ensemble, which we co-founded in 2010, using a humanities approach with a platform of public musicology that combines a research-based narrative, archival imagery, live music, and theatrical elements. Our programs about Emily Dickinson and her musical experiences illuminate Dickinson's musical activities through the digitized content of her bound music book, animated by the context of her correspondence, poetry, and other sources. Each of these programs presents unique content, providing fresh perspectives on the role music played in Dickinson's daily life and in her transformation from accomplished musician to immortal poet. Beginning with Dickinson's musical encounters in the parlor, included in these programs are Dickinson's boundary crossings into the musical world of the servants, Dickinson's engagement with her home and the natural world as reflected in the contents of her music book, her immersion in the Christian hymn tradition, and the music from her bound volume that reflected the events leading up to the Civil War.[30]

Building from the scholarship of the Red Skies Music Ensemble programs which also informed two published articles and blog posts of mine on Dickinson and her bound music book, and incorporating the work of Dickinson scholars, biographers, and musicologists, this book offers an expanded *musical* context from which literary scholars and others can examine Dickinson the poet.[31]

Starting with the music in her bound music book and the Dickinson family correspondence, we will become engaged with Emily Dickinson's musicality at the piano, encompassing her musical ability, ambition, and taste. The music Dickinson collected reflects and radiates out to the significant local and national cultural, educational, and political events of her time with which she was fully engaged. The final chapters examine her musical experiences both within and outside her bound music volume which gave Emily Dickinson critical opportunities to cross musical, social, cultural, and class boundaries. These collective experiences would have a lasting effect on shaping Dickinson's personality of performance, informing first her correspondence and, later, her verse. During her lifetime this process was an intensely private one. Ultimately it proved to be her "letter to the World."[32]

FIGURE 1. Emily E. Dickinson volume of American piano and vocal music, ca. 1823–1851, front cover. EDR 469, Houghton Library, Harvard University.

Emily Dickinson's Bound Music Volume

The study of bound volumes of music is a subject that has emerged only over the last decades, and is now an important cross-discipline area of interest for musicologists and cultural historians. Recent studies of women's bound music volumes by the musicologists Petra Meyer-Frazier, Candace Bailey, and others have been central to the movement for bringing the culture of bound music volumes to the fore.[33] Both Meyer-Frazier and Bailey position these bound volumes as engaging artifacts centered on women's lives and home music-making. Their scholarship has greatly assisted my own work on Dickinson and music in allowing new discoveries and perspectives to eclipse earlier observations about the young Emily Dickinson and the context and significance of her bound music volume and the larger musical world.

In the concluding decades of the eighteenth century and well into the nineteenth, music publishers, participating in the wave of industrial and economic expansion, were able to realize unprecedented advancements in the production and marketing of sheet music to a growing segment of eager consumers in both the United States and Europe. It was during this time that bound music volumes came into existence as an important and popular cultural artifact. As individually published sheet music titles collected and bound into a book, these musical keepsakes were assembled primarily by women of the middle and upper classes during their formative years of musical training, the conclusion of which often coincided with adulthood or marriage. These sheet music volumes were a vital accessory to the culture of home music-making. The practice of collecting, performing, and binding music was ubiquitous and widespread, even extending into the homes of some very notable amateur musicians and active consumers of sheet music. Jane Austen and her family collected eighteen volumes of bound music, hand copied as well as printed editions of solo keyboard music, harp music, and vocal music published between circa 1785 and 1820.[34]

Candace Bailey argues that these bound volumes were similar in their musical documentation to that of eighteenth-century commonplace books.[35] In Emily Dickinson's time, the music contained in these bound volumes exemplified the antebellum era's values of feminine gentility and social decorum, which found appropriate expression in domestic displays of musical talent, refinement, and taste.

The average bound music book generally contained thirty-five to forty-five pieces of the most popular and engaging music of the day. The evidence as to the average size of a bound volume of music is consistent across library collections, including those held by The New York Public Library for the Performing Arts, and the Harvard Theatre Collection (Houghton Library), as well as those volumes physically surveyed and analyzed by Petra Meyer-Frazier for her seminal dissertation and published book on American women's "parlor song collections."[36] In general, vocal music was the medium of choice because of its potential for participation between the performer and the listener. This vocal repertoire encompassed parlor "home" songs, opera selections, patriotic songs, sacred songs, and sentimental ballads. Some women were able to make two albums of about equal size of the separate mediums of vocal and instrumental music.

In contrast with the average bound music volume, Emily Dickinson's music book is extraordinarily robust, more than twice the average size of volumes one would normally encounter in libraries, archives, and other collections. The Dickinson family had the financial means to acquire a great deal of sheet music at considerable expense and, of course, a piano on which to play it. Without a doubt, Emily Dickinson was an eager consumer of sheet music.

While she was certainly attracted to the standard vocal repertoire, the majority of her bound music book consists of a broad spectrum of instrumental selections of piano music. These include a four-hand opera overture, variation sets on operatic arias and other music, military marches, lively quicksteps, waltzes, polkas, and a quadrille; the book also contains Irish, Scottish, and American fiddle tunes, as well as parlor songs, concluding with three pieces of music from the popular minstrel repertoire of the day.

Dickinson's first mention of the music she owned and played, as documented in her correspondence, appears in 1845, when she was thirteen years old. She would continue to acquire sheet music for at least another six or seven years until around the time her music was bound and the writing of her first poems in 1850–1852. The last firmly dated composition in Emily Dickinson's music book was published in 1850 (see no. 60 in Appendix A and online Appendix B). Other music might be dated to 1851 (see no. 45). According to Dickinson scholar Jay Leyda, in July 1851, Emily's father, Edward Dickinson, advertised in the local *Hampshire and Franklin Express* for mechanics, laborers, and "a book binder of the best kind."[37] Given the dating of the music in Emily's bound volume, the family sent at least one collection of loose sheet music off to a bookbinder later in 1851 or in early 1852; and one documented bound volume of music was returned to the family months later. On March 24, 1852, Lavinia Dickinson wrote to her brother Austin: "My music is bound very nicely. It came home yesterday. It pleased me exceedingly that you liked my music. You don't know how much your favor encouraged me. I shall practice with a great deal more interest now than before."[38] Both Dickinson sisters were avid sheet music collectors, although there appears to be no extant bound music book that belonged to Lavinia; this is the only known mention of a volume of bound sheet music that "came home" to the Dickinson household.

Musicologists and music librarians have long referred to these bound aggregates of individual pieces of music as "binder's volumes," considering the principal role of the binder as the creator of the physical object. A more accurate term used by rare book and special collections librarians is "composite volumes."[39] Musicologist and music librarian Robert Kosovsky notes that these volumes contain "a variety of music whose challenging descriptions arises from the music's various associations, relationships and uses."[40] With those words as a guide, throughout this book I refer to Emily Dickinson's "binder's volume" or "composite volume" as her "music book" or "bound volume of music." The assembly of this music was guided by Dickinson's own interests and experiences with the music that she enjoyed, performed, heard, and collected. In that regard, her bound music volume is typical for its time. But the fact that this bound volume of sheet music is unusual in its size and scope, and that it belonged to Emily Dickinson and was likely bound around the time that her first poems were written, gives her music book an added value that is inestimable in its association with the poet, and certainly invites continued research.

With the digitization of Emily Dickinson's music book in 2013, a new and immediate relationship arises with the music that Dickinson acquired and played at home. Access becomes instantaneous and transforming as we download the music and perform it at home just as Dickinson did in her family's parlor. Through this digital surrogate and its detailed cataloging and metadata, we can easily grasp the volume's content, organization, and scope.[41] In the front of the music book is a handwritten index (in a hand other than Dickinson's, likely belonging to the bookbinder). The index lists each piece of sheet music in order by title, sometimes in an abbreviated form (see figures 2 and 3). The pieces are grouped into distinct categories with headings—"Duett," "Variations," "Marches," "Quicksteps," and "Waltzes"—followed by two unnamed miscellaneous groupings: quadrilles/polkas and Irish/Scottish/American fiddle tunes. The final category of "Songs" includes an aggregate of seventeen pieces of vocal music followed by three popular minstrel songs bound at the very back.[42]

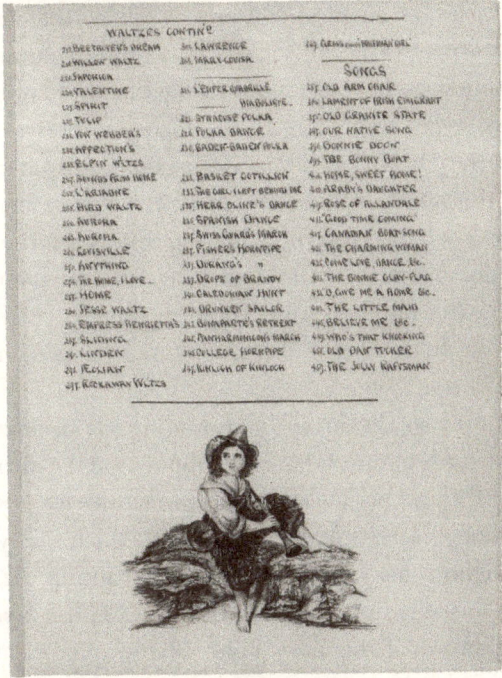

FIGURES 2 AND 3. Emily Dickinson's music book, index. EDR 469, Houghton Library, Harvard University.

The organization of her bound music book reflects the progress of Dickinson's musical studies as well as her evolving musical taste. Upon opening the volume, the casual viewer immediately takes in the more difficult music, which is bound in the front. This includes a four-hand opera overture and thirteen variation sets on opera arias and other melodies. At the back of the book, the last two groupings of vernacular music and songs can be viewed as a single aggregate of easier pieces which Dickinson acquired and played during her earliest years of study. These include the "tunes," as she referred to them, the popular "fiddle tunes" that were advertised by the music publishers as "Dances, Hornpipes, & Easy Lessons."[43] In between, the marches, quicksteps, and waltzes serve as an intermediate bridge between the two end groupings. The "newer" dance forms, the polka and quadrille, are positioned directly after the waltzes, reflecting a musical chronology and an enthusiasm for the newer forms that was supplanting the once popular waltzes of the day. The organization of the music book's content gives a distinctive arc to Emily Dickinson's early musical life.

Each of the first nine chapters of this book follows that arc by exploring a different aspect of Dickinson's bound music volume. From her early years of music study to around the time the music was bound and her first poems began to emerge in the 1850s, music was an important activity in the Dickinson home. All of the family members were engaged with the music of their day as active purchasers, collectors, performers, or listeners. Reaching beyond Emily's music book, the final chapters document the hymns she sang, and the popular ballads she knew and heard, and how all of these encounters both within and beyond her music book shaped the unique musical personality of the poet Emily Dickinson.

Chapter 1 chronicles Dickinson's early singing school experiences and her first years of study at the piano. Her happiness at the instrument, her eagerness to learn, and her curiosity and propensity for both the technical and emotional aspects of the music with which she was engaged is evident throughout her early correspondence and in the substantial amount of music she acquired during this time. Those first years represent a major portion of the music in her bound volume. Just over one third of the music book's content can be dated to the years 1844–1846. Those years would include two stays in Boston with her aunt Lavinia

Norcross: first for a month in May 1844, and again from late August to mid-September of 1846. Of the thirty-two pieces in her bound volume that can be dated to those years, twenty-four of them came from the local Boston music publishers; and out of the twenty-three most popular pieces of 1843 and 1844 listed in Julius Mattfeld's reference book *Variety Music Cavalcade*, eleven of them are represented in Dickinson's bound volume of sheet music.[44]

In chapter 2 we follow Emily Dickinson from her early schooling at the Amherst Academy through her time at the Mount Holyoke Female Seminary, where she was enrolled for the 1847–48 school year. Founded by Mary Lyon in 1837, Mount Holyoke was one of the many female seminaries and academies that were part of a robust movement to advance education for women, and music was an important part of their curricula. The music that Dickinson was exposed to at Mount Holyoke is reflected in the content of both her music book and the hymnbooks that were part of the Dickinson family library. Dickinson's music book also documents the groundswell of music that was produced and heard in other seminaries, shedding light on a few of the leading institutions of her day and the individuals who contributed to their success. As part of her musical education, Dickinson was also the beneficiary of a brilliant age of music pedagogy both imported from Europe and homegrown. Much of this music was featured on programs in the seminaries and academies, and it filtered down into Emily Dickinson's music book.[45]

Dickinson returned home from Mount Holyoke in August 1848, a home that she would eventually refer to as "a bit of Eden."[46] Chapter 3 explores some of the wide-ranging selections in Dickinson's bound music volume that give a descriptive depth to her musical taste and her avid collecting habits; this in turn helps us appreciate the many facets of Dickinson's home music-making. Through the thirty-two waltzes in her music book, we become engaged with the variety of their descriptive subjects and the lives of those who composed them. Of particular interest are those titles that support the Dickinson family's love of home. Within that domestic sphere, several of the waltzes in her music book evoke Dickinson's passion for her garden, and for collecting and cultivating exotic plants, which sparked her imaginings of homes far from Amherst. Although she traveled little, her passionate curiosity about these far-off lands is expressed in some of the music she acquired.

Chapter 4 explores the age of the musical virtuosi, an era that informed all aspects of America's expanding public musical life. During the 1840s and 1850s, professional touring ensembles, singing families, pianists, and other musical virtuosi from Europe were being introduced to American audiences. Emily Dickinson's music book is filled with the music associated with these performers. This was also the age of the American band movement, when nearly every city and town formed its own local wind or brass band, emulating the virtuosic performances of the renowned bandleaders of the day. The Dickinsons heard these bands, and Emily collected their repertoire. The Dickinsons also witnessed the Swedish soprano Jenny Lind at a concert in Northampton in 1851. "*Herself*, and not her music, was what we seemed to love," wrote Dickinson, whose early poems from around this time may have had something to say about Jenny Lind as well.[47]

In chapter 5 the musical consumerism of the Dickinson sisters is on full display. When their brother Austin was teaching in Boston and later attending Harvard Law School, he regularly filled requests from his sisters to send home sheet music from the local Boston music stores. Emily mostly asked him for instrumental piano music. Vinnie had a penchant for new vocal pieces as sung by the latest vocal stars. Their correspondence about music is animating, opening a window onto other family members and their connections to Emily Dickinson's bound volume of music.

The music book content and Emily Dickinson's correspondence provide insight into the Dickinson family personalities. These family portraits are brought to life beginning in chapter 6. Emily Dickinson's father, Edward, "the Squire of Amherst," was the leading citizen of the town. Emily's bound volume introduces us to Edward Dickinson's passionate interest in bringing the local railroad to Amherst and his involvement with militia groups and Whig Party politics. Edward enjoyed hearing the familiar songs, marches, and quicksteps from his militia days and political rallies. He sometimes used music to impose a sense of orderliness in the Dickinson home, especially if his daughters had been out and about in the evening. Edward's gratification at hearing his daughter Emily play was consistent with antebellum mores, in that his daughter was finally home, "fruitfully occupied, indoors and at a suitably feminine musical activity."[48]

In chapter 7, Emily's wit and humor enliven the setting of the family parlor and home music-making. The musical dynamic between Emily and Lavinia enhances our perspective on the two sisters, who engaged with music in very different ways. Lavinia gave the fullest expression to vocal sentimentality when she performed touching ballads at the family piano. Her singing evoked a style of performance that was encouraged and widely practiced in American parlors of the period. Emily, the polar opposite, enjoyed the more introspective side of musical expression afforded by instrumental music. A good amount of this instrumental piano music required above-average technique, something we can observe in the dynamic between the two sisters. When Emily tried to enlist Lavinia in performing a four-hand piano duet, she eventually wrote to her brother, "Vinnie cannot learn it."[49]

Chapter 8 offers an exploration of the music Dickinson collected which animates the social and political struggles that would lead to the outbreak of the Civil War. Some of the pieces in Dickinson's bound music volume would become staples of the regimental bands on both sides of the conflict. The compromises of political and personal freedoms that were exacerbated by westward expansion, the splintering of the Whig Party, and the US government's treatment of Native Americans all become palpable when viewed through this music in Dickinson's bound volume.

The vernacular tunes in Dickinson's music book are examined in chapter 9. These include the Irish airs and ballads, the Scottish jigs, reels, and hornpipes, tunes associated with the American fiddle repertoire, and the minstrel music she collected, such as "Old Dan Tucker," which was also associated with countless fiddler's tunebooks. These traditional fiddle tunes connected Emily with the lives and the music of the Dickinson servants, some of whom played musical instruments and taught the local children to play. By her twenties, Emily was known by family and neighbors to be an expert improviser at the keyboard. She borrowed from this vernacular music, fashioning "weird and beautiful" melodies, improvising a tune that she laughingly called "The Devil."[50] These improvisations were on display at family gatherings, or late at night, when her cousin John Graves recalled that he would be awakened by this "heavenly music." Emily would explain in the morning, "I can improvise better at night."[51]

Chapters 10 and 11 offer an examination of Dickinson's engagements with music both within and beyond the music book as a constituent to the poetry that began to emerge more fully as the 1860s began, when she wrote in one of her letters that "the noise in the Pool, at Noon — excels my Piano."[52] Dickinson scholars have shown that in many of her poems she was thinking musically. When her musicality is observed and distilled through a performative lens of historical musicology, it becomes clear that Dickinson's engagement with the hymns she sang, and the popular, vernacular, and concert music that was in her ears as a listening and performing musician, helped to shape a poetic means of expression that would prove "Better — than Music."[53] While the ballads from her music book provided her with poetic language tropes, the hymnbooks from her father's library gave her a model on which to claim her poetic status as a writer. These hymnbooks would provide her, of course, with meter, but more importantly, she would use these hymnic relationships to fashion a poetic voice that sang of both conformity and dissent.[54]

Chapter 12 expands on this performative analysis to include her white dress. Dickinson's introduction of this iconic garment coincided with the poet's gradual retreat into the Homestead. These activities can be seen as a both a cultivation and culmination of a poetic performance persona that she had activated years earlier, directly reconnecting her to early concert-going activities and to the music associated with those experiences. Music had been her guide, her informant, and her metaphorical lexicon. When Dickinson died in 1886, she left an indelible mark of genius. She also left us a bound volume of music whose content becomes a transformative link to the life of Emily Dickinson the musician/poet.

The book's "Postlude" extends this musical transformation of Dickinson the musician/poet into the world of contemporary music, offering an interpretive view of Dickinson that illuminates the sheer adaptability and malleability of her verse, a topic regularly explored in Dickinson scholarship. This concluding essay is a paean to the poet's compositional musicality, celebrating the extension of those musical qualities across disciplines and across generations. Poems such as "Musicians wrestle everywhere" and others exemplified the musical consonances and dissonances in Dickinson's poetic voice that sang "New Englandly."[55] These poems embraced a performative musical aesthetic that finds a similar resonance in the compositional qualities of the New England composer Charles Ives. Although they were a generation apart, in the context of the long nineteenth century they were musically concurrent. Both Dickinson and Ives captured a deep and earnest memory of the New England of the 1850s in their respective creative lives. Charles Ives drew from earlier sources, composing an underpinning of remembered and borrowed musics, overlaying that remembrance with a dissonance of transcendent beauty and discovery—"ultra-modernist" tendencies that were adopted by composers of the next generation. As with Ives, much of Emily Dickinson's verse was also underpinned by borrowed and remembered musics, the ballads and hymns from her early years, supported by a dissonance of rhythmic punctuation, with their glimmers of American modernism—something that confounded her early editors.

Emily Dickinson was an active participant in the "flowering of New England."[56] Ives, too, re-created that same flowering period in his music: the literary time of Emerson (whom the Dickinsons knew), Thoreau, the Alcotts, the deep musical resonances of the hymns of Isaac Watts, and the memorable tunes associated with the music of the day. In Dickinson's time, there was a sense of exuberance in this "crowded air" of New England, which, for Emily Dickinson, provided a lively accompaniment to a musical and poetic life that would remain in the air for generations to come.[57]

The book concludes with an appendix containing transcribed citations for each of the pieces in Dickinson's bound volume (Appendix A). Two online appendices accompany this book. Appendix B is an annotated bibliography addressing all of the music in Dickinson's bound volume of sheet music. Beyond the detailed citations, the annotated bibliography draws on the holdings of major library collections, offering in-depth information on editions, variant editions, publication histories, publishers, engravers, and lithographers, as well as supplemental biographical information on the composers, dedicatees, and associated performers not included in the main text. Tune etymologies are provided for the vernacular fiddle repertoire. Appendix B also contains twenty-one recorded audio performances of selections from Emily Dickinson's bound volume of sheet music. Thirteen recordings feature pianist Kit Young performing on instruments contemporary with Dickinson's time. Another eight recordings feature arrangements of music from Dickinson's music book performed by The

Red Skies Music Ensemble from live programs co-authored by the ensemble's co-founders George Boziwick and Trudy Williams. Appendix C is a checklist of citations concerning a good deal of the music mentioned in the Dickinson family correspondence that is not in Emily Dickinson's bound music book.

So much has been written about Emily Dickinson, yet so much about her remains enigmatic. That, as her biographer Lyndall Gordon notes, is exactly what "beckons us"; "its teasing insistence suggests something to be solved."[58] And so it is with Dickinson the musician/poet—something new about Dickinson to indulge in, or to be understood. The variety of interpretations of Dickinson's life and work sometimes seems limitless. This book exults in that, offering those who love Emily Dickinson an exuberant excursion into the musical life of the musician/poet, both within and beyond her bound music book, encompassing everything musical that surrounded her.

Even though the binding of Dickinson's music book may have signaled a closing off of her daily engagements with music, initiating a much larger gesture from which the early poetry could take hold and develop, Dickinson would not abandon the music she knew and collected; rather she used every bit of it to infiltrate, infuse, and inform a body of verse whose musicality continues to "sing," inviting continued exploration from literary scholars, or composers in search of a musical setting, or those who simply want to know more about Dickinson.

Finally, Dickinson's iconic poetic words "I dwell in Possibility — " are placed here as a musical caveat, a reminder that tracing the circuitous routes of the music that ended up in her bound volume of published music will be an adventure laden with both discovery and speculation, tempered by "Possibility."[59] In Dickinson's day, acquiring and collecting sheet music was so ubiquitous that finding traces of this activity becomes ephemeral, a loss that must be accepted and acknowledged as part of the activity itself.[60] What we know for certain though is that the stories behind the music in her bound volume commemorate both the ordinary and notable lives of people who in some way share a connection through music with the life of our extraordinary American poet Emily Dickinson.

CHAPTER 1

....

Childhood

"I attend singing school"

EMILY DICKINSON WAS BORN IN 1830 at the Homestead, the Dickinson family home on Main Street in the town of Amherst, Massachusetts, which is situated in Hampshire County in the Connecticut River Valley. She lived there with her father, Edward Dickinson (1803–1874); mother, Emily Norcross Dickinson (1804–1882); her older brother William Austin Dickinson (1829–1895), known as Austin; and younger sister Lavinia Dickinson (1833–1899), often referred to as Vinnie.

The Homestead, which is today the Emily Dickinson Museum, was built in 1813 in the Federal style of the period by Emily's grandfather Samuel Fowler Dickinson (1775–1838). It was purportedly the first brick house in the village, an edifice befitting one of the leading families of the town.[1] In helping to found the Amherst Academy in 1814 and Amherst College in 1821, Squire Fowler Dickinson incurred a great deal of personal debt, which, along with his legal practice, he passed on to his son Edward. In 1828 Samuel Dickinson sold the Homestead and property to John Leland, treasurer of Amherst College, and Edward Dickinson's cousin Nathan Dickinson. Edward was able to buy back the west half of the house from them, while his parents lived in the east half; but with a growing family to support, he was unable to financially sustain his portion of the Homestead. In 1833, the year Lavinia was born, Samuel Fowler Dickinson took a position at the Lane Seminary in Ohio, and Edward sold his portion of the Homestead back to John Leland and

Nathan Dickinson. Within days the house was sold to General David Mack Jr. (1778–1854). Edward Dickinson remained in the Homestead for several years, squeezing his family into the east half of the house, which he rented from the Macks.[2]

By 1840, with a thriving legal practice under way, Edward was solvent enough to move his young family to a house on West Street, today's North Pleasant Street, which fronted the town burial ground. (The house was razed in 1926 and on the site today is a gas station.) Until Edward Dickinson was able to reclaim the Homestead in 1855, it was here in the West Street home that Edward finally had the means to supply both of his daughters with music lessons and Emily's first piano.

After living in half of the Homestead, the West Street house seemed like a "Mansion" to Emily's brother Austin.[3] Emily and Austin were very close, and life in the house on West Street was an idyllic childhood time for Emily, "'where congregations ne'er break up,' and Austins have no end!"[4] It was here that music would become for Emily Dickinson a cherished outlet for expression, fostering a creativity that would allow her to excel well beyond the confines of her New England parlor and the years of her first piano.

"I go to singing-school Sabbath evenings to improve my voice"

The first reference to music in Emily Dickinson's surviving correspondence is from October 14, 1844. Thirteen-year-old Emily wrote to her brother Austin, who was attending the Williston Seminary: "I attend singing school. Mr. Woodman has a very fine one Sunday evenings and has quite a large school. I presume you will want to go when you return home."[5]

Emily Dickinson grew up with the local singing schools, which were still thriving in the 1840s in rural communities such as Amherst, where it was still a common practice to hire an itinerant singing master to set up a temporary school in the town. These took place in the church, the meetinghouse, or other local gathering places, usually in the late fall or winter, after the harvest and before spring planting. In the published histories of Amherst, parish records show that on April 30, 1795, a Mr. Stibbins was issued payment for a singing school he had taught the previous winter, and that "$40 was appropriated to procure a singing master" in 1801.[6] Emily's mention of a Mr. Woodman referred to such a hired teacher, who would have "boarded round" from week to week as part of his pay.⁷

In Amherst, singing schools took place in the local meetinghouse, the original home of the First Church, which opened in 1829 and which is today part of Amherst College.⁸ The singing school served as an important nexus of musical and social activity, where people from within the community could gather and learn the art of amateur music-making. Musicologist Christopher Small argues that "musical performance [such as Dickinson's singing school] was part of that larger dramatic enactment which we call ritual, where the members of the community acted out their relationships and their mutual responsibilities and the identity of the community as a whole was affirmed and celebrated."⁹ In a similar way, Emily's letters consistently indicate that she was both musically and socially engaged with her local community. In 1845 she reported to her friend Abiah Root: "I go to singing-school Sabbath evenings to improve my voice as a matter of [ ], & have the pleasure of a glimpse at nearly all the [ ] and [ ] in the town. Don't you envy me? ... I hope this letter wont be broken open. If it is folks will wonder who has got so much nonsense to tell, wont they?"¹⁰

Chief among the hymn repertoire in the Pioneer Valley were the hymns of Isaac Watts (1674–1748), which had taken hold in the (Jonathan) Edwards Church in Northampton, the nearest large town, which was eight miles from Amherst. These hymns migrated throughout New England and into hymnbooks such as Watts's *Psalms, Hymns and Spiritual Songs*, Asahel Nettleton's *Village Hymns*, and later Lowell Mason's *Church Psalmody*, copies of which were part of the Dickinson family library.¹¹ These volumes contained the "Sabbath-going" church hymns with which, as a child, Emily Dickinson would become and remain intimately familiar, finding resonance in her correspondence and, later, her poetry.

"She calls it the moosic": Emily Dickinson and the Piano

As early as age two and a half, Emily Dickinson was showing signs of an aptitude for music and a curiosity about the piano, as evidenced in a note from Emily's aunt Lavinia Norcross to her brother-in-law Edward Dickinson, written in 1833. Emily's mother was recuperating from an illness after the birth of her third child, Lavinia, when little Emily was sent to stay for a month with her aunt in Monson, a day's travel south of Amherst.[12] "I have but a few moments of leisure," she wrote, "but I will just let you know that Emily is perfectly well & contented—She is a very good child & but little trouble—She has learned to play on the piano—she calls it the <u>moosic</u>."[13]

Emily Dickinson began her piano lessons at age eight, at the time a typical age for a girl to begin lessons. In 1839–40 Dickinson studied piano for one year at the home of sixteen-year-old Ann Eliza Houghton of Amherst. Houghton's students included "Fanny Sellon daughter of Dr[.] S. of Amherst, Dr. Gridley's daughter Jane, two daughters of [Amherst College] Pres[ident] Hitchcock's (Mary and Kate), Lutheria [Luthera] Cutler (now Mrs. Judge Conkey) & lawyer Dickinson's daughter Emily."[14] At the conclusion of that year of music study, Houghton left Amherst to take a position at the Wilbraham Academy.[15] On September 7, 1840, Emily Dickinson began her first year at the Amherst Academy.[16]

Dickinson was an ambitious student, and her ambition showed itself fairly early. Emily wrote to Abiah Root: "We'll finish an education sometime, won't we? You may then be Plato, and I will be Socrates, provided you won't be wiser than I am."[17] Emily showed a similar ambition for her music studies, which continued during her time at the academy through its offerings of instrumental music instruction.[18] Although there are no details of Dickinson's musical studies between 1840 and 1844, it's clear from her 1845 letters and the piano method book that she was using (Henri Bertini, *Progressive and Complete Method for the Piano-forte*) that her studies in piano had progressed and that she was a serious student.[19] "I also was much pleased with the news [your letter] contained especially that you are taking lessons on the 'Piny,' as you always call it," she wrote to Abiah Root in May 1845, "but remember not to get on ahead of me. Father intends to have a Piano very soon. How happy I shall be when I have one of my own."[20] Three months later, on August 3, 1845, Emily reported to Abiah that she had got her piano and was happily playing it.[21]

Dickinson biographer Richard Sewall notes that Emily's talent for music was not recognized and rewarded with her own piano sooner than 1845 because "Edward's household, it seems, was all too typical of late-Puritan, small-town New England families in their insensitivity to extraordinary abilities in their children, especially those of an imaginative or artistic turn. Life was real, earnest, and mostly 'Prose.'"[22]

Emily was certainly musical, but during those early years her father was preoccupied with the financial constraints of the Homestead, and the move to the West Street house to accommodate his growing family, leading him to defer the substantial investment in a piano for his young daughter's musical education until 1845. But Edward Dickinson may have been intending to acquire a piano for some time.

The previous year Emily had been sent for a month-long stay with her aunt Lavinia Norcross's family in Boston. Dickinson was to conclude her Boston trip with a visit to her father's brother William in Worcester. On June 4, 1844, Edward Dickinson wrote to his daughter in Boston: "I want to have you see the Lunatic Hospital, & other interesting places in Worcester while you are there. . . . Tell Uncle William that I want a Piano when he can buy good ones, at a fair price. I hope he & Mr. Leland will go to Boston, this week, & find two good ones. I prefer *Rosewood*—3 pedals—& a stool. I want all together."[23]

When the Dickinsons' piano finally arrived, it was a welcome addition to the home. Musical instruments were signifiers of the burgeoning prosperity and cultural aspirations of the growing middle and upper-middle classes.[24] A small organ, square piano, or other instruments such as a violin, flute, or guitar were essentials in the well-to-do American parlor.

"I am taking lessons this term, of Aunt Selby"

In Dickinson's time, "music was considered a necessary component of a genteel education," and piano instruction came with an expectation that the student would achieve a "high degree of competency." Like most young women, and some young men engaged in the study of piano and voice, these efforts and ambitions were a lively topic of conversation.[25] On August 3, 1845, fourteen-year-old Emily wrote enthusiastically to Abiah Root about her new piano and about her studies:

> When I tell you that our term has been 16 weeks long & that I have had 4 studys & taken Music lessons you can imagine a little how my time has been taken up lately. . . . How do you like taking music lessons. I presume you are delighted with it. I am taking lessons this term, of Aunt Selby who is spending the summer with us. I never enjoyed myself more than I have this summer. For we have had such a delightful school and

such pleasant tea[c]hers, and besides I have had a piano of my own. Our Examination is to come off next week on Monday. I wish you could be here at that time. Why cant you come. If you will—You can come and practice on my piano as much as you wish to. . . . Are you practising now you are at home—I hope you are, for if you are not you would be likely to forget what you have learnt. I want very much to hear you play. I have the same Instruction book that you have, Bertini [*Progressive and Complete Method for the Piano-forte*], and I am getting along in it very well.[26]

Emily Dickinson displayed a genuine interest in and ambition for music.[27] Her happiness at the instrument, her eagerness to learn, her curiosity, and her propensity for both the technical and emotional aspects of the music with which she was engaged are evident throughout her early correspondence and in the music that she acquired during this time. In the same 1845 letter to Abiah Root, Dickinson admits that "Aunt Selby says she shant let me have many tunes now for she wants I should get over in the [Bertini method] book a good ways first." The "tunes" Dickinson refers to would have included the "easy lessons," traditional fiddle tunes in her music book such as "Basket Cotillion," "The Girl I Left Behind Me," "College Hornpipe," "Fisher's Hornpipe," "Caledonian Hunt," "Durang's Hornpipe," and "Herr Cline's Dance," and the two short pieces titled "Spanish Dance." Boston music publisher Oliver Ditson's 1844 catalog lists all of these and more under the category "Dances, Hornpipes, & Easy Lessons, etc."[28] This vernacular repertoire arranged with simple piano accompaniments would have been available from the music publishers, with these tunes serving as steppingstones to more challenging repertoire.[29]

It is clear that the fingerings and directional markings such as "Fine" and "D.C." (da capo) penciled into the music of "Basket Cotillion" in Dickinson's music book were made by a teacher, in this case Aunt Selby, who provided Emily with some of these easy pieces (see figure 4). Thus, these "tunes" find a distinct place and function in the young Emily Dickinson's music book among her beginner repertoire.

Even though Aunt Selby was telling Emily that she should be devoting more time to her piano method (Bertini), it is clear from the content of her music book that Emily loved her "tunes." Dickinson continues in her letter to Abiah that she has "been learning several beautiful pieces lately. The Grave of Bonaparte is one. Lancers Quick Step—Wood up, and Maiden Weep no more, which is a sweet little song. I wish much to

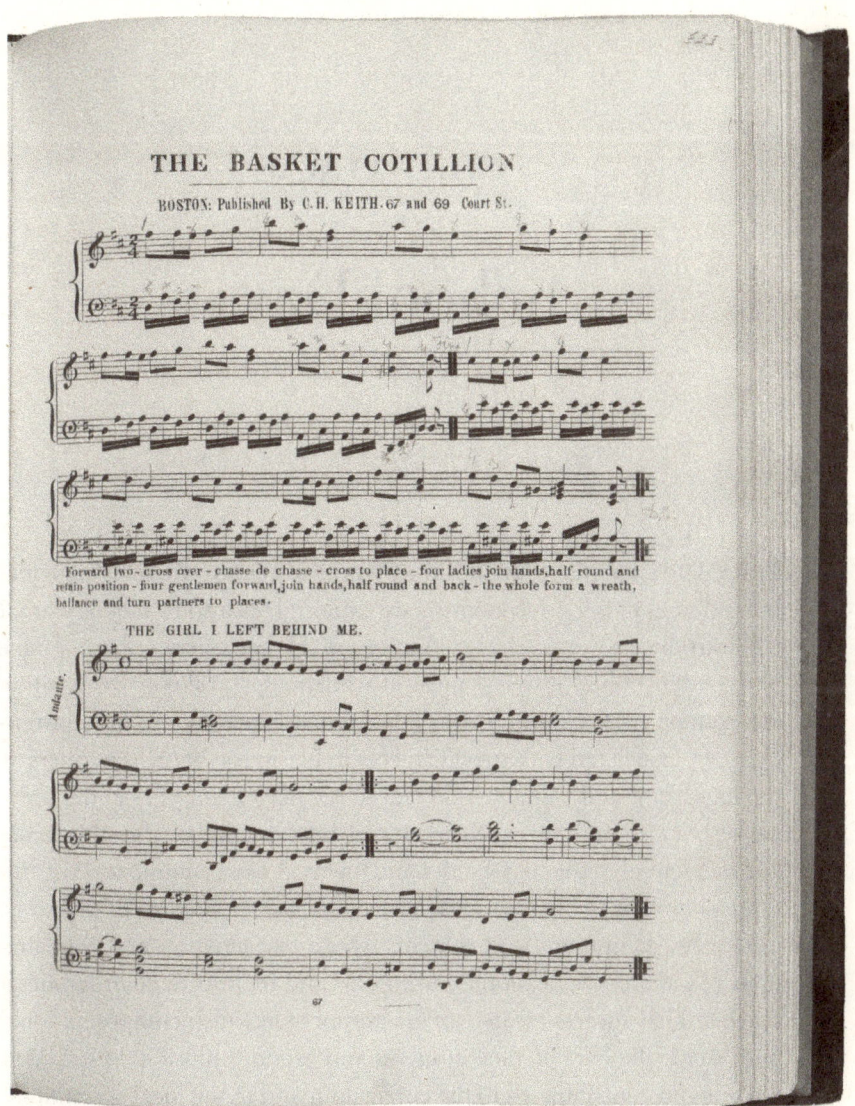

FIGURE 4. "The Basket Cotillion." Emily Dickinson's music book, EDR 469, Houghton Library, Harvard University.

see you and hear you play."[30] The power of the piano and its "tunes" that populated her music book would provide a musical accompaniment for Emily Dickinson throughout her formal education and into adulthood and the years of her first poems.

CHAPTER 2

School Days

"You know what it is to 'love school'"

EMILY DICKINSON'S MUSIC BOOK REVEALS a treasure trove of information relating to her education. As we explore Dickinson's school years, I will introduce several other institutions of higher learning both female and coeducational, as well as musical academies, and situate them within the context of Dickinson's own educational experience. These institutions are associated with specific pieces in her music book, reminders of the important and valuable role that music played not only in the seminaries but also through the formation of instrumental or choral societies and academies in the major cities and towns. A close examination of this music allows us to discover and pay tribute to the founders, benefactors, musicians, composers, and students whose participation and contributions made these educational institutions and their local communities a success. That success created an environment in which composers could both shape the lives of their students and produce music that served as meaningful contributions to the curriculum and to the local community. The music that these composer/teachers created was recognized and disseminated by the major music publishers. This music intersected with Emily Dickinson's musical world, and she acquired it.

The Amherst Academy

Emily Dickinson's first five years of schooling were spent at the town's district primary school on West Street.[1] From the ages of nine to sixteen

(1840–1847), Dickinson attended the Amherst Academy on Amity Street, an institution founded in 1814 by her grandfather Samuel Fowler Dickinson. Lexicographer Noah Webster (grandfather of Dickinson's childhood friend Emily Fowler), who had moved to Amherst in 1812, served on the school's board of trustees.[2] The academy had direct ties to Amherst College, so most of Dickinson's instructors were senior students or recent graduates of the college.

Instrumental music instruction at the Amherst Academy was taught by an unidentified "lady of distinguished talents and reputation."[3] Dickinson's involvement with music instruction seems to have continued uninterrupted during her early school years, as music continued to be part of the academy's curriculum. In her graduating year of 1847, the *Hampshire and Franklin Express* (August 13, 1847) reported on the exhibition exercises that concluded the school year at the academy: "The music too, ought not to be passed over in silence, being excellent, and appropriate to the occasion. And indeed everything combined to make the afternoon pass off in a very agreeable manner to the large audience which was assembled on the occasion. May we attend many such in the same place."[4]

At the Amherst Academy, Emily Dickinson was introduced to the teaching of Dr. Edward Hitchcock (1793–1864), a theologian, geologist, and Amherst College president (1845–1854). Hitchcock was a frequent lecturer at the academy, and his textbooks, including *Elementary Geology*, were an important part of the curriculum. Hitchcock was "as precise an observer [of nature] as he was far reaching as a speculator."[5] His *Religious Lectures on Peculiar Phenomena in the Four Seasons* had a profound effect on Emily, positioning science and the natural world as a means of explaining and enriching religious belief.[6] The influence of Hitchcock, her "Scientist of Faith," shaped Emily's lifelong and passionate bond with nature as a congenial agent for the divine.[7] This integrated perspective allowed Dickinson to "[keep her] Believing nimble," a quality that would play an important role in shaping her into the poet that she would become.[8] Edward Dickinson, like his father, Samuel Fowler Dickinson, was an advocate for public education. He served on the Amherst school committee, and in 1835 was appointed a trustee of the Amherst Academy. In August of that same year, he became treasurer of Amherst College, serving in that position until 1873, when he was succeeded by his son Austin.[9]

Since his college days at Yale, Edward Dickinson had maintained a keen and sincere interest in education for women. When Emily was seven and Edward was away on business, he was direct in wanting to know about his children's schooling. He wrote to Emily, "Keep school, and learn, so as to tell me, when I come home, how many new things you have learned, since I came away."[10] According to Dickinson's biographer Richard Sewall, Edward Dickinson "wanted his children's feet planted firmly on the ground, and he set out to see that they had a fine, solid education that would 'do them good' in many senses of the word."[11] Although Edward encouraged his daughter's continued education, it was with a nineteenth-century protectionist veneer. "He buys me many Books—," wrote Emily years later, "but begs me not to read them—because he fears they joggle the Mind."[12] As her studies at the Amherst Academy neared their conclusion, Dickinson prepared for the entrance examinations to the Mount Holyoke Female Seminary, today Mount Holyoke College, in South Hadley, Massachusetts.[13]

Emily Dickinson's Music Book and the Seminary Movement

Emily Dickinson benefited from the reforms that were expanding women's education during the 1840s. Taking center stage were the flourishing female seminaries and academies, including Emma Willard's Troy (New York) Female Seminary, founded in 1821; Catharine Beecher's Hartford (Connecticut) Female Seminary (1832); and the Mount Holyoke Female Seminary, founded in 1837 by Mary Lyon (1797–1849). These and other academies, seminaries, and institutes offered a college-level curriculum, usually for two or three years, emphasizing fundamentals including the sciences, mathematics, and English grammar. Some institutions included studies preparing young women for teaching, and still others the "useful" studies that could be applied to running a household.[14] Many seminaries enhanced their curricula to include "ornamental studies" such as art and music. The scholar Margaret A. Nash notes that "many historians have argued that the seminaries reinforced the ideology [of separate spheres] by training women for passive and 'traditional' family roles, while others have argued that some antebellum leaders, such as Mary Lyon, almost single-handedly challenged female domesticity by urging women to assert themselves."[15] At Mount Holyoke, Mary Lyon trained her students to be teachers and missionaries, and during Dickinson's time, an increasing number of women entered the seminaries in order to acquire the advanced training that educators agreed was necessary for the teaching profession.[16]

Mount Holyoke was one of the many female seminaries where music was an important part of the curriculum. The seminary network provided employment for hundreds of music educators, who fostered a high standard of pedagogy in the female seminaries and academies. Dickinson's music book documents some of the music that was produced and heard in these seminaries, shedding light on a few of the leading institutions of her day and the individuals who contributed to their success. One of those institutions represented in her music book was the Cherry Valley Female Academy in Cherry Valley, New York.

The Cherry Valley Female Academy

Emily Dickinson's music book contains the "Syracuse Polka," a widely published popular piece that reveals the reputational glow attached to its prolific composer, Jonathan Amos Fowler (1817–1878), who was a professor of music at the Cherry Valley Female Academy from 1842 to 1860.[17]

In Dickinson's time, Cherry Valley, New York, was a hub of regional commerce and culture. Established in 1738 along a westward Iroquois route through the northern foothills of the Catskill Mountains, Cherry Valley had become a settlement for Scotch-Irish immigrants. A turnpike establishing a direct route between Albany to the east and Ohio to the west made the town both a stopping point and a destination for travelers. According to a history of Cherry Valley: "The large number of old and wealthy families also gave the place great social prominence. Indeed the whole history of Cherry Valley during this period shows a prominence and activity that would be deemed incredible in a village of a thousand inhabitants, did not the official records testify to its truth."[18]

No longer a western wilderness, the village prospered, and in 1796, four years after New York State had established its Board of Regents, designed to supervise and support its institutions of higher learning, the Cherry Valley Female Academy was formed, one of the first such institutions in the state.[19] By the 1840s it had a thriving music department, headed by Fowler, who "attracted hither many students of music."[20]

Vocal music classes at Cherry Valley were mandatory. In addition, instrumental music instruction was offered in piano, harp, guitar, and organ. One of the required method books used was Henri Bertini's *Progressive and Complete Method for the Piano-forte*, the same book that Emily Dickinson had used since at least the age of thirteen. Other required music instruction books for piano at Cherry Valley were those by Franz Hünten and Carl Czerny (spelled Czerney in the school's 1854 catalog), whose pedagogical pieces and piano arrangements are represented in Dickinson's bound music book. Public rehearsals were held every other week. Under Jonathan Fowler's direction, the quality of the music at Cherry Valley was quite high, as reported approvingly by the institution's oversight committee:

> The Soiree Musicale, which closed the anniversary exercises on the evening of the 10th, was a most brilliant and delightful entertainment. . . . Among the distinguished gentlemen from abroad, we observed Ex-Governor Seward, of Auburn. . . . The perfect ease with which some of the most difficult pieces of the best Masters were executed, was a matter of the most agreeable surprise to all present. It could not but be apparent to all, that while this Institution is second to none in the opportunities afforded for the acquirement of a finished education in all the branches of Literature and Science, it also affords very superior advantages for those who have a taste for Music, and who desire to perfect themselves in that beautiful art. The Principal in this department has few equals as a teacher; and the Institution is located among an eminently musical people.[21]

It would appear that Fowler's efforts earned him not only great praise but a promotion as well. Fowler is listed as a trustee in the 1854 Cherry Valley catalog. The following year a profile on Fowler was featured in the journal *The Musical World*, edited by Richard Storrs Willis, highlighting Fowler as co-principal of the institution and director of the "Musical Department" at Cherry Valley. The article quoted from Fowler's publisher, whose catalog stated that "Mr. Fowler is widely and favorably known as one of the most successful teachers in America."[22] In 1860 Fowler moved to Englewood, New Jersey, where, until his retirement, he was co-proprietor of the Englewood Seminary for Young

Ladies. He died in Englewood in 1878 and was interred in the Cherry Valley Cemetery.

Fowler's "Syracuse Polka" in Dickinson's bound music book is dated 1848. First published the previous year, it was by far his most popular work. By 1856 the piece had reached ten editions (see online Appendix B). No other compositions by Fowler are in Dickinson's bound music book, but some of them are noted here as a reflection of his popularity and prolific output. Fowler's music appeared in the 1850 edition of *The Bouquet of Melody*, a notable annual anthology of songs, published in New York by William Hall and Son.[23] Fowler's *Banks of the Mohawk* from 1851, also published by William Hall, commemorates the Mohawk River, which runs near Cherry Valley in the Mohawk Valley region of the state. Fowler's many polkas were equally commemorative of New York State with the titles "Syracuse," "Sharon," and "Otsego."[24]

The Cherry Valley Female Academy trustees were proud of the quality of the institution's offerings and the rigor of its programs. Female seminaries sought to prove that their lofty educational goals were worthy of "the experiment" of female education, and in the case of the Amenia Seminary in Dutchess County, New York, a coeducational enterprise too.

The Amenia Seminary

The "Home Quick Step" (1842) in Dickinson's music book was composed by William Smith and dedicated to Dr. L.W. Stanton of Ameniaville, New York, home of the Amenia Seminary. A coed boarding and day school, the seminary was founded by a group of Methodists in 1835 in the town of Ameniaville (now Amenia), located in Dutchess County, near the Connecticut border. All but two of the seminary's early principals between 1838 and 1858 were alumni of Wesleyan University. Many Amenia Seminary graduates went on to study at Wesleyan and would return to occupy faculty positions at the school.[25] The overarching goal of the Amenia Seminary "was to prove the success of its perilous experiment, certainly carried through, to eminent success, a co-educational scheme, which gave the girls as good a chance for a liberal education as it gave their brothers."[26]

Both the composer and the dedicatee of the piece in Dickinson's bound music book, William Smith and Dr. L. W. Stanton, were from Ameniaville, which had been founded in 1762.[27] Smith was a graduate of the seminary, class of 1836. Dr. Luke W. Stanton (1806–1869) was a prominent citizen who owned a productive farm, a successful medical practice, and a pharmacy. He had a long association with the seminary, serving on its board of trustees as secretary, and was chairman of the executive committee until 1843. The school's annual year-end program of examinations and exhibitions featured a procession of students, a brass band, and Dr. Stanton as the grand marshal.[28]

There were no music offerings at Amenia during the time that William Smith was a student and Stanton was a trustee, but it did offer drawing and painting. By 1847 instruction was given in "all the branches of polite and ornamental education usually pursued in Female Seminaries. . . . Faithful attention is also given to music on the Piano Forte." The most notable instructor of music was Miss Julia Lines of Utica, New York. The seminary closed its doors in 1886 when public schools opened in the area.[29]

The Amenia Seminary reunion catalog of 1906 remembered Dr. Stanton as "a stirring and public-spirited citizen, active in all good enterprises."[30] William Smith's composition and its dedication to Dr. Stanton support that claim. Smith's quickstep found a home in many bound music volumes. The year the Amenia Seminary closed its doors, Smith's "Home Quick Step" was still in the catalog of Boston music publisher Oliver Ditson.

The Utica Female Academy and the Utica Musical Academy

Farther upstate in the Mohawk Valley region, the city of Utica was a cultural center with a connection to both Emily's music book and the Dickinson family. Two of Emily Dickinson's friends, her future sister-in-law Susan Gilbert and Susan's sister Martha, were enrolled in the prestigious Utica Female Academy between 1848 and 1850.[31] Of the three Utica-related pieces in the Dickinson bound music book, two of these pieces were composed by Utica resident George Dutton: "'Speed the Plough,' A Favorite Dance Arranged with Brilliant [but uncredited] Variations" (see online Appendix B), and "'Hope Again,' an Air with Variations for the Piano Forte."

George Dutton (1789–1854) was a composer, conductor, arranger, and publisher. He served as organist at Utica's Trinity Church after a new organ was installed there in 1821 and was also the proprietor of Utica's first music store. Dutton served as conductor of the orchestra of the Utica Musical Academy, which was founded in 1840 for the "promotion of skill and taste in both sacred and secular music." The academy was in operation until 1844, giving "a marked impulse to musical art" in the city.[32]

Dutton dedicated his composition "Hope Again" to Rudolph Snyder (1778–1861), a prominent Utica citizen. A cabinetmaker by trade, Snyder prospered and was active as a trustee of the village and later its president. Snyder also served as trustee on various boards, including that of the Utica Savings Bank, which was chartered in 1821.[33]

Utica had a vibrant, thriving cultural community, and the Music Academy and Female Academy are signifiers of that prosperity, status, and growth. Those signifiers are supported by the music in Dickinson's bound music book, which reminds us of those flourishing communities and the important local relationships that existed then but might not otherwise be known to us today. In Dickinson's day and for some time after, it was common for these relationships to be expressed and commemorated by a piece of music, corroborating stories about the important communities and circumstances from which this music emanated, and those who aided in its creation, publication, and dissemination.

Thomas Hastings and Lowell Mason

One of the musical advisors listed in the catalog of the Utica Female Academy with a connection to the Dickinson family was Thomas Hastings of New York (1784–1872). Hastings was one of the major contributors to the Eurocentric reforms in sacred music instruction and education that were under way in churches throughout the Northeast. Originally a resident of upstate New York, Hastings taught singing schools in Clinton, Troy, Albany, and Utica, introducing the works of Handel and other European composers as well as composing many well-known hymns such as "Rock of Ages."[34] His efforts in composing and compiling hymnbooks resulted in the publication of *Musica Sacra* by the Oneida Musical Society in 1823.

Hastings moved from Utica to New York City in 1832, where he founded the Academy of Sacred Music, a training ground for amateur choral singers. As part of his reform work, he was able to systematically organize and apply instruction in music and performance for a great number of church choirs and congregations in the city.

Emily Dickinson's uncle Mark Haskell Newman (1806–1852), a New York publisher, brought out seven sacred and secular tunebooks by Hastings, including *The New York Choralist* (1847) and *Congregational Harmony* (1849). He also published seventeen compilations by William Bradbury, a student of another music educator, Lowell Mason. While not all of Newman's published music books are in the Dickinson Collection at Harvard, author Carlton Lowenberg notes that "because Newman's music books, especially those of William Bradbury and Thomas Hastings, went through many printings and were widely circulated, the Dickinsons could well have known about them."[35] That so many important vocal music collections were available to Emily Dickinson helps us understand her intimacy with the hymn and choral traditions of her day, a medium that would both sustain and inform the work of Emily Dickinson the musician/poet (see chapter 11).

Another person with ties to Dickinson's musical world was the Boston music educator Lowell Mason (1792–1872). Mason composed sacred music to great success. During her time at Mount Holyoke, Dickinson used at least one of the sacred tunebooks Mason compiled, which featured his popular hymn tunes "Missionary Hymn" (sung to words by Reginald Heber as "From Greenland's Icy Mountains") and "Watchman! Tell us of the night" (words by John Bowring). Mason saw a need to elevate secular vocal music to the same standards of literacy that sacred music had recently achieved under choralists like Thomas Hastings. More importantly, Mason envisioned that the teaching of secular music should share an equal status with the major subjects of the school curriculum.

To set this project in motion on a large scale, Mason, along with George James Webb (1803–1887) and others, founded the Boston Academy of Music in 1833, a school devoted to teaching instrumental and vocal music. Mason utilized the systematized instructional literacy methods of Johann Heinrich Pestalozzi (1746–1827), which he found to be particularly applicable to vocal music instruction. The success of the Boston Academy catapulted Mason into the position of superintendent of music in the Boston Public Schools, making Boston the first city in the country to implement music as part of everyday instruction in the school curriculum. Mason went on to set up nationally organized secular singing schools called "Musical Conventions," which trained hundreds of teachers in vocal music instruction.[36]

One of those teachers influenced by Mason's teaching was Mary Lyon, founder of the Mount Holyoke Female Seminary. Lyon had taught at the Ipswich Female Seminary in Ipswich, Massachusetts, from 1828 to 1834, where she was assistant principal to Zilpah P. Grant (1794–1874). At Ipswich, Lyon came to know Lowell Mason, who was a visiting professor teaching vocal music during the 1830–31 school year. Mason's year at Ipswich had a lasting effect on Mary Lyon, as evidenced by a letter to Zilpah Grant written several months after Mason's departure from Ipswich:

> Ever since vocal music was introduced into our seminary, I have had an increasing sense of its great practical importance. By our influence, and the influence of our pupils on this subject, probably hundreds may be benefitted for a succession of generations. Those who have been able to sing from childhood, do not know by experience the feelings which *some* have who cannot sing. When passing near the music-room last summer, and thinking that a large part of the choir, probably, had no more of a musical voice than myself, I found it necessary to restrain, with firm determination, a rising murmur. I have sometimes felt, that I would have given six months of my time, when I was under twenty, and defrayed my expenses, difficult as it was to find time or money, could I have enjoyed the privileges for learning vocal music that some of our pupils enjoy.[37]

Lyon carried this memory with her, bringing Mason's standards and practices to South Hadley. She would remind her students, "Singing exerts a mighty moral influence, and, young ladies, I have no doubt that if you cultivate your musical powers here, you will sing and enjoy the song of Moses and the Lamb as those can not who have hidden their talent."[38] These remarks from Lyon are the best evidence we have as to why vocal music was emphasized over instrumental music at Mount Holyoke. Lyon's own deficiencies in music, her longings in that regard, and her grasp of the success of Mason's teaching methods were clearly the root cause for the emphasis on vocal music instruction, with supporting evidence coming from Lowell Mason himself.[39] Shortly before founding Mount Holyoke, Lyon received a note from Mason in which he seems to have set the tone for music instruction at Mount Holyoke. He advised her, "I am more and more convinced that while you ought not to make any exertion to introduce instrumental music—you can hardly do too much in favor of universal vocal music."[40] Mason's instructional methods played a vital role in making the vocal music curriculum at the Mount Holyoke Female Seminary a magnet for prospective students already well trained in music. Emily Dickinson was one of those students.

The Mount Holyoke Female Seminary

Given its academic reputation and proximity to Amherst, the Mount Holyoke Female Seminary was a natural choice for Emily's continued education, as no one in her immediate family liked being too far from home.[41] Mount Holyoke's stated mission to make education attainable to those in the middle class who could not otherwise afford the higher cost of tuition in similar institutions found resonance with Edward Dickinson, whose competing financial priority at the time was retaking possession of the Homestead.[42]

Emily Dickinson commenced her studies at the Mount Holyoke Female Seminary on September 30, 1847. Her first cousin Emily Lavinia Norcross (1828–1852) from Monson was in the senior class, and the two Emilys were roommates.[43] Twelve teachers were in charge of the record 235 students registered at the school for the 1847 fall term.[44] Like Dickinson and her cousin, most hailed from New England, but like many other schools, Mount Holyoke could boast an enrollment from a broad geographical area.

Emily's time at the Mount Holyoke Female Seminary was happy and formative. It was also rich in musical experiences, as reflected in the quantity and quality of music she encountered there that finds representation in her bound music book. Her own and her classmates' correspondence and recollections give us a vivid picture of the culture Dickinson experienced at Mount Holyoke. Amelia D. Jones (class of 1849) of Springfield, Massachusetts, recalled the first sight of her new classmate Emily Dickinson at the opening of the school term:

Companions of our student years! Again we see them, a flock of newcomers, as they crowd into the hall [i.e., Seminary Hall] for the opening exercises, some comely and graceful, and some destined to win admiration by their shining virtues and talents. We mark one modest, pale-faced maiden crowned with a wealth of auburn hair. Who could have divined that Emily Dickinson's brain teemed with rare notes that would ring through the land? . . . Truly we had opportunity to study character as well as text books, and to find congenial spirits with whom to form a strong and lasting friendship.[45]

"Things seem much more like home than I anticipated," Dickinson wrote to Abiah Root. "The teachers are all very kind & affectionate to us."[46] She also found herself to be well liked.[47] Dickinson embarked on a program of study that included algebra, chemistry, physiology, and later astronomy and rhetoric. There was also daily practice of calisthenics, and music, which for Emily included singing in one of the three graded choirs and the sacred music choir.[48] Since she was trained as a pianist, Dickinson was afforded the opportunity to practice the piano for about one hour each day. Soon after arriving at Mount Holyoke, she wrote to Abiah Root detailing her schedule, which included almost two hours of music each day of both piano and voice: "At 9. we all meet in Seminary Hall, for devotions. . . . [A]fter dinner, from 1 ½ until 2 I sing in Seminary Hall. From 2 ¾ until 3 ¾. I practice upon the Piano."[49]

Singing hymns at daily devotions was integral to the curriculum at the seminary. Books such as Nettleton's *Village Hymns* and Watts's *Psalms, Hymns, and Spiritual Songs* were required textbooks and served as a constant reminder of the mission of the school and its preceptress (principal/founder), Mary Lyon. Just as her academic programs were demanding, so too was Lyon's embrace of the sweeping fervor of evangelical Protestantism in that she expected each of her students would make a profession of faith and a commitment to Christ. Within days after the school year began, the pressure to make this religious commitment commenced.[50] Activities surrounding religious conversion were particularly acute during the revival year of 1846 and remained in the air "silent and unseen" when Dickinson arrived at Mount Holyoke in September 1847.[51] Most of the seminary's students did make this commitment, and many of them went on to missionary life in remote corners of the world. During her time at Mount Holyoke, Dickinson had come close to answering Mary Lyon's call to commit her life to Christ but instead found herself among the students Miss Lyon referred to as "No Hopers."[52] In a letter to Abiah Root, Dickinson expressed that she had been resolute and sober, not defiant in her unwillingness to accept Mary Lyon's call to Christ: "There is a great deal of religious interest here and many are flocking to the ark of safety. I have not yet given up to the claims of Christ, but trust I am not entirely thoughtless on so important & serious a subject."[53] This "serious subject" would surface again for Dickinson, most notably in 1850.

Music at Mount Holyoke

While the Mount Holyoke curriculum did not include instrumental music instruction, according to the seminary catalog "those who have attended to instrumental music can have the use of a piano a few hours in a week."[54] Dickinson, like other students trained in instrumental music, made regular use of the two or three pianos available for practice. Those who could play the piano were kept busy as accompanists for the calisthenics classes. These were a substitute for dancing, which was not permitted at Mount Holyoke.[55]

Dickinson's classmate Marion P. Harwood (class of 1849) noted that "on study day, [the] piano [was] never silent an hour." During those study days, preparations for examinations included perfecting piano pieces that were to be included in Mount Holyoke's public examination exhibitions.[56] These pieces provided a programmatic musical contrast to the recitations, delivering of prepared compositions (essays), and of course singing. These exhibition programs were open to the public, were well attended, and were often reviewed in the local press. Emily Dickinson's music book contains quite a few of the piano pieces found on seminary examination programs: the enormously popular variation sets on "The Last Rose of Summer," or "Believe Me If All Those Endearing Young Charms"; Kreutzer's Overture to *Lodoïska*; and the ubiquitous march from *The Battle of Prague* were all favorites on these programs.[57]

Public examination exhibitions drew large and enthusiastic audiences from around the community. One such visitor was Amherst College sophomore William Gardiner Hammond (1829–1894), who attended the final examinations in 1847:

A class in Virgil were on the floor when I came and the little I could catch was highly creditable to their scholarship. Then the first four books of Euclid: very well done: the teachers gave out the captions, and then the girls drew their own figures and demonstrated them without the use of letters. Then a class in Botany, . . . then History and one or two other things of the kind, very good and very dull: then Calisthenics, . . . everyone dressed in white, with green wreaths for this special occasion.—Then music from the piano, and singing: very fair: then five compositions: very good indeed, though rather for style than ideas: even in the style it was often easy to detect traces of some popular author. Then more music, and the performance closed.[58]

Commenting on one of these Mount Holyoke exhibitions, the *Springfield Daily Republican* noted the performers' skill: "[After the recitations] followed singing, with the piano accompanying; first by a large choir, and afterwards in duets and solos. We think we never listened to better or sweeter vocal music . . . rich and powerful. It was gratifying to witness such perfection in this delightful art—one which has heretofore received too little attention in our schools and seminaries."[59]

There was no official faculty position of music instructor at Mount Holyoke until 1862.[60] In Dickinson's time, students who were proficient enough to serve as teachers conducted the vocal music classes. During 1844–1848, vocal music was taught by Miss Harriet Hawes of Boston (class of 1848).[61] The choirs were under the general supervision of staff member Susan Tolman (1826–1912).[62] With three active choirs, and a fourth devoted to the performance of sacred music, the student instructors received assistance from as many as ten other students.[63] Thus, many of Mary Lyon's students were well trained in the performance and instruction of vocal music, and Lyon eagerly supported their musical activities even beyond their student years.

In September 1848, Susannah Fitch of Hamilton, Ohio, who had graduated the previous year, corresponded with Mary Lyon to inquire if Lyon could recommend someone who could teach music. In her detailed response to Fitch, Lyon recommended Emily Norcross, Dickinson's cousin. Lyon wrote: "Do you recollect Miss Norcross one year behind you[?] She has devoted considerable time to music. I am not quite certain that she considers herself qualified to teach." Lyon offers to write to Norcross and to Harriette C. Haile of Hinsdale, New Hampshire, of the 1848 graduating class. In closing Lyon writes: "If I fail of finding a teacher, I will let you know as early as I can. Affectionately yours, Mary Lyon."[64] Once again we see the gravitational pull that music had on Mary Lyon, and she responded to it with a passion.

The Music Books Used at Mount Holyoke

According to the 1847–48 Mount Holyoke catalog: "As Books and Stationery can be had at the Seminary on very low terms, young ladies need not purchase them elsewhere, though it is desirable that they bring with them any of the regular text books which they may own; also a Bible, an English Dictionary, a Modern Atlas, Watts' Psalms and Hymns, [Nettleton's] Village Hymns, the Carmina Sacra [by Lowell Mason], the Vocalist and the Odeon, together with any other musical works they may possess; and other books containing selections for improvement in reading, and standard poetical works."[65]

This kind of musical encouragement serves as an excellent indicator of the level of immersion in music that took place at Mount Holyoke. It also indicates that Emily Dickinson may have brought with her to Mount Holyoke music books already in the family library, as well as some of her own sheet music (see chapter 7).[66]

Mary Lyon told her students: "Secular music gives spirit and zest. We should thank God that he has so made us that we can enjoy it. It is a wonderful kindness."[67] The secular music books used by the vocal music instructors at Mount Holyoke served both as manuals for vocal music instruction and as a robust collection of music suitable for performance in both the singing school class and the family circle.[68] One of the required music books cited in the Mount Holyoke catalog was *The Odeon: A Collection of Secular Music Arranged and Harmonized for Four Voices* (1837) by G. J. Webb and Lowell Mason. Webb had co-founded the Boston Academy of Music in 1833 and, like his colleague Mason, was an experienced educator, hymnist, and tunebook compiler. *The Odeon* contained a repertory of about seventy-five accessible adaptations of well-known music by European composers as well as newly composed pieces in a similar style.[69] Some of these choral arrangements of secular music that Dickinson sang at school are represented as vocal and instrumental pieces in Dickinson's bound music book. These include songs such as "The Bonny Boat," "Home, Sweet Home," the "Canadian Boat Song," and "Bonnie Doon."[70]

According to the musicologist Jewel Smith, another music book used at Mount Holyoke was *The Social Choir* (1838), edited by educator, performer, and composer George Kingsley (1811–1884). [71] Again we see where Dickinson gained intimate familiarity with an arranged vocal and choral repertoire of operatic selections by Bellini, Rossini, Meyerbeer, Mozart, and Weber as well as the English composer and singer Charles Edward Horn (1786–1849) and the American composer and hymnist Augusta Browne (1820–1882), not to forget the ubiquitous vocal music staple of the period "Oft in the Stilly Night," arranged by John Stevenson, with words by Thomas Moore.[72] In a similar way, some of the music in *The Social Choir* can be found in Dickinson's music book, in the form of variation sets on operatic arias or other instrumental music, and vocal ballads such as "The Last Rose of Summer." Additional composers represented in Kingsley's compilation whose music Dickinson collected include Michael William Balfe, Samuel Nelson, and Henry Rowley Bishop. Of particular interest is Kingsley's vocal duet arrangement of the popular Irish air from Dickinson's music book "Araby's Daughter."[73]

According to the annual catalog for 1847–48, another vocal music collection used at Mount Holyoke which Dickinson owned was *The Vocalist: Consisting of Short and Easy Glees* (1844), compiled by Lowell Mason and George J. Webb. This compilation featured music by Felix Mendelssohn and a host of important but long-forgotten composers.[74] An entry from the Mount Holyoke journal letter written by Susan Tolman brings this music book to life.[75]

On Thursday, June 22, 1848, about 135 students participated in the school's annual mountain excursion to the top of Mount Holyoke. When they reached the summit, many brought out music books and began to sing from them. Susan Tolman, in the Mount Holyoke journal letter, describes in real time the details of that excursion: "Now our second company have reached the Holyoke Hotel—When they are leaving their carriages—Now a little cluster of songsters that [we] took with us are vieing [sic] with the feathered ones above them in their melody—They are seated on that rock overlooking Northampton, just now they sung 'When Up the Mountain Climbing,' then 'The Silver Moon,' and now 'Love Not.'"[76]

"When Up the Mountain Climbing" is the first line of "Mountain Song" from *The Vocalist: Consisting of Short and Easy Glees*, a required text which the students seem to have put to good use. "The Silver Moon" by Joseph W. Turner (1846) and "Love Not" by John J. Blockley were well known and could easily have been sung from memory. Dickinson's music book contains a quickstep arrangement of Blockley's "Love Not."

Whatever Emily Dickinson absorbed from her early singing schools, the vocal music curriculum at Mount Holyoke and the books used there would further extend her musical knowledge and abilities. Another charming anecdote, this one by classmate Amelia Jones of Springfield about her hometown friend Emily Bowdoin, illustrates the range and familiarity of the music to which the students at Mount Holyoke were exposed and the facilitation of its performance:

> One day E. came to my room, singing-book in hand. "I can stand it no longer," she said. "Come with me." We took the road to the ferry as the most sequestered, and having walked our required distance, we ventured to delay in the broad spaceway bounded by the horizon. Then, perched upon the top most rail of a fence, we opened the book and our mouths, drew the diapason stops of our vocal organs, and sang tune after tune,—long metres, short metres, hallelujah metres, et id omne genus,—chants, rounds, fugues, anthems, etc., etc., carrying two parts, and by snatches three or four, as the score demanded. We sang and sang till the valley rang "with our hymns of lofty cheer." Our only visible auditors were two or three cows that had been quietly feeding in a pasture near. They were too well-bred to obtrude with double-base bellowing or with horn accompaniment, but they ceased their cropping and stood in silent amazement at the unusual sight and sound. We needed no plaudits, for we were a joy to ourselves. We had found a remedy for depressions, repression, suppression and oppression, and no two maidens returned that day from open-air exercise more exhilarated than we. The seminary choirs were ere long arranged for regular practise, which was the tonic and safety-valve we needed.[77]

The sheer joy derived from this musical outing is evident. This anecdote also sheds light on what Amelia Jones meant when she said that her friend could "stand it no longer." The extreme regimentation imposed upon the students at the Mount Holyoke Female Seminary (and other institutions) extended to a mandatory isolation from the outside world and the local community.[78]

The Mexican American War

In the fall of 1847, far beyond the doors of the seminary, a war between the United States and Mexico over control of the territories of Texas, New Mexico, and California was raging and a presidential election was brewing; and while Dickinson, in a letter to her brother, may have been humorous in her account of not knowing what was happening, the isolation of the seminary from the outside world was clearly a concern.

On October 21, Dickinson wrote to Austin from Mount Holyoke:

> Wont you please to tell me when you answer my letter who the candidate for President is? I have been trying to find out ever since I came here & have not yet succeeded. I dont know anything more about affairs in the world, than if I was in a trance, & you must imagine with all your 'Sophomoric discernment,' that it is but little & very faint. Has the Mexican war terminated yet & how? Are we beat? Do you know of any nation about to besiege South Hadley? If so, do inform me of it, for I would be glad of a chance to escape, if we are to be stormed. I suppose Miss Lyon. would furnish us all with daggers & order us to fight for our lives, in case such perils should befall us.[79]

On the very day of Dickinson's letter, the *Springfield Daily Republican* noted that General Winfield Scott (1786–1866) had been in control of Mexico City, and with the help of the local Mexican police force had established and maintained order in that city. Scott was "reported to have called on the Mexican States for commissioners, to be vested with full powers to make a treaty."[80]

In Dickinson's music book there are several tunes that became important contrafacta during the Mexican-American War (1846–1848): the minstrel tune "Lucy Neal" (which is in the quickstep section of Dickinson's music book) would be adapted as a wartime melody with new lyrics by the prolific composer/arranger Joseph W. Turner (1818–1894) as "The Coast of Mexico."[81] "The Girl I Left Behind Me" was similarly fitted with new words as "The Leg I Left Behind Me," commemorating the victory of US troops over the Mexican army under the command of General Santa Anna.[82] Not surprisingly, "Yankee Doodle" was a tune that was in constant motion with US soldiers deployed to the Rio Grande.[83]

"The Home That I Love"

Five weeks after writing to her brother asking for some news of the Mexican war, Emily came home for the Thanksgiving recess. Upon her return to Mount Holyoke, she reported to Abiah Root that the days following Thanksgiving

> were as happily spent as the eventful Thanksgiving day itself.... Monday came so soon & with it came a carriage to our door & amidst tears falling thick & fast away I went again. Slowly & sadly dragged a few of the days after my return to the Seminary and I was very homesick, but "after a storm there comes a calm" and so it was in my case. My sorrows were soon lost in study & I again felt happy, if happiness there can be away from "home, sweet home."[84]

Here of course Dickinson references the song "Home, Sweet Home" from her music book. Her homesickness would be prematurely relieved, however, as she would be leaving Mount Holyoke sooner than anticipated. For years Emily's health had been an ongoing issue. At the Amherst Academy in 1846, she wrote to Abiah Root that she had been "an exile from school two terms on account of my health, and you know what it is to 'love school.'"[85]

Despite the fact that she was out of school at that time, in the winter term (January 1846), at the urging of her father, she attended a recitation in German at Amherst College conducted by the president of the Amherst Academy, Lyman Coleman (1796–1882). January 1846 would be Coleman's last term in Amherst (before moving on to a position in Princeton), so there was some urgency in Edward's wanting his daughter to have this opportunity to study with the Reverend Coleman. Aside from the German class, Emily reported to Abiah Root that she continued to take music lessons and practiced for two hours each day.[86]

In March of 1847 Emily wrote that she was "quite sick" with "the Influenza" which had been "very prevalent."[87] These bouts of illness continued into the Mount Holyoke period (1847–48), possibly the result of a pulmonary condition accompanied by a persistent cough.[88] She may also have developed a "nervous condition" brought about by weathering the storms of religious conversion at Mount Holyoke.[89] Whatever the reason, Emily Dickinson would attend the Mount Holyoke Female Seminary for only one year (two terms). The school was not averse to students staying only one year, and many did. According to the catalog from 1848–49: "No pledge is required for continuance in the Seminary for more than one year. A commencing of the regular course in order is all that is expected. All enter the institution for only one year at first. The question of returning the second is left for future decision."[90] In other words, the first year was probationary.[91]

When Emily Dickinson returned home from Mount Holyoke in August 1848, home she would remain. From that vantage point she watched many of her classmates go on to graduate and make their way as missionaries to the then exotic lands of India, Syria, Ceylon, and Persia.[92] Stories and objects from their adventures returned home to Amherst in abundance, in the form of curios, scientific specimens for the Amherst College "cabinet," and other artifacts. Most Americans of the period shared a fascination with travel and foreign lands, and this same curiosity finds expression in Emily Dickinson's music book. The next chapter explores the depth of Dickinson's music collecting through her imaginings of travel, from the "Chinese Museum" to the "Spice Isles," as well as simply the "Sounds From Home" and her garden, just as she experienced it all while seated at her piano in the family parlor.[93]

CHAPTER 3

The Avid Music Collector

"Home as a Waltz"

THE DICKINSON HOUSEHOLD APPEARS TO have been a quiet haven in that all the family members, particularly Emily, when away, wrote of missing home. This was a characteristic trait inherited from the Norcross side that, according to Dickinson biographer Alfred Habegger, "was a strong and exclusive adhesiveness to house and family."[1] For Emily, home was also a place where the undertow of both companionship and anxiety coalesced in a delicate balance of domestic sentiment and familial attachment.

At age fifteen, Emily was kept out of the women's sewing circle. "Mother thinks it not best for me to go into society so soon," she wrote to Abiah Root.[2] Edward Dickinson depended on Emily and Lavinia remaining at home not only for the comfort and companionship of family but also to help with the housework and the constant flow of visiting relatives and other houseguests. The sisters often expressed relief when these guests departed. On January 2, 1851, Lavinia reported in her diary that "The Hadley cousin visit is over and gone." A similar entry for October 23 reads "Uncle Alfred come & gone."[3]

Befitting the treasurer of Amherst College and a prominent lawyer, Edward Dickinson's home was a stopping point for visitors such as Civil War general George McClellan, publishers of the *Springfield Daily Republican* Samuel Bowles and Josiah Holland, Judge Otis Lord of Salem, and many others, including Dickinson relations from far and wide.[4] "We live in constant fear of some other visitation—," Emily wrote to her brother.[5]

[46]

These visits sometimes lasted for days or even weeks. Then there was the annual Amherst College commencement, a four-day affair which included an afternoon commencement tea at the Dickinson home and grounds. All of this activity kept Edward's two daughters tethered to a busy home life.

When she did go out, Emily's occasional absences from home caused her father "great agitation at my protracted stay—and mother and Vinnie in tears, for fear that he would kill me."[6] Although Emily was humorous in her correspondence regarding her father's concerns, Alfred Habegger notes that her "father's anxieties [were] as infectious as they were insistent."[7] Wendy Martin writes that Edward Dickinson's "children alternately feared and were fascinated by him. Emily Dickinson often refers to him as 'my master,' a habit common to Victorian women, and Austin and Lavinia were always careful to defer to him."[8]

Paternal worries on the part of the "Old Folks," as Emily amusingly referred to them, also centered on her health. She was often excused from church services during inclement weather, but by 1854, her interest in attending church services was waning: "They will all go but me, to the usual meetinghouse, to hear the usual sermon; the inclemency of the storm so kindly detaining me."[9] By 1861 poet Emily Dickinson would write, "Some keep the Sabbath going to Church — / I keep it, staying at Home — ."[10] Emily and her sister remained at home, and neither would marry.[11] Austin too remained at home, or at least nearby. His plan was to go west, but his father had other ideas. Edward took his son into his law firm as a partner and built him and his new wife, Susan, an elegant home next door that was christened The Evergreens.[12]

"The Home That I Love"

According to Dickinson scholars Vivian Pollack and Marianne Noble, home became Emily Dickinson's "model of perfection,"[13] complemented by nature as her choir and the bobolink as her singing master. The familial landscape of home and hearth in which Dickinson participated is reflected in the popular sentimental ballads and some of the instrumental selections in her music book. Women were prime consumers of sheet music, and music publishers celebrated the feminine sphere in much of their musical merchandise, which Dickinson eagerly acquired.[14] "The Home That I Love," "Home, Sweet Home," "Sounds From Home," "Home Quick Step," and "Home as a Waltz" in Dickinson's bound music book serve as performative signifiers which aided in the development of a musical sentiment that would find expression in her correspondence, and later, appropriations of colloquial language, tropes, and ballad meter from these songs would inform some of Dickinson's most beloved poems (see chapter 11).

"Home, Sweet Home" is ubiquitous in music volumes. Dickinson's volume features not just the usual vocal ballad but an instrumental waltz version, "Home as a Waltz," which is inscribed by Emily to "Lavinia N. Dickinson Jan. 15, 184[6]." According to the historian Jay Leyda, Emily presented Lavinia with this as her first piano piece.[15] Of the thirty-two waltzes in Dickinson's bound music book, there are many with interesting titles that evoke stories and associations with the Dickinson home and its surroundings. The waltzes also serve to animate the Dickinson family personalities, giving added meaning to the music. One of those titles is the "Aurora Waltz."

"Aurora Waltz"

Edward Dickinson's home, his family, and the community of Amherst were of paramount importance to him. He directed his children's attention to specific items of interest that engaged him and that he thought would engage them. The presence of two adjacent pieces in Emily Dickinson's music book with the title "Aurora Waltz," by Ferdinand Unger (1808–1871) and Joseph Labitzky (1802–1881), is a reminder of one such memorable event that greatly moved Edward Dickinson. On Monday, September 29, 1851, a magnificent aurora borealis blanketed the sky over Amherst. Emily wrote to her brother:

> There was quite an excitement in the village Monday evening. We were all startled by a violent church bell ringing, and thinking of nothing but fire, rushed out in the street to see. The sky was a beautiful red, bordering on a crimson, and rays of a gold pink color were constantly shooting off from a kind of sun in the centre. People were alarmed at this beautiful Phenomenon, supposing that fires somewhere were *coloring the sky*. The exhibition lasted for nearly 15. minutes, and the streets

were full of people wondering and admiring. Father happened to see it among the very first and rang the bell *himself* to call attention to it.[16]

Years later, Emily Dickinson, in a letter to her sister-in-law Susan Dickinson, included a poem, albeit about the sunrise, which she dedicated to her father:

> That shall Aurora be
> East of Eternity!
> One with the banner gay,
> One in the red array —
> *That* is the Break of Day![17]

Philadelphia

The following year, on December 17, 1852, Edward Dickinson was elected to the United States Congress as the representative from the Tenth District of Massachusetts.[18] He would be away from home frequently, but only for a single term. In February and March 1855 Emily and Lavinia visited their father in Washington, DC, where they spent three weeks. On their return trip to Amherst, they stopped in Philadelphia, staying two weeks with their second cousin Eliza Coleman. The Coleman and Dickinson families, related by marriage to Mrs. Dickinson, were very close. Eliza's father, the Reverend Lyman Coleman, was the former head of the Amherst Academy (1844–1846). After Amherst the Colemans moved to Princeton. While in Princeton their older daughter Olivia died suddenly of tuberculosis on September 28, 1847. A year later the Colemans moved to Philadelphia, where the Revered Coleman assumed the position of principal of the Presbyterian Academy.[19]

Beginning in the late eighteenth century, Philadelphia was a center for music publishing and could boast several major publishing houses, some of them family owned, such as those of the Benjamin Carr family and the Klemm brothers. Other publishing firms included those of George Willig and George E. Blake, which in their day would grow to become two of the largest publishing houses in the city, if not the country.[20] Many of these music publishers provided outlets for consumers to purchase music. Dickinson scholar Georgiana Strickland notes that Dickinson herself may have taken advantage of the music stores in Philadelphia, purchasing sheet music during her visit.[21] There are four Philadelphia imprints in the Dickinson music book: Philippe Musard's arrangement of the contra dance tune "The Celebrated Baden Baden Polka" was available at Lee & Walker's Music Store & Circulating Library, which in 1855 was located at 188 Chestnut Street.[22] If Eliza Coleman was a paid subscriber to Lee and Walker's circulating music library, she would have been able to borrow music, or simply purchase it directly from their music store.[23] Other Philadelphia imprints in Dickinson's music book include "L'Enfer Quadrille Diabolique" by Henri Bohlman, published by Augustus Fiot at 196 Chestnut Street; an instrumental arrangement of "Gems from *The Bohemian Girl*" the opera by William Balfe, published by Edmund Ferrett; and the "Bird Waltz" by Francis (Francesco) Panormo, published by John G. Klemm.

During their stay in Philadelphia, it is widely thought that the Dickinson sisters were taken to services at the Colemans' church, the Arch Street Presbyterian Church.[24] There they heard the preaching of the Reverend Charles Wadsworth (1814–1882). Wadsworth's preaching left a marked impression on Emily, and she and Wadsworth became correspondents.[25] After their visit, Eliza Coleman wrote often to Emily, sending her copies of Wadsworth's sermons. Depending on exactly when Dickinson's music was bound, perhaps Eliza also sent along some pieces of sheet music which Dickinson included in her music book as an affectionate reminder of her Philadelphia visit.

"Affection Waltz"

By far the most significant Philadelphia music connection in Dickinson's bound volume of music is the "Affection Waltz" by "W. H. F." (William Henry Fry, 1813–1864). Fry was a native of Philadelphia and one of the most important American composers of the nineteenth century. This waltz adaptation from Fry's opera *Leonora* was enormously popular, seeing dozens of editions and arrangements including a notable variation set by Carl Czerny.[26] *Leonora* had its premiere in Philadelphia at the Chestnut Street Theatre on June 4, 1845. Fry and his older brother, librettist Joseph Reese Fry (1811–1865), claimed that *Leonora* was the first grand opera written in the United States by an American librettist and composer.[27] Long before the Czech composer Antonín Dvořák visited America in 1892 and called on American composers to build their music from "American" sources (offering his *Symphony from the New World* as an example), Fry's efforts on this front were already in motion. As both a composer and a journalist, Fry had repeatedly encouraged US composers not just to emulate European musical models but instead to "work with their materials until they create a distinctly American style."[28] Fry frequently lectured audiences and composers on the state of music in America, arguing: "Until the American public shall learn to support American artists, Art will not become indigenous to this country, but will only exist as a feeble exotic, and we shall continue to be provincial in Art. The American composer should not allow the name of Beethoven, or Handel or Mozart to prove an eternal bugbear to him, nor should he pay them reverence; he should only reverence his Art, and strike out manfully and independently into untrodden realms, just as his nature and inspirations may invite him, else he can never achieve lasting renown."[29]

Fry was certainly not without his detractors; chief among them were the composer/critic Richard Storrs Willis and journalist John Sullivan Dwight, founder of the seminal *Dwight's Journal of Music*.[30] Both welcomed the Europeanization of America's musical culture and were not averse to engaging Fry in an all-out journalistic war of words on the subject.[31] But Fry was going against the prevailing tide. While his efforts on behalf of American music will reverberate more fully in the next chapter, we also have to remember that a similar scenario was playing out in the domestic sphere of the American parlor.

Beethoven, Labitzky, and Gung'l

Concurrently with the growing interest in Beethoven filtering out from the larger US cities, there had been a waltz craze going on, sweeping up many aspiring amateur musicians, including Emily Dickinson, and what better way to introduce the music of the leading European masters to these amateur American musicians than through a waltz. Of the thirty-two waltzes in Dickinson's bound music book, one third of the book's entire content, nine of those waltzes are misattributed to Ludwig van Beethoven (1770–1827). As evidenced in the concerned words of William Henry Fry, the music of Beethoven was on the ascendancy in the United States as a model to be imitated by American composers and aspired to by listeners and amateur performers, as well as a commodity to be exploited by music publishers. Beethoven's works were still a brand-new attraction to the burgeoning American sheet music market.[32] Until Beethoven's music was firmly established on America's shores and his published compositions were more widely available, these waltzes served as an accessible and popular means of attracting a broad and eager audience of consumers like Emily Dickinson. The music publishers who were monitoring the heartbeat of the movement then under way to elevate America's musical taste through the works of Beethoven and others did all they could to promote anything that could be grasped as being associated with Beethoven. According to musicologist Michael Broyles: "Beethoven wrote only two waltzes, in 1824, minor pieces for the Viennese actor Carl Friedrich Muller, both of which would have been unknown to American publishers who thought that combining Beethoven with waltz guaranteed success. This, however, did not stop publishers from printing many supposed waltzes by Beethoven. Any piece by Beethoven in three-quarter time was fair game, and if the music bore no relation to anything Beethoven composed, that mattered little also. That is particularly true after he had become well known."[33] While the true authorship of many of these waltzes attributed to Beethoven is not known, "Beethoven's Dream" in Dickinson's music book was actually composed by Carl Maria von Weber (1786–1826), whose presence in the music book is distinguished by another of his compositions, "Von Weber's Last Waltz."

Beyond the nine waltzes misattributed to Beethoven, Dickinson's propensity for waltzes continues with "The Elfin Waltzes" and the "Aurora Waltz" by Joseph Labitzky (1802–1881), two pieces that are representative of this major German-Bohemian composer, violinist, and conductor. Labitzky's elegant and spirited dance music was extremely popular both in the United States and abroad. Eventually Labitzky's popularity, and his music, would be eclipsed by the Hungarian oboist, orchestra leader, and composer Josef Gung'l (1809–1889) and later by the perennially popular works of the "Waltz King," the younger Johann Strauss (1825–1899).[34] The two works by Gung'l in Dickinson's bound music book are the "Fest March" and his waltz set "Sounds from Home." Performed on tour by Gung'l's Steyermarkische Orchestra, "Sounds from Home" took the United States by storm, stimulating sales of the sheet music. "Sounds from Home" is memorialized both in Dickinson's bound music book and in her correspondence.[35]

"The Louisville Waltz"

"The Louisville Waltz," by W. C. Peters, from Dickinson's music book, is noteworthy because it lets us trace the ultimately tragic story of a famous nineteenth-century American music publisher. In Dickinson's day the family of William Cumming Peters (1805–1866) operated a dynasty of publishing houses in Louisville, Baltimore, Cincinnati, and later New York and St. Louis.[36] Peters opened one of the first music shops in Pittsburgh in the 1820s. He moved to Louisville in 1832, where he was first a "Professor of Music" and later opened a music store.[37] With his publishing business firmly established, Peters issued his "Louisville March and Quick Step" and his "Louisville Waltz," which became very popular. Peters's biographer Richard Wetzel cites twenty-three editions of the "Louisville March and Quick Step," a title that, he notes, dated "probably from his early years in Louisville."[38]

In the 1830s Peters composed a great deal of instrumental arrangements and parlor music that was also brought out by the major music publishers in New York, Philadelphia, and Boston. Peters's name recognition was such that often only his initials would appear on a piece of published music, as is the case with his "'Louisville March and Quick Step,' *By W.C.P.*," in Dickinson's music book. Dickinson collected both the march and quickstep and his "Louisville Waltz."

A contemporary source describes Peters as the most "favorably known publisher in the west. [He] employs one title engraver, three music engravers, and about six printers. They keep their copper-plate presses constantly employed and issued seven to ten thousand pages of music per week."[39] Music publishers used title engravers to engrave the covers of the sheet music and the caption titles which served as a header on the first page of music. Dickinson's music book showcases some of the major title engravers of her time, as well as engravers of music (see online Appendix B).

Peters moved to Baltimore in 1849 and then to Cincinnati around 1851 and established successful publishing firms in both locations. He remained in Cincinnati for fifteen years. In March of 1866 a fire at the Pike Opera House, the home of Peters's publishing firm, destroyed his entire inventory. One month later, on April 20, 1866, Peters was dead of a heart attack. The Peters family publishing operation continued into the next generation, ceasing business around 1892.[40] While the firm is largely forgotten today, the music published by William Cumming Peters, especially his original compositions, live on in bound music volumes as a reminder of this once very successful music publishing family.

"The Glenmary Waltzes"

Emily Dickinson read widely and was fully aware of the important musical, cultural, and literary happenings of her time. The three waltz sets in Dickinson's music book, *The Glenmary Waltzes* (1847) by composer Richard Storrs Willis (1819–1900), are one such example, offering up engaging music with an equally engaging connection to America's literary and cultural history. Willis had a highly successful career as a music journalist, author, critic, compiler of choral music editions, and editor for the *Musical Times* (1849–1852) and later the *Musical World*.[41] As a composer, Willis is best remembered today for his tune "Carol" with words by Edmund Hamilton Sears (1810–1876) as "It Came Upon the Midnight Clear" (1850).[42]

Better known to the world at large was Willis's older brother, author and poet Nathaniel Parker Willis (1806–1867). Originally from Maine, the Willis family moved to Boston in 1812, where the nine Willis children were exposed to the city's literary and publishing circles. Their father, Nathaniel Willis Sr., was publisher of the *Boston Recorder* (1816) and later, in 1827, the first newspaper for children, the *Youth's Companion* (to which the Dickinsons subscribed).[43] The boys' sister Sara Payson Willis (1811–1872), under the name Fanny Fern, would become enormously successful as a writer of both novels and newspaper columns and an author of children's books.[44]

After his graduation from Yale in 1821, the junior Nathaniel Willis's poetry began appearing in his father's publications. Willis moved to Europe in 1831 to take a post as the foreign editor for the *New York Mirror*, chronicling that era in his lively book *Pencilings By the Way*. Moving to London in 1835, Willis met and married Mary Stace (1816–1845). He also became acquainted with Charles Dickens.[45]

Upon their return to the United States in 1837, the Willises settled by Owego Creek in Tioga County, New York, on an estate they called Glenmary. There they lived among other notables, including James Fenimore Cooper, and circulated in the company of Melville, Emerson, and Longfellow. Composer/singer Henry Russell recounts a pleasant visit that occurred in 1838:

After a short stay [in New York City], however, I determined to go on tramp again, so I proceeded up the North [Hudson] River to Albany and thence to Owego, by way of Schenectady, the seat of the Knickerbockers. Fenimore Cooper whose home was in Owego invited me to stay with him, and for a week I enjoyed the cordial hospitality of the distinguished novelist. Many famous men were among my fellow guests, including Longfellow (then quite a young man), Cullen Bryant, the poet, N. P. Willis, General George [Pope] Morris, and [poet] Epps [sic] Sargent.[46]

Willis's engaging book *Letters from Under a Bridge* memorializes his experiences as a gentleman farmer on the Glenmary estate.[47] This was not the only creative piece to take inspiration from that idyllic setting.

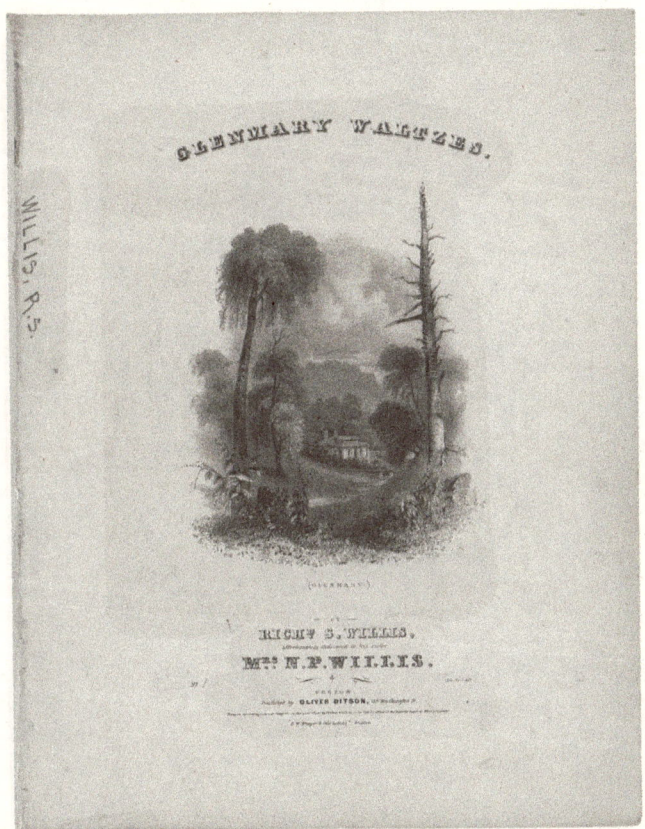

FIGURE 5. *The Glenmary Waltzes* (1842). Music and Recorded Sound Division, The New York Public Library for the Performing Arts, Astor, Lenox and Tilden Foundations.

Willis's brother Richard composed three sets of his *Glenmary Waltzes*, "affectionately dedicated to his sister[-in-law] Mrs. Nathaniel P. Willis" (see figure 5). They were published by Oliver Ditson in 1842. The illustrated cover from the firm of B. W. Thayer of Boston depicts the lushly wooded Glenmary estate. A second edition of the three sets was reissued by Ditson in 1845, containing a similarly illustrated cover, this one by illustrator John Henry Bufford. In 1842 the Willises had a daughter, Imogen. Shortly thereafter, financial troubles, and the death of Mary Willis in 1845, forced Nathaniel to give up the estate. He and Imogen moved to New York City, later settling at Idlewild, an estate in Cornwall, New York, on the Hudson River. There, Willis founded the *Home Journal*, a magazine dedicated to suburban living. It is still in publication today as *Town and Country*.[48]

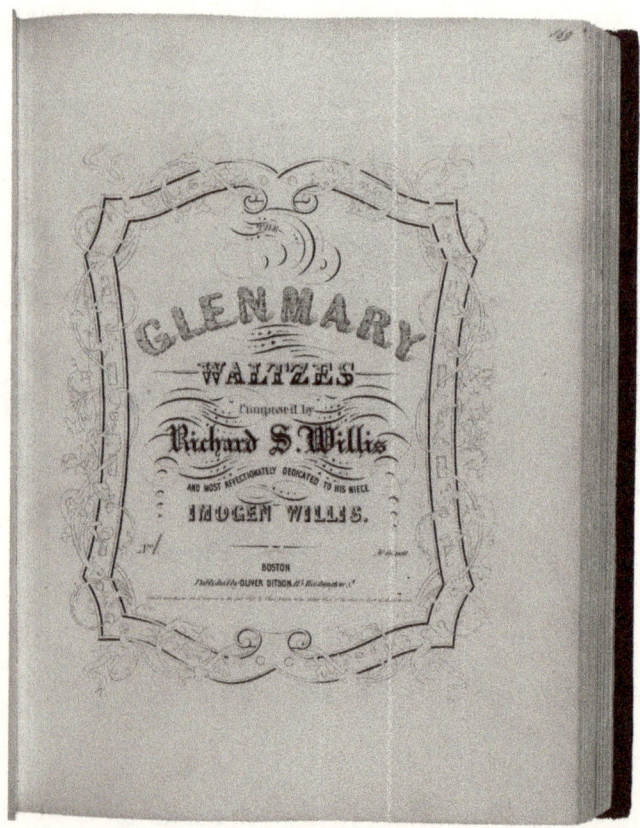

FIGURE 6. *The Glenmary Waltzes* (1847). Emily Dickinson's music book, EDR 469, Houghton Library, Harvard University.

The Glenmary Waltzes remained popular. They were reissued in 1847, and re-dedicated to Imogen Willis (see figure 6). Emily Dickinson's music book contains all three waltz sets from 1847. Sadly, no splendid illustration graces the title page of the sets in Dickinson's music book, just a simple decorative rustic wreath, perhaps a memorial to Mary Willis and the Glenmary estate. The three sets of *The Glenmary Waltzes* contain five or six waltzes each with titles like "Cottage," "Lawn," "Shade," "Meadow," "Glade," and "Voice of the River," recalling the woodland estate of Nathaniel Willis, the gentleman farmer, on New York State's southern tier.

Dickinson would have been familiar with the poetry of Nathaniel Willis from a music book she used at Mount Holyoke *The Social Choir* (1847), which contains the solo song "Andre's Request to Washington" by George Kingsley, set to Willis's poetry.[49] In addition, Susan Dickinson owned a copy of Willis's 1847 collection of poems, which is in the Dickinson family library at Harvard. With her passion for waltzes and her love of nature, it's not surprising that Emily Dickinson collected all three sets of *The Glenmary Waltzes*.

Emily Dickinson's Newfoundland Dog Carlo

Dickinson's love of nature and the outdoors also found expression in her extensive herbarium of plant and flower specimens, which she had begun around 1845 while studying botany at the Amherst Academy, gathering flowers in the woods, or if she had participated in Mount Holyoke class trips led by geologist and Amherst College president Dr. Edward Hitchcock.[50] Starting in 1849, she was accompanied on her long walks by her dog Carlo (ca. 1849/50–1866), which was given to her by her father.

Dickinson scholars agree that Carlo was a Newfoundland. There were other dogs named Carlo in contemporary literature that would have been familiar to Dickinson. In December 1849, around the time that Carlo came into Dickinson's life, she read Charlotte Brontë's *Jane Eyre* (1847), in which the character St. John Rivers owns a dog named Carlo. In Dickinson's correspondence, she refers to a favorite novel, *Reveries of a Bachelor* (1850) by Donald Grant Mitchell (a.k.a. Ik Marvel), which also features a dog named Carlo.[51] In addition to the contemporary literature there was also music. Composer Henry Russell, whose music Dickinson knew and collected, wrote a song called "The New Foundland Dog," which is not in her music book. Published in 1843, the song, billed as "a descriptive ballad," commemorates a dramatic and probably apocryphal event: The packet ship *Montezuma* was in the midst of an Atlantic crossing when a passenger, a young child, went overboard. A Newfoundland dog by the name of Carlo, which happened to be onboard and nearby, jumped into the water, grabbed the child, and swam to a waiting lifeboat. Both dog and child were saved.[52]

For sixteen years Emily Dickinson's Carlo would be a constant presence, providing her with both companionship and protection. With her "Shaggy Ally," Dickinson was able to remain outdoors on her own for long stretches in the woods without her parents worrying that "I might pick a poisonous flower, or Goblins kidnap me."[53] Recent Dickinson research points to the fact that after Carlo died in 1866, Dickinson began staying closer to home, spending more time in her beloved and beautiful garden.[54]

Waltzes and Emily Dickinson's Gardening Life

In Dickinson's day, while walking the grounds of the Dickinson home, we might have heard the strains of *The Glenmary Waltzes*, the "Tulip Waltz," "Japonica Waltz," "Linden Waltz," "Willow Waltz," or the "Bird Waltz," coming from the parlor piano. If the wind was blowing, the Dickinsons' aeolian harp might have been heard through an open window, accompanied by the sounds of the "Æolian Waltz" on the piano.[55] This music, like the Dickinson garden, spoke of gentility, refinement, and taste. These nature, flower, and plant-themed waltzes in her music book offer reminders of Emily Dickinson's passion for her flowers, plants, and garden. According to Judith Farr, Dickinson's flower garden, like her poems, was "a means of creating order and beauty."[56] The same could be said about Dickinson's bound volume of sheet music.

The Dickinsons cultivated their natural surroundings for both pleasure and sustenance. Behind the house was a barn for the horses, pigs, chickens, and cows. Under the care of Jeremiah Holden or Wells Newport, the animals grazed across the street in the "Dickinson meadow."[57] Alongside the barn were Mrs. Dickinson's "prize winning" figs, and grapes climbed the trellis.[58] Down the flagstone path were fruit trees—cherry, apple, and pear—and hedges of pussy willow. Dickinson referred to the pussy willow as "Nature's buff message — ."[59] The nature-themed waltzes in Dickinson's music book furnished a descriptive nod to the garden and grounds of the Dickinson home, for example, "Tulip Waltz":

> *The Tulip*
> She slept beneath a tree
>   Remembered but by me.
> I touched her cradle mute;
> She recognized the foot,
> Put on her Carmine suit, —
> And see![60]

Dickinson's niece Martha ("Mattie") remembered her aunt's garden as "a meandering mass of bloom,"[61] rich with peonies, lilacs, lily of the valley, nasturtiums, marigolds, and roses. There were also bulbs. Emily admitted that she had "long been a Lunatic on Bulbs."[62] Just as the "Tulip Waltz" in her music book and the "Carmine suit" tulips in her garden could be enjoyed again and again, she was known to force her bulbs to produce indoors, "one of Dickinson's stratagems against winter gloom."[63] Gardening was so important to cultivating Dickinson's "Eden" and the life of the Homestead that in 1855 Edward Dickinson added a conservatory to the house, enabling Emily and her sister to tend their plants year-round.[64] In winter, Emily coaxed her hyacinths into bloom in her conservatory and on her bedroom windowsills.[65]

"Willow Waltz"

While there were no willows on the Homestead property, Emily Dickinson Museum gardener in residence Marta McDowell notes that

> [Dickinson] likely would have seen weeping willow (*Salix babylonica*) during her 1846 visit to Mount Auburn Cemetery in Cambridge. The weeping willow was introduced to North America before 1800. Like all willows it is easy to propagate, thus popular with nurserymen. From the start it was common as a graveyard and later cemetery motif—both planted and on gravestone carvings—for its weeping form and foliage habit. It is among the last trees to drop leaves in the fall and first to green up in spring, reminders of everlasting life.[66]

In a letter to her future sister-in-law Susan Gilbert, Dickinson alludes to such a setting when she writes, "I remember you, Susie, *always*—I keep you ever here, and when *you* are gone, then I'm gone—and we're 'neath one willow tree."[67]

"*Japonica Waltz*"

Emily Dickinson also cultivated japonica plants. Using a japonica reference to admonish her friend Maria Whitney for not paying her a visit, Dickinson wrote, "You failed to keep your appointment with the appleblossoms—the japonica, even, bore an apple to elicit you, but that must be a silver bell which calls the human heart."[68] In Dickinson's time japonica was a popular plant found in most American conservatories.[69]

According to Marta McDowell:

> The word japonica is a specific epithet used for many different plant genera from Asia, especially, as one would guess, Japan. In the 19th century, as Japanese plants started coming into the U.S. [after Commodore Matthew C. Perry's visit to Japan in 1853–54], "japonica" was also picked up as a common name for different plants, including camellia. But for Dickinson, I'm confident that she was applying it to Chaenomeles japonica, what I call quince or flowering quince. One still grows at near the front piazza of The Evergreens (southwest corner). Dickinson's japonica a.k.a. flowering quince does bear fruit (though it isn't grown as an edible). It is related to the apple in that both are members of the Rose family. Note that it is not the quince fruit popular for preserves in the UK, which is Cydonia oblonga.[70]

Inside the Dickinson conservatory, Emily's flowers were "near and foreign, and I have but to cross the floor to stand in the Spice Isles."[71] Dickinson's fascination with distant shores far from her home and garden is evidenced in her music book, reflecting an aspect of the American imagination that was promoted by the music publishers.

"*The Swiss Waltz*"

"The Swiss Waltz" in Dickinson's music book, with variations by P. K. Moran (d. 1831), was a traditional tune (presumably of Swiss origin) and associated with the Scottish, Irish, and American traditional tune repertoire. Moran's variations were first published in the United States and in Moran's hometown of Dublin and proved to be a very popular piece in Dickinson's day. Peter K. Moran's first documented appearance in New York City was in 1817, the year his "Swiss Waltz" variations first appeared in print in New York, Philadelphia, and Baltimore.[72]

Moran embarked on an active and notable career as a composer, arranger, music teacher, publisher, and church organist. He advertised himself in the *New York Evening Post* as the organist of Grace Church in Manhattan. Moran was a regular on the New York concert scene, most notably as organist for the inaugural performance of the New York Choral Society in 1824. His various arrangements for piano were widely published. Also in Dickinson's music book is Moran's variation set of "Kinlock of Kinlock," a tune claimed equally as Scottish, English, and Irish.[73]

"The Chinese Museum is a great curiosity"

According to Krystyn Moon, author of the book *Yellow Face: Creating the Chinese in American Popular Music and Performance*, "with the increasing emphasis on spectacle in the nineteenth century, American and European composers, librettists, and producers found that Chinese exoticism worked well on the stage."[74] By far one of the most important pieces in Dickinson's music book representing Western imaginings of the Far East is not a waltz but the "Aladdin Quick Step" from "Favorite Melodies from the Grand Chinese Spectacle of *Aladdin; or the Wonderful Lamp*," which was produced at the Boston Museum in the winter and spring of 1847 by Thomas Comer and Silas Steele.

Dramatist Silas Sexton Steele (b. 1812) was the first in the United States to offer a treatment of Antoine Galland's French translation of *One Thousand and One Nights* (best known in English as *The Arabian Nights*). Steele's treatment of Aladdin "brought China to the Museum's stage, for the scene of action was transferred from Persia to China."[75] Featuring the music of the museum's musical director Thomas Comer (1790–1862), *Aladdin* was just one of many spectacles at the museum for which Comer would supply the music.[76]

The Boston Museum and Gallery of Fine Arts was a museum and theater that was in existence from 1841 to 1903. The museum's founder and impresario in charge of programs was Moses Kimball (1809–1895). The museum offered a variety of olios, musicals, operettas, comedies, and theatrical spectacles.[77] To expand the geographic reach of his audience, Kimball hired carriages to bring in customers from the outer reaches of the city. In the cover illustration of Dickinson's copy of the sheet music, the carriages are arriving at the museum's entrance on Tremont Street between School and Court Streets, delivering a throng of patrons to see the museum's enormously popular production of *Aladdin; or, the Wonderful Lamp*, which ran from January 25 to March 22, 1847. This was one of many theatrical spectacles presented by the museum's resident stock companies.[78] Another museum offering featured performances of Jacques Offenbach's "Celebrated Polka Dance," which is also in Dickinson's bound music book. Both pieces serve as mementos of Dickinson's 1846 stay in Boston.

On August 25, 1846, Emily Dickinson was sent to Boston for health reasons, to stay with her aunt Lavinia Norcross. She would remain there until mid-September. On a previous trip to Boston and Worcester two years earlier, Dickinson's father had directed her to visit "interesting places. . . . while you are there."[79] What really caught her attention among the "interesting places" on this visit was a blockbuster exhibit of artifacts on view at the Chinese Museum. In an engaging letter to Abiah Root she wrote:

> I left for Boston week before last. I had a delightful ride in the cars and am now quietly settled down, if there can be such a state in the city. I am visiting my aunt's family and am happy. . . . I have been here a fortnight to day & in that time I have both seen & heard a great many wonderful things. Perhaps you might like to know how I have spent the time here. I have been to Mount Auburn, to the Chinese Museum, to Bunker hill. I have attended 2 concerts, & 1 Horticultural exhibition. I have been upon the top of the State house & almost everywhere that you can imagine. . . . The Chinese Museum is a great curiosity. There are an endless variety of Wax figures made to resemble the Chinese & dressed in their costume. Also articles of chinese manufacture of an innumerable variety deck the rooms.[80]

The Chinese Museum exhibit was indeed "a great curiosity," offering viewers a revelation of tangible physical evidence of what they had theretofore only read in print concerning China, its culture, and its people.

The Chinese Museum was located in the Marlboro' Chapel on Washington Street in Boston. The exhibit ran from September 8, 1845, until February 6, 1847. As a result of the 1844 Wangxia Treaty between the United States and China, a unique display of artifacts was brought over by former Massachusetts congressman Caleb Cushing, the official envoy to the negotiations. The exhibition catalog notes that some of the artifacts were acquired with the help of Christian missionaries. Mary Lyon's Missionary Society at Mount Holyoke fostered awareness of and identification with the cultures infiltrated by her network of missionary graduates, so interest in and knowledge of the Chinese people and their culture would have been significant at Mount Holyoke.[81] Lucy Lyon, the niece of Mary Lyon, left her teaching position at Mount Holyoke to marry and take a missionary post in China beginning in 1846. Whether Lucy Lyon or any of the other missionaries in China from Mount Holyoke played a role in the selection and transmission of those artifacts is not known.

The exhibit contained two gentleman "informants," who as Dickinson explained "went with the exhibit." They were identified as calligrapher T'sow Chaoong and musician Le-Kaw hing. While the two were positioned to animate the exhibit with their writing and music, a detailed description in the *Boston Daily Atlas* gave the impression to an enthralled public (including Dickinson) that the men were among the exhibition's artifacts.[82] Many, again including Dickinson, thought their music too exotic.[83] Ultimately, though, she was edified by their performance and moved by their humanity and dignity:

> Two of the Chinese go with this exhibition. One of them is a Professor of music in China & the other is teacher of a writing school at home.... The Musician played upon two of his instruments & accompanied them with his voice. It needed great command over my risible faculty to enable me to keep sober as this amateur was performing, yet he was so very polite to give us some of his native music that we could not do otherwise than to express ourselves highly edified with his performances. The Writing Master is constantly occupied in writing the names of visitors who request it upon cards in the Chinese language—for which he charges 12 1/2 cts. apiece. He never fails to give his card besides to the person[s] who wish it. I obtained one of his cards for Viny & myself & I consider them very precious.[84]

They were indeed precious, and Dickinson scholar Hiroko Uno reminds us that Dickinson's "experiences in the Chinese Museum were so impressive that images of the East resonated for decades in her adult imagination."[85] Thus the music from the "Grand Chinese Spectacle" in Dickinson's music book is both a memento of her visit to Boston and a signifier of this aspect of the musician/poet's imagination, as precious as it is prescient.

During her 1846 visit to Boston, Dickinson wrote to Abiah Root that she had attended two concerts. The first, which took place on August 27, was reviewed in the *Boston Daily Journal* of August 29, which noted that a "concert [of secular music and songs] given by the Teachers Class of the Boston Academy on Thursday evening was numerously attended." The other concert took place on September 3 at the Melodeon, a major concert venue on Washington Street, home to Boston's Handel and Haydn Society. The concert was given, again by the teachers' class, "on which occasion [Franz Joseph] Haydn's *Creation* [was] performed, with full orchestral accompaniments."[86] The performance was reviewed in the September 4 issue of the *Daily Evening Traveller*: "The oratorio of *The Creation* was performed last evening at the Melodeon under the direction of Mr. Baker with tolerable success. The heat in the room was quite oppressive, yet the choruses were sung with much energy."[87]

Dickinson concludes her travelogue on a wistful note concerning news from home, not failing to incorporate the titles of two perennially popular songs, "Auld Lang Syne" and "Long, Long Ago," the first of which is represented in her music book: "Mr Taylor, Our old Teacher, was in Amherst at Commencement time. Oh! I do love Mr. Taylor. It seemed so like old times to meet Miss Adams & Mr Taylor again. I could hardly refrain from singing Auld Lang Syne. It seemed so very apropos. Have you forgotten the memorable ride we all took with Mr Taylor, 'Long, Long, ago.'"[88]

Dickinson's musical references and the content of her music book demonstrate her interest in both the intellectual refinement she sought through home music-making and her engagement with the public musical sphere of her day, where she witnessed performances by some of the most important virtuosos of her time. At least one of these concert-going experiences would resonate with Dickinson for years to come.

CHAPTER 4

The Age of the Virtuosi

"I never heard <u>sounds</u> before"

DURING THE 1840s AND 1850s, America's musical life outside the home was taking on a new shape, moving beyond the traditional singing schools and the sacred music of the meetinghouses. Big and small cities and some larger towns were witnessing the formation of an active musical culture of public performances by both local groups and professional touring ensembles from abroad. This activity was supported by a bourgeoning middle class of eager consumers, and the Dickinsons were active participants.[1] Not surprisingly, much of what Emily Dickinson heard in concert found its way into her bound book of sheet music. Who were these performers and composers who so excited the American public then, when all but a few are largely forgotten today?

Dickinson and her siblings came of age at a time when the American band movement was in flower, when brass and wind ensembles were springing up in nearly every city and town. The most celebrated professional bands from New York and Boston toured extensively, performing a variety of music to the delight of enthusiastic audiences. The Dickinsons saw some of the most famous groups of the era, such as the American virtuoso bugler Ned Kendall and his Boston Brass Band, and the Dodworth brass band from New York City. Both groups visited Springfield, Northampton, and Amherst.[2] In their day, these individuals and groups were household names, and a great deal of published sheet music from their respective repertoires made its way into Emily Dickinson's music book. Nine marches and twelve lively quicksteps in the Dickinson bound music book gave Emily and her siblings ample music with which to re-create a memorable band concert on the parlor piano.[3]

In Dickinson's time there were local bands in the nearby towns of Hadley, Hatfield, Belchertown, Northampton, and Springfield. These bands provided accompaniments to community events such as the opening of a local railroad, fairs, picnics, weddings, and funerals.[4] On October 22, 1851, the Belchertown Brass Band provided entertainment during the second annual Amherst Cattle Show.[5] In later years, Emily Dickinson's niece remembered the Cattle Show with its "bucolic sweetness and simplicity, which Emily loved afar; especially the strains of military music on the air, at intervals."[6] The high degree of talent displayed by these local bands fostered a spirit of civic pride, and their performances often received accolades in the press. On July 6, 1849, the *Springfield Daily Republican* noted that the Westfield band's leader, a "Mr. Hull, is a second Kendall on the bugle."

The bugle referred to in the review was an innovation of its day: a keyed bugle. Unlike the traditional bugle, the keyed instrument allowed the player additional dexterity and possessed a greater range and brighter timbre than the original instrument. The popularity of the keyed bugle owed much to Richard Willis (1790–1830), the first bandmaster of the United States Military Academy at West Point. Willis brought his keyed bugle over from Dublin, setting in motion a virtuosity on the instrument that was imitated by countless numbers of bands, including those led by the Dodworths and Ned Kendall.[7]

Brothers Ned and James Kendall were no strangers to the local Amherst music scene. Ned Kendall's Boston Brass Band, which he had been directing since the age of twenty-seven (1835), performed numerous times at Amherst College commencement exercises. On August 10, 1849, the *Springfield Daily Republican* reported on a Kendall concert given on the Wednesday of commencement week, August 8, which included works by Bellini, Rossini, Boldieu, and Strauss, stating: "The Kendalls' Boston Brass Band, who are furnishing the music part of the Commencement exercises gave a grand Concert in the evening. You know their quality and need not be told that it was the very perfection of concord and sweet."[8]

The Concert Scene in Dickinson's Day

Often invited to be guests of local ensembles as band soloists or as chamber musicians, the Kendalls and other well-known musicians performed throughout the Northeast; these appearances provided frequent opportunities for their talent to be heard and emulated. On Friday, January 5, 1849, the Kendalls appeared at the fourth annual Fireman's Ball of the Niagara Fire Company at Hampden Hall in Springfield. The music was provided by "Eastcott's Instrumental and Vocal Quadrille Band, assisted by Messers E[dward]. and J[ames]. Kendall of Boston and [pianist Jason] Collier of Albany, [New York]."[9]

The British-born bandleader Richard Eastcott (1817–1880) was a notable on the regional music scene. Eastcott was a violinist and music instructor in Springfield. Emily Dickinson playfully mentions him in her correspondence with Abiah Root. In February 1845 Root had transferred out of Amherst Academy and enrolled in Mary B. Campbell's school in Springfield, where Eastcott taught music. On August 2, 1845, Emily wrote to Abiah about one of Eastcott's two concerts which had taken place in Springfield on June 13 and July 2: "I don't know about this Mr. Eastcott giving you concert tickets. I think for my part it looks rather suspicious. He is a young man I suppose. These Music teachers are always such high souled beings that I think they would exactly suit your fancy."[10]

Eastcott had a "Music Room in Dwight's Building, over Covell's Drug Store" in Springfield and was providing music lessons on the piano and violin. He also sold pianos.[11] The following January, Dickinson wrote to Abiah Root: "I suppose you are getting along finely in music. I had forgotten to ask after your adorable Mr. Eastcott."[12]

Better known was Eastcott's wife, the celebrated soprano Lucy Evans Grant (1829–1895) of Springfield. They were married in 1846 and soon thereafter on April 10 presented a concert in Springfield which included vocal selections from Michael William Balfe's popular opera *The Bohemian Girl*. The Eastcotts subsequently moved to Albany, where Lucy was employed by St. Paul's Church. There they intersected with Albany pianist and music store owner Jason Collier. In 1852 the Eastcotts settled in Florence, Italy, and from that home base Lucy Evans Grant had a very successful touring career in Italy, England, and the United States.[13]

The Kendalls hosted, or were frequent participants in, these local chamber music concerts. Lavinia's diary mentions a Kendall concert on May 15, 1851: "Sunderland Aunts dined here. Walked with Howland, Displeased Mother thereby. Attended Kendall Concert with Austin & Emilie."[14] The concert the Dickinsons attended was advertised in the weekly *Hampshire and Franklin Express* on the previous Friday, May 9, 1851: "A Grand Musical Olio will be given at Howe's Hall, on Thursday evening next, by the celebrated Musicians, the Kendalls in connection with Mr. [George F.] Hayter, the distinguished *Pianist* [and organist of the Handel and Haydn Society, Boston], and Mr. Joseph Proctor, the *Tragedian*, who will appear in appropriate Dramatic Selections in *Costume.*"[15]

Concerts such as these would have featured Edward (Ned) Kendall (1808–1861) on bugle, and his brother James Kendall (1803–ca. 1874) on "clarionett" and ophiclyde (a bass keyed bugle). Mary Jane Kendall and Ned Kendall's wife, Emily, often performed as vocalists. A typical program would include arias from one of Vincenzo Bellini's operas, *La Sonnambula* or *Norma*, and by request the very popular "The Lament of the Alpine Shepherd Boy," by F. H. Brown sung by Miss M. J. Kendall "with Clarionett echo by J. K. Kendall"; a solo clarinet air on "The Last Rose of Summer"; and "Can I My Love Resign" from the opera *Cinderella* (Rossini) as sung by Mr. Wood.[16]

In addition to chamber music concerts, Ned Kendall also spent a great deal of time performing as a keyed bugler with circuses. In 1847 he toured with the Spaulding and Rogers North American Circus (where he intersected with drummer/composer Daniel Decatur Emmett).[17] In 1850 Kendall signed on with the John Robinson Circus.[18] Dickinson's fascination with the circus is well documented in her correspondence, and the Spaulding circus visited the area many times, so the Dickinsons would likely have seen them as they passed through Amherst.[19]

Dickinson's music book and her correspondence bring to life some of Ned Kendall's most notable repertoire. The music book contains a quickstep arrangement of the minstrel tune "Lucy Neal," which was featured on Kendall's programs. In her correspondence, Dickinson mentions that she has been learning "Wood Up," John Holloway's enormously popular encore piece, a quickstep he wrote in 1834 and which Ned Kendall made famous. Kendall's spectacular E-flat bugle solos elicited legendary accounts of his virtuosity and were long remembered by audiences and performers alike.[20] The fact that Emily Dickinson collected the sheet music for the "Lucy Neal Quick Step" and singled out "Wood Up" in her correspondence as one of her favorites documents the wide appeal of this music and Dickinson's enthusiastic engagement with its home performance. Both pieces even in their published piano reductions contain cues for the bugle solo to be played on the piano. Dickinson's copy of "Wood Up" is not in her music book but is part of the Dickinson holdings in the Houghton Library at Harvard University.[21] Various editions of the piece can be located in major library collections. See online Appendix C.

Dickinson's music book contains other piano pieces whose arrangements for band were found on typical Kendall programs. These included selections from popular operas such as Bellini's *Norma* and *The Bohemian Girl* by Michael William Balfe, or the band piece the "Bay State Quick Step." She also collected pieces written by Kendall's fellow performer the composer and vocalist Thomas Comer (1790–1862).[22]

The Dickinsons also saw "Dodworth's celebrated Band from New York City" as it led the commencement holiday procession on Thursday, August 8, 1850, when Austin Dickinson graduated from Amherst College. That evening the band gave a concert at Hampden Hall in Springfield.[23] The Dodworths' programs of popular opera excerpts, marches, and quicksteps also featured new American compositions such as selections from William Henry Fry's opera *Leonora* arranged for military band.[24] Dickinson's music book contains a version for piano of Fry's "Affection Waltz," which Fry drew from his opera.

The English-born Dodworth family was extraordinarily influential. Bandmaster Thomas Sr. and his children were all active musicians: Thomas J. (trombone), Charles R. (flute), Harvey B. (violin/bandmaster), and Allen (violin/bandleader/dance instructor). The Dodworths significantly altered the US band music landscape with their musicianship and versatility not just in performance but also in composing, arranging, publishing, and teaching. The Dodworths were founding members in 1842 of the Philharmonic Society of New York (today the New York Philharmonic).[25] Allen Dodworth was a renowned dance instructor whose students included the young Theodore Roosevelt, his brother Elliott, and sister Corinne.[26]

Another of the renowned "Boston bands" was the Boston Brigade Band, organized in 1821. One of its early leaders was the formidable composer, arranger, and educator Benjamin Augustus Burditt

(1810–1866). Two pieces of the Boston Brigade Band's repertoire are in the Dickinson bound music book: Burditt's quickstep arrangement of the famous ballad "The Blue Juniata," and "The Celebrated Spanish Retreat," arranged by the equally celebrated trombonist and guitarist José De Anguera (1810–1882).[27]

The Age of the European Virtuosi

Coinciding with the proliferation of these American bands, there was much talent coming in from outside the United States. Beginning in the late 1830s and into the following two decades, when Emily Dickinson would actively begin acquiring sheet music, economic growth along with improvements in local and national transportation brought a large influx of European virtuosi to America's shores, concertizing to enthusiastic audiences in the big cities and some of the smaller towns.[28] Legendary European concert artists were taking America by storm, and some of their repertoire was filtering into Emily Dickinson's music book in the form of variation sets on opera arias and popular melodies. According to Carleton Sprague Smith, "this was the era of the embellished theme, and Americans heard variations on Scottish, Irish, English, French, German, Italian, and their own patriotic melodies with never-ending delight."[29] One of the concert stars whose programs featured this repertoire was the Austrian pianist Henri Herz (1802–1888); his "Celebrated Henrietta Waltz" is in the Dickinson music book. Other instrumental virtuosi touring the United States included the Austrian pianist/composer Leopold de Meyer (1816–1883) and the Norwegian violinist Ole Bull (1810–1880), both of whom wowed American audiences with their variations on "Yankee Doodle." According to the musicologist R. Allen Lott: "Nearly every visiting artist felt obliged to compose a musical homage to his host country based on patriotic or popular tunes [such as 'Yankee Doodle' or 'Hail, Columbia']. . . . Audiences greeted them with gusto, and they demonstrated that the line between popular and art music had yet to be drawn decisively."[30] Dickinson's music book contains a similar repertoire. The fact that her music book includes an uncredited set of variations on "Yankee Doodle" (1842?) should not be underestimated in what it tells us about America's evolving musical taste.

The monumental English composer and ballad singer Henry Russell, who resided in the United States from 1836 to 1841, was another fixture on the US concert scene, particularly throughout New York State and New England. Russell greatly enjoyed his time in the United States, paying tribute to America with his vocal ballad "Our Native Song." Not long before he departed the States, Russell's newly published song "The Old Arm Chair" captivated American audiences. Russell himself said, "My songs were of the kind that reached the hearts of my audiences, my melodies were taking, and the poems to which they were wedded were of a high order."[31] Dickinson's music book contains both "Our Native Song" and "The Old Arm Chair."

Americans were also thrilled by the Hungarian Singers and the Euterpean Vocalists, who were in the vanguard of groups popularizing a new genre of close harmony singing. The Rainer Family, who were billed as the "Tyrolese Minstrels," arrived from Austria in 1838, influencing the formation of popular "singing families," which would reach a crest in the 1840s with the arrival of the Peak Family (billed as "Germanian" bell ringers), the Harmoneon Family (an American minstrel troupe), the Baker Family, and the famous Hutchinson Family.[32] The Harmoneons and especially the Hutchinsons were of great importance to Dickinson and her music book. There were also traveling opera troupes, the orchestras of the Germania Musical Society under the direction of Charles Lenschow (1821–1890), Josef Gung'l's Steyermarkische Company, and the Moravian composer, pianist, and concert impresario Maurice Strakosch (1825–1887). The ranks of these orchestras were filled with enormously talented musicians, many of them virtuosos on their respective instruments.[33] Dickinson saw the Germanians perform. Their highly polished programs included the repertoire of Josef Gung'l, Carl Maria von Weber, and Joseph Labitzky, a repertoire that finds representation in Dickinson's music book.

Among the famed singers touring the United States, many were of interest to the Dickinson family, and Emily and her sister Lavinia enjoyed performing some of their repertoire. There was the Scottish superstar Mary Anne Paton Wood (1802–1864), in whose song repertoire Lavinia Dickinson indulged, as well as Henriette Sontag (1806–1854) from Germany and the Irish soprano Catherine Hayes (1818–1861), both of whom Austin Dickinson saw in Boston, and whose repertoire Emily preserved in her music book. There was also the soprano Anna Bishop (1810–1884), who at one time was married to the composer of "Home, Sweet Home," Henry Rowley Bishop (1786–1855), whose perennially popular song was ubiquitous in bound music volumes, including Dickinson's.

The Dickinsons, who in many respects were typical concertgoers and above-average consumers of sheet music, likely witnessed and would have been familiar with many more of the virtuosos and star performers than has previously been known through their correspondence and other sources.[34] To judge from the content of her music book, Dickinson was certainly aware of these performers, and because she collected so much of their performance repertoire in the form of instrumental arrangements and variation sets, we do know that all of this musical virtuosity was rubbing off on the musician Emily Dickinson.

Musical Virtuosity on the Stage and at Home

Emily Dickinson knew of and acquired music by some of the most prominent composers, arrangers, and musical pedagogues of her day: Henri Herz (1803–1888), Joseph Labitzky (1802–1881), Henri Bertini (1798–1876), Johann Friedrich Franz Burgmüller (1806–1874), Jacques Claude Adolphe Miné (1796–1854), Carl Czerny (1791–1857), Franz Hünten (1793–1878), Thomas Valentine (1790–1878), and the Americans William Cumming Peters (1805–1866) and Edward Little White (1809–1851). She enjoyed performing instrumental variation sets based on memorable arias from the major operas of Bellini (arranged by Franz Hünten) and Rossini (arranged by Edward White), as well as popular fare by the arranger Thomas Valentine. A piece that no bound music book of Dickinson's day and long after would be without was the enormously popular "Battle of Prague" by Franz Kotzwara (c1750–1791).[35] From its first performances in the United States in the 1790s, Kotzwara's rousing battle piece became a pianist's showpiece and remained so, well into the nineteenth century. Dickinson's music book features a "March and Quick Step in the Battle of Prague." These variation sets and instrumental arrangements provided the American concert-going public, including Emily Dickinson, with accessible music, of pedagogical value, which also provided delightful entertainment in the home parlor.

During the 1840s and into the following decades, these visiting virtuosi and touring groups increasingly infiltrated cities and towns of even moderate size, which had recently been connected by good turnpikes and were served by stagecoaches.[36] Access to these star performers allowed nineteenth-century concert audiences to experience a remarkable display of musical refinement and virtuosity. The musicologist Daniel Cavicchi notes that "in the world of genteel Americans, professional musicians did not simply make music but shared social prestige; concert-goers did not only listen to music but cultivated aesthetic sensibility and knowledge; amateur musicians did not simply socialize through music but sought to copy and display staged virtuosity."[37] Nowhere was this aspect of "staged virtuosity" more engaging to American audiences, and to Emily Dickinson, than in the concerts of the Swedish soprano Jenny Lind.

Dickinson scholar Cristanne Miller notes that Dickinson "was vitally engaged with multiple aspects of her culture—literary, social, cultural, religious, and political."[38] The same is certainly true for music. It's clear that what she was attuned to musically is reflected equally in what she chose to collect in her bound music volume as in what she chose not to collect. The latter is certainly the case with the music associated with Jenny Lind, the most celebrated and significant performer witnessed by Emily Dickinson. Dickinson's correspondence vividly recounts Lind's Northampton concert in July 1851. She even quotes from Lind's concert repertoire in her correspondence, yet she chose to collect virtually none of the music associated with Lind's performances. "*Herself*, and not her music, was what we seemed to love," wrote Dickinson.[39]

Billed as the "Swedish Nightingale," Jenny Lind (1820–1887) made her American debut in New York City in September 1850. The Dickinsons saw her perform the following July. Lind's American tour was the brainchild of the impresario Phineas T. Barnum (1810–1891). Barnum's buildup of Lind's historic visit began at least ten months before her arrival, when the *Springfield Daily Republican* and other papers reported that negotiations were under way to bring Lind to the United States.[40] Well before the moment of her arrival in New York on September 1, 1850, and her first performance at New York's Castle Garden on the eleventh, "Lindomania" was everywhere: "Songs, quadrilles and polkas were dedicated to her, and poets sung her praise. There were Jenny Lind gloves, Jenny Lind bonnets, Jenny Lind riding hats, Jenny Lind shawls, mantillas, ropes, chairs, sofas, pianos—in fact everything was Jenny Lind. Her movements were constantly watched, and the moment her carriage appeared at the hotel door, it was surrounded by multitudes, eager to see her."[41]

The review of a Lind concert from the *Springfield Daily Republican* indicates how much the public embraced the hype and worshipped the performer in their midst:

> At last, the long coveted vision was revealed, and Jenny stood before her audience, bowing to the floor almost, under the storm of cheers that swept over her. She commenced "I know that my Redeemer liveth," and performed that noble solo from "the Messiah" with a touching and earnest tenderness that brought emotion to the brim of many a trembling lip and moistened eye, and sweetly hallowed her own pure presence.... Her good will is appreciated abundantly, and in the name of the community we thank her for her consideration. She consented to repeat almost every song, and her Springfield audience will remember her kindness as long as any she has ever delighted with her music.... We rejoice that this region is to be so highly favored with her sweet and noble music, and still entertain the hope that we may have a second Concert in Springfield. There is no question that it would be most abundantly patronized.[42]

Everyone flocked to Lind's concerts, and there were multiple opportunities to do so, although not often at reasonable prices.[43] In June 1851 Susan Gilbert, the Dickinson family friend who would marry Austin, went to New York to see a Jenny Lind concert. Lind performed at Tripler Hall on June 2 and at Castle Garden on June 4 and 6.[44] The Dickinson sisters made plans to see one of Lind's performances in Boston (June 18–27, 1851, some of which were at the Tremont Temple), but they were deluged with houseguests, and only Austin, who was in Boston at the time, attended the concert.[45]

Austin wrote to Emily about the concert he saw. While his letter is not extant, we know from Emily's reply that she was more than pleased with his "discreet opinion" of Jenny Lind:

> Permit me to accord with your discreet opinion concerning Swedish Jennie [sic], and to commend the heart brave eno' to express it—.... We have all been rather *piqued* at Jennie's singing so well, and this first calumnious whisper pleases us so well. We rejoice that we did not come—our visit is yet before us.... Father perused [your] letter and verily for joy the poor man could hardly contain himself—he read and read again, and each time seemed to relish the story more than at first. Fearing the consequences on a mind so formed as his, I seized the exciting sheet, and bore it away to my folio to amuse nations to come.[46]

Perhaps the Lind mania was too much for Austin, but his critique set a tone that would inform Emily's own reaction to the great soprano when she witnessed Lind herself. With Austin's "calumnious whisper" on their minds, Emily and her family took the stagecoach to Lind's concert in Northampton. The performance took place at the First Congregational Church on Thursday, July 3, 1851. Dickinson wrote to her brother in great detail about the concert. She mistakenly notes the day of the concert as Friday instead of Thursday, but perhaps because she arrived home so late (past midnight), in her mind it was still "the night of Jennie Lind."

> I wanted to write you *Friday*, the night of Jennie Lind, but reaching home past midnight, and *my room* sometime after, encountering several perils starting, and on the way, among which a *kicking horse*, an inexperienced driver, a number of Jove's thunderbolts, and a very terrible rain, are worthy to have record. All of us went— . . . how the rain did not abate, how we walked in silence to the old Edwards Church and took our seats in the same, how Jennie came out like a child and sang and sang again, how boquets [sic] fell in showers, and the roof was rent with applause—how it thundered outside, and inside with the thunder of God and of men—judge ye which was the loudest—.[47]

For Dickinson it was the setting and the Lind persona—rather than the music—that caught her attention. Judith Pascoe notes that "the singularity of a woman taking the place of a male minister [at the front of the church] was surely not lost on Dickinson, whose propensity for imaginative flights from the confines of the church pews is a matter of record."[48] Lind's manager, P. T. Barnum, had chosen the venue wisely. For most of the nineteenth century, women of the stage had to contend with a popular perception of immorality. Dickinson biographer Lyndall Gordon notes that "it did not escape Emily that her father did not take kindly to a woman who made herself conspicuous in public," and Emily was certainly aware of this prevailing attitude.[49] Barnum counteracted this perception by successfully projecting an image of Lind as pure as birdsong.[50] Thus it was the associated persona, and not her actual singing, that resonated with Dickinson:

> How we all loved Jennie Lind, but not accustomed oft to her manner of singing did'nt [sic] fancy *that* so well as we did *her*—no doubt it was very fine—but take some notes from her "Echo"—the Bird sounds from the "Bird Song" and some of her curious trills, and I'd rather have a Yankee.

Herself, and not her music, was what we seemed to love—she has an air of *exile* in her mild blue eyes, and a something sweet and touching in her native accent which charms her many friends—"Give me my thatched cottage" as she sang grew so earnest she seemed half lost in song and for a transient time I fancied she *had* found it and would be seen "na mair," and then her foreign accent made her again a wanderer—.[51]

Dickinson was commenting on three selections from Lind's concert repertoire, including her musical execution of the "Bird Song" by Wilhelm Taubert (1811–1891) and Lind's signature and pyrotechnical warhorse the "Herdsman's Song" ("Herde sang"), commonly called the "Echo Song," composed by Jacob Niclas Ahlström (1805–1857), with its spectacular echo effects. The third selection was "Home, Sweet Home," the only piece from Lind's concert in Dickinson's music book, and here Dickinson makes the most of it. In describing Lind as having "an air of exile," Dickinson is citing the opening line of verse two of the song, where, like Lind, the singer of the song is "an exile from home." Dickinson goes on to quote from the song's second verse, "O! Give me my [lowly] thatched cottage [again]."[52] According to a review of the Northampton concert in the *Republican* the following day, "'Casta Diva' [from Bellini's *Norma*], the 'Bird Song,' and 'Home, Sweet Home' were all repeated at the demand of the audience";[53] so Dickinson had a thorough immersion into this portion of Lind's song and Italian bel canto repertoire.[54] Dickinson's observations on Lind's "manner of singing," particularly her "curious trills," and her statement that "I'd rather have a Yankee," were not a sign of an "untrained" ear as early biographers have suggested; instead they were a reaction to what she perceived as the "foreignness" of Lind's vocal qualities as interpreted by Dickinson's own predisposed listening ear. Thus, the fact that Dickinson collected little of Lind's repertoire actually speaks volumes.

Emily's letter to Austin continues:

Father sat all the evening looking *mad*, and *silly*, and yet so much amused you would have *died* a laughing—when the performers bowed, he said 'Good evening Sir'—and when they retired, 'very well—that will do,' it was'nt *sarcasm* exactly, nor it was'nt *disdain*, it was infinitely funnier than either of those virtues, as if old Abraham had come to see the show, and thought it was all very well, but a little excess of *Monkey*! She took 4000$ / *mistake* arithmetical/ for tickets at Northampton aside from all expenses.[55]

While the staged virtuosity of Barnum's circus-like musical presentation of Lind did not go unnoticed by Emily or her father, Emily may have been girding herself against the Lind worshippers and the Barnum hype. "The Show is not the Show / But they that go — ," poet Emily Dickinson would later write.[56] While Emily accepted herself as part of "The Show," she may have been primed by Austin to anticipate Lind's vocal foreignness. Poet Dickinson would also write, "The Robin's my Criterion for Tune — ," situating her preference for the "Yankee" song of the robin over that of the "Swedish Nightingale" and Lind's vocalizations of the "Bird Song."[57] To Dickinson, it was not birdsong but an "otherness," contextualized through Dickinson's own attempt at mimicking a foreign accent in the finality of her critical words "na mair" (no more).

At a time when American anti-immigrant sentiments were cresting, Barnum's ingenious marketing of the Scandinavian Lind as angelic and pure was hugely successful with well-to-do white audiences.[58] While Lind's voice had been described in the New York press as that of "the perfect bird," she was not without her detractors. Henry Coad Watson (1818–1875) of *The Albion* criticized Lind for singing transpositions of her music upwards of more than a third, "far into the unsympathetic regions of the voice." This would have been a contributing factor for those who took issue with her ornamentation and an icy "coldness" in her voice. Many believed that these extreme registers hampered her ability to ingratiate herself successfully into the warmer regions of the Italian bel canto repertoire, which was a regular feature on her programs, including the one in Northampton.[59] These extreme registers nevertheless elicited a sonic purity that caught the ears of American audiences, who had been cool for some time toward the ornamental performance style associated with Italian opera.[60] Dickinson seems to have been cool toward this aspect as well, as there are no vocal opera arias of this type in her bound music book.

"I dinna choose to tell"

Emily Dickinson was not alone in her discomfort with Lind. In New York, critic Richard Storrs Willis had been voicing an opinion about Lind as well, albeit obliquely. Willis did not "*altogether* like Jenny Lind's singing of 'The Last Rose of Summer.' Despite the many moist eyes, [he] could not quite assent to the *taste* of the performance."[61] For Dickinson, Lind's performance in Northampton of the familiar Scotch-Irish song "Comin' thro' the Rye" (which Lind had transposed from A-flat up to C) proved less representational and thus less attractive to Dickinson's ear than the familiar Hiberno-English musical hues that she heard at home, spoken and sung by laundress Rosina Mack, maid of all work Margaret O'Brien, and, later, Dickinson's beloved Maggie Maher and the other Irish domestics with whom she regularly intersected as she went about her daily chores. We should not underestimate the importance to her listening ear of these sounds and timbres complemented by the Scotch-Irish music that Dickinson collected, played and heard that was associated with the Dickinson servants.[62]

What Barnum promoted and what audiences heard in Lind's voice is exactly what Dickinson saw in Lind "*Herself.*"[63] For Dickinson, Lind emanated an alternate version of whiteness. Contemporary images of Lind with her signature costume of a white dress would remain with Dickinson and resurface a decade later as Emily's *own* otherness, once her poetic persona began to take shape.

"I don't think her songs compare with Jenny Lind's"

After Jenny Lind's historic US tour, Austin Dickinson saw other singers, including the German soprano Henriette Sontag (1806–1854) and Catherine Hayes (1818–1861), who was billed as the "Swan of Erin."[64] Comparing other singers with Jenny Lind was an almost universal occupation among concertgoers, and we are fortunate to have a firsthand example from Austin Dickinson himself. Appearing in the United States just after Lind, the Irish soprano Catherine Hayes gave a concert on Sunday, October 26, 1851, in Boston, which Austin Dickinson attended. The concert was held at the Melodeon. It was sponsored by the Handel and Haydn Society of Boston, and as a result, the majority of Hayes's program decidedly favored those two composers.[65] Austin wrote to his future sister-in-law Martha Gilbert about it: "I went to hear Catherine Hayes sing last Sunday evening. I like the woman, but dont think her songs compare with Jenny Lind's. I will tell you about it Wednesday."[66] Austin also saw Henriette Sontag perform at the Boston Music Hall. Sontag's performances took place on December 7, 10, and

11, 1853, accompanied by an orchestra of the famed Germania Musical Society under the direction of Carl Bergmann.[67]

Although Catherine Hayes and Henriette Sontag attracted large audiences of enthusiastic admirers, their concerts have largely been eclipsed in the collective memory by those of Jenny Lind. But Dickinson's music book does remind us of the once enormous popularity of Sontag and Hayes at a time when audiences enjoyed at home the repertoire from their concerts: the Irish and Scottish ballads, and the opera arias, in particular the enormously popular "I Dreamt I Dwelt in Marble Halls" and "Then You'll Remember Me" from Michael William Balfe's 1843 opera *The Bohemian Girl*, both typically found in music volumes, including the instrumental versions and variation sets in Emily Dickinson's music book.

"I have a Bird in spring"

As a postscript to the Lind performance, it was around the time of Jenny Lind's US tour that Dickinson began to produce her first extant poems. Emily's observations about Lind may have created an initial stimulus, a "transcendental prospect" from which Dickinson could observe and begin to express poetically what she was hearing musically.[68] Just as she had heard the "Swedish Nightingale," so too would she begin capturing in verse a memory of her "Bird in spring" singing "[a] Melody new for me."[69] During this time, Dickinson began to observe, distill, and appropriate what would eventually emerge as a persona of musical performance from which she could draw and shape the musical metaphors that would inform her poetry. As she continued to attend concerts and collect and perform music, we see Dickinson using her correspondence to capture and experiment with opportunities for both musical and poetic expression.

"The Luxury to apprehend"

On April 19, 1853, Emily and Lavinia and their cousin John Graves witnessed a performance by the touring instrumental ensemble the Germania Serenade Band, an offshoot of the larger Germania Musical Society, which had arrived in the United States in 1848 for an extended

[80] CHAPTER 4

FIGURE 7. The Germania Musical Society. The Joseph Muller Collection of Music and Other Portraits, Music and Recorded Sound Division, The New York Public Library for the Performing Arts, Astor, Lenox and Tilden Foundations.

stay (see figure 7). Dickinson saw the Germanians in a performance that concluded the Spring Exhibition at Amherst College, and she recounted the event in a letter to her brother. The ensemble's exquisite musical presentation and cultivated performance persona did not escape Dickinson's ears or eyes in her melding of a musical experience into an opportunity for metaphoric and poetic expression: "The Germanians gave a concert here the evening of Exhibition day. Vinnie and I went with J. I never heard <u>sounds</u> before—they seemed like <u>brazen Robins</u>, all wearing broadcloth wings, and I think they were, for they all flew away as soon as the concert was over. I tried so hard to make Susie go with us, but she would'nt consent to it. I could not bear to have her lose it."[70]

In describing this flock of musicians as "brazen Robins," Dickinson iterates her own observations of the performance, indulging in imaginative and colorful poetic metaphors. We are reminded again of her 1854 poem "I have a Bird in spring." Here we can situate the "<u>sounds</u>" Dickinson heard, followed by the abrupt departure of the musicians, with a visual image of her own poetic robin whose song obligingly ends when the bird departs soon after the arrival of spring: "And as the summer nears / And as the Rose appears, / Robin is gone."[71] So too in the case of the Germanians; with the conclusion of the Spring Exhibition, the musicians "flew away as soon as the concert was over."

Dickinson's letter to her brother was first published in 1894. Subsequent published versions of Dickinson's letter transcribed by Mabel Loomis Todd (1931), Millicent Todd Bingham (1955), and most notably Theodora Ward and Thomas Johnson (1958) do Dickinson a musical disservice by including a parenthetical insertion in the line "I never heard [such] *sounds* before."[72] Inserting the word "such" dilutes the aural perspective of musical awe that audiences, including Emily Dickinson, must have experienced. The thrill she must have sensed in her "Luxury to apprehend" whatever those "<u>sounds</u>" were to her is lost in these later interpretations.[73] Even if Dickinson was exaggerating, or "posing," as Austin claimed she sometimes did, the true meaning, which we can only imagine either way, is at least hanging in the air, just as she wrote it: "I never heard <u>sounds</u> before." At this time, the poetry was clearly in the air as well. Later, poet Emily Dickinson would reach back to reuse her memory of the Germanians, transforming them from "brazen Robins" into a "'band' — in brass and scarlet" in her 1861 poem "Musicians wrestle everywhere."

Cultivating a "Higher Music"

The Germanians gave repeat performances of the recent symphonic repertoire of Mendelssohn, Mozart, and Beethoven, whose music was still new to US audiences, so Dickinson's response to the Germanians was certainly typical. The Germanians' precision and flawless execution of orchestral showpieces was a revelation to listeners whose ears had never been exposed to such virtuosity or to music of "so high an order."[74]

Even in large cities, permanent orchestras with competent musicians were not yet in place to present demanding works such as the titanic symphonies of Ludwig van Beethoven. New Yorkers did not hear Beethoven's Fifth Symphony (1808) in its entirety until February 11, 1841. "The occasion was a giant concert at the Tabernacle, given for the benefit of the German Society" featuring some of New York's top musicians.[75] This was one year before America had its first permanent orchestra, the Philharmonic Society of New York (today the New York Philharmonic).

Boston would not have its own symphony orchestra until 1888. Within days of the Fifth Symphony's premiere in New York, the city of Boston on February 13 received its first hearing of Beethoven's First Symphony, performed at the Boston Academy of Music. It took some time for Beethoven's published symphonic works to be exported to America, and once these works arrived and were prepared for performance and introduced, additional time was needed for American audiences to comprehend Beethoven's stylistic grandeur and abstraction. It also took some time to establish orchestras that could dedicate themselves to performing this music on a regular basis. As to the establishment of these permanent orchestras, the musicologist Michael Broyles notes that the "symphony orchestra more than any other institution came to represent high culture in most American cities. . . . Transcendental writers, extolling the virtues of abstract music, applied to instrumental, especially symphonic, music the same religious-oriented rhetoric that the Presbyterian-Congregation reformers had used when describing church music."[76]

According to musicologist Douglas Shadle, the symphony orchestra, with its precision and teamwork, was heralded as a model of individual cooperative efforts toward a common good, tantamount to the American idea of an emerging republican selfhood. "These politicized interpretations of instrumental music had gained traction in the 1840s among New England Transcendentalists, and they persisted through the 1850s."[77] In large part because of promoters such as the Boston music critic, Transcendentalist, and utopian community Brook Farm participant John Sullivan Dwight (1813–1893), a growing exposure to and attendant uplift toward this "higher music" flourished in Boston and other large cities, but in the 1840s there was much less of a roar in the smaller towns.[78]

Americans' awareness and knowledge of the "higher" works of Beethoven was in its early stages when Emily Dickinson was doing the major portion of her music collecting. Access to such music was limited, and the attendant musical aspirations were not yet shaped into a directive of "connect[ing] the elevation of taste with class," as Dwight and others would soon claim.[79] Perhaps the nine waltzes misattributed to Beethoven in Dickinson's bound music book reflect an attempt to cultivate a higher musical taste. More likely her primary interest was simply in perfecting her own talents, albeit through music newly in vogue. In that regard we should be looking elsewhere in Dickinson's music book. Her emphasis on variation sets speaks loudly in articulating the European influence on America's changing musical taste, which was trending away from contemplative ballad forms toward a more challenging and engaging musical experience thanks to the virtuosic showpieces that were brought here by the pianists, composers, and pedagogues whose work populates Dickinson's music book. Family members and early biographers such as George Whicher and Millicent Todd Bingham clearly misread Dickinson's seeming lack of an earnest pursuit of cultivating a taste for this "higher music," which by the twentieth century had firmly established camps of lowbrow and highbrow musical engagement.[80] Instead, as we have seen in her descriptions of both Jenny Lind and the Germanians, Emily Dickinson's responses to the music she encountered more importantly assisted her in setting the stage not so much for a "higher" *musical* standard but rather for a musically informed and integrated form of *poetic* expression.

CHAPTER 5

....

Home Music-Making

"Sounds From Home"

IN IDENTIFYING WITH CONCERT STARS and attending their performances, nineteenth-century concertgoers used those experiences as a means of artistic comparison, self-reflection, and inspiration to refine their own music-making in the home parlor setting.[1] According to Millicent Todd Bingham, after seeing Jenny Lind, "Vinnie tried to improve her singing."[2] Certainly, after the Lind concert in July 1851, the Dickinson family correspondence indicates an increased interest and activity in purchasing sheet music and attending live performances.

This increased purchasing activity was precipitated in part because Austin Dickinson had taken a teaching position in Boston. The family regularly asked him to send books, clothing, jewelry, fabric, even an ottoman for Lavinia. "Get any sort of *ottoman* that pleases you," she wrote. "I sent for a black bracelet & a song, 'When do the Swallows homeward fly.'"[3] Lavinia was asking for the popular parlor song "When the Swallows Homeward Fly" by the German composer Franz Abt (1819–1885). In an earlier letter, after pining for her brother, Lavinia asks for yet another piece of music, this one on behalf of her sister: "I do want to see you Austin very much. Emilie wants cousin E. to get the Polka which she plays, for her, & send it by Father. Hope you'll have a nice visit with him"[4] There are three polkas in Dickinson's music book. Emily's request for the polka that her Norcross cousin played for her points to "The Celebrated Polka Dance" by Jacques Offenbach (1819–1880), "as performed with enthusiastic applause at the Boston Museum." Offenbach's polka (published in 1844) was part of the offerings in operetta that the Boston Museum's impresario Moses Kimball had briefly introduced by the 1843–44 season.[5] Offenbach's "Celebrated Polka Dance" remained popular with music publishers into the 1850s.

Had Austin been looking for umbrellas as gifts, the music stores sold those as well. According to Christine Merrick Ayars: "From about 1825 to 1850 there was in Boston a peculiar business combination of umbrellas and music. John Ashton, Jr. followed by John Ashton & Co. ([with] E. H. Wade as a partner) were umbrella makers (1820–1843) at 18 Marlboro St. and later 197 Washington St. They added music and musical instruments to their line in 1825."[6] In his first shop at 52 Court Street, the Boston music publisher Henry Prentiss sold umbrellas along with sheet music, method books, and musical instruments such as keyed bugles, which Prentiss imported and stamped with his shop name.[7]

The local music stores in Springfield such as Marsh's Music Saloon (opposite Court Square) also sold parasols and umbrellas. William H. Weed advertised the latest sheet music or, more often, "collections of church and secular music."[8] A much larger selection of music was to be had in the Boston music stores and music publishing houses on Court and Washington Streets or Tremont Row. Hence most of the music in the Dickinson bound music book is associated with the major Boston music publishers of the time: Charles H. Keith, Oliver Ditson, George P. Reed, Charles Bradlee, and Henry Prentiss.

The two Dickinson sisters' tastes in music were quite different. Emily's requests were primarily for instrumental selections, while Lavinia's were consistently aimed at sentimental vocal ballads—so much so that she was constantly hounding Austin to send her new pieces by the popular composers of the day or the music associated with the latest vocal stars:

26 January 1852

Dear Austin

The song, "Merry Days When We Were Young" is not the one, I sent for, & I want to have you exchange it, if you will, the one I want you to get is sung by *Mrs. Wood* & not by "Mr. Leffler." I do not want this one any how. I think you can find the right one, at some of the music stores. I'm anxious to have it. Olivia Coleman used to sing it & tis a beautiful thing. Remember that tis sung by Mrs. Wood & no other, the tune begins with these words, "Oh! the merry days, the merry days when we were young."⁹

Lavinia obviously knew the song she wanted. The last line quoted in her letter is the complete opening line of the song, as if she were singing it directly into Austin's willing (or unwilling) ear. "Oh the Merry Days When We Were Young" was associated with the Scottish singer Mary Anne Paton Wood (1802–1864) and promoted by the publisher as "Sung with unbounded Applause by Mrs. Wood." There is no authorship credited on the music.

The celebrated superstars Mrs. Wood and her husband, Joseph (1801–1890), made their United States debut in 1833, performing in concerts and operas at the major theaters on the East Coast and west to Buffalo, Cincinnati, and St. Louis. The Woods returned to the United States twice more. Their last visit in 1840 coincided with the publication of "Oh the Merry Days When We Were Young." What Lavinia received from Austin was a completely different song by the same title, written by the English composer Edward James Loder (1813–1865), a song that was associated with the English bass-baritone Adam Leffler (1808–1857).¹⁰ Accompanying the Woods on their return to the United States in 1840, Leffler made his American debut, sharing the stage with them in New York in a performance of *La Sonnambula* at the Park Theatre on September 28 and the *Messiah* at the Tabernacle on November 19.¹¹

What appeals to Lavinia most about the song sung by Mrs. Wood is that she remembers it from touching parlor performances by Olivia Coleman, the Dickinsons' second cousin. A particular poignancy is expressed in Lavinia's letter to Austin, memorializing Olivia, who, five years earlier, had died suddenly of tuberculosis. She was twenty years old.¹²

On February 18, 1852, the correct song was delivered to Lavinia through William Kellogg's general store. Emily wrote to Austin conveying thanks from Vinnie for the music, telling him that "it is correct." Lavinia enclosed her own note saying: "The music is all right & I thank you very much for it. I have learned most of it."¹³

"Oh the Merry Days When We Were Young" as sung by Mrs. Wood is indeed a poignant song, typical of the expressions of sentimentality common in Dickinson's day. It is a textbook example of the genre in that its power "is derived from its ability to stay 'in the moment,' even if that moment consists of contemplating the distant past."[14] Antebellum America's engagement with the sentimental song was tethered to the uncertainties of a rapidly industrializing country with its evaporating agrarian identity and its rural population migrating to cities, often resulting in the disruption of families. Most importantly, the specter of early death, particularly for infants and young women, was a topic of great concern often expressed through music. For Lavinia, the song's association with Olivia Coleman certainly supports this.

In purchasing the incorrect song for Lavinia, Austin seems to have been misled by a common marketing ploy. According to musicologist Nicholas Tawa, music publishers would "affix the title of a well-liked song to different music," in this case to sell the version of "Oh the Merry Days When We Were Young" associated with Adam Leffler on the coattails of Mrs. Wood's fame.[15] The sheet music to "Oh the Merry Days When We Were Young" that was associated with Mrs. Wood remains a relative staple in major library collections, the E. J. Loder song by the same name much less so. Since the title associated with Mrs. Wood was requested by Lavinia, it is not in Emily's bound music book and is not extant in any Dickinson-related collection; nevertheless, despite its ephemerality as a piece of popular sheet music of the day, its permanence in documenting the Dickinson family's lively musical engagements is obvious and should not be underestimated.

Mrs. Wood does have a place of note in Emily's music volume with a theme and variations set on "Take Them, I Implore Thee" ("Deh conte") from the opera *Norma* by Vincenzo Bellini (1801–1830), a duet popularized in the United States by the Woods. *Norma* premiered at La Scala in 1831 and had its US premiere in New Orleans in 1836, where it was presented by the traveling Montresor Opera Company.[16] *Norma* was performed in New York (in Italian) on September 20, 1843, by an Italian opera troupe from Havana which had been booked for several engagements at Niblo's Garden.[17] But what really established an audience for Bellini's music in America were European singers such as the English soprano Elizabeth Austin (1800–1835) and the Woods. They were the main force behind the growing popularity of Italian opera in the United States, bringing Bellini's *La Sonnambula* to New York on November 13, 1835, and *Norma* to Philadelphia on January 11, 1841.[18] Excerpts from

Norma made their way into concert programs in the Springfield area as early as 1845.[19] Dickinson's piano arrangement with variations dates from 1847. She was sixteen years old and would have been at full steam in her practicing and home performances. Indeed, any and all sheet music associated with the Woods' repertoire sold widely.

In the same letter of October 10, 1852, in which Lavinia asks Austin to exchange the sheet music, she immediately continues: "& I should like two other pieces 'You and Me' & 'the Ossian Serenade.' If you can, please send them by W. Kellogg or Mr. Sweetser. I don't know but t'will trouble you to select these songs. If you are busy & cant conveniently attend to them, let them go till another time."

The Dickinsons often had their packages delivered to the businesses of William Kellogg or Luke Sweetser, each of whom owned a general store in Amherst. The sheet music titles Lavinia requested are not part of the Dickinson or other related collections, and the personal copies that belonged to Lavinia have heretofore not been located. Fortunately, both titles are found in major library collections. The song "You And Me" is a love ballad composed to words by Thomas Hood.[20] "Ossian's Serenade" by Ossian Dodge is associated with an unusual incident that occurred before Jenny Lind's first Boston concert in 1850, an event that will intersect with Emily Dickinson in chapter 12.

Lavinia's persistent requests for sheet music eventually elicited an exasperated reaction from her brother. On October 10, 1851, having just received from Austin the song "Nelly Bly," Lavinia, writing to her brother, commented on the lyrics as "exquisite," and went on to make an additional request: "I wish you'd get me a song called 'Blanche Alpine,' and bring it with you for the Cattle show."[21] Lavinia was asking for the sentimental vocal ballad "The Song of Blanche Alpen" by the popular composing team of Charles Jefferys (1807–1865) and Stephen Glover (1812–1870). Glover was the composer of the song "Charity," a favorite of Lavinia's (see chapter 7), and Jefferys's work is represented in Emily's music book.

It seems that Austin had had enough. The next evening he wrote to his future wife, Susan Gilbert: "Emily writes me every week—and always something I like to read—Vinnie pencils a line occasionally—generally when she happens to want something—I received about a half a line from her last night—merely to inform me that she was in want of some new music."[22]

Several years before her marriage to Austin, Susan Gilbert and Emily Dickinson, who had been friends in Amherst, were becoming intimate correspondents.[23] Through Susan, who as a young woman spent much of her time in New York State, we see the scope of the music in Dickinson's bound volume radiating out beyond its local New England geographical sphere.

Susan Gilbert and the Dickinson Music Book

Susan Huntington Gilbert (1830–1913) was born in Deerfield, Massachusetts, the youngest of seven children. After the death of their mother in 1837 and father in 1841, Susan and her sister Martha (1829–1895) were sent to live with their aunt Sophia Arms Van Vranken in Geneva, New York, in the Finger Lakes region of the state. Susan and Martha also boarded for a time with their married sister Harriet Gilbert Cutler, who lived on Amity Street in Amherst. Susan attended the Amherst Academy in 1846–47 and was briefly a classmate of Emily Dickinson. While in Amherst, Susan and Martha both became friends of Emily's, but the sisters welcomed opportunities to escape Harriet's difficult husband, William Cutler, and they often returned to Geneva, particularly during the holidays.

Beginning in 1848, the Gilbert sisters attended the prestigious Utica Female Academy in Utica, New York, in the Mohawk Valley region of the state. Shortly after arriving at the academy, Susan met her "vivid friend" and classmate Kate Scott Anthon (1831–1917) of Cooperstown, New York. Kate would remain a longtime friend and was someone with whom Emily Dickinson would become close. After graduation, Susan kept up her ties with Utica. Dickinson biographer Alfred Habegger writes that Susan's "alma mater had a stated policy of providing 'suitable testimonials' for former pupils."[24] Through that connection she secured an appointment at Mr. and Mrs. Archer's Boarding and Day School for Young Ladies in Baltimore. In the summer of 1852, after a year of teaching, Susan moved back permanently to Amherst, where she and Austin Dickinson began a courtship, becoming engaged the following year. They married in Geneva on July 1, 1856. The next year, Martha married John Williams Smith (1822–1878), owner of the J. W. Smith Dry Goods Company in Geneva.[25] The Geneva, New York, connection extends to Samuel Bowles, editor of the *Springfield Daily Republican*, a very close friend of the Dickinsons: in 1848 he married Mary Schermerhorn of Geneva.

Susan Dickinson would return many times to Geneva, sometimes "making a long visiting tour in the state of New York" which would include stops in nearby Aurora to visit her uncle Eben's family.[26] Later, Susan took the children on yearly autumn excursions to Geneva to visit her sister Martha.[27] There are eleven musical compositions affiliated with New York State in Emily Dickinson's music book, eight of them associated with either the Finger Lakes region, where Susan grew up, or the Mohawk Valley region, where she went to school in Utica. These musical geographical associations include the villages and cities of Auburn, Aurora, Rochester, and Syracuse in the Finger Lakes region and Cooperstown, Cherry Valley, Clinton, and Utica in the Mohawk Valley region, as well as Albany in the capital region.

According to Ellen Louise Hart and Martha Nell Smith, there was an "intellectual intimacy between Emily and Susan." This is apparent from their earliest correspondence, which began around 1850. "In her letters to Susan, Emily frequently refers to the novels she is reading and [music, using] various metaphors or codes to relate her feelings about herself and Susan, and comment about friends, relatives, and literary and political luminaries and events."[28] Both women were musical and both played the piano.[29] Given this close relationship and the ubiquitous and constant exchange of letters, books, and other items between Emily and Susan, it would have been common to give gifts of sheet music. It's a fair assumption that the provenance of these eleven New York State–themed compositions cuts a clear personal and geographical path between the two women.

Emily Dickinson's Music Book and New York State

Three pieces in Dickinson's volume of bound music hold associations with Utica, in New York State's Mohawk Valley. Two of them are by Utica resident George Dutton (1789–1854): "'Speed the Plough,' A Favorite Dance Arranged with Brilliant Variations," and "Hope Again, an Air with Variations for the Piano Forte" (see chapter 2). Dutton was associated with the Utica Musical Academy, which was founded in 1840, continuing until 1844. The mission of the academy was "the promotion of skill and taste in both sacred and secular music." With a student body of over eighty, the academy was able to maintain both a chorus and an orchestra. George Dutton conducted the orchestra, while the vocal music was under the direction of John Finley Smith.[30] Smith was also a composer. His touching personal story comes alive through Dickinson's music book and Smith's humorous composition "Any Thing, a new waltz, composed for Every Body, and respectfully dedicated to *Any Body*."

John Finley Smith was born in Cooperstown, New York, on July 14, 1815. He attended Hamilton College in Clinton, New York (class of 1834), and went on to the Auburn Seminary, graduating in 1838. Smith returned to Hamilton, first as a tutor (1838–1839) and then as a professor of Latin and Greek (1839–1843).

Smith's "Any Thing" waltz was first published by Auburn resident Henry Ivison Jr., a trustee of the Auburn Seminary from 1839 to 1846 and later a book publisher in New York.[31] Ivison's publication of John Finley Smith's waltz includes an "Andante" for piano and flute by Smith. The "Any Thing" waltz was subsequently published in 1847 by George P. Reed of Boston and by C. Holt in New York. The Holt imprint is what we find in Dickinson's bound music book.

John Finley Smith died in Urbana, New York, on October 4, 1843, at the age of twenty-eight.[32] Reflecting on the infectious humor of his compositions, Smith was recalled as a genial if earnest soul in a touching tribute from a prominent Hamilton College colleague: "We often met him in a social way, and in religious meetings, and were captivated, as all others were, by his generous and brilliant qualities. His joyous nature found an easy natural expression in song and instrumental music. To human prophecy a bright and enviable future was before him. But his marriage [on] April [8], 1840, to [Adelaide Gridley] the only daughter of Deacon Orrin Gridley, of Clinton, was followed by her death early in 1842, and his own death, October 4, 1843."[33]

Smith was obviously beloved. He was eulogized in a published sermon delivered at Hamilton College. When the Utica Musical Academy was reestablished in 1858, fifteen years after his death, the published remarks spoke repeatedly of his character and accomplishments in service to the earlier academy.[34] John Finley Smith wrote other lighthearted pieces, including "A Frog He Would a Wooing Go, a sentimental song."

(Additional compositions by Smith are listed in the online Appendix B.) Henry Ivison was listed as a reference in the 1871–72 catalog for the Utica Female Academy. Also listed as a reference is composer Thomas Hastings, some of whose tunebooks were published by Emily Dickinson's uncle Mark Haskell Newman (see chapter 2).[35]

Syracuse, New York

Farther north on our "visiting tour" in the state of New York, the "Syracuse Polka" in Dickinson's music book was composed by Jonathan A. Fowler of Cherry Valley, New York. Fowler attended Amherst College during 1835–36.[36] During his second year, Fowler and four other students petitioned the faculty for permission to organize a society called the Amherst College Band.[37] The petition was denied. If funds were involved as part of the petitioning process, approval would have been needed from Amherst College treasurer Edward Dickinson, whose long tenure had just begun the previous year. In that regard Edward Dickinson would have come across Fowler's name. Fowler is listed in the Amherst College alumni catalog as being associated with the class of 1839. Fowler went on to become a noted music teacher, composer, and director of the music department at the Cherry Valley Female Academy (see chapter 2). His "Syracuse Polka" is dedicated to "Miss R. H. Loomis of Syracuse, N.Y."[38] Many of Fowler's compositions were written for and are dedicated to his students, a number of whom were from prominent families in Cherry Valley (see online Appendix B).[39]

Originally published in 1847, Fowler's enormously popular composition was brought out by at least ten different publishers. The copy in Dickinson's bound music book was published in New York by Atwill in 1848. Polkas were still new to the United States, and Fowler may have taken the opportunity to introduce a fresh teaching piece into his students' repertoire. It's certainly a highlight in Dickinson's music book.[40]

Another Syracuse connection is Elizabeth C. Adams, one of Dickinson's favorite teachers at the Amherst Academy. Before coming to Amherst, Adams had been associated with an academy in Syracuse, where she had served as principal of the female department from 1840 to 1842.[41] In March of 1847, just a few months before Emily Dickinson was to graduate from the academy, she reported to Abiah Root that

Miss Adams had left the Amherst Academy for Syracuse "to make her 'wedding gear.'"[42]

Edward Dickinson had a cousin in Syracuse, Pliny Dickinson, who visited the Amherst Dickinsons in April 1852 with his two daughters. The cousins stayed for what Emily described as a "long, and unexpected visit" of about three days. When Emily wrote to Austin of Pliny Dickinson's announcement that he "might stay around a month, visiting old acquaintances—if it was'nt for his business," she quipped to her brother, "Fortunate for us indeed, that his business feels the need for him, or I think he would *never* go."[43]

Three additional New York State–themed compositions in the Dickinson bound music book will be of interest to us in the next chapter: the "Locomotive Quick Step" composed by Auburn, New York, resident L. Thayer Chadwick, which honors the development of the local railroad; "Bayeaux's Quick Step," written for the Albany Burgesses militia group; and the "Camp Barnum Quick Step," written for the Rochester Union Grays. Those and other pieces will assist in animating the character and personality of the "Squire of Amherst," Edward Dickinson.

CHAPTER 6

Edward Dickinson

"Hail to the Chief"

THE PRESENCE IN EMILY DICKINSON's music book of "Roderick Dhu's March," the tune we know today as "Hail to the Chief," provides good theme music to commence a musical nod to Edward Dickinson, Amherst's chief citizen.

Despite the financial setbacks incurred by Samuel Fowler Dickinson in the founding of Amherst College, which he subsequently passed on to his son, Edward Dickinson was able to recover and prosper. He owned the leading law practice in Amherst; he was the treasurer of Amherst College; and he helped to found the Massachusetts Agricultural College, which became the University of Massachusetts, Amherst. He served on the boards of numerous institutions, including the "lunatic hospital" in Northampton and the Home Mission Society. He was elected to the United States Congress, serving in the House of Representatives for one term. Edward Dickinson was central to all manner of civic projects, including bringing the telegraph and railroad to Amherst and the building of a modern waterworks.[1] Three things that interested and inspired him—the militia, the opening of the local railroad, and Whig Party politics—all find a place in his daughter Emily's music book.

The Amherst and Belchertown Railroad

The developing network and technological progress of railroads was of great interest to Edward Dickinson, who believed that such progress was essential to the economic future of Amherst. Ever since the Amherst Branch Railroad Company was granted a charter in 1848, Edward Dickinson and others in the community had been lobbying for its construction so that Amherst could establish commercial connections to lines running west to Albany and east to Boston.[2]

On June 29, 1851, Emily shouted the news to her brother: "The railroad is a 'workin.'"[3] The next day, the Amherst and Belchertown Rail Road Company was granted its charter with Luke Sweetser, Ithamar Conkey, Myron Lawrence, Joseph Brown, and Edward Dickinson chosen as directors.[4] Construction on the branch to run between Amherst and Palmer commenced early in 1852, when "two hundred Irish laborers were at work at Logtown, southeast of Amherst." Edward Dickinson conveyed his unbridled excitement to his son Austin: "You will see by the Editor's glorification article in to-day's 'Express,' that the Am. & Bel. r. road is 'a fixed fact.' The contract is made—the workmen will be digging, in 'Logtown,' next week—& we shall see those animating shantees [along the route], smoking through an old flour barrel, for a chimney, before many days. . . . [T]he whole thing seems as much like a dream." The Amherst–Belchertown railroad opened on May 9, 1853.[5]

In her poem "I like to see it lap the miles," Dickinson alludes to those "shanties by the sides of roads," some of which remained inhabited after the railroad was completed. Dickinson's poem, titled "The Railway Train" by her first editors, Mabel Loomis Todd and T. W. Higginson, was included in *Poems by Emily Dickinson* (second series, 1891):

The Railway Train

I like to see it lap the miles,
And lick the valleys up,
And stop to feed itself at tanks;
And then, prodigious, step

Around a pile of mountains,
And, supercilious, peer
In shanties by the sides of roads;
And then a quarry pare

> To fit its sides, and crawl between,
> Complaining all the while
> In horrid, hooting stanza;
> Then chase itself down hill
>
> And neigh like Boanerges;
> Then, punctual as a star,
> Stop — docile and omnipotent —
> At its own stable door.[6]

Even with Dickinson's conflicting poetic imagery of the train, it's clear that she shared her father's enthusiasm for the railroad. In a letter to her brother in May 1853, one week after the opening of the railroad, the musical imagery is of course all Emily: "While I write, the whistle is playing, and the cars just coming in. It gives us all new life, every time it plays. How you will love to hear it, when you come home again!"[7]

Dickinson was clearly responding to a new musical soundscape, as was everyone in the industrializing North. Ralph Waldo Emerson wrote that the railroad was "the voice of the civility of the Nineteenth Century saying, 'Here I am.'"[8] With each mill, factory, and railroad, the sounds of everyday life were changing, animating towns, putting them "on the road to economic progress." Small towns like Amherst were urbanizing, as the railroad brought a new "bustle and stir" that was a welcome sound to many, including Emily Dickinson.[9]

Exactly one month after the Amherst–Belchertown line opened, Edward Dickinson led a visiting delegation of 325 people from New London, Connecticut, who came to celebrate the new railway. Emily wrote to her brother: "The New London Day passed off grandly—so all the people said—it was pretty hot and dusty, but nobody cared for that. Father was as usual, Chief Marshal of the day, and went marching around the town with New London at his heels like some old Roman General, upon a Triumph Day."[10]

The railroad brought more and more visitors to Amherst, many of them to the Dickinson home. Writing to her brother the following week, Emily was singing a slightly different tune: "We have been free from company by the 'Amherst and Belchertown Railroad' since [uncle] Joel went home, tho' we live in constant fear of some other visitation—.... The cars continue thriving—a good many passengers seem to arrive from somewhere, tho' nobody knows from where—.... I expect all our Grandfathers and all their country cousins will come here to pass

Commencement, and dont doubt the [railroad] stock will rise several percent that week."[11] Edward's stature with the railroad certainly rose. In 1862 one of the locomotives was "thoroughly renovated" and rechristened the "Edward Dickinson."[12]

"Locomotive Quick Step"

The Dickinsons' interest in the progress of mass transportation and those who were responsible for its development finds representation in Emily's music book with the "Locomotive Quick Step" by L. Thayer Chadwick, dedicated to C. C. Dennis of Auburn, New York. (Auburn is situated midway between Syracuse to the northeast and Geneva to the southwest in the Finger Lakes region of New York State.)

The Auburn & Syracuse Railroad opened on January 8, 1838, with support from former New York State governor and US senator William H. Seward (1801–1872), an Auburn resident who would later serve as President Lincoln's secretary of state. The railroad would connect remote and rural Auburn to a segment of the Erie Canal in Syracuse. Eventually it would become a branch of the New York Central Railroad.

The "Locomotive Quick Step" commemorates C. C. Dennis, builder of the first high-speed locomotive for the Auburn & Syracuse Railroad. The engine, christened the "Owasco," was given a test run on December 15, 1840, making all stops between Auburn and Syracuse in a then record time of fifty-eight minutes. The locomotive had been built in Auburn by the Commercial Iron Works, which was founded and operated by brothers-in-law Cyrus C. Dennis, David D. Thomas, and Charles P. Wood. Dennis was a civil engineer who worked on the Erie Canal. He arrived in Auburn in 1838 and played an active role in the Auburn & Syracuse Railroad and the Auburn & Rochester Railroad, eventually serving on both boards of trustees. When Auburn was incorporated as a city in 1848, Dennis became the city's first mayor.[13]

Auburn, New York, would serve as part of the figurative Underground Railroad, becoming a community of both Black and white residents. William Seward hid fugitive enslaved people in his home in Auburn before the Civil War. Antislavery hero Harriet Tubman (b. 1822) owned a home in Auburn sold to her by the Seward family. Tubman died in Auburn in 1913.[14]

Major Edward Dickinson

The "Locomotive Quick Step" is one of twelve quicksteps in the Dickinson music book. These and the nine marches allow us to reflect on Edward Dickinson's long-standing interest in and association with militias. According to Alfred Habegger: "It was in 1824 that Edward received his commission as ensign in his state's militia. Quickly promoted to major, he acquired the sword, sash, and plume that were part of the correct parade regalia. . . . [H]e was an earnest participant in musters and encampments."[15]

Before there was an official organization of armed forces in the United States, volunteer militias were formed as state-controlled aggregates of citizen soldiers. They were also fraternal organizations whose pomp and circumstance included parades, musters, and encampments, with music as an active and lively component.[16] Both Massachusetts and New York were states with a large network of militias, some of the oldest in the country.

From his early years of service as a militiaman, Edward Dickinson retained a quality of discipline that sometimes amused Emily. She wrote often, both ruefully and admiringly, of her father, with his stentorian tone and patrician demeanor. Emily wrote to her cousins, "Father steps like Cromwell when he gets the kindlings."[17]

Edward remained active in the Massachusetts militia at least into the mid-1840s, and the majority of the militia-related music in Emily's bound music book can be dated to that period.[18] As a militiaman Edward Dickinson fraternized with members of other local militias, and those fraternizations are a distinct feature of some of the stories behind these marches and quicksteps in Emily Dickinson's music book. For Edward Dickinson, this music offered up reminders of pleasant experiences, which he passed down to his daughter in the form of musical memories for her to perform.

Leading off the quickstep section in the bound music book is "The Celebrated Spanish Retreat," with its attractive lithographed cover containing the caption title "Shoulder Arms" (see figure 8). Dickinson's copy of the music has a copyright date of 1841 by Henry Prentiss of Boston (see Appendix A and online Appendix B). "The Celebrated Spanish Retreat" was performed for the first time by the Boston Brigade Band at the encampment of the Hancock Light Infantry in July of that year. The

FIGURE 8. "Shoulder Arms," the illustrated cover for "The Celebrated Spanish Retreat." Emily Dickinson's music book, EDR469, Houghton Library, Harvard University.

Hancock Light Infantry of Boston was under the command of Captain Noah Lincoln, and the Boston Brigade Band was under the direction of Benjamin Augustus Burditt. On August 25, 1845, the Hancock Light Infantry of Boston paid a visit to Springfield, where the *Daily Republican* reported: "They are accompanied by Kendall's Brass Band and are a guest of the 'Blues.' From the attention which is being paid them, we should judge this visit will be one of interest, alike to themselves and their military friends."[19]

Another splendid example of a period piece associated with the activities of a local militia is "Bayeaux's Quick Step." The Albany Burgesses Corps of Albany, New York (formed in 1833), commissioned the piece from the prolific composer William Cooper Glynn (1816–1877), whose

"Bay State Quick Step" and "Rockaway Waltzes" are also found in Dickinson's bound music book. "Bayeaux's Quick Step" is dedicated to the officers and members of the Albany Burgesses Corps and named for corps captain Thomas Bayeaux, or Bayeux (1802–1844).[20] This quickstep became part of the repertoire of the Burgesses Band and was performed at their public concerts and events.[21]

One of those events occurred on Friday, June 17, 1843, when the Albany Burgesses Corps participated in the Boston celebration honoring the completion of the Bunker Hill Monument (which Emily Dickinson would visit three years later). President John Tyler attended and Noah Webster gave the keynote address. The *Springfield Republican* reported on June 24 that the Albany Burgesses Corps, on their way home from the celebration in Boston, arrived in Springfield at noon on Monday the twentieth. They stayed at the Hampden House, viewed the armory, and dined with a committee of dignitaries from the city. "This company is a highly respectable, richly dressed, and thoroughly disciplined corps," declared the *Republican*. "We were glad to improve this or any other opportunity to make Albany and Springfield better acquainted."[22]

"Bayeaux's Quick Step" is a superb example of the quality of the music written for these militia groups. The infectious programmatic beauty of this piece evokes the camaraderie and fraternization that was enjoyed by these organizations and documented in the local press.

Another militia group that fraternized with the Albany Burgesses Corps was the Rochester Union Grays, an artillery unit organized in 1838 and associated with the Fifty-fourth Regiment, based in Rochester, New York. The "Camp Barnum Quick Step" (1847) in Dickinson's music book was composed by Rochester music teacher Charles Wilson.[23] The piece commemorates the citizen-soldiers of the Grays and is dedicated to Grays member Mason A. Fisher (d. 1847). The band associated with this unit was formed in 1841 and achieved an international reputation under the leadership of Captain Jesse C. Adams.[24] The Albany Burgesses Corps also fraternized with the Rochester City Cadets, and the Rochester Light Guards. Each of these Rochester militia groups used the services of the Adams Brass Band, as did other groups and organizations such as the Independent Order of Oddfellows in Rochester.[25]

The National Whig Party

Edward Dickinson also had a strong and loyal affiliation with the Whig Party, which was formed in the 1830s to oppose the policies of Democratic president Andrew Jackson. It wasn't until 1840 that the Whigs had their first successful presidential nominee in William Henry Harrison. The "Prize Banner Quick Step" (1841) in the Dickinson music book commemorates the activities of the national Whig Party of 1840. According to the *Springfield Republican* of September 19, 1840, the Prize Banner of Boston would be issued to the "ward which shall give the greatest Whig gain at the coming election." The cover of the sheet music shows the Prize Banner being waved in celebration, and the music is "Dedicated to the Whigs of the Prize Banner Ward." William Henry Harrison was elected President in 1840 but died on April 4, 1841, just thirty-one days after assuming the presidency.

Four years later, Henry Clay would become the Whig Party's 1844 presidential nominee, and Henry Clay clubs sprang up across the country. In Boston, the local Henry Clay Club no. 1 was singing the popular song "The Bonnie Clay Flag," which was written for them and which Emily Dickinson was able to acquire for her music book. When the Whigs established their own Henry Clay Club in Amherst on May 21, 1844, Edward Dickinson became its first president.[26]

"I like an obedient daughter, played & sang a few tunes"

Edward Dickinson enjoyed hearing songs such as "The Bonnie Clay Flag," "The Prize Banner Quick Step," and other familiar "tunes" from his militia days and political rallies. This music was arranged and issued by the music publishers to provide accessible and suitable band and military music to be re-created on the home parlor piano. Music was a family affair for the Dickinsons, not only in what Emily collected but also in how and when the music was performed at home.

Edward Dickinson often requested that his daughters play music for him, and they complied. Music was sometimes used to convey a sense of orderliness in the Dickinson home. According to Dickinson biographer Genevieve Taggard, Emily performed dutifully for her father, which was "Edward's way of bringing Emily back when she escaped, absorbed in a book."[27]

In January 1852 Emily was in the midst of a letter to Abiah Root: "I left you here and went down to prepare the tea; I thought to return to you so soon as tea was done, but father asked for some music, and I could not deny him."[28]

Another instance took place the evening of Thanksgiving Day 1847, while Emily was on recess from Mount Holyoke. That night she spent a long evening out with friends, and in a letter written months later, she recounted the experience to Abiah Root:

> At about 7. o'clock, Father, Mother, Austin, Viny, Cousin Emily & myself to bring up the rear, went down to Profr. Warner's, where we spent an hour delightfully, with a few friends & then bidding them good eve, we young folks, went down to Mrs. S. Mack's accompanied by *Sister Mary*.
>
> There was quite a company of young people assembled, when we arrived and after we had played many Games, we had in familiar terms a "Candy scrape." We enjoyed the evening much & returned not until the clock pealed out 'Remember 10 oclock my dear, remember 10, oclock.' After our return, Father wishing to hear the Piano, I like an obedient daughter, played & sang a few tunes, much to his apparent gratification.[29]

Edward's "apparent gratification" was consistent with antebellum mores, in that his daughter was finally home, obediently and "fruitfully occupied, indoors and at a suitably feminine musical activity."[30] While Emily would not deny a request from her father to "sing and play a few tunes"—"Edward's way of bringing Emily back" after her long evening out—it should be noted that the large number of marches and quicksteps in Emily Dickinson's music book point directly to Edward Dickinson as an active musical participant and influence in the content of Emily's music book, and a source of encouragement for Emily to excel at the piano.[31]

As a postscript to our musical chapter on Edward Dickinson, Alfred Habegger notes that "there was a definite military quality in Edward—a sense of discipline, of readiness for combat, of standing at attention for life."[32] These same qualities often defined the atmosphere in the Dickinson home. On December 15, 1851, Emily wrote to her brother, confessing that since Austin had left for Boston to teach school, "we dont *have* many jokes tho' *now*, it is pretty much all sobriety, and we do not have much poetry, father having made up his mind that its pretty much all *real life*. Fathers real life and *mine* sometimes come into collision, but as yet, escape un-hurt!"[33]

Making fun of her father was both an outlet and "a favorite sport in her letters—Father and the railroad; Father at Jenny Lind's concert; Father and the 'amazin raw' weather," which we shall encounter in the next chapter.[34] Dickinson had ample opportunities to celebrate both the achievements and the foibles of her father. Family music-making in the Dickinson parlor presents opportunities for us to further witness this family dynamic. In the next chapter we shall also see some of Emily's stretching of the truth, sometimes through wit and humor, a habit her brother Austin dubbed her "posing."[35]

CHAPTER 7

Music-Making and the Dickinson Family Correspondence

"Vinnie is at the instrument"

EMILY DICKINSON FILLED HER CORRESPONDENCE with quotes from literature, poetry, the Bible, and the music of the day. Her letters served as a canvas on which she could observe and comment on the family dynamic, filtered through musical activities in the home parlor. On Sunday, June 8, 1851, Emily wrote to her brother, who had left home the previous day to take up a teaching post in Boston:

> We are enjoying this evening what is called a "northeast storm"—a little north of east, in case you are pretty definite. Father thinks "it's amazin raw," and I'm half disposed to think that he's in the right about it, tho' I keep pretty dark, and don't *say* much about it! Vinnie is at the instrument, humming a pensive air concerning a young lady who thought she was "almost there." Vinnie seems much grieved, and I really suppose *I* ought to betake myself to weeping; I'm pretty sure that I *shall* if she dont abate her singing.[1]

The chill of the evening both outside and inside the Dickinson parlor is palpable, but leavened once again with Emily's humor; she obviously enjoys mocking Vinnie's earnest but overwrought performance:

Lavinia "like an obedient daughter played & sang a few tunes," while Emily "keep[s] pretty dark."[2]

The "pensive air" hummed by Lavinia was the enormously popular song "Are We Almost There?" by the poet Florence Vane, which details the last hours of a dying young woman. Lavinia emulated a sentimentality of performance that was encouraged and widely practiced in American parlors of the period. Its distinctive features included expressions of sighing, sobbing, or murmuring.[3] Here, Lavinia could be the Dickinson family's "warbling teller" from Emily's 1882 poem "The Bible is an antique Volume — ." The practice of expressive sentimentality in music was considered both attractive and appropriate—so much so that Lavinia's performance finds resonance with Dickinson's line from the same poem "Had but the Tale a warbling Teller — ."[4] Not only does this characterization assist us, along with Emily, in poking fun at Lavinia but also, more importantly, just as Dickinson's poem is a "spoof of established [biblical] doctrine," the poem's "slant" lines perfectly animate, exemplify, and perhaps de-sacralize the sentimentality of performance that was so enormously popular in Dickinson's day, and in which Lavinia was so completely engaged.[5]

Emily, the polar opposite, is posing.[6] Five years earlier, Emily had expressed her own esteem for Florence Vane's poem, writing to Abiah Root: "Have you seen a beautiful piece of poetry which has been going through the papers lately? *Are we almost there?* is the title of it." Thomas Johnson notes that the poem "Are We Almost There?" had its first newspaper printing in 1833.[7] Vane herself set the poem to music, and Oliver Ditson published the song in 1845. A prefatory note on the title page explains the song's inspiration: "A young lady had visited the South for her health, but finding she hourly grew worse, her friends hurried her home. On the journey she was very much exhausted, and continually enquired 'Are we almost there?' She died just before reaching home. A friend who accompanied her wrote the song."[8]

While this popular ballad is not in the Dickinson bound music book, Emily's reference to it illuminates for us Lavinia's attraction to the sentimental ballads that so defined the era, with their evocation of ties of human affection and bonding centering on the home.[9] Lavinia had regular occasion to perform "Are We Almost There" and other sentimental songs and ballads such as "Comin' thro' the Rye" at levees, such as the annual senior class event at the home of Amherst College president the Reverend William Augustus Stearns (1805–1876), with whose family the Dickinson's were "all intimately friendly," or at teas hosted by Amherst merchant and Dickinson neighbor Deacon Luke Sweetser (1800–1882).[10] Dickinson's music book contains a few similar sentimental vocal pieces. Most of these are evocative of home or of missing someone at home, such as "The Old Arm Chair," "The Rose of Allandale," and of course "Home, Sweet Home."

Lavinia gave the fullest expression to vocal sentimentality through the performance of touching ballads around the family piano. Emily, by contrast, enjoyed engaging in the more introspective side of musical expression afforded by instrumental music. Her collecting focus was on variation sets on arias from Rossini's *Tancredi* and Bellini's *Norma* and other tunes such as "Speed the Plough" and "Believe Me If All Those Endearing Young Charms," or a four-hand arrangement of the overture to the opera *Lodoïska* by Rodolphe Kreutzer. A good deal of this music required above-average piano technique, something that we can observe in the dynamic between the two sisters.[11]

"Thank you for the music Austin"

On December 15, 1851, Emily wrote to her brother: "Thank you for the music Austin, and thank you for the books. I have enjoyed them very much. I shall learn my part of the Duett, and try to have Vinnie her's. She is very much pleased with Charity. She would write you now but is busy getting her lesson." Vinnie was "much pleased" because Austin had just sent her another song by the composer Stephen Glover, whose music she favored. This one was Glover's popular religious song "Charity." Perhaps the new song was the focus of Lavinia's lesson which Emily had overheard.[12]

But something seems to have gone awry with Emily's plans for the duet. Six weeks later Emily followed up on her sister's progress: "You sent us the *Duett*, Austin. Vinnie cannot learn it, and I see from the outside page, that there is a piece for *two* hands. Are you willing to change it. Dont be in haste to send it; any time will do! Shall write when I hear from you, more fully."[13]

The duet she refers to in her letters points to Kreutzer's Overture to *Lodoïska* arranged for piano four hands by Carl Czerny (1791–1857). The overture is the first composition, and the only four-hand piece, in

Dickinson's music book. Emily and Lavinia intended to produce a rousing home performance of this robust work, but according to Emily's letter, that did not come to pass, nor is there evidence that she returned the music. A clue to the legitimacy of Dickinson's claim that "Vinnie cannot learn it" is in the music itself. The first five pages of the piece are filled with handwritten fingerings, beat alignments between the staves, and note names written above those notes requiring ledger lines, something a beginning student would do.[14] The overture consists of a slow section (pages two through four) followed by a more difficult fast section commencing on page five; after page five, however, the handwritten markings cease. The speed and complexity of the overture's allegro section had caught up with Lavinia, and any hopes of a performance ended right there.

Emily Dickinson's Piano

The duet in Dickinson's bound music book offers evidence that it was around this time, in late 1851 or early 1852, that the Dickinsons acquired a new and larger piano. The duet, the variation sets, and some of the quicksteps and other pieces in Dickinson's bound music book would have exceeded the range of the earlier square pianos manufactured in 1845. By the date of Dickinson's letter to her brother on December 15, 1851, when she was twenty-one, her playing had obviously reached a more advanced level, and her requests for the more difficult compositions such as the four-hand Overture to *Lodoïska* demanded a larger piano. Dickinson's niece Martha Dickinson Bianchi (1866–1943) described Emily's piano as "an old-fashioned square in an elaborately carved mahogany case."[15] What Bianchi was remembering was the much larger ornately carved 1851 Hallet and Davis square piano, which is on view in the Emily Dickinson Room at Harvard University's Houghton Library.[16] Americans favored "old-fashioned" square pianos well into the 1880s, and the Dickinsons favored them too.[17]

Whatever the reason for abandoning the four-hand duet, it forever maintains pride of place as the first piece in Dickinson's bound music book. Perhaps Dickinson had in mind that the four-hand duet from Kreutzer's opera should set the tone for the casual viewer who opens her music volume for the first time, as evidence of her abilities, accomplishments, and taste.

Rodolphe Kreutzer's Lodoïska

Rodolphe Kreutzer (1766–1831) was a virtuoso violinist and composer. He is best remembered as the dedicatee of Ludwig van Beethoven's "Kreutzer Sonata" for violin and piano, opus 47.[18] Kreutzer's opera was based on the novel *Les Amours du Chevalier de Faublas* by Jean-Baptiste Louvet de Couvray (1760–1797). *Lodoïska* opened in Paris in 1791. The opera was not staged in New York City until 1837, an indication of how long it could take for major symphonic and operatic productions, with their attendant resources, to make the transatlantic route into American theaters and opera houses.

The opera situates the listener centuries ago in the deep forests of Poland, a country viewed at the time as a land of "mystery and romance for Western audiences."[19] In the story, Count Floreski searches for his lover, Lodoïska, who has been sent away by her father to prevent her marriage to the count. Eventually Floreski finds Lodoïska confined to the castle of Baron Dourlinski, deep in the uncharted Polish forest. Lodoïska's father has since died, but Dourlinski refuses to release Lodoïska, wishing instead to take her as his bride. Floreski and his servant disguise themselves as two brothers who have been sent by Lodoïska's mother, forcing Baron Dourlinski to release her from captivity.

After Kreutzer's death in 1831, excerpts from *Lodoïska* continued to be a feature on local concert programs. "Selections from the works of celebrated composers," including an uncredited "Overture de Lodoiski," was part of a program given by the Springfield Musical Society on May 25, 1836. The following week, the *Springfield Republican* reprinted the "Tale of Poland" recounting the legend of Lodoïska.[20] The legend was attractive to other composers who also brought the story to life on the operatic stage. These included Johann Simon Mayr (1763–1845), Stephen Storace (1763–1796), and the more well-known Luigi Cherubini (1760–1842).

Kreutzer's Overture to *Lodoïska* remained a favorite composition on the nineteenth-century concert stage and in the home parlor. This arrangement by Carl Czerny places Dickinson in an important musical and historical context. Czerny (a former pupil of Beethoven and teacher of Franz Liszt) was a composer/arranger and pedagogue whose work was in high demand. According to Thomas Christensen, "Beethoven told his publisher that he had neither the time nor the patience to reduce [his full opera score] *Fidelio* [into a piano-vocal format] and was happy to turn the job over to Czerny."[21] Thus the Czerny arrangement of Kreutzer's Overture to *Lodoïska* which Dickinson collected provides important insight into her world as a knowledgeable practicing musician, contextualizing both the pedagogical and historical musical moment in which she was engaged.

We know that there were other published editions of Kreutzer's overture for one piano two hands, which supports the fact that Dickinson, while perusing the "outside cover," requested that her brother procure a two-hand version which she could perform by herself.[22] The "outside cover" of these publications was often a protective wrapper, which mainly served as a marketing vehicle advertising other sheet music offered by the publisher, including other versions of the work in hand. According to bibliographer Donald Krummel, these wrappers were "generally [of a] paper quite different from the paper used in the main text, and, if present, generally occur when there is a full title page (but not when there is only a caption title [at the head of the first page of music])."[23] Dickinson was clearly perusing one of these wrappers, but unfortunately for today's musicologists, wrappers were often discarded, especially if the music was to be collated and bound so as to reduce the size of the bound volume.[24] That certainly seems to be the case with this and a few other pieces in Dickinson's music book. See online Appendix B.

Music publishers appealed to consumers like Dickinson by marketing a variety of music, from simplified vocal versions to instrumental arrangements or challenging variation sets on opera arias, songs, and other well-known melodies, a mainstay of a music publisher's output.[25] Dickinson would have been well aware of the popularity of sentimental songs such as John J. Blockley's "Love Not," or the perennial tune "Auld Lang Syne," the popular "Blue Juniata" by Marion Dix Sullivan, or the Irish air "The Last Rose of Summer" with words by Thomas Moore. Her decision to collect instrumental quickstep arrangements or variation sets of these popular melodies, instead of the original published songs, suggests a preference for the privacy of tasteful serious practice, and individual accomplishment afforded by instrumental music, rather than an outward display of vocal talent.[26] This is an aspect of Dickinson's musical life that warrants further exploration, situating her within the cultural discourse of musical literacy in the nineteenth-century American parlor. Dickinson certainly had a great deal of musical knowledge and taste, and put it to good use acquiring these variation sets, some of which are representative of the most distinguished arrangers of her day.

"Believe Me If All Those Endearing Young Charms"

One of the premier arrangers of piano music in Dickinson's day was Thomas Valentine. There are three examples of his work in her music book: The "Aria alla Scozzese" with variations by Valentine; his arrangement of "The Much Admired Waltz" (with music misattributed to Beethoven); and his variation set on the Irish/English air "Believe Me If All Those Endearing Young Charms," or "My Lodging Is on the Cold Ground."[27]

Thomas Valentine (1790–1878) was an English composer and a prolific arranger. He also published instruction books.[28] The song "Believe Me If All Those Endearing Young Charms" had long been a familiar tune, first seeing print in London in 1775 with the words "My Lodging is on the Cold Ground." The words we know today were written by Thomas Moore and first published in *A Selection of Irish Melodies* (1807–8). In Dickinson's day the tune was still known by both titles, and for those consumers who were familiar with this tune under its earlier title, an exact re-publication of this set of variations by Valentine "to the Admired Air of 'My Lodging is on the Cold Ground'" was published by George P. Reed in Boston, sometime in the 1840s, ten pages of music at a price of seventy-five cents. In addition to the variation set of "Believe Me If All Those Endearing Young Charms," Dickinson also collected the vocal score to this popular air.

As a Harvard Law School graduate, Austin Dickinson would have been familiar with the tune in its 1836 reincarnation by the Reverend Samuel Gilman (1791–1858) as the new ode "Fair Harvard." The "Ode Sung at the Second Centennial Celebration" would become Harvard's alma mater. The words and music were published by the Boston publishing firm of Samuel H. Parker and Oliver Ditson, who had a publishing partnership between 1836 and 1842.[29]

Emily Dickinson's letter of February 17, 1848, written from Mount Holyoke to her brother contains a diamond-shaped sticker on which she printed "Believe me," along with the first bar of music to the tune "Believe Me If All Those Endearing Young Charms."[30] It's clear that some of her personal sheet music went with her to Mount Holyoke and she played it there.

In Dickinson's time, incorporating musical references into one's correspondence was a common practice, not just for Emily Dickinson. Her extensive knowledge of the musical repertoire of her day and the ubiquity of some of this music in women's bound music volumes animate the discourse between Dickinson and her correspondents. References to songs such as "Believe Me If All Those Endearing Young Charms," "The Last Rose of Summer," "John Anderson My Jo," "Bonnie Doon," and much more are found in her letters and later in some of her poems.[31]

Throughout her teenage years and into early adulthood, Emily and her friends eagerly exchanged information about their musical activities. Emily's second cousins Olivia and Eliza Coleman kept their friends up to date on their activities and music purchases. In May of 1846, Olivia Coleman wrote to their mutual friend Emily Fowler, "We discovered a new Music Store, and I purchased the song 'I'm alone—all alone,' for I am truly alone without you."[32] Olivia was missing the companionship of her friends back home in Amherst since her father, the Reverend Lyman Coleman, had taken a position at the College of New Jersey (Princeton) two months before.[33]

In 1850 Dickinson wrote to her friend Jane Humphrey echoing Olivia's letter by quoting the same lyric: "Vinnie you know is away—and that I'm very lonely is too plain for me to tell you—I am *alone—all alone*."[34]

Another Coleman family connection that inspired a musical reference from Dickinson appears in an 1865 letter to her cousin Louisa Norcross. "Loo" was preparing to visit Eliza Coleman in Middletown, Connecticut, where the Coleman family had moved from Philadelphia in 1858. In Middletown, Eliza Coleman met John Langdon Dudley, a noted clergyman. They became engaged and would marry in June 1861. An Amherst College graduate of 1844, Dudley was introduced to Emily Dickinson when he and his fiancée attended the Amherst commencement in 1860.[35] Dickinson's Norcross cousins (Louisa and Frances, ages eighteen and thirteen) also attended, with Eliza serving as their festive guardian for the event, which made for a very spirited and bonding occasion. "I knew she would guard my children, as she has often guarded me, from publicity," Emily wrote to her Norcross cousins afterwards.[36] It's clear that Emily Dickinson and the Dudleys remained close, evidenced by the fact that it was at those commencement exercises that Emily and Lavinia made plans to visit them in Middletown two months later, in October 1860.[37] Thus Dickinson was obviously thrilled that her Norcross cousin from Boston would be visiting the Dudleys at Middletown, and her 1865 letter to Louisa shows it, emphatically punctuated with a reference to the instrumental waltz set from her music book "Sounds From Home" by Josef Gung'l: "I am glad to the foot of my heart that you will go to Middletown. It will make you warm. Touches 'from home,' tell Gungl, are better than 'sounds.'"[38]

Dickinson's knowledge of music repertoire certainly went beyond the contents of her music book. In another letter to her childhood friend Emily Fowler, Dickinson enclosed a lock of her hair and used a musical reference to the song "John Anderson My Jo" as a signifier of their enduring friendship: "Dear Emily—this is all—It will serve to make you remember me when locks are crisp and gray, and the quiet cap, and the spectacles, and 'John Anderson my Joe' are all that is left of me."[39]

In a letter to her brother, we see Dickinson making another musical reference, this time to the hymnbook *Village Hymns* by Asahel Nettleton. Soon after Austin left for Harvard Law School in March 1853, Emily wrote to him teasingly about his devotional accommodations and his religious nourishment: "Trust you enjoy your closet, and meditate profoundly upon the Daily Food! I shall send you Village Hymns, by earliest opportunity."[40] Dickinson was being playful in offering to send *Village Hymns*. According to Dickinson biographer Alfred Habegger, "That was in 1853, when she and Austin were the family's only unconverted members." Emily was "well aware that this now old-fashioned compilation was the last thing he wanted."[41]

One of the more deliberate and amusing yet prescient musical references in Dickinson's correspondence is contained in a letter to Austin dated November 14, 1853. Monday, November 14, was Election Day in Massachusetts, and the Dickinsons supported Ithamar Frank (Francis) Conkey (1823–1875), who was voted in as the representative from Amherst to the Massachusetts House of Representatives.[42] Austin was expected to come home and vote. As Lavinia told her brother, "Father expected you *certainly* & we had a splendid dinner ready for you

& Sue came down to see if you were here."⁴³ But when the hour came for his arrival, Austin didn't appear. On the one hand, Emily may have been teasing again when she wrote to Austin, "Father seemed perfectly sober, when the afternoon train came in, and there was no intelligence of you in any way." On the other hand, the bond between father and son was very strong,⁴⁴ so Emily's summation of universal disappointment was confirmation of the truth behind her words:

> Mother got a great dinner yesterday, thinking in her kind heart that you would be so hungry after your *long ride*, and the table was set for you, and nobody moved your chair, but there it stood at the table, until dinner was all done, a melancholy emblem of the blasted hopes of the world. And we had new custard pie, too, which is a rarity in days when hens dont lay, but mother knew you loved it, and when noon really got here, and you really did not come, then a big piece was saved in case you should come at night. Father seemed perfectly sober, when the afternoon train came in, and there was no intelligence of you in any way, but "there's a good time coming"!⁴⁵

The song "There's a Good Time Coming" from Dickinson's music book is based on a melody by Henry Russell (but not credited to Russell in this published musical arrangement as "composed & sung by the Hutchinson Family"). Russell's music for "There's a Good Time Coming" was set to a text by Charles Mackay (1814–1889). The Hutchinsons co-opted parts of Russell's tune and composed their own song with assistance from arranger Edward Little White. "There's a Good Time Coming" proved to be one of the Hutchinsons' most popular creations. The chorus is out front here, Mackay's lyrics setting the tone, longing for a world united in peace and tranquillity:

CHORUS

There's a good time coming boys,
A good time coming,
There's a good time coming boys,
Wait a little longer.

VERSE 1

We may not live to see the day,
But earth shall glisten in the ray
Of the good time coming.

> Cannon-balls may aid the truth,
> But thought's a weapon stronger;
> We'll win our battle by its aid
> Wait a little longer.[46]

While Dickinson's letter gently satirizes her prominent Amherst family as the center of their own local universe, with Austin's empty chair standing in as a "melancholy emblem of the blasted hopes of the world," soon "the blasted hopes of the world" would loom far beyond the Dickinson family's Amherst home. There would be no "Good Time Coming," and as in Dickinson's poem about a clock stopping, the sheet music titles that we shall encounter in the next chapter are, like the broken clock, frozen in time within the pages of her music book—witnesses to the political and cultural crises developing in the 1840s and 1850s, "Decades of Arrogance" that would soon rend the nation apart into civil war:

> A Clock stopped —
> Not the Mantel's —
> Geneva's farthest skill
> Cant put the puppet bowing —
> That just now dangled still —
>
> An awe came on the Trinket!
> The Figures hunched — with pain —
> Then quivered out of Decimals —
> Into Degreeless noon —
>
> It will not stir for Doctor's —
> This Pendulum of snow —
> The shopman importunes it —
> While cool — concernless No —
>
> Nods from the Gilded pointers —
> Nods from the Seconds slim —
> Decades of Arrogance between
> The Dial life —
> And him — [47]

CHAPTER 8

The American Political Struggle

"Decades of Arrogance"

THE NEWS OF THE day came to the Dickinson household through a variety of print sources. As regular readers of the *Springfield Daily Republican*, the *Hampshire and Franklin Express*, the *Atlantic Monthly*, *Harper's*, *Century Magazine*, the *New York Observer*, *Scribner's*, and other publications, the Dickinson family kept abreast of all manner of local and national, cultural, and world affairs. A number of pieces in Dickinson's music book rally around some of the major social and political issues of the day: "The "Bonnie Clay Flag," "The Prize Banner Quick Step," "The Juniata Quick Step," "The Girl I Left Behind Me," "Yankee Doodle," "Oh Give Me a Home If in Foreign Land," "Old Dan Tucker," and "Home, Sweet Home" all contribute a musical commentary to the news of the day and the crises unfolding during the 1850s that would lead to the outbreak of the Civil War in 1861.

Emily Dickinson was an avid reader of the *Springfield Daily Republican*. Founded in 1821 by Samuel Bowles II (1797–1851), it was originally a single-sheet Saturday weekly newspaper. In March 1844 the paper expanded to a four-page evening daily and became the area's leading news organ.[1] The editors, Samuel Bowles III (1826–1878) and Josiah Gilbert Holland (1819–1881), were close friends of the Dickinsons and were frequent visitors to Amherst, especially Bowles. Emily and Lavinia would visit them in Springfield, and Emily engaged in regular correspondence with Samuel Bowles and his wife, Mary Bowles (1827–1893), and Dr. Holland and his wife, Elizabeth Holland (1823–1896). Emily's 1853 letter to Elizabeth Holland reflects her intimate engagement with the paper, as she reacts to the news of the day:

> I thought of you all last week, until the world grew rounder than it sometimes is, and I broke several dishes. . . . One glimpse of *The Republican* makes me break things again—I read in it every night.
>
> Who writes those funny accidents, where railroads meet each other unexpectedly, and gentlemen in factories get their heads cut off quite informally? The author, too, relates them in such a sprightly way, that they are quite attractive. Vinnie was disappointed to-night, that there were not more accidents—I read the news aloud, while Vinnie was sewing. *The Republican* seems to us like a letter from you, and we break the seal and read it eagerly.[2]

"The Bonnie Clay Flag"

In Emily Dickinson's day, the *Springfield Daily Republican* was advancing the cause of the Whig Party, and Emily's music book was a direct beneficiary of those politics. On Friday, September 20, 1844, the *Republican* reported on a rally that had taken place the previous day in Boston. In anticipation of the November presidential election, the Boston Clay Club (a local outpost of the National Whig Party) held a procession and a "great Mass Meeting of the Whigs of Massachusetts, joined by large delegations from every section of the Union." The paper noted that "over thirty bands of Music were in the procession at different points."[3] The meeting was held on the Boston Common in celebration of the nomination of their party's presidential candidate, Henry Clay (1777–1852). The nomination, which had taken place in May, pitted Clay against the Jacksonian Democrat James K. Polk (1795–1849). Clay lost in November, and Polk became the eleventh president of the United States.

In Dickinson's music book, "The Bonnie Clay Flag" is dedicated to the "Boston Clay Club No[.] 1" and is commemorative of those Whig rallies of 1844. The song was appropriated from a well-known Scottish Highland Fling, "Hey the Bonnie Breast Knots," composed by the Scottish opera singer John Sinclair (1791–1857), with new words as "The Bonnie Clay Flag" by John Henry Warland (1807–1872).[4] Warland combined his new pro-Whig text with some of the original words from the tune's chorus, giving the song a parodic nod to an anti-Irish sentiment that was on the rise, particularly in Massachusetts. Within weeks of its publication in January 1844, the song was being advertised by music publishers from Boston to Cleveland.[5] In May of 1844 the song was in the air when thirteen-year-old Emily Dickinson was visiting her aunt Lavinia's family in Boston.

The Whig Party was the party of the Dickinsons, and the political sentiments of the family and of Samuel Bowles's *Springfield Daily*

FIGURE 9. "The Bonnie Clay Flag." Emily Dickinson's music book, EDR469, Houghton Library, Harvard University.

Republican, her "interpreter of world events," were trickling down to Emily.[6] Dickinson's copy of "The Bonnie Clay Flag" is inscribed in pencil "To the Editor with the compliments of the publisher please notice" (see figure 9). "The Editor," passed his copy of "The Bonnie Clay Flag" on to Emily Dickinson. Several months later, with sheet music in hand, Dickinson wrote to Abiah Root: "Please send me a copy of that Romance you was writing at Amherst [Academy]. I am in a fever to read it. I expect it will be against my Whig feelings."[7]

The editor did "notice," and on April 3, 1844, the *Springfield Daily Republican* ran a review of *The National Clay Melodist*, edited by John H. Warland. This was a "songster," a little book full of Whig-style contrafacta, topical lyrics sung to familiar tunes. The first selection in this songster was Warland's own "The Bonnie Clay Flag."

The paper crowed:

> We have received from the publisher, Benjamin Adams, Boston, a copy of the *National Clay Melodist*, a little volume of 100 pages, filled with capital and appropriate songs for the coming Presidential campaign. The work is edited, and many of the best songs written by J. H. Warland Esq.—a well known and popular Whig editor.[8] The Melodist should be in the hands of every singing Whig, and every Clay Club in the country. The singing of songs, set to popular and spirit stirring tunes, so general and taking in the Harrison campaign, we are glad to notice is reviving in the present. There certainly can be no harm in singing, however much our opponents may sneer and despise it. It is a natural and pleasant way of expressing one's feelings, and we doubt not that it will be extensively followed during the coming season, and help to swell the gushing tide for Harry of the West.

The paper concluded its review with another tune from the songster that had an even louder crow to it: "So, 'Get out of the way, you're all unlucky / Clear the track for old Kentucky.'"[9] That topical lyric contained multiple references that contemporary audiences would have understood. The words served as the chorus of "The Moon Was Shining Silver Bright," a paean to the 1844 Whig Party candidate, Kentuckian Henry Clay. Set to the popular minstrel tune "Old Dan Tucker," this Whig appropriation was audacious, in that the words of the chorus were aimed directly at the Hutchinson Family Singers, whose abolitionist leanings were viewed by the Whigs as excessive. The Hutchinsons' appropriation of the same tune, "Old Dan Tucker," which they titled "Get Off the Track," had its own familiar chorus: "Get out the way! every station, Clear the way for [e]'mancipation." The rhythms of "Old Dan Tucker" were indeed infectious, encouraging appropriations from all corners, especially those who wished to join in with their own brand of subversion, political or otherwise.[10] These types of musical activities and appropriations would only grow louder as the 1850s progressed.

"The Solid Men"

As a prominent member of the Massachusetts Whig Party, Edward Dickinson aligned himself with "[Daniel] Webster's class of 'solid men.'"[11] Edward was a "law and order" man who opposed slavery, particularly in the opening of new territories. Yet he too, according to Millicent Todd Bingham, was "united in deploring the fanaticism of the abolitionists, who, they said, were by their very fervor widening the breach between the two sections of the country, a view with which Edward Dickinson was in complete agreement."[12] In 1852 Edward Dickinson took his political ideals to the people and was elected to the Thirty-third United States Congress as the representative from the Tenth District of Massachusetts.

As the 1850s wore on, the Whig Party began to splinter over the issues of slavery, immigration, territorial expansion, and the displacement of Native Americans. Even the Dickinson family correspondence was showing signs of strain, not just for Emily but for Austin as well. After he graduated from Amherst College in 1850, Austin thought he might want to teach school and secured a post in nearby Sunderland. In a letter to his future wife, Susan Gilbert, he complained about his dislike of teaching and how his free time seemed to be limited socially by his having to "answer to the *Free Soilers* for all the sins of omission as well as commission of the whole whig party."[13] But it was while teaching in Boston a year later that Austin seems to have allowed some "Know Nothing" sympathies to surface. The "Know Nothings" were a short-lived political party, a movement whose chief motivation was to tamp down the influx of immigrants, especially the Irish Catholics, some of whom were under Austin's charge at Boston's Endicott School.[14] In response to one of his letters, Emily wrote to him coolly, perhaps teasingly: "Father remarks quite briefly that he 'thinks they have found their master,' mother bites her lips, and fears 'you will be *rash* with them' and Vinnie and I say masses for poor Irish boys souls."[15]

One thing that Austin did know was that he had had enough of teaching. He returned to what he and Emily both called "My Father's House." There he settled down and began working in Edward's law office while making preparations to enter Harvard Law School the following year.

"The Blue Juniata"

Another ongoing social and political struggle during this time concerned the eradication of the Native American population, which is reflected in "The Juniata Quick Step" in Dickinson's bound music book. This is a quickstep arrangement of the popular vocal ballad "The Blue Juniata," "as played by the Boston Bands."

Written by Marion Dix Sullivan (ca. 1820–after 1855) and first published in 1844, "The Blue Juniata," also called "The Indian Girl, or Bright Alfarata," was the first song written by an American woman to achieve commercial success in the nineteenth century.[16] The song's lyrics (see figure 10) captured the imagination of the public, echoing the image of the noble savage as portrayed by Henry Wadsworth Longfellow (1807–1882) and James Fenimore Cooper (1789–1851).[17] "The Blue Juniata" romanticizes the plight of Native Americans as their population dwindled and their culture was being eradicated along with the country's wilderness landscape.

The presence of "The Juniata Quick Step" in Dickinson's bound music book opens a door to Emily's childhood friend Helen Fiske Hunt Jackson (1830–1885). Jackson is best remembered as the author of *A Century of Dishonor* (1881) and the novel *Ramona* (1884), both powerful indictments of the US government's treatment of Native Americans. Although Jackson's books were published long after Emily acquired "The Juniata Quick Step," Jackson's groundbreaking work does provide some important background.

In *A Century of Dishonor*, Jackson chronicles the US government's attempts to establish treaties with various Native American tribes,

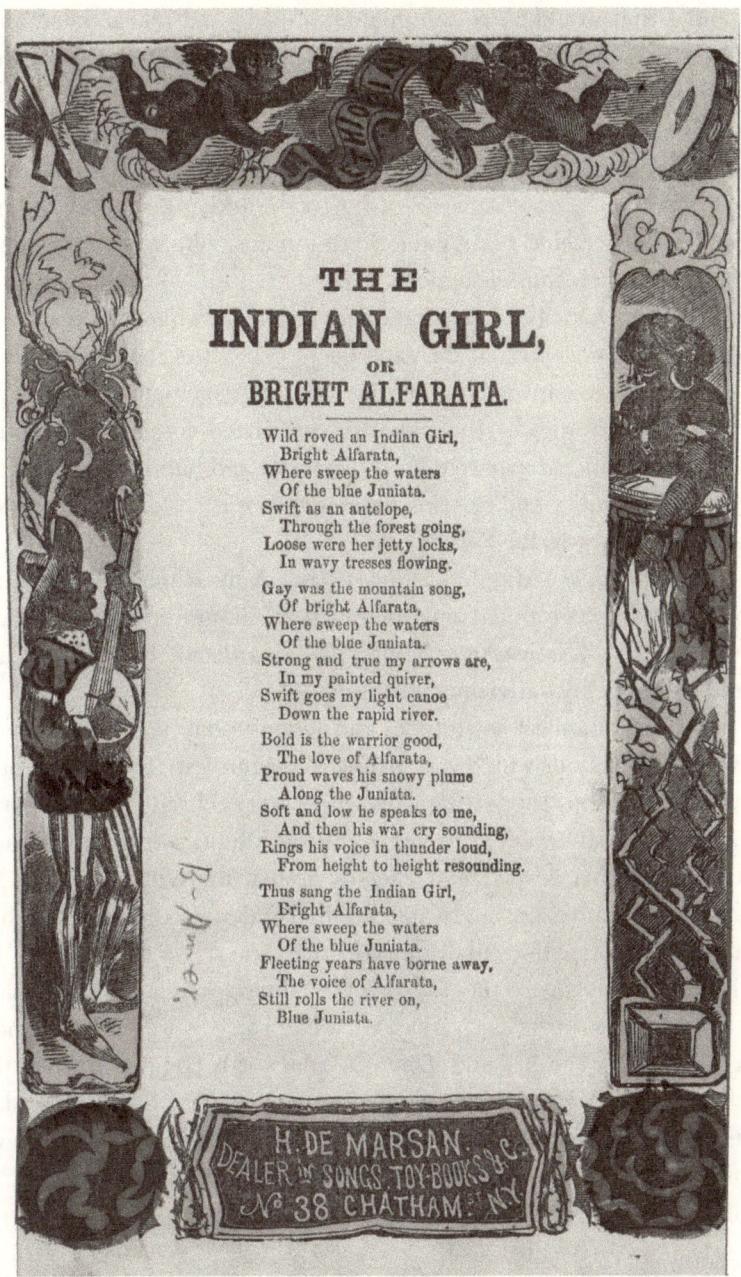

FIGURE 10. "The Indian Girl, or Bright Alfarata." American Broadside Collection, Music and Recorded Sound Division, The New York Public Library for the Performing Arts, Astor, Lenox and Tilden Foundations.

treaties that would be consummated, broken, and renegotiated anew. The government's attempts to limit the geographical freedom formerly enjoyed by Native American peoples precipitated unrest and rebellion, and the government ultimately restricted Native Americans to confined areas designed to serve as self-governing territories. Within these territories it was the government's wish that the Indians should "assume a fixed residence, and occupy themselves in agriculture . . . abandoning the chase as a means of support."[18]

The simultaneity of territorial expansion by whites, the encroaching railroad system, and the subsequent growth of the industrial sector caused constant friction as the local management of these "permanent" territories by the Indians experienced continual disruption. White interlopers trespassed on Indian land and hunting grounds, and by cutting timber and clearing grasses and brush, claimed these paths as rights-of-way to the West.[19]

In her article "Manifest Domesticity," Amy Kaplan situates these homesteaders as rationalizing their right to claim territory by "rendering [the] prior [Native American] inhabitants alien and undomesticated and by implicitly nativizing newcomers."[20]

We understand these attitudes and actions today as the systemic racism of the period, which was justified by Manifest Destiny and other widely held ideas supporting white superiority. Philip J. Deloria writes that "Americans wanted to feel a natural affinity with the continent, and it was Indians who could teach them such aboriginal closeness. Yet, in order to control the landscape they had to destroy the original inhabitants."[21] It was within this framework that Americans could situate, justify, and acknowledge the tragedy of the disappearing Native peoples.

Jackson's writings on Native American subjects forged an immediate bond between her and Thomas Wentworth Higginson when they chanced to meet at a boardinghouse in Newport, Rhode Island, in about 1866. Talk of Emily Dickinson surfaced quickly, and Jackson was off to Amherst soon thereafter to search out Dickinson and her poems.[22]

The Hutchinson Family: "Get Off the Track"

In the decades preceding the Civil War, another issue that gripped the nation in both politics and song was the abolition of slavery, and the

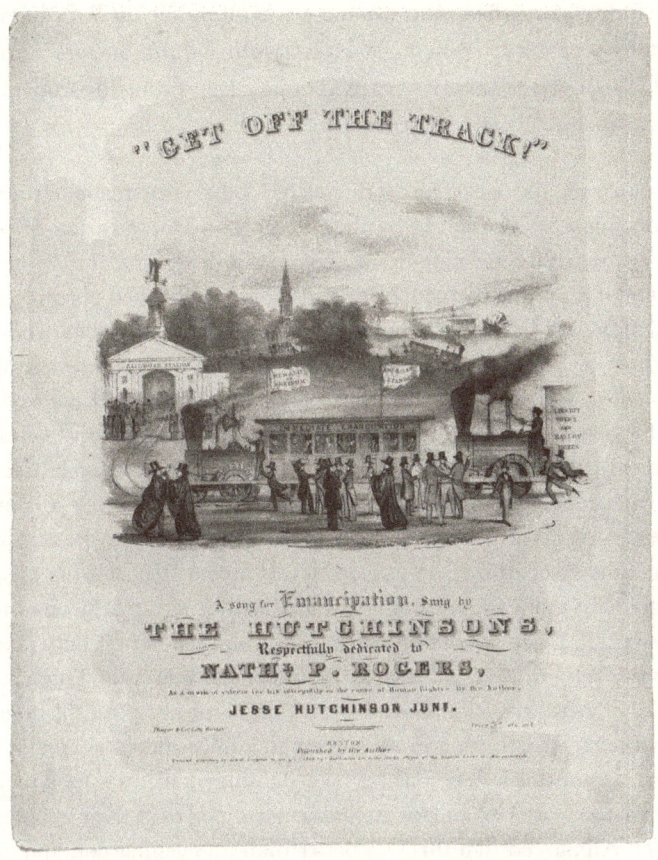

FIGURE 11. Jesse Hutchinson, "Get off the track!" Music and Recorded Sound Division, The New York Public Library for the Performing Arts, Astor, Lenox and Tilden Foundations.

music of the Hutchinson Family Singers rang out loudly in this cause. Traveling throughout the eastern seaboard and eventually to England, the Hutchinsons garnered wide acclaim for their concerts devoted to songs of abolition, temperance, and family living. They performed in Amherst and in Northampton, where they had an association with the nearby utopian community in Florence, which they visited frequently. Formed in 1842, the Northampton Association of Education and Industry, with its promotion of communal living, was modeled on the Transcendentalist experiment at Brook Farm.[23] Thus the Hutchinson Family's local performances were well within the Dickinsons' concert-going sphere. Dickinson may have had an opportunity to see the group while she was attending the Mount Holyoke Female Seminary.[24] When the Hutchinson Family Singers came to South Hadley, news of their visit caused quite a stir among the students, as one of Dickinson's classmates recalled:

> One morning the early birds discovered bills posted about town announcing a vocal concert by the Hutchinson Family to be given that evening in the meeting-house. A number of the students wished to attend. Great was their surprise and indignation when permission was withheld. Miss Lyon told us that present arrangements would not admit of our sparing the time for an evening entertainment, and requested us to bear in mind the principle that one should not ask a favor for herself which could not be granted to all. Poor Jane W— was the chief mourner and considered herself a martyr. The Hutchinsons were friends of her family and on that account had sent her a complimentary ticket which she thought it very impolite not to use. She found many sympathizers. A few said it was inconsistent in Miss Lyon to urge us to cultivate vocal music and then not let us hear any but our own. . . . Early the next morning, the young ladies on duty near the parlor passed the word that Mr. Hutchinson was calling on Miss Lyon. . . . After devotions, Miss Lyon told us of her pleasant interview with Mr. Hutchinson in which he had kindly offered to give us a concert. Upon this a door was opened, the singers filed in, took their places on the platform, and for an hour entertained us in their happiest manner. All agreed that this was better than an evening out, and no face expressed more pleasure than Miss Lyon's.[25]

If Dickinson had seen the Hutchinson Family at Mount Holyoke, she would have been swept up in the urgency of the song "Get Off the Track," an adaptation of the enormously popular minstrel tune "Old Dan Tucker," which is in Dickinson's music book. Giving the popular tune new words, the Hutchinsons fashioned it into a powerful antislavery anthem, extolling the work of the Underground Railroad (see figure 11). The song's rousing chorus celebrating the fast-approaching railroad car of "Immediate Emancipation," pulled by the engine "Liberator," told listeners to "Get out the way! every station, Clear the way for [e]'mancipation." The power of both the music and the message is palpable even today, and the song's historical significance as a vehicle for political and cultural appropriation is considered a milestone in American music history.[26]

At the first performance of "Get Off the Track" on February 22, 1844, "the enthusiasm of the audience was so great that the singers could scarcely go on to the end. This was the song upon which the Hutchinsons' audiences were to split wide open, the abolitionist sympathizers shouting with approval, the opposition hissing and howling their derision and anger."[27]

> VERSE 1 *(to the tune of "Old Dan Tucker")*
> Ho! the Car Emancipation
> Rides majestic thro' our nation
> Bearing on its Train, the story,
> LIBERTY! a Nation's Glory
> Roll it along, Roll it along,
> Roll it along, thro' the Nation
> Freedom's Car, Emancipation[28]

Slavery's polarizing effects on the country are embedded in the reception of "Get Off the Track," as evidenced by this response in the *Philadelphia Courier* after the Hutchinsons had given three concerts there: "It is really time that someone should tell these people, in a spirit of friendly candor, that they are not apostles and martyrs, entrusted with a 'mission' to reform the world, but only a company of common song-singers, whose performances sound very pleasantly to the great mass of the people ignorant of real music."[29] The Hutchinsons remained active into the 1850s. They made their last tour in 1855, setting their sights on Kansas, hoping to show support for the emigrating Free Soilers, who were determined that the new territory should remain free from slavery.[30]

"It is a kind of gone-to-Kansas feeling"

In the spring of 1855 Edward Dickinson reacquired the Homestead from the family of David Mack, and in mid-November after renovations were completed, the Dickinsons returned to their ancestral home. Emily wrote to Elizabeth Holland recounting the family's journey from the West Street house back to the original Homestead on Main Street:

> I cannot tell you how we moved. I had rather not remember. I believe my "effects" were brought in a bandbox, and the "deathless me," on foot, not many moments after. I took at the time a memorandum of my

several senses, and also of my hat and coat, and my best shoes—but it was lost in the *mêlée*, and I am out with lanterns, looking for myself.

Such wits as I reserved, are so badly shattered that repair is useless—and still I can't help laughing at my own catastrophe. I supposed we were going to make a "transit," as heavenly bodies did—but we came budget by budget, as our fellows do, till we fulfilled the pantomime contained in the word "moved." It is a kind of *gone-to-Kansas* feeling, and if I sat in a long wagon, with my family tied behind, I should suppose without doubt I was a party of emigrants!

They say that "home is where the heart is." I think it is where the *house* is, and the adjacent buildings.[31]

Emily's comparison of the settlement of new territories to the act of settling into a new home contextualizes exactly how, during the 1850s, "the language of domesticity suffused the debates about national expansion."[32] Scholar Amy Kaplan continues:

> One of the major contradictions of imperialist expansion is that while the United States strove to nationalize and domesticate foreign territories and peoples, annexation threatened to incorporate non-white foreign subjects into the republic in a way that was perceived to undermine the nation as a domestic space. The discourse of domesticity was deployed to negotiate the borders of an expanding empire and divided nation. Rather than stabilizing the representation of the nation as home, this rhetoric heightened the fraught and contingent nature of the boundary between the domestic and the foreign, a boundary that breaks down around the questions of the racial identity of the nation as a home.[33]

The song "Oh Give Me a Home If in Foreign Land" in Dickinson's music book was part of the repertoire of the Harmoneon Family, a blackface minstrel troupe.[34] The song's lyrics, with their various associations of domesticity and freedom anticipated by territorial expansion, can be construed as emblematic in articulating the fear of destabilization inherent in domesticating the "other." This fear is expressed in the song's lyrics, where "the ones I meet are those of a few, / Who greet the stranger with feelings true." The right to expansion is claimed by those "whose hearts and hands are open and free, / As waves that play on the bounding sea." These "freedoms" were manifestly articulated as the "bounding sea" of annexation, conquering Mexican and Native American territories, so vividly described in Helen Hunt Jackson's novel *Ramona*.[35] Those encroachments destabilized the country by privileging the nation's white racial identity over that of the "foreign." Dickinson appropriated a similar language directly from the song in her music book when she wrote to Samuel Bowles, who was in Europe recuperating from a bout of ill health: "We hope you are more well, than when you lived in America—and that those Foreign people are kind, and true, to you."[36]

As these parties of emigrants moved west, music went with them. "The Rose of Allandale," from Dickinson's music book, which was as popular in Scotland as it was in the United States, accompanied emigrants on their sea voyages across the Atlantic or from the East Coast to California by way of Cape Horn.[37] "From songs sung during the actual [overland westward] journey to music played at events and for entertainment, emigrants imported familiar eastern music to the West and used it to comfort, inspire, and reassure themselves and each other during the trip and in their new homes."[38]

"The Girl I Left Behind Me" from Dickinson's music book is a song with a long and complex history. It was claimed as an eighteenth-century British military march, "Brighton Camp." During the 1849 California gold rush, "The Girl I Left Behind Me" was a staple in the dance halls of western towns. It was later appropriated into the cowboy repertoire as "The Gal I Left Behind Me," or "That Pretty Little Gal," with its "expressed fear of Indian encounters along the westward trail."[39]

This history of mixed usage animates the converging political, social, ethnic, and psychological discourse that was cresting in the late 1850s. As much about nostalgia and loss as it is about heroism and gain, "The Girl I Left Behind Me" would resurface in military dress sometime after April 12, 1861, when shots rang out at Fort Sumter in Charleston, South Carolina, engulfing the nation in civil war. During the war the song would become the musical property of both Union and Confederate armies.[40]

The Civil War: "[I] sang off charnel steps"

By 1858 Dickinson had already commenced writing poetry, and once the war came, she responded to it, her poems sometimes reflecting "the martial backdrop against which they were written."[41]

> From marshallings as simple
> The flags of nations swang.[42]

Dickinson's music book contains similar "marshallings" in the form of music that would be adapted and appropriated to the war effort. When the first troops were mustered out of Amherst, Edward Dickinson helped to preside over their departure, a ceremony that sent them off to war to the heroic strains of "The Girl I Left Behind Me" and "Yankee Doodle."[43] During the war years, these songs and other tunes Dickinson collected, such as "Roderick Dhu's March" ("Hail to the Chief"), were adapted for various uses, becoming staples among Civil War regimental bands.[44] "The Girl I Left Behind Me" was used to signal the departure of a regiment from one camp or town to the next. Of the other tunes in Dickinson's music book, "Drunken Sailor" was often played by fifers during the war as a call to camp duties, and "Believe Me If All Those Endearing Young Charms" was used as a bugler's tattoo ("lights out").[45] A report in the *Philadelphia Press* noted that "'Yankee Doodle' was just as powerful in 1861 as it was when Cornwallis marched forth from Yorktown to its inspiring music."[46] Considered a rallying anthem, "Yankee Doodle" was often heard in the moments when rebel strongholds succumbed to Union forces.[47] The tune was said to be a favorite of General Ulysses S. Grant, commander of the Union Army.

"After a review of the Army of the Potomac during the siege of Petersburg . . . General Grant and President Lincoln were discussing the various elements of the army when, Lincoln [hearing a nearby regimental band] exclaimed to Grant, 'That's a good band.' Grant replied, 'It's the best band in the army, they tell me. But you couldn't prove it by me. I know only two tunes. One is 'Yankee Doodle' and the other isn't."[48]

The regimental band that Lincoln heard was under the direction of George Edward Ives (1845–1894), the father of the American composer Charles E. Ives (1874–1954). The Union Army's youngest bandmaster at age seventeen, George Ives was attached to the Connecticut "Heavies" (Heavy Artillery), which later joined forces with the Army of the Potomac under General George McClellan. This band story circulated around the Ives family for generations. We will circle back to Charles Ives and his father in the Postlude.

A tune in the repertoire of the Ives regimental band, and indeed in every Civil War band book, was "Home, Sweet Home."[49] The sentimentality of the song was so powerful that there was an official attempt to remove it from regimental performances lest it undermine the morale of the soldiers. But the song continued to be heard in both Northern and

Southern encampments, and was thus considered "common property" of both sides in the conflict. Sometimes at the end of a long day of fighting, troops from opposing sides would set up nearby encampments, and the bands would engage each other in a friendly competition. One notable occasion happened in Fredericksburg, a battle in which the "Amherst Boys" of the Twenty-first Regiment of Massachusetts Volunteers participated.[50] The Northern band would play "The Battle Cry of Freedom," while the Southern musicians would counter with "The Bonnie Blue Flag" or "Dixie." Sooner or later the sentimental strains of "Home, Sweet Home" would fill the air as both bands joined in. While the song brought forth "loud cheers for home from both sides," most soldiers quietly wept.[51]

Emily Dickinson's brother Austin was not among those soldiers who dreamt of "Home, Sweet Home" because he did not go to war. Instead, he and many others of his economic and social class paid the enormous sum of $500 to send a substitute.[52] Nevertheless, the tragedy of the Civil War did not spare the Dickinsons. Austin's friend Frazar Stearns was killed in the Union victory at New Bern, North Carolina, on March 14, 1862. Stearns, the first Amherst casualty of the war, was the son of Amherst College president the Reverend William Augustus Stearns.[53] Dickinson scholar Martha Ackmann notes that "the twenty-one-year-old was considered the crown prince of Amherst, beloved, amiable, and as passionate about music as he was science."[54]

On March 24, 1862, Emily wrote to her Norcross cousins:

Dear Children,

You have done more for me—'tis least that I can do, to tell you of brave Frazer—'killed at Newbern,' darlings. His big heart shot away by a 'minie ball.' I had read of those— . . .

He went to sleep from the village church. Crowds came to tell him goodnight, choirs sang to him, pastors told how brave he was—early-soldier heart. And the family bowed their heads, as the reeds the wind shakes.

So our part in Frazer is done, but you must come next summer, and we will mind ourselves of this young crusader—too brave that he could fear to die. We will play his tunes—maybe he can hear them; we will try to comfort his broken-hearted Ella, who, as the clergyman said, "gave him peculiar confidence." . . . Austin is stunned completely. Let us love better, children, it's most that's left to do.[55]

'Tis not that Dying hurts us so —
'Tis Living — hurts us more —
But Dying — is a different way —
A Kind behind the Door —

The Southern Custom — of the Bird —
That ere the Frosts are due —
Accepts a better Latitude —
We — are the Birds — that stay.

The Shiverers round Farmers' doors —
For whose reluctant Crumb —
We stipulate — till pitying Snows
Persuade our Feathers Home.[56]

CHAPTER 9

Fiddle Tunes, Minstrel Music, and Musical Borrowing

"No Black bird bates His Banjo —"

EMILY DICKINSON'S MUSIC BOOK CONTAINS a host of vernacular music which includes at least twenty titles associated with the Irish, Scottish, English, and American traditional fiddler's repertoire, and three popular songs from the minstrel stage.[1] The inclusion of these musics serves as a testament to Dickinson's wide-ranging taste and her interest in and intersection with the musical and cultural life of her town. The well-known fiddle tunes in her music book, "Durangs Hornpipe," "Fisher's Hornpipe," "Drops of Brandy," and others, are easy pieces that would have been part of her early music lessons.

Dickinson was among the growing ranks of American consumers who indulged in an expanding vernacular music market, one enlivened by a cultural shift brought on by industrialization and immigration. Musicologist Charles Hamm notes:

> As early as the first decades of the nineteenth century, it was becoming clear that Americans liked novelty—songs in musical styles drawing on the various schools of national song brought to America by new immigrants. The aristocratic cultures of eighteenth-century Europe that had spawned and nourished the Classical style were of little or

no concern to vast numbers of Americans who preferred the fresh and "wild" sounds of Irish and Scottish song, the cloying seductions of the new school of Italian opera, the exciting and amusing minstrel songs combining the neo-African sound of the banjo with Irish-Scottish melodies.[2]

The Minstrel Music

Some of this vernacular and minstrel music to which Emily Dickinson was attracted and that she collected into her bound music book would eventually find expression in her poetry, most notably in the line "No Black bird bates His Banjo — ."[3] Dickinson scholar Cristanne Miller interprets this as an anthropomorphized reference to the illustrated sheet music covers of the minstrel music in Dickinson's book, "Who's That Knocking at the Door," "The Jolly Raftsman," and "Old Dan Tucker."[4]

In light of our contemporary understanding of racism, examining the blackface minstrel repertoire in Dickinson's music book and viewing the graphically illustrated covers of the songs she collected, with their offensive depictions of Black people as created by white performers in blackface, is a painful reminder of this music's past popularity. Musicologist Dale Cockrell writes:

> The word "minstrel" would not be applied to those who performed in comic blackface until 1843. But "blackface minstrelsy" was already in place by 1834. There is no question that the skeleton around which this popular entertainment was built was the denigration of black people. There is also no doubt that its muscle consisted of stereotypes of black Americans, many of which tragically prevail to the present. And—too often forgotten—there is no question that its enormous, century-long appeal was because of the music and dance that gave it flesh.[5]

The form's most widely recognized progenitor in the United States was Thomas Dartmouth "Daddy" Rice. As early as 1830 he performed his own "Ethiopian creations," songs such as "Old Zip Coon," the words of which Rice married to the popular Scotch-Irish fiddle tune "Turkey in the Straw" (also called "Natchez Under the Hill"). These were the tunes and dances that set this music on its course.[6]

By 1842 there were other blackface performers filling the theaters. At the Bowery and Chatham theaters in New York City, two of these were R. W. (Dick) Pelham and William (Billy) Whitlock, author of "Who's That Knocking at the Door," a song that is in Dickinson's music book. Pelham and Whitlock, along with dancer Frank Brower, formed the Virginia Minstrels, led by Daniel Decatur Emmett (1815–1904), who claimed authorship of the songs "Dixie" and "Old Dan Tucker." Emily Dickinson owned the sheet music to "Old Dan Tucker" and would make oblique references to this minstrel music in her correspondence and her poetry.

Emmett's "Old Dan Tucker" originated from music that he had heard in the 1830s while working on the Ohio River, where Irish and Black laborers intersected through a shared riverine culture.[7] Another tune from Dickinson's music book associated with Emmett, "The Jolly Raftsman," was cited by Mark Twain in *The Adventures of Huckleberry Finn*, as a group of boatmen share music-making and a jug of whiskey.

It did not take long for "Old Dan Tucker," "Clare de Kitchen," "Jim Along Josey," and other songs of this type to infiltrate the popular urban venues where this music was featured nightly in bars and brothels or the more reputable "concert saloons" throughout the border areas of large northeastern cities.[8] In his 1841 book *Extraordinary Popular Delusions and the Madness of Crowds*, Charles Mackay wrote of the obsession with "Jim Crow": "The uncouth dance, its accompaniment, might be seen in its full perfection on market-nights in any great thoroughfare; and the words of the song might be heard, piercing above all the din and buzz of the ever-moving multitude."[9] This urban soundscape with its accompanying music and dance animating locales such as the Five Points district in New York City was experienced by all classes and any number of noted tourists, including Charles Dickens and Davy Crockett.[10]

Just as quickly, the major music publishers engaged in a type of cross-pollination by issuing and marketing sheet music arrangements of these songs, harnessing the raw energy of the concert saloons and melding it into the gentility of the parlor, embellished with simple piano accompaniments and elaborate caption titles or illustrated title covers.[11] The propulsive rhythms of the instrumental accompaniment and the persistent hammering recitative-like melody of the verse made a song like "Old Dan Tucker" one of the most representative, successful, malleable, and addictive tunes of the genre.[12]

Musicologist Christopher Smith writes: "Participation was both a fundamental part of Afro-Caribbean and African American performance, powerfully attractive as a target not only of observation but also imitation, and, as a result of this attraction, powerfully subversive. The music and dancing made audiences want to participate. This desire for participatory pleasure is at the root of [this] popular music's appeal."[13]

The *Springfield Daily Republican* regularly advertised local concerts by groups such as the Virginia Serenaders, the Ethiopian Vocalists, the (Jerome B.) Fellow's Ethiopian Opera Troupe, and the New Orleans Serenaders Opera Company. These ensembles presented burlesques of *La Sonnambula, Bohemian Girl,* and *Leonora,* examples of the "bizarre, hybrid product resulting from whites masquerading as blacks, parodying Italian [and other] opera."[14] While these titles offered a veil of respectability, this racialized product was clearly on the minstrel spectrum. One wonders what Edward Dickinson's opinions were on all this, as he perused the pages of the *Springfield Republican* with its concert notices for the Fellow's Ethiopian Troupe performing for two nights at Hampden Hall, featuring "S. A. Wells the original tambourineist and Primo Basso of Dumbolton's Ethiopian Serenaders; G. Warren White, formerly of the same troupe; and E. Horn, alias Brudder Bones, the great original Ethiopian performer, making in all, the most talented corps that has ever visited this place."[15]

During a trip to Boston in September 1851 with her sister, Lavinia reported in her diary that she had "heard Ordways [Aeolians] in [the] evening [with Uncle] Joel & Austin."[16] This framing of the blackface minstrel idiom as an organized, professional product presented by these groups, promoted by newspapers, and marketed and disseminated by music publishers enabled this theatrical form and its attendant subversive music and lyrics to become a popular mainstream product for middle-class consumption.[17] This same vein of subversive participation attracted Emily Dickinson, giving her permission for activating a means of boundary crossing within the parlor setting. She had long been familiar with songs such as "Old Dan Tucker," which had only recently hit the Boston music stores when Emily visited her aunt Lavinia in 1844. Scholar Sandra Runzo's take on the character of "Old Dan Tucker" as being rebellious and "energizingly subversive" fits well with Dickinson, as Runzo compares the rebelliousness of Tucker with Dickinson's own pleasure at being the trickster, "a spirit that Dickinson embraced and cultivated."[18]

"I misbehaved tonight," Dickinson wrote in an August 1860 letter of apology to Samuel Bowles, who had spent a merry evening with the Dickinsons while he was in Amherst covering commencement week.[19] While there have been many interpretations of this letter, it's clear that Dickinson's reference to "Mrs. Jim Crow" and her "misbehaving" characterization of "Bob o' Lincoln" tells us that Dickinson's musical and cultural "staging [of] racial categories, boundaries, and types" was furtive, familiar, and purposeful, and that she had been embracing opportunities for such subversions for quite some time.[20]

Ten years earlier, in February 1850, Dickinson sent a letter to preceptor (Amherst College senior teaching assistant) George H. Gould. The letter was published anonymously as a valentine in *The Indicator*, an organ of Amherst College. In this letter, nineteen-year-old Emily Dickinson lifts the phrase "Magnum bonum" from verse three of "Old Dan Tucker." With sheet music in hand, Dickinson used the persistent rhythmic energy of the tune while making up new words (some employing a pseudo-Latin) to complete the verse: "Magnum bonum, 'harum scarum,' zounds et zounds, et war alarum, man reformam, life perfectum, mundum changum, all things flarum?"[21] Just the previous month Dickinson had auditioned this idea in a letter to her uncle Joel Norcross (1821–1900) when she wrote, " — *magnum bonum* promise maker — harum scarum promise breaker — ."[22]

Later, poet Dickinson would write:

> I cannot dance opon my Toes —
> No Man instructed me —
> But oftentimes, among my mind,
> A Glee possesseth me.[23]

Sandra Runzo notes that "the 'Glee' that 'possesseth' the speaker denotes high spirits as well as song" and, in Dickinson's poem, a "minstrel-style comic ballet."[24] Derived from the eighteenth-century English choral tradition and associated with "entertainment [and] fun," glees were popular with English singing societies and clubs.[25] Dickinson would have been familiar with glees from books such as *The Vocalist: Consisting of Short and Easy Glees*, which was used at Mount Holyoke. Usually arranged for three or four voices, glees were popular with nineteenth-century singing groups like the Hutchinson Family Singers. The form crossed over onto the minstrel stage and was exploited by groups such as the Virginia Minstrels and the Harmoneon Family, whose music Dickinson collected. These groups often referred to their songs as glees, and this music was compiled into published vocal arrangements such as Elias Howe's *Ethiopian Glee Book*.[26]

Emily Dickinson had many opportunities to cross over the social, cultural, and musical boundaries that defined her time. This activity is verified through the music in her music volume with its vernacular flavors—not just the popular minstrel music but the jigs, reels, hornpipes, and other traditional music. These Scotch-Irish and American fiddle tunes were part of a body of music that she would have easily absorbed both through her lessons and across the threshold of the kitchen as her daily chores, particularly her bread-making duties, intersected with the lives, the sounds, and the music of the Dickinson servants.

"She makes all the bread for her father only likes hers"

When Edward Dickinson and Emily Norcross married, their "mutual interests and values, [and] a desire for the comforts of a shared life" informed the Dickinson household.[27] Those shared values helped to sustain the "frugal housewife," Mrs. Dickinson, who ascribed to the then popular philosophy that servants were not a necessity, and so she assumed all of the housework herself.[28] As they came of age, much of this philosophy of frugal "self-sufficiency" fell to Mrs. Dickinson's two daughters in "support [of their] mother's gentle reign."[29] Housework to Mrs. Dickinson also meant exercise as a means of improving the health of her older daughter. When Emily was kept out of school in September 1845 because of illness, that was when her bread making commenced. "You asked me if I was attending school now. I am not," Emily wrote to Abiah Root: "Mother thinks me not able to confine myself to school this term. She had rather I would exercise, and I can assure you I get plenty of that article by staying at home. I am going to learn to make bread tomorrow. So you may imagine me with my sleeves rolled up, mixing flour, milk, saleratus [baking soda], etc., with a deal of grace. I advise you if you don't know how to make the staff of life to learn with dispatch."[30]

The results of her bread making were evidently successful, because Edward Dickinson would designate Emily the official baker of bread in the Dickinson home. Years later Thomas Wentworth Higginson reported to his wife that Dickinson's father would consume only the bread made by his daughter.[31] Emily's breads and desserts were legendary. Her black cake was a regular feature at the Dickinsons' annual commencement reception at the Homestead, and in October 1856 she won second prize for her rye and Indian bread at the Amherst annual autumn Cattle Show.

By 1850 Edward Dickinson had begun hiring permanent domestic help. From this point forward, Emily's kitchen duties provided her with a setting in which she consistently intersected with this expanding household staff of maids, stablemen, and groundskeepers. In her book *Maid as Muse: How Servants Changed Emily Dickinson's Life and Language*, Aífe Murray notes that when the Homestead was renovated in 1855, access to the kitchen was made easiest through the back door rather than through the parlor, and as a result, "Dickinson headquartered in the kitchen was more reachable by peddlers and stablemen than by her Yankee peers."[32]

Between the Homestead and The Evergreens next door, where Austin and his family lived, the Dickinsons employed over time as many as eighty servants. As a steadier presence of domestic help relieved Emily and her sister of a good deal of the housework, Emily had more time, sometimes concurrently with her kitchen duties, to engage in poetic activity.[33] While working in the kitchen, she frequently made use of scraps of paper, old grocery lists, or the backs of envelopes, jotting down phrases or even whole poems.[34] From this vantage point, Dickinson was always observant, particularly when a new hired hand crossed the grounds of the Dickinson Homestead.

> New feet within my garden go —
> New fingers stir the sod —
> A Troubadour opon the Elm
> Betrays the solitude.[35]

As she went about her daily work in the kitchen, Emily grew closer to many of the servants. Laundress Rosina Mack and maid of all work Margaret O'Brien were two of the earliest arrivals of Irish domestics at the Homestead. The daily activities of Jeremiah (Jerry) Holden and

Richard (Dick) Matthews, the Dickinsons' stablemen, groundskeeper "old Amos" Newport, and laborer Tom Kelley all find animation and affection in Dickinson's correspondence. None of these servants was closer to Emily than Margaret Maher, who began working at the Homestead in 1869. "Maggie is with us still," Dickinson wrote to her cousins in 1884, "warm and wild and mighty."[36] After Emily's death two years later, Maher stayed on until Lavinia passed away in 1899. Maher lived next to the Amherst train depot with her brother-in-law and Dickinson laborer Tom Kelley. Over time, Tom was able to purchase additional nearby buildings from Edward Dickinson, establishing his family in a comfortable residential compound known as "Kelley Square."[37]

Emily's poem about the railroad, "I Like to see it lap the miles," includes a reference to the settlements along the railroad tracks, home to Black and Irish laborers, some of whom worked for the Dickinsons.[38] It was in these outlying settlements along the railroad tracks and the Connecticut River that members of both groups enjoyed a proximity conducive to habitual intersections and cultural exchanges that included the sharing of traditional dance and fiddle repertoire. Vernacular artworks from the period document the fact that these groups freely exchanged, integrated, and melded Afro-Caribbean and Irish expressive forms of dance and music.[39] The seasonal migrations of these laboring groups brought their music into the towns and villages, often providing the middle class with musical accompaniments to their social dancing.[40]

It was not unusual for Dickinson to visit the homes of these servants, witness their music-making, and borrow from it for her own inspiration and enjoyment. In an 1854 letter, Emily, age twenty-three, wrote to her brother about her errands and visits: "Then I worked until dusk, then went to Mr. Sweetser's to call on Abiah Root, then walked around to Jerry's [African American stableman Jeremiah Holden] and made a call on him—then hurried home to supper." Dickinson was known to reach out to all classes,[41] and the vernacular tunes that informed her music book were the same ones that she would have heard from the servants and others who provided opportunities for listening or music-making both inside and outside the parlor setting, and in which Dickinson herself participated. On June 22, 1851, Emily wrote to Austin: "Our Reading Club still is, and becomes now very pleasant—[Milan] *Stebbins* comes in to read now, and [John] *Spencer*—t'would not be so if *you* were here—the *last* time *Charles* [Fowler] came in when we had finished reading, and we broke up with a *dance*—make your own reflections at the story I just told you—the Tutors come after us, and walk home with us—we *enjoy that*!"⁴²

Millicent Todd Bingham reminds us that these clubs were gatherings of women joined by "tutors," men who were Amherst College seniors and, in this case, former classmates of Austin's (class of 1850). On this particular night there was indeed an element of fun. One of the tutors was Austin's college friend Charles Fowler, the brother of Emily Dickinson's close friend Emily Fowler (Ford).⁴³ There is no evidence that Charles Fowler played an instrument, but in making one's own reflections on the story Dickinson is recounting, we can sense in her words that there was a great deal of furtive fun going on—dancing, of course, and if there was a piano nearby, Dickinson would have been in the middle of it.

According to Susan Dickinson: "Emily Fowler had what she called P.O.M. [Poetry of Motion] meetings at her house, impromptu dances,—if our floundering attempts to get through a Virginia Reel, or Lancers could be called that,—to the sharp voice of an attenuated piano! It was great fun and seemed real,—Beside it was contraband."⁴⁴

At least one of the Dickinson servants, Charles Thompson, played a musical instrument. Originally from Maine, Charles was taken in by the Reverend William A. Stearns and his family in 1838, when he was fifteen. At the time, the Stearnses lived in Cambridge, where the Reverend Stearns was pastor of the Prospect Street Presbyterian Church. Thompson left the Stearnses in 1847, spending six years at sea on whaling ships. He followed them to Amherst around 1855, when the Reverend Stearns was appointed president of Amherst College (1854–1876).⁴⁵ Thompson worked as a janitor for the college and was also a laborer for the Dickinsons. He was beloved by the Amherst College students and was known affectionately as the "Professor of Dust and Ash."⁴⁶

Charles Thompson was a fiddler, and he taught some of the local children to play. He was fondly remembered in a pamphlet published in 1902 by the Stearnses' daughter Abigail Eloise Stearns Lee: "But it was Charley's musical ability that made us love him, as a companion in the evening, for Charley owned a fiddle, and when he played 'Money Musk' or some lively jig, the children could not help dancing. 'Just keep your fingers going and bumby [by and by] you'll get it,' was his advice to my brother, who tried to play."[47] Thompson likely learned his tunes from his father, who, according to Thompson, "was a great fiddler."[48] "Money Musk," which is not in Dickinson's music book, was one of the most popular tunes in antebellum New England dance circles, and fiddler's tunebooks.[49] It remains a staple in today's traditional fiddle repertoire.

The ever-observant Emily Dickinson may have been remembering Charles Thompson and his fiddle in her 1859 poem "New feet within my garden go — " as her "Troubadour opon the Elm," when Charles would have been working on the property.[50] Dickinson's accounts of visiting and spending time with the servants, dancing with the members of the reading club, Emily Fowler's clandestine meetings, or Charles Thompson and his fiddle attest to the fact that these dance tunes were readily transmitted, borrowed, adapted, and performed from the oral tradition as well as from published parlor piano editions such as the "tunes" that Dickinson owned and played. This music was also compiled and printed in instrumental tunebooks and method books enjoying wide circulation among the performing musicians reading or improvising on the banjo, fiddle, flute, and other instruments.

The major publishers of these tunebooks were Edward Riley (1769–1829) in New York, George E. Blake (1775–1871) in Philadelphia, and Elias Howe (1820–1895) in Boston. Howe and others also published cotillion pamphlets for social dancing.[51] In addition to the fiddle tunes, popular melodies such as the "Battle of Prague," "Swiss Waltz," "Russian March," "Louisville March," "Hail to the Chief," "Grand March in *Norma*," "Panharmonic March," "Auld Lang Syne," and "Home, Sweet Home," all from Dickinson's music book, were included in these instrumental fiddler's tunebooks.[52] Many of these publications, particularly those of Elias Howe, were being brought out concurrently with the piano editions of the mainstream music publishers—again a type of cross-pollination from the street, to the dance hall, and into the parlor—and into Dickinson's music book. Musicologist Paul Wells notes that these popular traditional fiddle tunes were in such wide circulation that tracing the source of the published piano editions in Dickinson's bound music book to any particular fiddler's tunebook is likely not possible.[53] (For more information on these tunes and tunebooks, see the online Appendix B.)

While the history, transmission, and publication of these traditional tunes were fluid, according to musicologist Chris Goertzen, "this nineteenth-century stream of publications, with stable tune titles and stable tunes, was known to some degree all over the United States, but had its greatest influence in New England and across the northern part of the country."[54] Many of the vernacular fiddle tunes in Dickinson's music book were of this type: standardized and popular. They include the many Irish and Scottish dance tunes, ballads, and songs that occupy a distinct presence in Dickinson's volume of sheet music. While Irish ballads were enormously popular in bound music volumes, Dickinson also favored traditional fiddle tunes, jigs, reels, and hornpipes, which were less common in genteel music volumes. These tunes were fitted out by the music publishers with accessible piano accompaniments underneath the familiar melodies, facilitating lively performances and dancing in the family parlor. Among the popular and traditional tunes throughout Dickinson's bound music book associated with the Irish and Scottish tunebook repertoire, "Fisher's Hornpipe," "College Hornpipe," "Bonaparte's March Crossing the Rhine" "Speed the Plough" "Drunken Sailor," and "Durang's Hornpipe" are all tunes that would have been familiar to the Dickinson servants. This was also key repertoire for the general performing and contra dancing population of amateur and professional musicians. This would also become key repertoire for Emily Dickinson, who, as early as 1850, began using this vernacular music from her music book in remarkable and imaginative ways.

"I can improvise better at night"

In Dickinson's correspondence and in some of her first poems from the early 1850s, we see her beginning to fashion a form of poetic expression from the music that was in her ears, the concerts she attended, and the music she enjoyed and played. We also see her seeking a similar means of creative absorption and expression at the piano through improvisation, an activity that was witnessed and reported by her family, friends, and neighbors. These improvisations first surface in 1854.

That spring, most of the Dickinson family left for a trip to Washington, DC, leaving Emily and Susan Gilbert alone with Emily's cousin John Graves, who at the time was attending Amherst College (class of 1855).

Under Edward's directive, Graves was in residence at the Dickinson home while the family was away. This was obviously a memorable visit, because years later Emily reminisced about "those triumphant days" in a letter to Graves, recalling when she played those "old, odd tunes" on the piano "after honest hours," which would "wake dear Sue, and madden me, with their grief and fun."[55] John Graves described these improvisations as "heavenly music." Graves's daughter recounted that during that 1854 visit, when her "father would be awakened from his sleep by this 'heavenly music[,]' Emily would explain in the morning, 'I can improvise better at night.'" During other visits Emily would make music for him as well.[56]

MacGregor Jenkins, who was a Dickinson neighbor, also witnessed these improvisations, which often took place during gatherings at The Evergreens next door:

> [Emily] went often across the lawn to her brother's house. It was through him, and his handsome wife, the "Sue" of her letters and messages, that she kept in touch with the life of her circle, and to a considerable extent with the village and the world. It was here that she would fly to the piano, if the mood required, and thunder out a composition of her own which she laughingly but appropriately called "The Devil," and when her father came, lantern in hand, to see that she reached home in safety, she would elude him and dart through the darkness to reach home before him. This was pure mischief and there was much of it in her.[57]

According to Dickinson scholar Martha Nell Smith, Dickinson's "Devil" improvisation made a lasting impression on Susan Dickinson.[58] Kate Scott Anthon, Susan's classmate from the Utica Female Academy, also recalled lively evenings at The Evergreens. In a letter to Susan Dickinson, Anthon wrote: "I am continually driven back into the *Past*—*our* own sacred Past—The golden days you & I have spent together—Oh! dear Sue how vividly I recal[l] them! Those happy visits at your house! Those celestial evenings in the Library—The blazing *wood* fire—*Emily*—*Austin*,—The music—The rampant fun—the inextinguishable laughter—the uproarious spirits of our chosen—our most congenial circle."[59] Anthon remembered "the old blissful evenings at Austin's! Rare hours, full of merriment, brilliant wit, and inexhaustible laughter, Emily with her dog, & Lantern! often at the piano playing weird & beautiful melodies, all from her own inspiration, oh! She was a choice spirit!"[60]

Dickinson's cousin Clara Newman Turner, who also witnessed these improvisations, which included "The Devil," recalled that Dickinson "had learned it on an old-fashioned piano, 2 octaves shorter than the modern 'Chickering' wh[ich] then stood in her home parlor,—& always before seating herself to play she covered these superfluous octaves that the key-board might accord with her education."[61]

Clara Newman (1844–1920) and her sister Anna (1846–1887) had relocated from Brooklyn to Amherst in 1853 as wards of Edward Dickinson after the death the previous year of their father, music publisher Mark Haskell Newman, and his wife, Mary, Edward Dickinson's sister.[62] In Amherst the Newman sisters lived quite near the Dickinsons until after 1856, when they moved into The Evergreens next door to the Homestead.[63] Clara spent much time at her uncle Edward's house. She and Emily would become close, which suggests that Clara, who played the piano herself, had ample opportunity to witness her cousin's piano improvisations and her habit of covering the octaves, both upper and lower, which were outside the range of Dickinson's first piano. Given the fact that the Dickinsons acquired a larger piano in late 1851 or early 1852, it's clear that Dickinson's improvisational seeds were sown much earlier than the time when cousin John Graves heard her improvise in 1854 or the Newmans' arrival in Amherst in 1853. Perhaps Dickinson's 1850 "Magnum bonum" reveries signaled an initial stimulus for improvisation, borrowing from the rhythms of "Old Dan Tucker" and the melodies of the vernacular tunes in her music book.

There is no concrete evidence as to the sound and texture of Dickinson's improvisations beyond the fact that they were described as "heavenly," or "weird and beautiful," or as Newman pronounced them to be, "weird and quaint enough to warrant the title ['The Devil']."[64] Dickinson's niece tells us that Emily "improvised brilliantly upon the piano all sorts of dramatic performances of her own, one she called the Devil being particularly applauded."[65] The fact that the execution of these improvisations employed a narrow melodic range, and that Dickinson herself often referred to the music she played as "tunes," suggests that her improvisations were sourced from the vernacular music she collected—the minstrel music; the traditional Irish and Scottish jigs, reels, and hornpipes; and others she heard and enjoyed firsthand.[66] She could easily have drawn on the local sounds of traditional music-making to which she would have been exposed, or just as easily exploited a wide variety of "brilliant" or "dramatic" musical tropes realized from her formal training, as it would not have been unusual for some type of extemporization to be a component of those lessons. She would have had much to draw from in creating her broad musical canvas. Her letters and poems allude to the variety of vernacular forms in her music book, giving evidence to the fact that she was intimately familiar with music that was performed and enjoyed by all classes. Dickinson's 1852 poetic reference to "Bonnie Doon," her surrealistic late-night comment from her correspondence, "and the lounge polka a little," her sentimental reflections on "Auld Lang Syne" and "Long, Long Ago," the jigs, reels, and hornpipes are all possible candidates for exploitation, sourced from the music she collected, performed, and enjoyed.[67]

But by the late 1850s, when these improvisations were seemingly at their most active and certainly most well documented, another type of "metaphorical" music-making was already taking shape. Dickinson's music book had been bound, and while the lives of other women of her age and her class would have been consumed by the looming commitments of marriage and family, Dickinson's music book, as evidenced by its size and scope, was not a musical "keepsake" that was going to be put away. This was a time of immense growth for Dickinson, as the music was receding and the poetry increasing. She had been an actively engaged musician, collecting a great deal of music and describing her musical engagements vividly in her correspondence, often employing musical and poetic metaphors from within and outside her music book. Other impulses were surfacing now, and what was forming in Dickinson's imagination was a type of musical borrowing that would allow her to use those same musical images, tropes, and metaphors as an egress into the world of the poet that she was becoming.

CHAPTER 10

The Poetry Takes Hold

" — and the noise in the Pool, at Noon — excels my Piano"

EMILY DICKINSON'S FIRST POEMS emerged slowly over the course of the 1850s.[1] We can imagine the "sounds" of those early poems as if they were elements of a musical improvisation, the building blocks of melodies and harmonies that emerged as early poetic and musical images, themes, and tropes. Her first extant poem from 1850, arises, bold like an anthem: "Awake ye muses mine, sing me a strain divine." In her second poem dating from 1852, "Sic transit gloria mundi," Dickinson borrows the imagery of "How doth the busy bee" from hymnist Isaac Watts's *Divine and Moral Songs for Children*.[2] According to Victoria Morgan, this is a signifying trope of both "reverie" and industry for Dickinson the developing poet.[3] Her fourth poem, written in 1854, introduces her beloved robin: "I have a Bird in spring / Which for myself doth sing — / . . . Melody new for me," as if Emily were alone at the piano in 1854, the year of her first documented piano improvisations.[4] Then from 1858 through the first years of the Civil War, she produced over eleven hundred poems, many of which are her most well-known. While this period would prove to be her most productive, it appears that the transition from the years of her piano to when the poetry took hold may not have been easy. She would allude to this transitioning time early in her correspondence with Thomas Wentworth Higginson.

Higginson (1823–1911) was an abolitionist, literary figure, and editor of the *Atlantic Monthly*. He would become a mentor to Dickinson, a lifelong friend, and after her death in 1886, the first editor (along with

Mabel Loomis Todd) of Dickinson's published poems, issued in 1890 and 1891. Higginson and Dickinson first corresponded over his "Letter to a Young Contributor," an essay that he had written for the April 1862 *Atlantic Monthly* offering guidance and advice to budding writers. Dickinson took that advice and sent Higginson four poems, among them "Safe in their Alabaster Chambers — ." But Higginson felt that Dickinson's poems "defied too many conventions of nineteenth-century verse" and harbored a concern "that her unconventional and startling poems might alienate a reading audience."[5] Dickinson responded to his first two letters: "You think my gait 'spasmodic'—I am in danger—Sir—You think me 'uncontrolled'—I have no Tribunal."[6] Their correspondence continued, and Higginson asked for more poems. These "gifts" of poems and letter-poems from Dickinson kept coming, yet he encouraged her to delay publishing.[7] Dickinson seemed willing to accept this recommendation. Her reply to one of his critiques is prescient: "If fame belonged to me, I could not escape her—if she did not, the longest day would pass me on the chase—and the approbation of my Dog, would forsake me—then—My Barefoot Rank is better—."[8]

When Higginson inquired about Dickinson's life and her poetic background, she replied obliquely yet alluded to something more powerful that had recently taken place: "You ask of my Companions[.] Hills—Sir—and the Sundown—and a Dog—large as myself, that my Father bought me—They are better than Beings—because they know—but do not tell—and the noise in the Pool, at Noon—excels my Piano."[9]

"Noon" had long fascinated Emily Dickinson. She termed it "Consciousness" because it was at that hour that the cacophony of nature was most active and alive to her.[10] As her poetry commenced, what Dickinson may have been hearing was no longer defined by her "Piano." By 1862 those sounds would claim superiority as poetic metaphors:

> Better — than Music!
> For I — who heard it —
> I was used — to the Birds — before —
> This — was different — 'Twas Translation —
> Of all tunes I knew — and more —
>
> 'Twas'nt contained — like other stanza —
> No one could play it — the second time —
> But the Composer — perfect Mozart —
> Perish with him — that keyless Rhyme![11]

From a musician's viewpoint, Dickinson understood well that any type of musical performance, even birdsong, was an impermanent art. She alludes to this impermanence in her 1862 poem "Better — than Music!": "No one could play it — the second time — ." As in the impermanence of her musical improvisations, Dickinson was realizing a similarly impermanent *poetic* state, wherein the poetic images she was drawing on, and the musical impulses she may have been hearing in the natural world around her, were not repeatable in the performative sense. Dickinson scholar Judith Farr uses Dickinson's poem "By my Window have I for Scenery" to illustrate that "the pine [tree] makes music that Dickinson finds 'divine.' Like Coleridge listening to the music of the wind in his aeolian harp, she considers herself dumb by comparison. Nor can she define its melody since the true music (of nature?) defies definition."[12]

> To hear an Oriole sing
> May be a common thing —
> Or only a divine.[13]

Of this 1862 poem, Farr argues that "unless one hears a birdsong as the otherworldly magic that it is, [Dickinson] says that, the 'tune' has not been translated into art, at least for that listener."[14]

In another poem, the persistent call of a distant unseen bird is identified by Dickinson as "a lonesome Glee — ," perhaps, as Dickinson scholar Jed Deppman notes, "by opposition to the choral connotations of 'Glee,'" a four-part choral form in which Dickinson was immersed at Mount Holyoke.[15] Here Dickinson hears only the merry solo song as the other voices of her "Glee" are missing. While it "Delight[s] without a Cause," the bird's song is as "Arrestless as [the bird is] invisible — ." About these qualities, invisibility, arrestlessness, causelessness, and independence (or lonesomeness), Deppman argues, "Could it be that [for Dickinson] there is no finality or teleology woven into the fabric of nature, [and] could that non-finality be a source of both affect and song?"[16]

Dickinson's relationship to sound was very powerful. As observed by Christina Pugh: "Dickinson does often wish to be captured by a sound whose amplitude would be great enough, or beautiful enough to absorb the self and to obliterate thought. On the other hand, however, Dickinson rejects—and sometimes fears—such captivating sound."[17]

Another Dickinson poem, "I dreaded that first Robin, so / But He is mastered, now" (1862), indicates that mastering this new and different kind of "listening ear," and metaphorical music that was informing her poetry, indeed presented a greater challenge than she was at first prepared to confront; but Dickinson continues in the same poem, "Not all Pianos in the Woods / Had power to mangle me — "[18] By this time, what she was hearing, "that keyless Rhyme!," may have been a musical epiphany toward her "perfect Mozart," a "higher" music, ascended to and sustained through a commanding and sometimes painful poetic transformation.

Later Dickinson would write:

> When they begin, if Robins may,
> I always had a fear
> I did not tell, it was their last Experiment
> Last Year.[19]

Knowing but not telling is a recurring trope for Dickinson as early as 1858, when she wrote to her uncle Joseph Sweetser:

There is a smiling summer here, which causes birds to sing, and sets the bees in motion.

Strange blooms arise on many stalks, and trees receive their tenants. I would you saw what I can see, and imbibed this music. The day went down, long time ago, and still a simple choir bear the canto on.

I dont know who it is, that sings, nor *did* I, would I tell!

God gives us many cups. Perhaps you will come to Amherst, before the wassail's done. Our man has mown today, and as he plied his scythe, I thought of *other* mowings, and garners far from here.

I wonder how long we shall wonder; how early we shall *know*.[20]

Dickinson biographer Richard Sewall suggests that this "letter is emblematic of the mood and style of the late 1850s, alternately transparent and opaque, and evasive where we (and perhaps Uncle Joseph) would most seek enlightenment. It is a sobering introduction to this phase of her life."[21] In her letter Dickinson observes, "The day went down, long time ago." In quoting the traditional American folk song "Long Time Ago," Dickinson may be alluding to both the present day and the past.[22] With her words "I dont know who it is, that sings, nor *did* I, would I tell!," she seems to be keeping quiet about her unique musical "Experiment" with nature in which she was intimately engaged and, in 1858, she seems to have just begun, with a burst of forty-two poems.[23] Whatever her concern was, it certainly consumed her, and may have found a later outlet of expression not only in her 1862 poem "Better — than Music!" but also in the often cited line from the same April 1862 letter to Higginson: "I had a terror—since September [1861]—I could tell to none—and so I sing, as the Boy does by the Burying Ground—because I am afraid—."[24]

Much has been written about her "terror," most often attributed to an acute eye condition requiring her to spend considerable time in Boston under the care of a physician.[25] Premonitions of her eye trouble; the opening years of the Civil War; the cascade of poetry that ensued at this time, with an attendant "fear that the loss of her muse would overwhelm her"; or a possible love interest manifested in her three mysterious and powerful "master letters"—all defining a transitional period for Dickinson: on that, there is wide agreement among Dickinson biographers and scholars.[26] Each one of these factors and more were contributing to a performative shift from the figurative transitioning music of her "Piano" to that of the poet's "fuller tune."[27] Again we turn to Richard Sewall, as he seems to be the first to have made a claim as to her musical ambitions, which, by the late 1850s, were certainly yielding both practically and metaphorically to the poetry that was then taking shape:

> That, at a certain point, she made a professional decision about music is suggested in Clara Bellinger Green's memory of [a] conversation [she had] with Dickinson: "She [mentioned] her early love for the piano and confided that, after hearing Rubinstein—I believe it was Rubinstein—play in Boston, she had become convinced that she could never master the art and had forthwith abandoned it once and for all, giving herself up then wholly to literature.[28]

Dickinson scholar Judy Jo Small notes that "this recollection [of Green's] suggests two rather remarkable things: first, that Dickinson may once have had serious musical ambitions that she relinquished for poetry, and second, that she had an auditory relationship to a town and its people that she had closed out of her sight. What part her persistent eye problems may have played in magnifying the importance of her hearing one can only guess."[29]

With her ample music book serving as evidence of her investment in music, it seems clear that Dickinson did indeed come to some sort of "professional decision." The binding of the music book around 1852, which coincided with the appearance of her earliest poems, may have been the signifier that her intense interest in music had begun seeking another means of self-expression; as Richard Sewall notes: "Her practical interest in music declined, [and] her metaphorical interest increased."[30] Dickinson also understood that it would have been inappropriate for a woman of her time, place, and class to position herself musically beyond the prescribed feminine domestic sphere.[31] Save for her letters to Higginson and her cousins, and the enigmatic letter to her uncle Joseph, as the poetry began to take hold, Dickinson kept silent about any remaining musical ambitions. Perhaps she was searching for a means of finally putting them quietly to rest, and found it, as Sewall's anecdote suggests, after she had witnessed a performance by the great pianist.

"The Show is not the Show"

No pianist of the nineteenth century had a greater musical hold on his audience than Anton Rubinstein (1829–1894).[32] Rubinstein's acclaimed American tour (1872–1873) featured a concert in Springfield, which was prominently advertised in the *Republican* and would not have escaped the notice of one of that paper's most avid readers.[33] The *Republican* advertised a single Springfield appearance by Rubinstein, on October 21, 1872. Later, a "farewell concert" was added for May 8, 1873.

In her poem "The Show is not the Show," written late in 1872, Dickinson associates herself with the menagerie of concertgoers. Just as with Jenny Lind, Dickinson's performative spirit is once again fully engaged, this time in the Rubinstein phenomenon and, perhaps, the concert itself:

> The Show is not the Show
> But they that go —
> Menagerie to me
> My Neighbor be —
> Fair Glee —
> Both went to see —[34]

By 1872, it is generally agreed by Dickinson scholars that she was likely no longer making herself available to public scrutiny; therefore, attending the Rubinstein concert in Springfield would have been exceptional. We do know from reports cited by Dickinson scholar Sandra Runzo that Dickinson's piano playing was heard by her nephew Ned Dickinson (b. 1861) and niece Martha Dickinson (b. 1866), and Dickinson's young neighbor MacGregor Jenkins (b. 1869). These reports imply that Dickinson was still playing into the 1870s, certainly around the time of Rubinstein's visit to Springfield.[35]

As the time for Rubinstein's October concert approached, Dickinson was invited to Springfield for a visit by Mrs. J. G. Holland. Her reply seems firmly negative, but her musical reference has a gravitational pull:

Thanking you tenderly as a child for a sweet favor I can never go. This will not retard my place in Affection will it?
    I shall still be mentioned when the children come?
    Some must seem a Traitor, not because it is, but it's Truth belie it. . . .
    This will make no difference in the daily dearness?
    You will keep the same Face and myself no other Heart, with the slight repairs Thought and Nature make—
    In adequate Music there is a Major and a Minor—
    Should there not also be a Private?
    Good Night—I am going to sleep if the Rat permit me—I hear him singing now to the Tune of a Nut.
    I could wish to know, be it by a Trifle, that you name me still.

                                                    Emily.[36]

Two months after the Rubinstein concert, Dickinson wrote to Thomas Wentworth Higginson:

When I saw you last, it was Mighty Summer—Now the Grass is Glass and the Meadow Stucco, and "Still Waters" in the Pool where the Frog drinks.
    These Behaviors of the Year hurt almost like Music—shifting when it ease us most. Thank you for the "Lesson."
    I will study it though hitherto

                Menagerie to me
                My Neighbor be.[37]

In stating that "these Behaviors of the Year hurt almost like Music," Dickinson ascribes a performative metaphor of shifting musical textures to the change of season then taking hold in Amherst. She appears to be letting out the memory of an emotionally charged musical experience, with which she was already intimately familiar, in the manner of an oblique comment on both an aspect of the Rubinstein concert and her own "professional decision" to no longer pursue music. As an accomplished musician, Dickinson would have certainly experienced for herself how a performer achieves the essential effect of tension and release in musical performance, an accretion of power and dynamics toward a musical and harmonic precipice, which, when executed precisely, permits the "hurt" to give way to "the fascinating chill that Music leaves." As Carolyn Lindley Cooley posits, "It is possible that Dickinson's poem, 'The fascinating chill that music leaves' . . . , had its origin in the Rubinstein music which had 'chilled' her so."[38] The fact that the music "hurt" also provides affirmation that her "Piano" was being supplanted by the shifting metaphorical tropes of musical sound and imagery which were informing her poetry.[39] It is certainly worth considering that the "terror" to which she referred in her 1862 letter to Higginson might have had some connection to music. If there *was* a "Rubinstein crisis," that "day went down, long time ago."[40] Nevertheless, her musical-poetic epiphany is palpable, as we shall see in the next chapter, when Dickinson applied the tension and release of those shifting behaviors so familiar to her in music to the surfaces and the internal structures of her verse. Just as it does in music, this activity would allow her to create "a fuller tune," or perhaps her "perfect Mozart."

The following May (1873), writing to her cousins Frances and Louisa Norcross, Dickinson offers performative imagery, again of Rubinstein and the "fascinating chill," indicating that she may indeed have been a witness to the great pianist the previous October: "Glad you heard Rubinstein. Grieved Loo could not hear him. He makes me think of polar nights Captain Hall could tell! Going from ice to ice! What an exchange of awe!"[41]

The Arctic explorer Captain Charles F. Hall (1821–1871) died in northern Greenland on November 8, 1871, during an unsuccessful expedition to reach the North Pole. The expedition concluded on April 30, 1873, with a dramatic rescue of nineteen crew members who had spent 196 days on an ice floe after the ship USS *Polaris* was crushed by ice. Thomas Johnson notes that reports of the expedition ran in the *Republican* from

May 10 to May 15, 1873. On May 12 the *Republican* reported that Captain Hall might have been the victim of a mutinous crew.[42]

Dickinson's observation contains an element of suggestion that she was thinking not only of what Captain Hall could have told had he survived his polar expedition but also of her own unarticulated musical feelings centering on Rubinstein. She understood the enormous power of Rubinstein to "compel" a mere mechanical instrument into becoming an agent of otherworldly emotion.[43] Similarly, Dickinson's own transformation from musician to poet echoes here. Even though by this time Dickinson had already made the shift, her letter demonstrates her own extraordinary ability to exchange an awe inspired by musical performance for that of a poetic metaphor for nature. By 1880 she seems to be evincing a calm sense of resolution on the whole matter, when she states simply to Mrs. Elizabeth Carmichael, "I am studying music now with the jays, and find them charming artists."[44]

Whenever this musical closure finally occurred, it did not stop her from thinking musically. Dickinson's engagements with music, and her decision to excel in that sphere, had long ago prepared her with the means to develop and gradually let out, through her poetry, the music of her "Piano," and to "Experiment," emulate, and even surpass poetically the "noise in the Pool, at Noon" that so preoccupied her in 1862. "If fame belonged to [her]," Dickinson would already have successfully grappled with, surpassed, and defined her own fame and destiny "on the chase," by using the music she knew, played, and danced to as informants to the language of her poetry.[45]

There were other musics engaging Dickinson the poet at this time, and she would use those as a model on which to claim her poetic status as a writer. What she needed in order to accomplish this would be close at hand in the hymnbooks of her father's library. As her poetic aspirations fully emerged, Dickinson's intimacy since childhood with the New England hymn tradition would assist her in navigating some difficult and turbulent waters that had been churning around her for some time.

CHAPTER 11

Hymns and Ballads: More Musical Borrowings

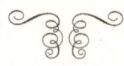

"Let Emily sing for you because she cannot pray."

IN 1850, DURING ONE OF the many religious revivals that swept through Amherst, nineteen-year-old Emily Dickinson wrote to Abiah Root:

> My rebellious thoughts are many, and the friend I love and trust in has much *now* to forgive. I wish I were somebody else—I would pray the prayer of the "Pharisee," but I am a poor little "Publican," "Son of David," look down on me! . . . The shore is safer, Abiah, but I love to buffet the sea—I can count the bitter wrecks here in these pleasant waters, and hear the murmuring winds, but Oh, I *love* the *danger!* You are learning control and firmness—Christ Jesus will love you more—I'm afraid he dont love me *any*![1]

Indeed, Emily Dickinson was an outlier. She withstood eight religious revivals that swept through Amherst between 1840 and 1862.[2] During the revival of 1850, "the ark of safety" took in nearly all of the Dickinson family except for Emily and her brother. The Christian tradition and the natural world both held her, a duality that would eventually allow the poet Emily Dickinson to conform and rebel, believe and disbelieve, sometimes simultaneously. Dickinson once wrote to Judge Otis Lord, "We both believe, and disbelieve a hundred times an Hour, which keeps Believing nimble."[3]

According to the scholar Emma Duncan, Dickinson displays this simultaneity of belief and disbelief in poems such as "I know that He exists" and "Going to Heaven!"[4] As an example of Dickinson's ability to both conform and rebel, Duncan pairs the hymn "Amazing Grace" with the opening lines of Dickinson's poem "If I'm lost — now — / That I was found — ." Here Dickinson's familiarity with the hymn engages her poetic and unbelieving voice to reverse the order of the hymn's lines "I once was lost, but now am found."[5]

In Dickinson's day it was certainly not unusual to have a firm grasp of scripture and hymn texts, referencing them in letters and conversation. Dickinson's propensity to quote from hymns and scripture is notable and can be seen as early as 1845. In a letter to Abiah Root, fourteen-year-old Emily wrote: "I think I could keep house very comfortably if I knew how to cook. But as long as I don't, my knowledge of housekeeping is about of as much use as faith without works, which you know we are told is dead. Excuse my quoting from the Scripture, dear Abiah, for it was so handy in this case I couldn't get along very well without it."[6] Even after this apology, Dickinson continues, "Since I wrote you last the summer is past and gone." Here Dickinson is singing—quoting the opening line, "The day is past and gone," from hymn number 512 in Asahel Nettleton's *Village Hymns*, "Evening Shade."[7]

Dickinson once wrote to her cousins, "Let Emily sing for you because she cannot pray."[8] In Dickinson's day this would have been an alarming admission; but this statement is emblematic of Dickinson's ability to set a strong conviction against a *scalding* fear and resolve it through musical metaphors and borrowings.[9] She understood well "the cordiality of the Sacrament" and took full advantage of that cordiality in articulating and legitimizing her belief in the sanctity of the natural world, letting her keen aural intelligence for music guide her to a safer shore where she could "sing," and where her poetry could reside.[10]

She achieved this by borrowing from the meters, imagery, and tropes of her New England hymn tradition. The hymn and scriptural references in her correspondence and later her poetry attest to the fact that although she gradually withdrew from attending church services, Dickinson's firm foundation in the New England Christian hymn tradition sustained her in imaginative ways.

That hymn meter and popular ballad meter served as an underpinning for a good deal of Dickinson's poetry has been thoroughly discussed by Dickinson scholars. Thomas Johnson in his 1955 *Emily Dickinson: An Interpretive Biography* was the first to elucidate her use of hymn meter. According to Johnson, Dickinson "did not have to step outside her father's library to receive a beginner's lesson in hymn metrics."[11] Asahel Nettleton's *Village Hymns for Social Worship* (1838), Isaac Watts's *Christian Psalmody* (1817) and his *Psalms, Hymns, and Spiritual Songs* (1834), as well as Lowell Mason's *Church Psalmody* (1831) and more were part of Edward Dickinson's library.[12] Johnson notes that when Dickinson employs these hymn meters, "a very large proportion of her poems are in common meter," which could be aligned with any number of hymn texts or set to any number of corresponding hymn tunes with which Dickinson would have been intimately familiar.[13] Dickinson biographer Richard Sewall writes: "And how did she come by that 'incredible ear'?—to which should be added at once a sense of rhythm that enabled her to make the tight, limited form of the Common Meter (the '8's and '6's of the hymnals) a medium of great flexibility, responsive to a wide range of mood and tone."[14]

"My *business is to* sing"

Through a relationship of metrics and imagery, we can see how Dickinson found a musical and an intellectual trajectory and congeniality in borrowing from her New England hymn tradition, which she had been steeped in since childhood, in particular the hymns of Isaac Watts, as a means of informing her verse. But there was more at stake: had she identified herself to her family and to the world as a secular poet, she would have been branded an outlier, positioning herself well beyond the orbit of her country town of Amherst.[15] Wendy Martin notes that it was "clear that her parents consider[ed] her poetry writing useless, perhaps even sinful."[16] While Dickinson was weathering the revival of 1850, she wrote to Jane Humphrey, "I dont wonder that the good angels weep— and bad ones sing songs."[17] But the secular song of the poet would have to be altered to fix the hymn as an acceptable means of expression: to "modify the Glee / To fit some Crucifixal Clef — / [to] Some Key of Calvary — ," altering the music's timbre, key, and clef from the bright and lively rhythms and contrapuntal textures of the secular glees that

Dickinson would have sung at Mount Holyoke (and experienced in a variety of birdsong) to the conforming homophonic voicings of the hymns she sang in church.[18]

This was her egress, her way into the world of the secular poet. According to scholar Victoria Morgan, Dickinson "was also willing to call her poems 'hymns.' In this we can interpret what must have been a conscious decision to express herself through the echoes of her own matrilineal heritage. This heritage of spiritual women had hymnody and Watts at its core."[19]

It was around 1862 that Dickinson wrote to Mrs. Holland, affirming, "*My* business is to *sing*."[20] Vocation and industry are both at play here.[21] We can see how Dickinson modifies her Glee by aligning and asserting herself musically, rhetorically, and poetically within the acceptable occupational boundaries of the Christian feminine hymnists of her day—Phoebe Hinsdale Brown (1783–1861), Eliza Lee Follen (1787–1860), and Julia Ward Howe (1819–1910)—as a justification of her poetic calling.[22] Dickinson was acquainted with the work of at least one of these writers.

Along with Betsey Fay Norcross (1777–1829), Dickinson's maternal grandmother, hymnist Phoebe Hinsdale Brown, served as a founding member of the Praying Circle, a women's group that was affiliated with the First Church in Monson, Massachusetts. Brown's early and best-known hymn, "I Love to Steal Awhile Away," a favorite hymn of Brown's personal friend Mary Lyon, appeared in Nettleton's *Village Hymns*, a compilation in which Nettleton incorporated a large number of Watts's hymns as well.[23] According to Victoria Morgan, "the fact that Dickinson's mother passed her copy of Watts's psalmody [*Psalms carefully suited to the Christian Worship*] on to the poet means that memories of Watts's tunes were inevitably bound with memories of her mother."[24] And whatever Dickinson would have known or remembered of the Monson Praying Circle and Phoebe Hinsdale Brown meant that Dickinson's literal relationship to hymnody was close at hand. Biographer Alfred Habegger observes: "If there was much that Dickinson took from the Norcross side, there was much she had to resist and reject, to define herself *against*. A part of this large maternal heritage was Phoebe H. Brown, public poet, the voice of congregations. To grow up with her as the accepted standard could spur a fresh mind into thinking about a more private form of authorship."[25]

"This is my letter to the World"

Martha Winburn England observes that "the formal influence in all [Dickinson's] poetry is the hymn. When music is considered along with hymn texts, that influence is seen as pervasive. Her poetry was written as Watts's was written, as most hymns are written *par-odia*, to an existing tune."[26] With that in mind, we can easily observe, as Richard Sewall articulates, how Dickinson makes "the tight, limited form of the Common Meter (the '8's and '6's of the hymnals) a medium of great flexibility."[27] But Dickinson took this hymnic appropriation a step further, aligning herself with Watts, as Victoria Morgan notes, in utilizing "a traditional means of Christian devotion as a form of dissent."[28]

This dissenting tradition, with its emphasis on autonomy and choice, was passed down from Watts through Phoebe Hinsdale Brown to Dickinson, questioning the established modes of worship and the religious experience. Consider the dissenting nature of Brown's "I Love to Steal Awhile Away" in a verse not published in Nettleton, here Brown circumvents the cult of domesticity, finding inner peace away from family, and alone with God:

> I love to steal awhile away
> From little ones and care,
> And spend the hours of setting day
> In gratitude and prayer.[29]

In poems such as "Some keep the Sabbath going to Church — / I keep it, staying at Home — / With a Bobolink for a Chorister — / And an Orchard, for a Dome — ," Dickinson rejects the uniform of the surplice and the constraints of the church service, finding her own choir, sexton, and preacher in solitude, on the peaceful grounds of the Dickinson Homestead.[30]

Another one of the hymnbooks from her father's library with which Dickinson would also have been intimately familiar was Lowell Mason's *Church Psalmody* (1831). Mason sourced hymns from a variety of collections, but the majority are those of Isaac Watts.[31] Considering the Watts hymn "Oh God Our Help in Ages Past" (from Mason's *Church Psalmody*) allows us to view Dickinson's borrowing from Watts on a variety of levels. Like Watts, she accesses the divine not through an orthodox rhetoric but on her own terms; as Victoria Morgan explains, "both [Watts and Dickinson] sought to redefine God in ways that were more compatible with their own experience."³² Within that means of expression we can see in Dickinson's poems that the "plain style" of Watts is evident.³³ Dickinson states in one of her poems, "My Faith is larger than the Hills — ."³⁴ Here Dickinson aligns her vision of the Pelham Hills to the east of Amherst with the lectures of geologist Edward Hitchcock, her "Scientist of Faith," and the third verse of the Watts hymn.³⁵

> Before the hills in order stood,
> Or earth receiv'd her frame;
> From everlasting thou art God;
> To endless years the same.³⁶

In Dickinson's poem "This is my letter to the World," which she wrote in 1863 at the age of thirty-two, her transformation of a common meter structure into a more flexible multilayered medium of expression comes alive when paired with the Watts hymn "Oh God Our Help in Ages Past," and its accompanying tune, "St. Anne." The familiar common meter of Watts in Dickinson's "Letter to the World" invites us to participate in the poem's sense of conformity, which satisfies the "hymnness" to which Dickinson aspired; Dickinson's text, however, freely presents an opportunity for dissent. In her poem, Dickinson asserts that the natural world around her is at the same time real, feminine, *and* divine. But as her poem concludes, Dickinson asks for tender judgment, a request that resonates far beyond the poem itself. On the surface, the poem's dissonant rhythms of punctuation may, in recalling Dickinson's own words, "hurt almost like Music — shifting when it ease us most"; but underneath this dissonance, there is indeed a borrowed hymn tune embedded in her verse.³⁷ And like many of Watts's hymn texts, Dickinson's poem aligns itself with any number of common meter tunes, but I believe most poignantly with the tune "St. Anne," as in "Oh God Our Help in Ages Past."³⁸

> This is my letter to the World
> That never wrote to Me —
> The simple News that Nature told —
> With tender Majesty
>
> Her Message is committed
> To Hands I cannot see —
> For love of Her — Sweet — countrymen —
> Judge tenderly — of Me³⁹

"Memory like Melody, / Is pink eternally — "

Dickinson scholar Cristanne Miller writes: "While there is ample evidence that Dickinson wrote with the rhythms of hymns in her ears, several aspects of her verse suggest that a more accurate formulation would be that she wrote in relation to song. Song in this context includes the hymns and ballads she sang, the poetry she read, and the popular music she played on the piano."[40]

Miller's observations are well illustrated in Dickinson's poem "Blossoms will run away — ."[41] Here Dickinson reminds us that "Memory like Melody, / Is pink eternally — ." This sentiment of an active and sustained memory finds expression in her music book in Henry Russell's enormously popular ballad "The Old Arm Chair." Russell's melody was set to a poem by Eliza Cook which addresses the lasting memory of motherhood and the role of mother, whose person and position in the home is the most revered. The intense expression of sentiment common to these period vocal pieces is emphatically represented in the song's second verse:

> I sat and watch'd her many a day,
> When her eyes grew dim, and her locks were gray,
> And I almost worshipp'd her when she smil'd,
> And turn'd from her bible to bless her child.
> Years roll'd on, but the last one sped,
> My idol was shatter'd, my earth star fled:
> I learnt how much the heart can bear,
> When I saw her die in that Old Arm Chair.[42]

Another example of Dickinson's borrowing of lyric sentiment and meter from the ballads in her music book is the English folk song "The Rose of Allandale." Here the song's text shares a similar sentiment to Russell's ballad, that of a remembrance, in this case, of the scent of the rose:

> The morn was fair the skies were clear,
> No breath came o'er the sea
> When Mary left her highland cot
> and wander'd forth with me:
> Though flowers deck'd the mountain's side
> And fragrance fill'd the vale,
> By far the sweetest flower there
> Was the Rose of Allandale.[43]

In her poem "I had a guinea golden," Dickinson models the ballad form, the colloquial language trope ("many a day"), and the sentiment of memory expressed in the vocal music of her bound volume in songs such as "The Old Arm Chair" and "The Rose of Allandale."[44] In stanza two of Dickinson's poem, the speaker describes holding a permanent place for the memory of a lost birdsong:

> I had a crimson Robin —
> Who sang full many a day
> But when the woods were painted —
> He — too — did fly away —
> Time brought me other Robins —
> Their ballads were the same —
> Still, for my missing Troubadour
> I kept the "house at hame".[45]

The variety of her performative musical and poetic experiences with the ballads from her music book and the hymns she had been familiar with since childhood ultimately did allow Emily Dickinson to find a safer shore, as she had expressed to Abiah Root in 1850. In the 1860s and 1870s she would continue this trajectory and boundary crossing by creating a performance persona that enabled her to move sometimes invisibly across a threshold where she would "select her own society" in order "to withdraw and witness, to observe but not to participate, to attract devotion but not have to return it."[46] But in doing so, she would once again have to "buffet the sea" of her small town and her enlarging role in it as the "Myth" of Amherst.

CHAPTER 12

....

The White Dress

"Ossian's Serenade"

SOMETIME IN THE LATE 1860s, Emily Dickinson adopted a simple white housedress as her daily costume, assisting her in achieving the same "air of exile" she had observed years before in Jenny Lind.[1] Contemporary images of Lind often portray her in a white dress, and descriptions of Lind's white dress have been recorded by those who attended her performances. One concertgoer wrote: "Jenny Lind was dressed in a heavy white silk under white lace [dress] with a large green bow—quilt on her bosom and green flowers in her hair. The dress was made very low in the neck, broad white chiffon with long ends around the waist, gold chain circled around the neck, numerous bracelets."[2]

While musical borrowings would contribute to the development of Emily Dickinson's poetic persona, the white dress would provide a branding of that persona, making it socially transportable across boundaries and eventually recognizable and assimilated as part of a Lind-inspired performance persona.

For someone of her social class who crossed boundaries, the simple working housedress permitted Dickinson a dual identity: as a servant to her poetic art, and as Emily Dickinson who engaged in boundary crossings and borrowings in the domestic sphere of her daily housekeeping, working alongside the servants at the Homestead, with whom she was in daily contact. Aífe Murray suggests that Emily "used her [Irish] maid [Maggie] to draw a line between herself and her peers; those who might make claims on her, Emily limited her contact to those familiar enough to use the back door."³

Similarly, in her book *Emily Dickinson: Personae and Performance*, Elizabeth Phillips states that Dickinson "enjoyed being enigmatic and dodging the inquisitive."⁴ In Dickinson's time, contemporary usage of the word "dodge" can be traced to the notorious Ossian E. Dodge, a composer/singer/performer who deceptively tried to associate himself with Jenny Lind. On Thursday, September 26, the *Springfield Republican* reported that

> the first bid for the first seat in Tremont Temple, Boston, for Jenny's first concert there [which would take place the following evening].... The ticket was finally struck off to Ossian E. Dodge, the vocalist, for SIX HUNDRED AND TWENTY-FIVE DOLLARS PREMIUM! The ticket being $3, would make the sum paid for the ticket $628.... The crowd at the sale was very large, and as the successive bids progressed each was met by cheers. When Dodge was announced as the purchaser he was greeted with a round of cheers. The second ticket sold for $24.⁵

This and other shrewd promotional tactics instigated by Lind's manager, P. T. Barnum, were widely circulated in the press. Eventually Lind put an end to Barnum's auction stunts just before her Northampton performance.⁶ As an avid reader of the *Springfield Daily Republican*, Dickinson was certainly aware of "that great Dodge of all Dodges."⁷ The sheet music cover of Dodge's composition "Ossian's Serenade" depicts his introduction to Lind by Barnum in an after-concert parlor setting, an event that, according to Daniel Cavicchi, "had not, to anyone's knowledge, actually occurred" (see figure 12).⁸

The auction event continued to be discussed long afterwards. One week after a January 19, 1852, story regarding Ossian Dodge appeared in the *Springfield Daily Republican*, Lavinia wrote to her brother, "I should also like two other pieces, 'You & Me,' & 'the Ossian Serenade.'"⁹ The fact that the Dickinsons appear to have owned a copy of the sheet music to "Ossian's Serenade" suggests that Emily still identified herself with the image of Lind and her white dress as seen in concert and depicted on the cover of the sheet music, adopting that image as her own. Judith Pascoe articulates Dickinson's "performance poems," such as "Publication — is the Auction / Of the Mind of Man — ," as connecting Barnum's auction stunt, and the white dress worn in concert by Jenny Lind, to Dickinson's

FIGURE 12. "Ossian's Serenade." Music and Recorded Sound Division, The New York Public Library for the Performing Arts, Astor, Lenox and Tilden Foundations.

own "literary performance," also utilizing a white dress.[10] The illustrated sheet music cover serves, then, as both corroboration and commemoration of this notorious event, making Dickinson's own white dress palpable as a signifier of performance art, remembered, borrowed, and aligned with her own musical memory of Jenny Lind from 1851, when Dickinson was twenty years old. Dickinson scholar Páraic Finnerty notes that "Lind offered Dickinson an important example of the complexity but also marketability of contradictorily maintaining allure, privacy, and mystery, while becoming a spectacle of communal fascination."[11]

In the end, it may not have been Dickinson who fashioned herself as a "spectacle of communal fascination." That final branding would find its greatest assistant in Austin Dickinson's mistress, Mabel Loomis Todd.[12] Dickinson scholar Martha Nell Smith states that "it is Mabel

Loomis Todd who sets in motion many of the fallacies that have since become Dickinson legend."[13]

Mabel Todd arrived in Amherst on August 31, 1881, with her husband, David Peck Todd (Amherst class of 1875). David, an astronomy professor, had been appointed head of the Amherst College Observatory. The Todds immediately became intertwined with the social life of Amherst and were regular visitors to The Evergreens. Austin Dickinson and Mabel Loomis Todd entered into an affair that began in 1882 and continued until Austin's death in 1895.

Mabel crossed the grounds to the Homestead often, playing the piano and singing while "Miss Emily in her weird white dress was outside in the shadow hearing every word."[14] Two months after arriving in Amherst, Todd was able to report to her parents:

> I must tell you about the *character* of Amherst. It is a lady whom the people call the *Myth*. She is a sister of Mr. Dickinson, & seems to be the climax of all the family oddity. She has not been outside of her own house in fifteen years. . . . She dresses wholly in white, & her mind is said to be perfectly wonderful. She writes finely, but no one *ever* sees her. . . . No one knows the cause of her isolation, but of course there are dozens of reasons assigned.[15]

Over time those "reasons" proliferated. Dickinson scholar Sandra Runzo observes that "the charismatic energy of the white dress has galvanized particular views of Dickinson so successfully that every quality that has been associated with the white dress has been associated with Dickinson herself."[16]

"I do not cross my Father's ground to any House or town," Dickinson wrote to Thomas Wentworth Higginson in 1869.[17] By her late thirties, with her gradual withdrawal under way, Emily Dickinson was already developing a satisfactorily intimate relationship with her own poetry and performance identity. Adrienne Rich notes that "genius knows itself; that Dickinson chose her seclusion, knowing she was exceptional and knowing what she needed."[18] It is likely Dickinson did not want or need contact with others who might bring her publicity or notoriety, instead preferring intimate contact only with the "rewarding person" who intersected with her daily activities—her family, her correspondents, and the Irish and African American servants.[19]

"Ye Banks and Braes of Bonnie Doon"

Emily was equally comfortable in the weird and the beautiful, the secular and the sacred, crossing from the parlor to the kitchen, where her eyes and ears were exposed to a variety of Hiberno-English accents and African American vernacular English, both spoken and sung.[20] Just as she used the Irish and other traditional tunes in her music book to inform her improvisations, or borrowed hymns and ballads to underpin her poetry, she also extended her daily conversations with the Irish servants into some of her verse. Ephemeral traces of Hiberno-English function as dialogic commentary, melding almost unnoticed into the short hymn meter that underpins her poem "Each Second is the last":

> Each Second is the last
> Perhaps, recalls the Man
> Just measuring unconsciousness
> The Sea and Spar between —
>
> To fail within a chance —
> How *terribler* a thing
> Than perish from the chance's list
> Before the Perishing![21]

Emily grew fond of the domestic servants and groundskeepers, and remained so to the end of her life, memorializing their musical qualities in the music she played and the verse she wrote. These servants had given her a space for work, musical and linguistic dialects for borrowing, and thresholds for crossing. Her final request had been that after her death, her white casket be borne from the house through the fields to the cemetery by the Irish servants to whom she had entrusted her daily activities.

The chief pallbearer was Tom Kelley, assisted by Dennis Scanlon, Pat Ward, Stephen Sullivan, Dennis Cashman, and Dan Moynihan. Dickinson identified with them as belonging to an outlier class, eager for assimilation yet wanting to retain their Irish identity. Emily did not reject the cultural structures of her own class or faith; rather, as evidenced by her "exultant proclamation of [her] artistic status," "Mine — by the Right of the White Election," she freely borrowed from them, claiming an ownership and a faith in the tunes and dialects that were part of the fertile surroundings of her beloved Connecticut River Valley.[22]

Emily once wrote to her cousin John Graves, "I play the old, odd tunes yet, which used to flit about your head after honest hours—and wake dear Sue, and madden me, with their grief and fun—How far from us, that spring seems—and those triumphant days—."[23] The "old, odd tunes" in Emily Dickinson's music book provide a new perspective on understanding how Dickinson's daily musical encounters, her ambitions, and her musical borrowings and boundary crossings became her proving ground, as they informed the developing musical metaphors of her unique poetic persona. Emily Dickinson's music book serves as both a document of past musical activity in the Dickinson home and a means of contextualizing that music within the era in which it thrived and was part of the everyday life of Emily Dickinson the musician/poet. Both of these aspects reveal a fuller picture and will continue to engage us in a broader understanding of the life of a great American poet, whose "business [was] to *sing*."

POSTLUDE

"Musicians wrestle everywhere"

In 1861, when Dickinson's most productive poetic period was under way, she may have poetically and musically reached her "fuller tune" when she composed her poem "Musicians wrestle everywhere — ":

> Musicians wrestle everywhere —
> All day — among the crowded air
> I hear the silver strife —
> And — waking — long before the morn —
> Such transport breaks opon the town
> I think it that "New life"!
>
> It is not Bird — it has no nest —
> Nor "Band" — in brass and scarlet — drest —
> Nor Tamborin — nor Man —
> It is not Hymn from pulpit read —
> The "Morning Stars" the Treble led
> On Time's first afternoon!
>
> Some — say — it is "the Spheres" — at play!
> Some say — that bright Majority
> Of vanished Dames — and Men!
> Some — think it service in the place
> Where we — with late — celestial face —
> Please God — shall ascertain![1]

Many of the musical references and events Dickinson incorporates into "Musicians wrestle everywhere — " occurred significantly earlier in time, when her poetry, still embryonic, was not yet a discernible vehicle for her powerful musical metaphors, musical borrowings, and rhythmic dissonances. Dickinson's memories and their attendant musical associations would be released full force beginning in the early 1860s, capturing the gamut of dialects and imagery available to her. "Musicians wrestle everywhere — " reaches back to those past musical experiences, creating images of the noises of the town, such as the musical ensemble the Germanians, once described by Dickinson as "brazen Robins," now "in brass and scarlet — drest — ," and the tambourine's association with minstrel music, both images resonating with the music in Dickinson's bound music book.[2] Finally, hymn references such as the "Morning Stars," led by the choir's treble voices, remind us of the hymnbooks of her youth.[3]

Cristanne Miller, editor of *Emily Dickinson's Poems: As She Preserved Them*, positions the chronology of this poem's composition to "c. late spring 1861."[4] I strongly believe and propose that this positioning holds a congruent resonance with a tangible historical moment in our nation's history: the aftermath of the first shots fired at Fort Sumter on April 12, 1861. "Musicians wrestle everywhere — " serves as a marker, signifier, and catalog of Dickinson's once musical and now poetic life, whose "Loaded Gun" of past musical experiences explodes onto the page one by one.[5] In her poem Dickinson may have used these images to reflect on and perhaps herald the oncoming cataclysmic "silver strife," a civil war whose outcome was as yet unknowable, a future for the country unknowable, and the future and identity of the young poet Emily Dickinson, also unknowable. Perhaps a poem such as "Musicians wrestle everywhere — " enabled her to make that transition: to wrestle with, and surrender her musical identity to, what she must have felt was the start of a "new life," as a poet.

"Because I see — New Englandly — "

"Musicians wrestle everywhere — " is emblematic of Dickinson's New England Americanness. Her ability to "see [and think] "New Englandly" is a trope that has long been addressed in Dickinson scholarship, and presents an opportunity for interpretation here based in part on the work of scholar Helen Vendler.[6] In her poem "Musicians wrestle everywhere — ," Dickinson reimagines her small provincial New England town as it once was, but now on a grand scale, all present and alive to her. Through a host of musical metaphors Dickinson simultaneously evokes a time both past and present, through a memory of now. According to biographer Richard Sewall, "the breathlessness of Emily Dickinson's poems comes from the urgency of her attempts to arrest the moment, to catch and preserve its essence. The exercise kept her nimble." Dickinson would later write, "Forever — is composed of Nows — ."[7]

Dickinson's poetic voice that sang "New Englandly" embraced a performative musical aesthetic that in its agency and urgency finds a similar resonance in the musical voice of the New England composer Charles Ives (1874–1954). Although they were a generation apart, in the context of the long nineteenth century they were concurrent musically and poetically. Both Dickinson and Ives sought to capture a deep and earnest memory of the New England of the 1850s in their respective creative lives. Ives was determined to evoke a New England of an earlier time, that of his father, the Civil War regimental bandmaster George Edward Ives (1845–1894), one of Dickinson's own generation. Ives biographer Stuart Feder states, "There is no question in the listener's mind that [Ives's melodic] episodes exist only in the now of memory."[8] Charles Ives created what the musicologist Carol Oja has called a "usable past."[9] By drawing from earlier sources, composing an underpinning of remembered and borrowed musics, Ives overlaid that remembrance with a dissonance of transcendent beauty and discovery. Composer Henry Cowell, a close friend, biographer, music publisher, and promoter of Charles Ives and other composers, identified Ives as the first to exhibit what he defined as "ultra-modernist" tendencies, something that Cowell himself adopted and promoted in the work of others.[10]

As with Ives's music, much of Emily Dickinson's verse was also underpinned by borrowed and remembered musics, supported by a dissonance of rhythmic punctuation, with glimmers of American modernism—something that confounded her early editors.[11] According to Willis J. Buckingham, "Modernism, nascent in the [eighteen] nineties, had to reach fuller self-understanding before it could find its expression in Emily Dickinson."[12] Dickinson was a modernist whose poetic voice was animated by a musical and compositional aesthetic, in that almost as soon as her poems saw publication in 1890, Dickinson's verse inspired an increasingly large number of musical settings. That same interest and enthusiasm for setting Dickinson's poems continues today unabated.[13] This not only invigorates a continuity of music-making from Dickinson's era to the present day but also connects once again the early musical Dickinson with the American modernist poet she would become.

Carol Oja observes that modernism in music "stood for one basic principle: iconoclastic, irreverent innovation, sometimes irreconcilable with the historic traditions that preceded it."[14] That observation is where I think the convergence of Emily Dickinson and Charles Ives rests, their artistic commonality resonating in the fact that both Dickinson and Ives abided by a long tradition of musical borrowing, blending together the past with something that was startlingly new.

Ives scholar J. Peter Burkholder reminds us that "using another work as a model was common for all types of music in the nineteenth century."[15] Cristanne Miller refers to Dickinson's stanzaic and metric forms as arising from the "intersections of elite and popular, printed and sung, religious and secular short-lined forms prevalent in the 1840s and 1850s."[16]

Dickinson crossed boundaries in the melding of the sacred with the secular, or in harvesting a poetically dissonant tonality of punctuation, acting in a "Behavior" much "like Music—shifting when it ease us most."[17] For instance, in recasting the meters of Isaac Watts's hymn texts, Dickinson more than just emulates Watts the hymnist. When her poem "This is my letter to the World" is paired with the common meter of Watts's "Oh God Our Help in Ages Past" and sung to the tune "St. Anne," the hymn tune's presence underneath a new "shifting" dissonant secular poetic text above it invites a "faith," not in religion, but in a performative *action* of capturing what Dickinson referred to as the "fuller tune," a divinity of performance to which Dickinson and Ives ultimately aspired.

Both Ives and Dickinson engaged in these borrowings as part of a musical and poetic affiliation that echoed from the small New England towns to which Van Wyck Brooks alludes in *The Flowering of New England* in the early decades of the nineteenth-century: "Ironically enough, it was Boston and Cambridge that grew to seem provincial, while the local and even parochial Concord mind, which had always been universal, proved to be also national. Whatever doubts the country at large felt regarding the other New England authors, Hawthorne, Thoreau and Emerson were clearly of the main stream, with Emily Dickinson, Whitman, Poe and Melville."[18]

Charles Ives's movement "The Alcotts" from his *Concord Sonata* for piano, and Dickinson's poem "Musicians wrestle everywhere — ," both recall "New Englandly" a similar time in the early decades of the nineteenth century. In both Dickinson's poem and Ives's music, what at first appears a provincial New England townscape eventually becomes a proving ground for the symbols of a higher art. "The Alcotts" evokes a walk down Main Street in Concord, Massachusetts, during the 1850s. Passing by the home of Bronson Alcott and his family, we hear "the little old spinet piano Sophia Thoreau gave to the Alcott children, on which Beth played the old Scotch airs, and played at the *Fifth Symphony*" of Beethoven.[19] Ives and others referred to this famous musical motive as "a human faith melody," "a tune the Concord bards are ever playing."[20] It can also be heard as a metaphor of knocking, trying to awaken the New England soul to the "higher" music of Beethoven and others that was then new to our American ears.

The same can be said of Dickinson's Amherst and her own musical and poetic metaphors. In the music of "the spheres at play," she is a musician wrestling like a Beethoven with his muse and, like Ives, attempting to fashion a New England soundscape of hymns and words, hewn out of past musical experiences, creating a *poetic* "human faith melody" that was also new to our American eyes and ears.

In her poem "It will be Summer — eventually" (1862), Dickinson unfolds her imagined provincial New England summer landscape through a memory of mixed meter and dissonant punctuation whose soundscape gradually cedes to the symbols that signal the sacrament of the concluding season. Richard Brantley observes that "the evangelically empirical dimension of [Dickinson's] imagination so creatively 'masters' the empirically evangelical aspect of her Anglo-American heritage that she does not so much 'escape' from her tradition as she gives it life and passes it on."[21] Like Charles Ives, Emily Dickinson filled her "crowded air" with musical memories and poetic metaphors that, as Richard Sewall notes, "grew out of a lifetime's association with the thing itself. She had shifted from the old music to the new, but the old lived on as part of her poetry," giving it "new life" and, as Brantley notes, "passing it on" in order to create what Dickinson called her "fuller tune."[22] And as Van Wyck Brooks observes of Dickinson, it was a tune that "fluttered a breast in Amherst that was to sing to better purpose than most of the famous poets of the eighteen-sixties."[23]

Charles Ives wrote:

> I think there must be a place in the soul
> all made of tunes, of tunes long ago: . . .
> I know not what are the words.
> But they sing in my soul of the things our Fathers loved.[24]

Dickinson expressed a similar sentiment when she wrote:

> The Bees — will not despise the tune —
> Their Forefathers — have hummed — [25]

   As with Charles Ives, Emily Dickinson's early years laid the groundwork for her musical memories and sensibilities and her longings not only to excel musically but also, more importantly, to not despise the tunes of her forefathers, but in a show of faith, to use them in imaginative ways and pass them on. By the time the poetry took hold, she had become fluent enough in those musics to use all of them as a means of conformity and rebellion in establishing, legitimizing, and fulfilling her poetic calling.[26] In Dickinson's poems, musical imagery both underpins and extrapolates her internal and external worlds. As in her long-ago 1850 letter to Abiah Root, by wishing she were somebody else, Emily Dickinson did not become one of the "bitter wrecks" of failed expectation, but rather she gained a sure foothold in the eternal ranks of those who have learned to sing the "fuller tune." *This* was Emily Dickinson's musical life, "and there was much of it in her."[27]

> It will be Summer — eventually.
> Ladies — with parasols —
> Sauntering Gentlemen — with Canes —
> And little Girls — with Dolls —
>
> Will tint the pallid landscape —
> As 'twere a bright Boquet —
> Tho' drifted deep, in Parian —
> The Village lies — today —
>
> The Lilacs — bending many a year —
> Will sway with purple load —
> The Bees — will not despise the tune —
> Their Forefathers — have hummed —
>
> The Wild Rose — redden in the Bog —
> The Aster — on the Hill
> Her everlasting fashion — set —
> And Covenant Gentians — frill —
>
> Till Summer folds her miracle —
> As Women — do — their Gown —
> Or Priests — adjust the Symbols —
> When Sacrament — is done — [28]

Appendix A

Contents Listing of Emily Dickinson's Bound Volume of Sheet Music

Emily Dickinson's bound volume of sheet music contains one hundred published pieces of music comprising 107 individual compositions. Each entry in this contents listing has been transcribed from the title page or the caption title on the first page of music, up to and including the publisher's imprint and year of copyright deposit, if one is present on the music. The date of copyright if present is cited as it appears on the music: "c1846" (i.e., © 1846). In the absence of a date of copyright, the date of publication is determined by the presence of a publisher's plate number or street address or other means. See Appendix B, the annotated online bibliography, for detailed descriptions and background information on each of these pieces (http://umpressopen.library.umass.edu/projects/emily-dickinsons-music-book). Each piece has been numbered, 1 through 107.

Title: *Emily E. Dickinson volume of American piano and vocal music, circa 1823–1851.* Emily Dickinson Collection, Houghton Library, Harvard University. Call number EDR 469.

DUETT

1. [Kreutzer, Rodolphe.] The Celebrated Overture To Lodoiska, composed by Kreutzer, Arranged for Two Performers on the Piano Forte by Charles [Carl] Czerny. New-York Published by Firth Hall & Pond 239 Broadway. And 1 Franklin Sq. [1846?].

VARIATIONS

2. Aria Alla Scozzese with Variations Composed for the Piano Forte, by T. Valentine[.] Keith's Music Publishing House 67 & 69 Court St. Boston. [1845?]. Plate number: 348–4.

3. Beleive [sic] Me if All Those Endearing Young Charms, or My Lodging Is On The Cold Ground: arranged with Variations for the Piano Forte, by Thos. Valentine. Correct Edition. Published by F.D. Benteen, Baltimore. [1843?]. Plate number: 271.

4. Hope Again[.] Air with Variations for the Piano Forte[.] Inscribed by Permission to Rudolph Snyder Esq. By Geo. Dutton. Utica, Published by Geo. Dutton, Sold By Wm. Dubois, Firth & Hall, & others, New York. Parker & Ditson, Boston. c1841 by G. Dutton.

5. Kinlock of Kinlock Arranged for the Piano Forte with Variations by P. K. Moran. Boston: Published by C. Bradlee 184 Washington Street. [between 1845 and 1847?].

6. [Bellini, Vincenzo.] Take Them, I Implore Thee Deh Conte Arranged from the Opera Norma with Variations By F. Hunten. Boston Published by Oliver Ditson 115 Washington St. [1847?]. Plate number: 1369.

7. [Rossini, Gioacchino.] Di Tanti Palpiti, A Favorite Air from *Tancredi* With Variations for the Piano Forte by Edward L. White. Boston: Published by C. Bradlee 135 Washington Street. c1834 by T.B. White.

8. The Swiss Waltz, with Variations by P.K. Moran. Boston: Published by C.H. Keith. 67 & 69 Court St. [between 1840 and 1842?]. Plate number: 26.

9. Auld Lang Syne with Variations for the Piano Forte or Harp by D. Ross. Boston Published by G.P. Reed. 17 Tremont Row. [1843]. Plate number: 206.

10. The Last Rose of Summer, with easy Variations by A. Mine. Boston: Published by Geo. P. Reed 17 Tremont Row. [184–?].

11. Bonny Doon with Variations composed by Wm. Wood Jnr. New York Pubd by Firth & Hall at their Piano Forte and Music Store. 1 Franklin Sq. [1844–45?]. Plate number: 2971.

12. A.B.C. A Favorite French Air With an Introduction and Variations Composed and Arranged as Exercises for the Piano Forte and Respectfully Dedicated to His Pupils by Edward L. White. Boston: Published by Wm. H. Oakes & for sale by John Ashton and Co. 197 Washington St. c1843 by W. H. Oakes. Plate number: 62.

13. Yankee Doodle Arranged with Variations for the Piano Forte. Boston: Published by C.H. Keith. 67 & 69 Court St. [1842?]. Plate number: 77.

14. Speed the Plough, A Favorite Dance Arranged with Brilliant Variations for the Piano Forte. Fourth Edition. New York Published by William Hall & Son. 239 Broadway. c1845 by Firth & Hall[.] Plate number: 3059.

MARCHES

15. The Fest March, or Warrior's Joy composed by Josef Gung'l. Boston: Published by Oliver Ditson 115 Washington St. [1849?]. Plate number: 1672.

16. Congress March. By J. Z. Hesser[.] Keith's Music Publishing House 67 & 69 Court St. Boston. [1845?]. Plate number: 339–2.

17. Massachusetts March, Composed for the Piano Forte by H.B. Under-

hill. Boston: Published by Oliver Ditson 115 Washington St. [1844–1847?]. Plate number: 15.

18. Russian March. Boston Published by Keith & Moore 67 & 69 Court St. [between 1839 and 1842]. Plate number: 5.

19. [Peters, William Cumming.] Louisville March and Quick Step Composed for and Dedicated to Mrs. A. Bowen. By W.C.P. Boston: Published by C. Bradlee 107 Washington St. [between 1834 and 1836?].

20. [Bellini, Vincenzo.] Grand March in *Norma*, No. 1. Composed and Arranged, for the Piano Forte, by Bellini. Boston Published by Oliver Ditson 115 Washington St. [184–?].

21. Roderick Dhu's March, Composed and Arranged for the Piano Forte. Boston Published by Oliver Ditson 115 Washington St. [1844–?].

22. [Kočzwara, František.] March and Quick Step in the Battle of Prague. New-York, Publish'd, by Firth & Hall, 358, Pearl St. [between 1823 and 1831?].

23. Bonaparte's March Crossing the Rhine, Composed and Arranged for the Piano Forte. [Boston]: [Oliver Ditson?], [1835?].

QUICKSTEPS

24. The Celebrated Spanish Retreat, Quick Step. Respectfully Dedicated to Mrs. D.B. Stedman. Arranged for the Piano Forte by J. De Anguera. Performed for the 1st time by the Brigade Band at the Encampment of the Hancock Light Infantry July 1841[.] Boston. Published by Henry Prentiss 33 Court Street. c1841 by Henry Prentiss. Plate number: 29. Cover title: Shoulder Arms with illus. of standing soldier. Boston. Published by Henry Prentiss 33 Court St. c1842 by Henry Prentiss. Price 25 cts. nett. B. W. Thayer & Cos. Lith. Boston.

25. [Blockley, John J.]. Blockley's Beautiful Melody of Love Not Arranged as a Quick Step for the Piano Forte by Edward L. White[.] Boston: Published by Oliver Ditson, No. [115?] Washington St. c1843 by Oliver Ditson.

26. Camp Barnum Quick Step, As Played by Adams' Band, Composed Arranged & Dedicated to Mason A. Fisher, of the Rochester Grays by Charles Wilson. New York, Published by Firth, Pond & Co. 1 Franklin Sq. c1847 by Firth Hall & Pond. Plate number: 4110.

27. Prize Banner Quick Step. Composed & Arranged for the Piano Forte, And Dedicated to the Whigs of The Prize Banner Ward, by D.H. Haskell. Boston Published by Henry Prentiss, 33 Court St. c1841 by Henry Prentiss. Plate number: 609. Cover illus. of four men waving the Prize Banner of the Whig Party.

28. Bayeaux's Quick Step Composed and Arranged for the Piano Forte. by Wm. C. Glynn. Published with the authority of the composer[.] Keith's Publishing House, 67 & 69 Court St. Boston. c1844 by CH Keith. Plate number: 254-2.

29. Locomotive Quick Step. Respectfully Dedicated to C.C. Dennis

Esq[.], of Auburn, N.Y. By the Author, L. Thayer Chadwick. Keith's Music Publishing House 67–69 Court St. Boston. [1844]. Plate number: 382 2.

30. Home Quick Step, Composed for the Piano Forte and Respectfully dedicated to Dr. L.W. Stanton (of Ameniaville N.Y.) by Wm. Smith. Boston; Published by C.H. Keith. 67 & 69 Court Street. c1842 by C.H. Keith. Plate number: 53.

31. Lucy Neal Quick Step as performed by the Boston Bands Introducing the Celebrated Airs[,] "Lucy Neal[,] Dandy Jim and Lovely Fan" Arranged for the Piano Forte By Joseph W. Turner. Boston: Published at Keith's Music Publishing House 67 & 69 Court St. c1844 by C. H. Keith. Plate number: 278–2.

32. Favorite Melodies from the Grand Chinese Spectacle of Aladdin or The Wonderful Lamp, As produced at the Boston Museum. Words by S.S. Steele, Esq. The Music Composed by T. Comer. No. 6 — [underlined in orange pencil] Aladdin Quick Step. Boston. Published by Prentiss & Clark. 33 Court St. c1847 by Prentiss and Clark.

33. Juniata Quick Step Played by the Boston Bands Arranged from the Popular Song of "The Blue Juniata" by B.A. Burditt. Boston Published by Oliver Ditson 115 Washington St. c1847 by Oliver Ditson. Plate number: 1311.

34. Coolidge Quickstep, Composed and Arranged for the Piano Forte, and Respectfully dedicated to Major Chs. Austin Coolidge, of the Brigade Staff by J.G. Jones. Boston: Published by C.H. Keith 67 & 69 Court St. c1844 by CH Keith. Plate number: 231–2.

35. Bay State Quick Step, As Performed by the Boston Brass Band, Arranged for the Piano Forte by William C. Glynn. Boston. Published at Keith's Music Publishing House, 67 & 69 Court St. c1844 by Chas. H. Keith. Plate number: 243–2. Thayer & Cos. Lith. Cover illustration of people strolling along Colonnade Row, Boston.

WALTZES

36. *The Glenmary Waltzes*[.] Composed by Richard S. Willis and Most Affectionately Dedicated to His Niece Imogen Willis. No. [1 written in orange pencil]. Boston Published by Oliver Ditson 115 Washington St. c1847 by Oliver Ditson.

37. *The Glenmary Waltzes*[.] Composed by Richard S. Willis and Most Affectionately Dedicated to His Niece Imogen Willis. No. [2 written in orange pencil]. Boston Published by Oliver Ditson 115 Washington St. c1847 by Oliver Ditson.

38. *The Glenmary Waltzes*[.] Composed by Richard S. Willis and Most Affectionately Dedicated to His Niece Imogen Willis. No. [3 written in orange pencil]. Boston Published by Oliver Ditson 115 Washington St. c1847 by Oliver Ditson. Plate number: 1257. Caption title on first page of music: Third Set of Glen Mary Waltzes.

39. [Misattributed to Beethoven.] Clara Waltz Beethoven's Last Com-

posed and Arranged for the Piano Forte. Keith's Music Publishing House 67 & 69 Court St. Boston. [1845?]. Plate number: 365 2.

40. [Misattributed to Beethoven.] La Doleur Waltz, composed by L.V. Beethoven. Boston Published by Oliver Ditson 115 Washington St. [1846?]. Plate number: 1172.

41. [Misattributed to Beethoven.] Grand Landler Waltz Composed by L.V. Beethoven. Boston Published by Oliver Ditson 115 Washington St. [1846?]. Plate number: 1155.

42. [Weber, Carl Maria von.] Beethoven's Dream, A Grand Waltz for the Piano Forte. Boston, Published by Geo. P. Reed, 17 Tremont Row. [between 1839 and 1850?].

43. [Misattributed to Beethoven.] Willow Waltz, Composed for the Piano Forte by L.V. Beethoven. Boston: Published by C. Bradlee 135 Washington St. [1841?].

44. [Misattributed to Beethoven.] Japonica Waltz Composed for the piano forte by L.V. Beethoven. Boston: Published by C.H. Keith. 67 & 69 Court St. [1842?]. Plate number: 84.

45. [Misattributed to Beethoven.] The Much Admired Waltz, Composed by Beethoven, arranged by [Thomas] Valentine. St. Louis: Published by Balmer & Weber. [1851?]. Plate number: 378 2.

46. [Misattributed to Beethoven.] The Spirit Waltz. by Beethoven. Boston: Published by C.H. Keith. 67 & 69 Court St. [1842?]. Plate number: 89.

47. [Misattributed to Beethoven.] Tulip Waltz by Beethoven. Boston: Published by C.H. Keith 67 & 69 Court St. [1845?] Plate number: 375 1.

48. [Weber, Karl Maria von.] Von Weber's Last Waltz. Boston: C. Bradlee 184 Washington Street. [1844–1847?].

49. [Fry, William Henry.] Affection Waltz. Composed by W.H.F. Boston: Published by Oliver Ditson 115 Washington Street. [1844].

50. [Labitzky, Joseph. Elfin Waltzes.] Firth, Pond & Co's. Collection of Celebrated Waltzes, by Joseph Labitzky. New York, Published by Firth, Pond & Co. No. 1 Franklin Square. [184?]. No. 5 [underlined in orange pencil] Elfin Waltzes. Plate number: 4045.

51. [Gung'l, Josef.]. Sounds from Home. A set of Waltzes played by the Steyermarkische Company by Gungl [sic]. Boston. Published by Oliver Ditson 115 Washington St. [1848?]. Plate number: 1601.

52. L'Ariadne Waltz, Composed by James Flint. Boston. Published by Wm. H. Oakes, & for sale by John Ashton & Co. 197 Washington St. [1842].

53. The Bird Waltz, for the Harp or Piano Forte, Composed by Francis Panormo. Philadelphia, Published by J. G. Klemm. 3. South Third Street. [between 1823 and 1825?]. Plate number: 116.

54. Aurora Waltz, Composed for the Piano Forte, by Ferdinand Unger. Boston: Published by C. Bradlee 107 Washington Street. [between 1834 and 1837?].

55. [Labitzky, Joseph.] Aurora Waltz. Labitzky. Boston. Published by E.H. Wade 197 Washington Street. [1845–?]. Plate number: 571.

56. [Peters, William Cumming.] The Louisville Waltz. Composed for the Piano Forte or Harp and Dedicated to Mrs. Atkinson, by Peters. New York, Published by Firth, Hall & Pond, 239 Broadway. c1835 by J. L. Hewitt & Co. Plate number: 2489.

57. [Smith, John Finley (1815–1843).] Any Thing, a new Waltz composed for Every Body and Respectfully dedicated to Any Body by John Smith. Published by C. Holt Junr. 156 Fulton St. New York. c1847 by C. Holt Junr.

58. The Home That I Love arranged as a Waltz By Edward L. White. Boston Published by Oliver Ditson 115 Washington St. c1846 by Oliver Ditson. Plate number: 1187.

59. Home as a Waltz. Boston: Published by C.H. Keith. [1842?]. Plate number: 75.

60. [Olds, Mark Lafayette.] Jessie Waltz Composed and Respectfully Dedicated to Miss J. M. by M. L. Olds. Boston Published by J. Prentiss. 81 Washington St. A. Reed. Columbus. Ohio. c1850 by J. Prentiss. Plate number: 700.

61. [Herz, Henri.] The Celebrated Empress Henrietta's Waltz Composed by H. Herz. Boston: Published by C.H. Keith 67 & 69 Court St. [between 1842 and 1843?]. Plate number: 107.

62. The much admired Sliding Waltz. Boston: Published by C.H. Keith 67 & 69 Court St. [1844?]. Plate number: 206-1.

63. [Burgmüller, Johann Friedrich Franz.] Linden Waltz Arranged for the Piano forte by F. Burgmüller. Boston Published by Oliver Ditson 115 Washington St. [1846?]. Plate number 1160.

64. Æolian Waltz, Composed for the Piano Forte with or without Colemans Attachment and Dedicated to Miss Anne B. Francis by Richard B. Taylor. Keith's Publishing House 67 & 69 Court St. Boston. c1845 by Chas. H. Keith. Plate number: 310—-3.

65. The Rockaway Waltzes, Composed and arranged for the Piano Forte and dedicated to Miss Georgiana Andrews, by William C. Glynn. Boston. Published at Keith's Music Publishing House, 67 & 69 Court St. c1844 by Chas. H. Keith. Thayer & Cos.. Lith. Boston[.] Plate number: 265_4. Cover illustration of children and adults dancing.

66. Lawrence Waltz. Composed and Arranged for the Piano Forte. By Henry Lemoine. Boston: C.H. Keith 67 & 69 Court St. [1843?]. Plate number: 167–2.

67. Mary Louisa Waltz, Composed & Inscribed to Miss Mary L. Snell by A.W. Bayley. Boston: Published by Geo. P. Reed 17 Tremont Row. c1844 by Geo. P. Reed.

MISCELLANEOUS I [Dances]

68. [Bohlman (Sauzeau), Henri]. L'Enfer Quadrille Diabolique, Performed at the Public & Private Assemblies, Composed for the Piano Forte by Henri Bohlman. New York. Published by Wm. Dubois 285 Broadway. Philadelphia A. Fiot 196 Chestnut St. [1843].

Contents Listing of Emily Dickinson's Bound Volume of Sheet Music [181]

69. [Fowler, Jonathan Amos (1817–1878).] Syracuse Polka, Composed & arranged for the Piano Forte, and very respectfully inscribed to Miss R.H. Loomis, of Syracuse, N.Y. By J. A. Fowler. Atwill, 201 Broadway, New York. c1848 by J. F. Atwill.

70. [Offenbach, Jacques]. The Celebrated Polka Dance As performed with Enthusiastic Applause at the Boston Museum Composed by J. Offenbach. Boston: Published at Keith's Music Publishing House 67 & 69 Court St. [1844?]. Plate number: 267–2.

71. The Celebrated Baden, Baden, Polka Pas Bohemian Arranged by Musard. Philada. Published at Lee & Walker's Music Store & Circulating Library 120 Walnut St. [1845?]. Plate number: 30–2.

MISCELLANEOUS II [Traditional dance and fiddle music, etc.]

72–73. The Basket Cotillion. [WITH:] The Girl I Left Behind Me. Boston: Published By C.H. Keith. 67 & 69 Court St. [1842?]. Plate number: 67.

74, 75, 76. Herr Cline's Dance. [WITH:] Spanish Dance. [WITH:] Spanish Dance. Boston: Published By C. H. Keith. 67 & 69 Court St. [1842?]. Plate number: 68.

77–78. Swiss Guards March. [WITH:] Fisher's Hornpipe. Boston: Published by Keith & Moore 67 & 69 Court St. [between 1839 and 1842?]. Plate number: 15.

79–80. Durang's Hornpipe. [WITH:] Drops of Brandy. Boston: Published by C. H. Keith. 67 & 69 Court St. [1842?]. Plate number: 65.

81–82. Caledonian Hunt. [WITH:] Drunken Sailor. Keith's Music Publishing House 67 & 69 Court. St. Boston. [184–?].

83. Bonaparte's Retreat From Moscow. Arranged by J. Schell. Boston: Published by C.H. Keith. 67 & 69 Court St. [1842?]. Plate number: 62.

84–85. Panharmonicon March. [WITH:] College Hornpipe. Boston: Keith & Moore. 67 & 69 Court St. [between 1839 and 1842?]. Plate number: 31.

86. Kinloch of Kinloch. Boston: Published by Keith & Moore, 67 & 69 Court St. [between 1839 and 1840?]. Plate number: 3.

87. [Balfe, Michael William]. Gems from the Bohemian Girl, Arranged for the Piano Forte. E. Ferrett & Co., Philadelphia—68 South Fourth St. New York—237 Broadway. [1845].

SONGS

88. The Old Arm Chair, A Ballad, The music composed and respectfully dedicated to Holton Olmstead, Esquire, by Henry Russell. [Words by Eliza Cook]. Twenty Third Edition[.] Boston Published by Geo. P. Reed, 17 Tremont Row. c1840 by Oakes and Swan. Plate number: 202. Price 50 cts. nett. Thayer and Co's. Lithogy.. Boston. Cover illustration of woman standing behind an empty chair once occupied by her mother.

89. The Lament of the Irish Emigrant. A Ballad, Poetry by the Hon.

Mrs. Price Blackwood. The Music composed and most cordially dedicated to Mrs. Isaac M͡cGaw. of New York, by William R. Dempster. Boston: Geo. P. Reed, 17 Tremont Row. c1843 by Geo. P. Reed. Plate number: 203. Price 50 cts. net. Cover illustration of man leaning on fence.

90. The Old Granite State, A Song, Composed, Arranged and Sung, by the Hutchinson Family. Boston, Published by Oliver Ditson Washington St. c1843 by John Hutchinson. Lith. Of Bouvé & Sharp. Cover illustration of four members of the Hutchinson Family: Judson, Abby, John, Asa.

91. Our Native Song, A National Refrain as Sung with great applause by Mr. H. Russell, at His Public Concerts. The Music Composed, Adapted, Arranged, & Most Respectfully Dedicated to the People of the United States by Henry Russell. New York Published by Firth Hall & Pond 239 Broadway. And 1 Franklin Sq. c1841 by Hewitt & Jacques.

92. Bonnie Doon Favourite Scotch Song For one or two voices arranged for the Piano Forte. Boston: Chas. H. Keith, 67–69 Court St. [1843?]. Plate number: 153–2.

93. The Bonny Boat. Boston: Pub. by C. H. Keith 67 & 69 Court Street. [1843?]. Plate number: 133.

94. Home, Sweet Home. Boston: Published by C.H. Keith. 67 & 69 Court Street. [between 1840 and 1841?]. Plate number: 20.

95. Araby's Daughter. Sung with Great Applause by Mr. Williamson Written by Thomas Moore Esq. Composed by G. Kiallmark. Boston: Published by C. H. Keith 67 & 69 Court St. [1843?]. Plate number: 134.

96. The Rose of Allandale a Ballad Written by Charles Jeffery[s] The Music by S. Nelson. Boston Published by Keith & Moore, 67 & 69 Court St. [between 1840 and 1841?]. Plate number: 18.

97. There's a Good Time Coming[.] Ballad Composed & Sung by the Hutchinson Family The Symphonies & Accompaniments by E[dward] L. White Written by Charles Mackay. Boston Published by Oliver Ditson 115 Washington St. c1846 by Oliver Ditson. Plate number: 1242. Pr. 37 ½ Cts. nett.

98. [Moore, Thomas]. The Admired Canadian Boat Song and Trio Written and Composed by T. Moore Esq. Boston, Chas. H. Keith. 67 & 69 Court St. [1843?]. Plate number: 140.

99. The Charming Woman[.] Words and Music by Mrs. Price Blackwood[.] Boston. Published by Kieth [sic] & Moore, 67 & 69 Court St. [between 1839 and 1842?]. Plate number: 29.

100. Come, Love, Dance the Polka An admired Song Adapted for the Piano Forte by F. Romani. Baltimore; Published by F. D. Benteen Baltimore St. c1844 by F. D. Benteen. Plate number: 474. Price 25 Cts. Nett.

101. The Bonnie Clay Flag music composed by John Sinclair words by John H. Warland, Esq. and respectfully dedicated to the Boston Clay Club No[.] 1. Boston: Published by C.H. Keith 67 & 69 Court St. c1844 by C.H. Keith. Plate number: 216–3.

102. Oh Give Me a Home If in Foreign Land[.] Song Sung by the Harmoneon Family as a Quartette Poetry by Marshall S. Pike Music Composed & Respectfully Dedicated to Mrs. Samuel Farrar of Bangor Me. by L.V.H. Crosby. Boston Published by Oliver Ditson 115 Washington St. c1845 by Oliver Ditson. Plate number: 1294. Caption title on first page of music: "Oh! Give Me a Home if in Foreign Land. Arranged as a Quartette by Edward L. White."

103. The Little Maid[.] A Little Song for Little Folks, To be sung in Little (or Large) Rooms with Little Exertion Composed by J.J. Hutchinson and Dedicated to Every One Who Sings It Especially Little Singers[.] Boston Published by Oliver Ditson 115 Washington St. c1846. Plate number: 1132.

104. Believe Me, If All Those Endearing Young Charms. Written by Thomas Moore. E. Ferrett & Co. New York, 237 Broadway. Philadelphia, 68 South Fourth Street. Boston, 30 Cornhill. [1845?].

105. Who's that knocking at the door. As Composed and Sung by Wm. Whitlock. New York Published by C.G. Christman. 404 Pearl St., c1846 by C. G. Christman. Lith. of E. Jones and G. W. Newman 128 Fulton St. Whitlock's Collection of Ethiopian Melodies As Sung With Great Applause at the Principal Theaters in the United States.

106. The Original Old Dan Tucker. Words by Old Dan. D. Emmit [sic]. As Sung by the Virginia Minstrels. Boston: Published by Chas. H. Keith, 67 & 69 Court St. c1843 by Chas. H. Keith. Plate number: 123. Old Dan Emmit's Original Banjo Melodies. Emmit, Brower, Whitlock, Pelham. As sung by the Virginia Minstrels with enthusiastic applause at the principal Theaters and Concerts in the Union, being an entire new collection of peices [sic] never before Published. Arranged for the Piano Forte by Rice. Bouvé & Sharp, Lith.rs Boston[.] Price, Each 25 cts. nett.

107. The Jolly Raftsman. Words by Andrew Evans And sung by him at his Concerts with Great Success. Keith's Music Publishing House 67 & 69 Court st Boston. c1844 by C. H. Keith. Plate number: 291–3. [Illustrated cover:] Second Series Old Dan Emmit's [sic] Original Banjo Melodies Never Before Published[.] Mr. D. D. Emmit. As Sung by Him with Unprecedented Success, at the Theatres & Concerts both in Europe and America. . . . Bouvé & Sharp, Lith., Boston. Price 25 cts. nett.

Notes

Preface

1. "When word images are potent and condensed, as are those of Emily Dickinson, the music seems to write itself." Charles W. Rassely to Carlton Lowenberg, 25 July 1990, in Carlton Lowenberg, *Musicians Wrestle Everywhere: Emily Dickinson and Music* (Berkeley: Fallen Leaf Press, 1992), 84. See also Carolyn Lindley Cooley, *The Music of Emily Dickinson's Poems and Letters: A Study of Imagery and Form* (London: McFarland and Co., 2003), 127.
2. Richard Benson Sewall, *The Life of Emily Dickinson* (New York: Farrar, Straus and Giroux, 1974), 407.

Prelude

1. Dickinson's correspondence is a treasure trove, documenting a great deal of musical activity. Chapters 5–7 of this book are central to the discussion of home music-making in the Dickinson parlor.
2. Emily E. Dickinson, volume of American piano and vocal music, ca. 1823–1851, EDR 469, Houghton Library, Harvard University, https://iiif.lib.harvard.edu/manifests/view/drs:46653089$1ii.
3. Judy Jo Small, *Positive as Sound: Emily Dickinson's Rhyme* (Athens: University of Georgia Press, 1990), 30.
4. Thomas H. Johnson, *Emily Dickinson: An Interpretive Biography* (Cambridge: Belknap Press of Harvard University Press, 1955), 84–86.
5. Martha Winburn England, "Emily Dickinson and Isaac Watts: Puritan Hymnodists," *New York Public Library Bulletin* 69, no. 2 (2 February 1965): 83–116.
6. Victoria N. Morgan, *Emily Dickinson and Hymn Culture: Tradition and Experience* (Farnham, England: Ashgate Press, 2010).
7. "Dickinson's use of bee imagery [from Watts] connotes a diverse relationality, thus making connection between poetry and industry, industry and revery, more explicit." Morgan, *Emily Dickinson and Hymn Culture*, 112.
8. Barton Levi St. Armand, *Emily Dickinson and Her Culture: The Soul's Society* (New York: Cambridge University Press, 1984).
9. Cristanne Miller, *Reading in Time: Emily Dickinson in the Nineteenth Century* (Amherst: University of Massachusetts Press, 2012), 49–81.
10. Sandra Runzo, *"Theatricals of Day": Emily Dickinson and Nineteenth-Century American Popular Culture* (Amherst: University of Massachusetts Press, 2019).
11. The four songs are "The Old Granite State," "The Little Maid," "The Lament of the Irish Emigrant," and "There's a Good Time Coming." The Dickinsons collected two other titles associated with the Hutchinsons that are not in Emily's bound music volume: "The Grave of Bonaparte" is mentioned by Emily Dickinson in *The Letters of Emily Dickinson*, ed. Thomas H. Johnson and Theodora Ward (hereafter Johnson, *Letters*), 3 vols. (Cambridge: Harvard University Press, 1958), no. 7 (Emily Dickinson to Abiah Root, 3 August 1845). Copies of the song are in the Dickinson Collection at the Jones Library, Amherst, and in the Dickinson Collection in the Houghton Library, Harvard University. The song "Oh the Merry Days When We Were Young," also associated with the Hutchinsons, is mentioned by Emily's sister

Lavinia in a letter to their brother Austin. See Millicent Todd Bingham, *Emily Dickinson's Home: Letters of Edward Dickinson and His Family* (New York: Harper and Brothers Publishers, 1955), 211–12. A copy of the sheet music to this song has not heretofore been located in any Dickinson-related collection, although it is a staple in most large library collections. For a comprehensive listing of Hutchinson Family repertoire, see *The Granite Songster: Comprising the Songs Performed by the Hutchinson Family Without the Music* (Boston: A. B. Hutchinson; New York: Charles Holt Jr., 1847), The New York Public Library for the Performing Arts (hereafter NYPL/LPA), call number Mus. Res. *MPW-Amer. The words to the song "Oh the Merry Days When We Were Young" can be found in *Book of Words of the Hutchinson Family* (New York: Baker, Godwin & Co., printers, 1853), 61.

12. Runzo, *"Theatricals of Day,"* 63–65, 94–100.
13. Martha Dickinson Bianchi, *The Life and Letters of Emily Dickinson* (Boston: Houghton Mifflin, 1924), 64.
14. Genevieve Taggard, *The Life and Mind of Emily Dickinson* (New York: Alfred A. Knopf, 1930), 45.
15. George Frisbie Whicher, *This Was a Poet: A Critical Biography of Emily Dickinson* (New York: Charles Scribner's Sons, 1939), 56.
16. Whicher's observation about Dickinson's study of philosophy adopts a similar tone: "The 'Mental Philosophy' recited by a girl of fifteen from [Thomas] Upham's [1842] manual cannot be taken seriously" (*This Was a Poet*, 47). Dickinson scholar Jed Deppman argues that Whicher's "main assumptions seem to have been that philosophy was too difficult, too esoteric, and simply not intended for students that young or that female." See Jed Deppman, "Dickinson and Philosophy," in *Trying to Think with Emily Dickinson* (Amherst: University of Massachusetts Press, 2008), 79.
17. Charles Hamm, *Yesterdays: Popular Song in America* (New York: W. W. Norton, 1979), 199–200.
18. Whicher, *This Was a Poet*, 56. In a conversation with the violinist Ole Bull, singer Henry Russell observed that "until the beginning of this [nineteenth] century, musical culture was a thing practically unknown outside such towns as New York, Philadelphia, and Boston. It is only now the denizens of the smaller towns are beginning to take an interest in things musical." Henry Russell, *Cheer Boys Cheer: Memories of Men and Music* (London: John Macqueen, 1895), 146–47.
19. Whicher, *This Was a Poet*, 56.
20. Jennifer Lynn Stoever, *The Sonic Color Line: Race and the Cultural Politics of Listening* (New York: New York University Press, 2016), 78. In chapter 2 of her book, Stoever discusses "how the collusive relationship between sight and sound deliberately interweaves the racial gaze and its aural counterpart, the listening ear." This relationship is explored in chapter 4 of this book in the discussion of Dickinson's reaction to the Swedish soprano Jenny Lind.
21. Bingham, *Emily Dickinson's Home*, 153.
22. Louise Winn Reglin, "Music in the Life and Poetry of Emily Dickinson" (master's thesis, North Texas State University, 1971), 125–26. Reglin cites 118 different musical terms Dickinson used in her poems.
23. Richard Benson Sewall, *The Life of Emily Dickinson* (New York: Farrar, Straus and Giroux, 1974), 407–9.
24. St. Armand, *Emily Dickinson and Her Culture*, 112.
25. Carolyn Lindley Cooley, *The Music of Emily Dickinson's Poems and Letters: A Study of Imagery and Form* (London: McFarland and Company, 2003), 20.
26. "MUSIC (list of all pieces in D House)," Millicent Todd Bingham Papers, Emily Dickinson, Source Documents and Research Notes, Jay Leyda notes, call number MS496D/Series V/box 104/folder 622, Manuscripts and Archives, Yale University.
27. Carlton Lowenberg, *Musicians Wrestle Everywhere: Emily Dickinson and Music* (Berkeley: Fallen Leaf Press, 1992).
28. George Boziwick, "Dickinson and the Composer," panel discussion on Dickinson and the performing arts, "'To another Sea': Dickinson, Environment, and the West," the Emily Dickinson International Society international conference, 9–11 August 2019, Asilomar, CA. See also Georgiana Strickland, *Emily Dickinson in Song: A Discography, 1925–2019*, available through the Humanities Commons website, https://hcommons.org/deposits/item/hc:28401/.
29. Lowenberg lists "a selection of the some hundreds of books and periodicals that are

documented in the Houghton Library Handlist and Daniel Lombardo's *Tales of Amherst*." Lowenberg, *Musicians Wrestle Everywhere*, xv.
30. The Red Skies Music Ensemble Emily Dickinson programs presented by Trudy Williams (Artistic Director/Curator) and George Boziwick (Curator/Music Director). "Emily and Lavinia: Music Making and Dickinson's Eden," performed at the Amherst Women's Club, Amherst, MA, 2018; "Dickinson's Musical Eden. Emily and Lavinia: Music Making at the Homestead," performed at the Emily Dickinson International Society annual meeting, Amherst, 2017; "'Musicians Wrestle Everywhere — ': Music, Nature, Hymnody, and the Poetic Conversion of Emily Dickinson," performed at the Institute for Sacred Music, Yale University, New Haven, 2017; "Emily Dickinson in Her Elements: Accomplished Musician, Emerging Poet," performed at the Emily Dickinson International Society annual meeting, Amherst, 2015; "'My Wars are laid away in Books — ,' Emily Dickinson's Music Book: A Prelude to the Civil War," performed at the American Repertory Theater's Oberon Theater, Cambridge, MA, sponsored by the Houghton Library and the Loeb Music Library, Harvard University, 2015; "'My Business is to Sing': Emily Dickinson, Musician and Poet," performed at NYPL/LPA, 2015; "The Musical Parlor of Emily Dickinson," performed at the First Congregational Church, Amherst, sponsored by the Emily Dickinson Museum, 2013; "The Musical Parlor of Emily Dickinson," performed at NYPL/LPA, 2012. Additional information and documentation on these programs can be accessed at TheRedSkiesMusicEnsemble.com.
31. George Boziwick, "Emily Dickinson's Music Book: A Performative Exploration," *Emily Dickinson Journal* 25, no. 1 (2016): 83–105; George Boziwick, "'*My* Business is to Sing: Emily Dickinson's Musical Borrowings," *Journal of the Society for American Music* 8, no. 2 (2014): 130–66. Other papers, presentations, and blog posts on Dickinson and her music book by George Boziwick include "'I wish I were somebody else': Emily Dickinson's Musical Longings," paper delivered at the Modern Language Association convention, 2021; "'*My* Business is to Sing': Emily Dickinson, Musician and Poet," New York Public Library blog post, 9 December 2014; "'I wish I were somebody else': Emily Dickinson's Musical Longings," paper delivered at the Society for American Music conference, Lancaster, PA, 2014; "Finding a Life at the New York Public Library: Emily Dickinson the Avid Music Collector," New York Public Library blog post, 10 December 2013; "Emily Dickinson's Music Book," blog post written for the Houghton Library on the occasion of the digitization of Dickinson's bound volume of sheet music, 5 September 2013; "The Musical Parlor of Emily Dickinson," paper delivered at the International Association of Music Libraries conference, Vienna, 2013.
32. *The Complete Poems of Emily Dickinson*, ed. Ralph W. Franklin (Cambridge: Harvard University Press, 1999), no. 519, "This is my letter to the World" (1863).
33. Petra Meyer-Frazier, "American Women's Roles in Domestic Music Making as Revealed in Parlor Song Collections: 1820–1870" (PhD diss., University of Colorado, 1999); Petra Meyer-Frazier, *Bound Music, Unbound Women: The Search for an Identity in the Nineteenth Century*, Monographs and Bibliographies in American Music (Missoula, MT: College Music Society, 2015); Candace Bailey, *Music and the Southern Belle: From Accomplished Lady to Confederate Composer* (Carbondale: Southern Illinois University Press, 2010). See also *Emily's Songbook: Music in 1850s Albany*, ed. Mark Slobin et al., Recent Researches in the Oral Tradition of Music, no. 9 (Middletown, WI: A-R Editions, 2012). This publication explores and reproduces the bound music volume of Emily McKissick of Albany, New York.
34. In 2015 the eighteen bound music books belonging to Jane Austen and her family were digitized as part of the University of Southampton's digital library project. See "The Austen Family Music Books," https://archive.org/details/austenfamilymusicbooks.
35. "Bound for Glory: Binder's Volumes in a 21st Century Reading," panel presented at the Music Library Association annual meeting, Portland, OR, 1 February 2018. Presenters included musicologist Candace Bailey (North Carolina Central University), whose topic was binder's volumes as commonplace books. See also Candace Bailey, "Binder's Volumes as Commonplace Books: The Transmission of Cultural Codes in the Antebellum South," *Journal of the Society for American Music* 10, no. 4 (November 2016): 446–69.
36. Meyer-Frazier, "American Women's Roles in Domestic Music Making," 5–6. Bound music volumes surveyed by Meyer-Frazier included those housed at the University of Colorado Boulder; the University of North Carolina, Chapel Hill; the University of Tennessee at Knoxville; and the private collection of Dr. Karl Kroeger. See also Appendix A in Meyer-Frazier's dissertation.

37. See the reproduction of the advertisement in Jay Leyda, *The Years and Hours of Emily Dickinson*, 2 vols. (New Haven: Yale University Press, 1960), 1:207.
38. Lavinia Dickinson to Austin Dickinson, 10 October 1852, Emily Dickinson Collection (1840–2005), call number MA.00167, ser. 1, Poems and Letters, box 7, folder 39, letter 592g, Amherst College Archives and Special Collections, Amherst College Library. See also Bingham, *Emily Dickinson's Home*, 237.
39. John Carter, *ABC for Book Collectors*, 6th ed., with corrections and additions by Nicholas Barker (London: Granada Publishing 1982), 77. See the use of the term "composite volume" in the entry under "Disbound." This term has been adopted by CILIP, the Chartered Institute of Library and Information Professionals. My thanks to Robert Kosovsky, librarian, Rare Books and Manuscripts, Music & Recorded Sound Division, NYPL/LPA.
40. Robert Kosovsky, "Binder's [?] Volumes," paper presented at the Music Library Association annual meeting, Portland, OR, 1 February 2018.
41. Detailed catalog record of Dickinson's bound volume of sheet music in the Houghton Library, Harvard University, Emily E. Dickinson volume of American piano and vocal music, ca. 1823–1851, https://hollis.harvard.edu/primo-explore/fulldisplay?context=L&vid=HVD2&search_scope=everything&tab=everything&lang=en_US&docid=01HVD_ALMA212102865430003941.
42. The three minstrel songs are "Who's That Knocking at the Door," "Old Dan Tucker," and "The Jolly Raftsman." In addition, in the quickstep section of Dickinson's book, the "Lucy Neal Quick Step" is an instrumental arrangement of the minstrel tunes "Lucy Neal," "Dandy Jim," and "Lovely Fan" (a.k.a. "Buffalo Gals"). Situated near the minstrel songs at the back of the book is a vocal quartet arrangement of the song "Oh Give Me a Home If in Foreign Land." Although not considered a song of the minstrel stage, it was associated with and performed by the Harmoneon Family, later called the Harmoneons, a blackface minstrel troupe. Other music Dickinson collected that was also heard on the minstrel stage includes "Fishers Hornpipe," "Durangs Hornpipe," and "The Blue Juniata" (a quickstep arrangement). See Sandra Runzo, "Popular Culture," in *Emily Dickinson in Context*, ed. Eliza Richards (New York: Cambridge University Press, 2013), 219.
43. See *Catalogue of Music and Musical Works: Instrumental music no. 2* (Boston: Oliver Ditson, 115 Washington Street, 1844–1857), broadsheet held by the American Antiquarian Society, call number BDSDS 1844 F.
44. Julius Mattfeld, *Variety Music Cavalcade, 1620–1969: A Chronology of Vocal and Instrumental Music Popular in the United States*, 3rd ed. (Englewood Cliffs, NJ: Prentice Hall, 1971), 63–67. The titles listed by Mattfeld that are represented in Dickinson's bound volume are "I Dreamt I Dwelt in Marble Halls" (an instrumental arrangement from the opera *The Bohemian Girl*), "The Lament of the Irish Emigrant," "Old Dan Tucker," "The Old Granite State," "Then You'll Remember Me" (an instrumental arrangement from *The Bohemian Girl*), "The Blue Juniata" (a quickstep arrangement), and "Lucy Neale" (a quickstep arrangement). The songs "The Grave of Bonaparte" and "Long, Long Ago," also listed in Mattfeld, are not in Dickinson's bound volume but are mentioned in her correspondence. See Johnson, *Letters*, no. 7 (Emily Dickinson to Abiah Root, 3 August 1845) and no. 13 (Emily Dickinson to Abiah Root, 8 September 1846).
45. These pedagogues include Henri Bertini (1798–1876), Johann Friedrich Franz Burgmüller (1806–1874), Jacques Claude Adolphe Miné (1796–1854), Carl Czerny (1791–1857), Franz Hünten (1793–1878), Thomas Valentine (1790–1878), and the Americans William Cumming Peters (1805–1866) and Edward Little White (1809–1851).
46. "Here seems indeed to be a bit of Eden." See Johnson, *Letters*, no. 59 (Emily Dickinson to Austin Dickinson, 25 October 1851).
47. Johnson, *Letters*, no. 46 (Emily Dickinson to Austin Dickinson, 6 July 1851).
48. James Parakilas, "A History of Lessons and Practicing," in *Piano Roles: Three Hundred Years of Life with the Piano*, ed. James Parakilas (New Haven: Yale University Press, 1999), 150.
49. Johnson, *Letters*, no. 71 (Emily Dickinson to Austin Dickinson, 28 January 1852).
50. Alfred Habegger, *My Wars Are Laid Away in Books: The Life of Emily Dickinson* (New York: Random House, 2001), 373; MacGregor Jenkins, *Emily Dickinson, Friend and Neighbor* (Boston: Little, Brown, 1930), 36.
51. Gertrude Graves, "A Cousin's Memories of Emily Dickinson," *Boston Globe*, 12 January 1930 (excerpt), reprinted in *Dickinson in Her Own Time: A Biographical Chronicle of Her Life, Drawn from*

Recollections, Interviews, and Memoirs by Family, Friends, and Associates, ed. Jane Donahue Eberwein, Stephanie Farrar, and Cristanne Miller (Iowa City: University of Iowa Press, 2015), 185.
52. Johnson, *Letters*, no. 261 (Emily Dickinson to Thomas Wentworth Higginson, 25 April 1862).
53. Franklin, *The Complete Poems*, no. 378, "Better — than Music!" (1862).
54. "Hymnic relationships" refers to the multiple elements of Dickinson's poems that make them "performative," in that they contain and convey identifiable actionable characteristics of hymns, such as rhythms and meter, language, and melody.
55. This line is "Because I see — New Englandly — " from Dickinson's poem "The Robin's my Criterion for Tune — " in Franklin, *The Complete Poems*, no. 256 (1861).
56. Van Wyck Brooks, *The Flowering of New England, 1815–1865* (New York: E. P. Dutton, 1936).
57. "Musicians wrestle everywhere — / All day — among the crowded air / I hear the silver strife — ." Franklin, *The Complete Poems*, no. 229 (1861).
58. Lyndall Gordon, *Lives Like Loaded Guns: Emily Dickinson and Her Family Feuds* (New York: Penguin Books, 2010), 9.
59. Franklin, *The Complete Poems*, no. 466, "I dwell in Possibility — " (1862).
60. "Very early in the education of an archivist, one learns something counterintuitive: the theory and practice of archives are not about saving records as much as they are about acknowledging and managing loss." Tom Hyry, "Convergence or Collision? Archival Appraisal and the Expanded Role of Special Collections in the Research Library," paper delivered at the Transformation of Academic Library Collecting: A Symposium Inspired by Dan C. Hazen, 21 October 2016, Harvard University, https://projects.iq.harvard.edu/files/hazen/files/convergence_or_collision_hyry.pdf.

Chapter 1: Childhood

1. Richard Benson Sewall, *The Life of Emily Dickinson* (New York: Farrar, Straus and Giroux, 1974), xvii.
2. Alfred Habegger, *My Wars Are Laid Away in Books: The Life of Emily Dickinson* (New York: Random House, 2001), 69, 83.
3. This is how Austin described the West Street house to his schoolmate Joseph Lyman. See Sewall, *Life of Emily Dickinson*, 322.
4. *The Letters of Emily Dickinson*, ed. Thomas H. Johnson and Theodora Ward (hereafter Johnson, *Letters*), 3 vols. (Cambridge: Harvard University Press, 1958), no. 42 (Emily Dickinson to Austin Dickinson, 8 June 1851). The hymn reference is from "Jerusalem, my happy home!" The line reads, "Where congregations ne'er break up, / And Sabbaths have no end." Johnson and Ward cite the William Burkitt version of 1693, when the word "congregations" was first introduced at the end of the second verse. For a citation from a hymnbook owned by the Dickinsons, see Lowell Mason and David Greene, *Church Psalmody: A Collection of Psalms and Hymns, Adapted to Public Worship. Selected from Dr. Watts and Other Authors* (Boston: Perkins and Marvin, 1831), 528, no. 640.
5. Johnson, *Letters*, no. 4. (Emily Dickinson to Austin Dickinson, autumn 1844). Austin attended Williston Seminary during the spring 1842 term, and returned for the 1844–45 school year. See Sewall, *Life of Emily Dickinson*, 98. This letter has been re-dated to 14 October. See Cristanne Miller, "Emily Dickinson's Letters: A Preview," *Emily Dickinson Journal* 30, no. 1 (2021): 29.
6. Edward Wilton Carpenter and Charles Frederick Morehouse, *The History of the Town of Amherst, Massachusetts, 1731–1896* (Amherst: Press of Carpenter and Morehouse, 1896), 214.
7. *Exercises at the Semi-centennial of Amherst College, July 12, 1871* (Springfield, MA: Samuel Bowles and Company, Printers, 1871), 44.
8. Susan Huntington Dickinson, "The Annals of The Evergreens, 1872–1892," unpublished typescript in the Dickinson Collection, Jones Library, Amherst, 17–18. See also Jane Donahue Eberwein, "'Is Immortality True?': Salvaging Faith in an Age of Upheavals," in *A Historical Guide to Emily Dickinson*, ed. Vivian Pollack (New York: Oxford University Press, 2004), 70–71.
9. Christopher Small, *Musicking: The Meanings of Performing and Listening* (Hanover: University Press of New England, 1998), 40.
10. Johnson, *Letters*, no. 5 (Emily Dickinson to Abiah Root, 23 February 1845). See also Ralph

W. Franklin, "Emily Dickinson to Abiah Root: Ten Reconstructed Letters," *Emily Dickinson Journal* 4, no. 1 (Spring 1995): 8–9. The deletions were made by Abiah Root Strong prior to the letter's first publication in 1894. All quotations adhere to Dickinson's original spelling, punctuation, and capitalization.

11. For a listing of the music books and books on music in the Dickinson library, see Carlton Lowenberg, *Musicians Wrestle Everywhere: Emily Dickinson and Music* (Berkeley: Fallen Leaf Press, 1992), 125–28. For a discussion of Watts's hymns in the Pioneer Valley, see Martha Winburn England, "Emily Dickinson and Isaac Watts: Puritan Hymnodists," *New York Public Library Bulletin* 69, no. 2 (2 February 1965): 83–116.
12. Elizabeth Phillips, *Emily Dickinson: Personae and Performance* (University Park: Pennsylvania State University Press, 1988), 10.
13. Lavinia Norcross (1812–1860), letters to Emily Norcross Dickinson (1804–1882), [1832]–33, Dickinson family papers, call number MS Am 1118.95 (196), Houghton Library, Harvard University,https://iiif.lib.harvard.edu/manifests/view/drs:46906955$7i.
14. Carol Damon Andrews, "Thinking Musically, Writing Expectantly: New Biographical Information about Emily Dickinson," *New England Quarterly* 81, no. 2 (June 2008): 331. Thanks to Dickinson scholar Georgiana Strickland through her contact with Christopher Benfey for bringing this to my attention. To situate the time frame of Dickinson's first piano lessons with that of her fellow student Fanny Sellon, see the letter from Emily Fowler to Mr. and Mrs. J. W. Hand, 16 February 1840, in Jay Leyda, *The Years and Hours of Emily Dickinson*, vol. 1 (New Haven: Yale University Press, 1960), 59: "Death is all around us and yet we have been spared—. . . Fanny Sellon one of my young companions is to be buried day after tomorrow—."
15. Andrews, "Thinking Musically," 331.
16. Sewall, *Life of Emily Dickinson*, xviii.
17. Johnson, *Letters*, no. 5 (Emily Dickinson to Abiah Root, 23 February 1845).
18. Frederick Tuckerman, *Amherst Academy: A New England School of the Past* (Amherst: Printed for the Trustees, 1929), 104.
19. Johnson, *Letters*, no. 7 (Emily Dickinson to Abiah Root, 3 August 1845).
20. Franklin, "Emily Dickinson to Abiah Root: Ten Reconstructed Letters," 10.
21. Johnson, *Letters*, no. 7 (Emily Dickinson to Abiah Root, 3 August 1845).
22. Sewall, *Life of Emily Dickinson*,326; *"real life,"* see also Johnson, *Letters*, no. 65 (Emily Dickinson to Austin Dickinson, 15 December 1851).
23. Edward Dickinson to Emily Dickinson, 4 June 1844, quoted in Leyda, *The Years and Hours of Emily Dickinson*, 1:86–87. On 29 April 1844, the death of Emily's friend Sophia Holland, age fifteen, left Emily in a "fixed melancholy." See Johnson, *Letters*, no. 11 (Emily Dickinson to Abiah Root, 28 March 1846). Her parents hoped that a stay in Boston would "be a benefit to [her] to be away from home a little while." Lavinia Norcross Dickinson papers (1839–1898), MS AM 1118.95, box 9, Houghton Library, Harvard University, quoted in Leyda, *The Years and Hours of Emily Dickinson*, 1:86.
24. See Katherine Preston, "Music in the McKissick Parlor," in *Emily's Songbook: Music in 1850s Albany*, ed. Mark Slobin et al., Recent Researches in the Oral Tradition of Music, no. 9 (Middletown, WI: A-R Editions, 2012), 14.
25. Nicholas E. Tawa, *Sweet Songs for Gentle Americans: The Parlor Song in America, 1790–1860* (Bowling Green, OH: Bowling Green Popular Press, 1980), 44, 48.
26. Johnson, *Letters*, no. 7 (Emily Dickinson to Abiah Root, 3 August 1845). Emily's first piano was a square piano, which was favored in American parlors. Despite the fact that "Boston was the liveliest American center for the development of new piano-making ideas before the middle of the [nineteenth] century, the upright piano did not become the standard in the United States for a long time. . . . [I]t was the square shape that remained Americans' overwhelming preference for nearly three generations." See Arthur Loesser, *Men, Women & Pianos: A Social History* (New York: Simon and Schuster, 1954), 462. Ann Elizabeth Vaill Selby (b. 1823), a Norcross family relative from Emily's grandfather Joel Norcross's second marriage, lived with the Dickinsons in the summer of 1845 in their home on West Street. She was designated an "honorary Aunt." See Habegger, *My Wars Are Laid Away in Books*, 129.
27. Just as in her other subjects, Dickinson was clearly engaged with the cumulative challenge of improving her musical mind, as was expected in the intense "pedagogical culture" in which she was raised. See Jed Deppman, *Trying to Think with Emily Dickinson* (Amherst: University of Massachusetts Press, 2008), 53–56.

28. See *Catalogue of Music and Musical Works: Instrumental music no. 2* (Boston: Oliver Ditson, 115 Washington Street, 1844–1857), broadsheet held by the American Antiquarian Society, call number BDSD 1844 F.
29. Chris Goertzen, *George P. Knauff's Virginia Reels and the History of American Fiddling* (Jackson: University Press of Mississippi, 2017), 170. According to Goertzen, this method of using fiddle tunes as early pedagogical aids is still practiced today by violin students of the Suzuki and O'Connor methods.
30. Johnson, *Letters*, no. 7 (Emily Dickinson to Abiah Root, 3 August 1845). Lyman Heath, "The Grave of Bonaparte," words by Henry S. Washburn (Boston: Oliver Ditson, 1843); John Holloway, "Wood Up (Boston: C. Bradlee, 1834); F. L. Raymond, "The Lancer's Quick Step" (Boston: H. Prentiss, n.d.). "Maiden Weep No More" is not easily located. It was, however, arranged for four voices and included in Lowell Mason and George J. Webb's compilation *The Vocalist: Consisting of Short and Easy Glees, or Songs in parts: Arranged for Soprano, Alto, Tenor, and Bass Voices* (Boston: Wilkins, Carter, 1844), 14. This was one of the required music books at Mount Holyoke. See Carlton Lowenberg, *Emily Dickinson's Textbooks* (Lafayette, CA: C. Lowenberg, 1986), 72. The first three of these individual pieces of sheet music (not in the music book) are part of the Dickinson Collection in the Houghton Library at Harvard University. See Lowenberg, *Musicians Wrestle Everywhere*, 126–27. A second copy of "The Lancer's Quick Step" is in the Dickinson Collection at the Jones Library in Amherst.

Chapter 2: School Days

1. Polly Longsworth, *The World of Emily Dickinson: A Visual Biography* (New York: W. W. Norton, 1990), 23; Richard Benson Sewall, *The Life of Emily Dickinson* (New York: Farrar, Straus and Giroux, 1974), 337.
2. Sewall, *Life of Emily Dickinson*, 337.
3. Frederick Tuckerman, *Amherst Academy: A New England School of the Past* (Amherst: Printed for the Trustees, 1929), 104.
4. Quoted in Tuckerman, *Amherst Academy*, 114–15. The exhibition took place on Tuesday, 10 August 1847.
5. Carlton Lowenberg, *Emily Dickinson's Textbooks* (Lafayette, CA: C. Lowenberg, 1986), 57.
6. Domhnall Mitchell, "Amherst," in *Emily Dickinson in Context*, ed. Eliza Richards (New York: Cambridge University Press, 2013), 13–14.
7. James R. Guthrie, *Emily Dickinson's Vision: Illness and Identity in Her Poetry* (Gainesville: University Press of Florida, 1998), 54–55. For Dickinson's poetic reference to her "Scientist of Faith," see *The Complete Poems of Emily Dickinson*, ed. Ralph W. Franklin (Cambridge: Harvard University Press, 1999), no. 1261, "The Lilac is an ancient shrub" (1872).
8. *The Letters of Emily Dickinson*, ed. Thomas H. Johnson and Theodora Ward (hereafter Johnson, *Letters*), 3 vols. (Cambridge: Harvard University Press, 1958), no. 750 (Emily Dickinson to Otis P. Lord, 30 April 1882).
9. Sewall, *Life of Emily Dickinson*, xvii.
10. Sewall, *Life of Emily Dickinson*, 335.
11. Sewall, *Life of Emily Dickinson*, 336.
12. Johnson, *Letters*, no. 261 (Emily Dickinson to Thomas Wentworth Higginson, 25 April 1862). For information on Edward Dickinson's education, see Alfred Habegger, *My Wars Are Laid Away in Books: The Life of Emily Dickinson* (New York: Random House, 2001), 45–50.
13. In January 1846 Dickinson wrote to Abiah Root explaining that she had been reviewing the course requirements of Mount Holyoke's first-year "junior class" so that she would be prepared to enter the second-year "middle class" of the institution's three-year curriculum. Her preparations paid off. When she entered Mount Holyoke in the fall of 1847, she was allowed to take a six-week-long review of the courses offered at the junior level, after which she was admitted to the middle class. See Ralph W. Franklin, "Emily Dickinson to Abiah Root: Ten Reconstructed Letters," *Emily Dickinson Journal* 4, no. 1 (Spring 1995): 4, 20–21; Habegger, *My Wars Are Laid Away in Books*, 195. See also the *Eleventh Annual Catalog of the Mount Holyoke Female Seminary, 1847–48* (Amherst: Press of J. S. & C. Adams, 1848), 6, Mount Holyoke College Archives and Special Collections, identifier rg10s01–1847. The firm of J. S. & C. Adams printed the catalogs for

Mount Holyoke, Amherst College, and the short-lived Amherst Female Seminary. The firm also printed Amherst College lecture materials such as those of Nathan Welby Fiske, father of author Helen Fiske Hunt Jackson, Dickinson's childhood friend. The Adams printing firm also published Edward Hitchcock's *Religious Lectures on Peculiar Phenomena in the Four Seasons* (1850). The Adams Company bookstore was an intellectual gathering place in Amherst. See Sewall, *Life of Emily Dickinson*, 344.

14. Margaret A. Nash, *Women's Education in the United States, 1780–1840* (New York: Palgrave Macmillan, 2005), 36.
15. Nash, *Women's Education in the United States*, 10.
16. Nash, *Women's Education in the United States*, 61, 109.
17. Fowler's starting date of teaching at the Cherry Valley Female Academy was likely 1842. See "Musical Progress," unsigned column in *Musical World and Times* 9, no. 14 (5 August 1854): 161, in *Music in the USA: A Documentary Companion*, ed. Judith Tick with Paul Beaudoin (New York: Oxford University Press, 2008), 156–57. Fowler's "reputational glow" is substantiated in this statement from an 1854 Cherry Valley catalog: "Optional Course. Department of Music. This department is under the charge of a gentleman who combines with a liberal education, a thorough acquaintance with the science of Music in all its branches. As an artist, he stands at the head of his profession, and his compositions have given him a wide spread popularity as an author. Possessing these attainments, together with a rare facility for imparting instruction, it is not strange that he should meet with unparalled [*sic*] success as a teacher." *Catalog of the Officers and Pupils of the Cherry Valley Female Academy for 1854, Cherry Valley, N.Y., 1854* (Kneeland, Printer, 57 Ann Street New York), 17. New York Public Library, General Research Division (hereafter NYPL/GRD), call number STGR.
18. John Sawyer, *History of Cherry Valley from 1740 to 1898* (Cherry Valley, NY: Gazette Print, 1898), 114–15.
19. Nash, *Women's Education in the United States*, 38; J[ohn] H[omer] French (1824–1888), *Gazetteer of the State of New York* (Syracuse: R. Pearsall Smith, 1860), 131; repr., Baltimore: Genealogical Publishing Co., [1995]).
20. Sawyer, *History of Cherry Valley*, 114–15.
21. *Catalog of the Officers and Pupils of the Cherry Valley Female Academy for 1854*, 23.
22. "Cherry Valley Female Academy," *Musical World: A Journal for "Heavenly Music's Earthly Friends* 12, no. 40, ed. Richard Storrs Willis (24 March 1855): 141. The article is quoting from the catalog of Fowler's New York publisher, William Hall and Son.
23. Vera Brodsky Lawrence, *Strong on Music: The New York Music Scene in the Days of George Templeton Strong*, vol. 1, *Resonances, 1836–1849* (Chicago: University of Chicago Press, 1988), 600.
24. Copies of this music are in the American Music Collection in the Music and Recorded Sound Division, NYPL/LPA.
25. Joel Benton, *Amenia Seminary Reunion, August 22, 1906* (New York: Broadway Publishing Co., 1907), 97, NYPL/GRD, call number AD 10–72.
26. Benton, *Amenia Seminary Reunion*, 24.
27. Newton Reed, *Early History of Amenia* (Amenia, NY: De Lacey & Wiley, Printers, 1875), 45.
28. Benton, *Amenia Seminary Reunion*, 22; Betsy Strauss (Amenia Historical Society), email correspondence with the author, 11–16 December 2018.
29. *Catalog of the Officers and Students of the Amenia Seminary, Dutchess County, New York, for the first session, including two quarters, ending April 6, 1836* (Poughkeepsie: Jackson and Schram, 1836). Amenia Seminary catalogs from the collections of the American Antiquarian Society, call number Schools Pams A560, Schools Amen (1836, 1842 and 1847); Benton, *Amenia Seminary Reunion*, 95; Betsy Strauss (Amenia Historical Society), email correspondence with the author, 11–16 December 2018.
30. Benton, *Amenia Seminary Reunion*, 47.
31. Habegger, *My Wars Are Laid Away in Books*, 266. The Utica Female Academy was chartered on 28 April 1837. Its classes were held in the United States Hotel until a building was constructed and began operation for the 1838–39 school year. See Moses Mears Bagg, *Memorial History of Utica, N.Y.: From Its Settlement to the Present Time* (Syracuse: D. Mason & Co., 1892), 464. In 1850–51, composer William Carey Wright (1825–1904), father of the architect Frank Lloyd Wright, commenced a teaching post at the Utica Female Academy, teaching piano, voice, and violin. See Paul Hendrickson, *Plagued by Fire: The Dreams and Furies of Frank Lloyd Wright* (New York: Vintage Books, 2019), 407–8.

32. Bagg, *Memorial History of Utica, N.Y.*, 147, 240.
33. Bagg, *Memorial History of Utica, N.Y.*, 94–95, 144, 584.
34. H. Wiley Hitchcock, *Music in the United States: A Historical Introduction*, 4th ed., History of Music Series (New York: Prentice Hall, 2000), 67–68.
35. For a list of music books published by Mark Haskell Newman, see Carlton Lowenberg, *Musicians Wrestle Everywhere: Emily Dickinson and Music* (Berkeley: Fallen Leaf Press, 1992), 129–31. See also Lowenberg, *Emily Dickinson's Textbooks*, 24. Newman published nine non-music books that Dickinson used during her schooling, including Edward Hitchcock's *Elementary Geology*. Thanks to Dickinson scholar Georgiana Strickland for bringing this to my attention.
36. Richard Crawford, *America's Musical Life: A History* (New York: W. W. Norton, 2001), 140–41; John Tasker Howard and George Kent Bellows, *A Short History of Music in America* (New York: Thomas Y. Crowell, 1957), 92–96.
37. Edward Hitchcock, *The Power of Christian Benevolence: Illustrated in the Life and Labors of Mary Lyon* (Northampton: Hopkins, Bridgman; Philadelphia: Thomas, Cowperthwait, 1851), 81–82.
38. Fidelia Fisk, *The Recollections of Mary Lyon with Selections from Her Instruction to the Pupils of Mount Holyoke Female Seminary* (Boston: American Tract Society, 1866), 106.
39. Jewel A. Smith, *Transforming Women's Education: Liberal Arts and Music in Female Seminaries* (Urbana: University of Illinois Press, 2019), 101–2.
40. Lowell Mason to Mary Lyon, Boston, 20 November 1832, Lowell Mason Papers, Irving S. Gilmore Music Library, Yale University, call number MSS 33, ser. 2, Correspondence, box 4, folder 62.
41. Habegger, *My Wars Are Laid Away in Books*, 28, 191; Sewall, *Life of Emily Dickinson*, 38–39.
42. Smith, *Transforming Women's Education*, 50; Habegger, *My Wars Are Laid Away in Books*, 130–31.
43. Johnson, *Letters*, no. 20 (Emily Dickinson to Abiah Root, 17 January 1848); Sewall, *Life of Emily Dickinson*, 194.
44. Mount Holyoke College Archives and Special Collections, Mount Holyoke journal letters and notebooks, letter 14 (September 1847–3 August 1848), entry for 26 April 1848, 70–71, identifier rg22-s01-b01-i013.
45. Amelia D. Jones, "Memorabilia," 86–88ff., Mount Holyoke College Archive, published in "Sunny Memories of Holyoke Life," *Mount Holyoke* 12, no. 6 (February 1903): 288.
46. Johnson, *Letters*, no. 18 (Emily Dickinson to Abiah Root, South Hadley, 6 November 1847).
47. George Frisbie Whicher, *This Was a Poet: A Critical Biography of Emily Dickinson* (New York: Charles Scribner's Sons, 1939), 67.
48. Smith, *Transforming Women's Education*, 101–2.
49. Johnson, *Letters*, no. 18 (Emily Dickinson to Abiah Root, 6 November 1847).
50. Mount Holyoke College Collections, Archives and Special Collections, Mount Holyoke journal letters and notebooks, letter 13 (30 September 1846–6 August 1847), 2, identifier rg22-s01-b01-i012. In the 3 October entry Susan Tolman wrote: "To day the names of those were taken who are professed of religion & those who are not. I am sorry to say that more than ninety almost half of our family are among that class who have no hope." In Dickinson's year, the journal entry for 11 October reads: "[Miss Lyon's] closing remarks were very solemn; there seemed to be solemnity at least, upon every one present. Some were in tears. Oh! for the spirit's influence now at the beginning of the year." Archives and Special Collections, Mount Holyoke journal letters and notebooks, letter 13 (30 September 1846–6 August 1847), 10.
51. Mrs. Sarah D. (Locke) Stow, *History of the Mount Holyoke Seminary, South Hadley, Mass., During its first half century, 1837–1887* (South Hadley: Published by the Seminary, 1887), 178.
52. Sydney R. McLean, "Emily Dickinson at Mount Holyoke," *New England Quarterly* 7, no. 1 (March 1934): 41; Mount Holyoke journal letters and notebooks, letter 15 (29 September 1847–3 August 1848), 28. According to Susan Tolman's Mount Holyoke journal entry of 24 December 1847, "There are 25 of the present Middle Class without hope."
53. Johnson, *Letters*, no. 20 (Emily Dickinson to Abiah Root, 17 January 1848).
54. Quoted in Edward Hitchcock, *The Power of Christian Benevolence*, 290–91. Beth Bradford Gilchrist, *The Life of Mary Lyon* (Boston: Houghton Mifflin, 1920). See also Smith, *Transforming Women's Education*, 130–33 for an overview of instrumental music in the female seminaries.
55. Smith, *Transforming Women's Education*, 84.
56. Smith, *Transforming Women's Education*, 117.
57. Smith, *Transforming Women's Education*, 122, 130–32.

58. Journal of William Gardiner Hammond, 1844–1849, copied from the original journals under the supervision of Juliet Hammond, vol. 2, 21 May 1847–5 June 1848, Amherst College Archives and Special Collections, Amherst College Library, call number x LD156 .H3 1928.
59. "Mount Holyoke Female Seminary," *Springfield Republican*, 1 August 1845.
60. Smith, *Transforming Women's Education*, 93.
61. Stow, *History of the Mount Holyoke Seminary*, 357.
62. On 14 October 1847, Susan Tolman wrote in the Mount Holyoke journal: "The singing was also commenced today. Miss Hawes is with us still. I am taking the general care of the choirs. One of these sings at 9.A.M., the other at 3 ¾ P.M. They sing three days in the week. All who can sing belong to one of these." Mount Holyoke College Archives and Special Collections, Mount Holyoke journal letters and notebooks, letter 14 (September 1847–3 August 1848), 10. Susan Tolman attended Mount Holyoke from 1842 to 1845, then taught at the seminary until 1848. Her last journal entry on 26 April reads, "You may be interested to know that my friend Mr. [Cyrus] Mills is designated to Batticotta, Ceylon." The writing of the journal was continued by Miss Harriet Johnson. Tolman and Mills married in September and departed for Ceylon. After returning to the United States, they co-founded what would become Mills College in Oakland, California.
63. Smith, *Transforming Women's Education*, 93.
64. Mary Lyon to Susannah Fitch, 17 September 1848. Mount Holyoke College Archives and Special Collections, Mary Lyon Correspondence, ser. A, 1818–1849, identifier ms0500-s01-ss01-b02-f08-i005. Norcross taught in Ohio for about one year. See Habegger, *My Wars Are Laid Away in Books*, 194.
65. Mount Holyoke College Annual Catalog, 1847–48, Mount Holyoke College Archives and Special Collections, catalogs, registers, and directories, https://compass.fivecolleges.edu/object/mtholyoke%3A46275.
66. Music in the Dickinson library at Harvard includes Watts's *Psalms and Hymns*, Nettleton's *Village Hymns*, the *Carmina Sacra* by Lowell Mason, and *The Vocalist*.
67. Fisk, *The Recollections of Mary Lyon*, 106.
68. Nicholas E. Tawa, *Sweet Songs for Gentle Americans: The Parlor Song in America, 1790–1860* (Bowling Green, OH: Bowling Green Popular Press, 1980), 57.
69. Charles Hamm, *Music in the New World* (New York: W. W. Norton, 1983), 169.
70. George James Webb and Lowell Mason, *The Odeon: A Collection of Secular Music Arranged and Harmonized for Four Voices Designed for Adult Music Schools and for Social Music Parties* (Boston: Wilkins, Carter, 1841).
71. Smith, *Transforming Women's Education*, 153.
72. George Kingsley, *The Social Choir* (Boston: Crocker & Brewster, 1835), copy owned by the author.
73. G. Kiallmark and Thomas Moore, "'Araby's Daughter,' Sung with Great Applause by Mr. Williamson. Written by Thomas Moore Esq. Composed by G. Kiallmark" (Boston: Published by C. H. Keith, 67 & 69 Court St., [1843?]). In December 1849 Dickinson had read her brother's copy of Thomas Moore's epic poem *Lalla Rookh*, from which the text for "Araby's Daughter" was drawn. See Jay Leyda, *The Years and Hours of Emily Dickinson*, vol. 1 (New Haven: Yale University Press, 1960), 161.
74. Lowenberg, *Emily Dickinson's Textbooks*, 72; *The Vocalist: Consisting of Short and Easy Glees* (Boston: Wilkins, Carter and Co.,1844), NYPL/LPA, call number JMC 89–171. These long-forgotten composers include, from Saxony, Johann Wilhelm Immler (1782); the Bohemian composer and pianist Johann Joseph Rösler (1771–1812); Swiss composers Hans Georg Nägeli (1773–1836) and Johann Heinrich Tobler (1777–1838); German composers Karl Karow (1790–1863), Albert Methfessel (1785–1869), and Philipp Friedrich Silcher (1789); and Austrian composer Leonhard de Call (1767–1815).
75. These annual journal letters documenting the activities at Mount Holyoke were compiled by the seminary staff and circulated around the world to former students engaged in missionary work.
76. Mount Holyoke journal letter, 14 (September 1847–3 August 1848), 94–95.
77. Jones, "Memorabilia." Among the students who, along with Dickinson, were enrolled in the 1847–48 middle class were Amelia D. Jones and Emily W. S. Bowdoin (both of Springfield), who is the "E" referred to in Jones's "Memorabilia." Further evidence that "E." is not Dickinson is provided by the fact that both Bowdoin and Dickinson faced removal from the school because of illness at the end of the 1847–48 term. While Dickinson returned home for good, Bowdoin and Jones are both listed in the seminary catalog as members of the senior class for

the following 1848–49 term. Bowdoin (class of 1849) taught vocal music at Mount Holyoke during 1849–50. See the annual catalog for 1848–49, Mount Holyoke College, Archives and Special Collections, catalogs, registers, and directories. For a listing of the faculty, see Stow, *History of the Mount Holyoke Seminary*, 357.

78. Keith Melder, "Mask of Oppression: The Female Seminary Movement in the United States," *New York History* 55, no. 3 (July 1974): 268.
79. Johnson, *Letters*, no. 16 (Emily Dickinson to Austin Dickinson, 21 October 1847). On 3 March 1848, Susan Tolman wrote in the Mount Holyoke journal letter: "There is also a great excitement in the prospect of a speedy peace with Mexico. We know little of the political world in our little community. I sometimes think too little." Mount Holyoke journal letter 14 (September 1847–3 August 1848), 49.
80. "Letter from Mexico," *Springfield Republican*, 21 October 1847.
81. Elise Kirk, "Sheet Music Related to the United States War with Mexico (1846–1848) in the Jenkins Garrett Library, University of Texas at Arlington," *NOTES* 37, no. 1 (September 1980): 14–30. An 1850 catalog from the Boston publishing firm of Oliver Ditson lists forty-two pieces associated with Joseph W. Turner. See "Catalog of Sheet Music and Music Books Published by Oliver Ditson," American Antiquarian Society, call number Book Dealers Cats. Dits., Bib ID 40111, 130.
82. During the Mexican-American War, "the war trophy which most excited America's public imagination" was the prosthetic leg and other belongings abandoned by Santa Anna as American forces pushed toward Mexico City. Michael Scott Van Wagenen, *Remembering the Forgotten War: The Enduring Legacies of the U.S.-Mexican War* (Amherst: University of Massachusetts Press, 2012), 26. See also Robert W. Johannsen, *To the Halls of the Montezumas: The Mexican War in the American Imagination* (New York: Oxford University Press, 1985), 240.
83. William McCarty, comp., *National Songs, Ballads, and Other Patriotic Poetry* (Philadelphia: Published by William McCarty, 1846). For contrafacta on the tune "Yankee Doodle," see no. 41, "Song," and no. 61, "Uncle Sam's Song to Miss Texas." For contrafacta on the tune "Old Dan Tucker," see no. 19, "Song of the Volunteers" (with its fourteen verses), and no. 45, "A Song for the Army." For more appropriations of the song, see also NYPL/LPA, call number AM2-V Emmitt, Old Dan Tucker, tune.
84. Johnson, *Letters*, no. 20 (Emily Dickinson to Abiah Root, 17 January 1848).
85. Johnson, *Letters*, no. 14 (Emily Dickinson to Abiah Root, late autumn 1846).
86. Johnson, *Letters*, no. 9 (Emily Dickinson to Abiah Root, 12 January 1846); Johnson, *Letters*, no. 14 (Emily Dickinson to Abiah Root, late autumn 1846). Dickinson was kept out of the Amherst Academy for the winter and fall terms of 1846. Regarding Coleman's German class: "In addition to his duties as Principal [at Amherst Academy], he taught Greek and German for two years [1844–1846] in the College. German had not heretofore been a required study at Amherst. In 1846–47 it appears for the first time in the curriculum." Tuckerman, *Amherst Academy*, 108.
87. Johnson, *Letters*, no. 15 (Emily Dickinson to Abiah Root, 14 March 1847).
88. Habegger, *My Wars Are Laid Away in Books*, 262–63.
89. Barton Levi St. Armand, *Emily Dickinson and Her Culture: The Soul's Society* (New York: Cambridge University Press, 1984), 110.
90. Gilchrist, *Life of Mary Lyon*, 449.
91. Martha Ackmann, *These Fevered Days: Ten Pivotal Moments in the Making of Emily Dickinson*. (New York: W. W. Norton, 2020), 36.
92. Gilchrist, *Life of Mary Lyon*, 324.
93. "Sounds From Home" by Joseph Gung'l was a popular set of waltzes. Dickinson acquired the sheet music and included it in her bound volume. For more on Dickinson and her interest in travel, see Cristanne Miller, "Becoming a Poet in 'Turbaned Seas,'" in *Reading in Time: Emily Dickinson in the Nineteenth Century* (Amherst: University of Massachusetts Press, 2012), 118–46.

Chapter 3; The Avid Music Collector

1. Alfred Habegger, *My Wars Are Laid Away in Books: The Life of Emily Dickinson* (New York: Random House, 2001), 28.
2. Ralph W. Franklin, "Emily Dickinson to Abiah Root: Ten Reconstructed Letters," *Emily Dickinson Journal* 4, no. 1 (Spring 1995): 4. About missing home, see *The Letters of Emily Dickinson*,

ed. Thomas H. Johnson, and Theodora Ward (hereafter Johnson, *Letters*), 3 vols. (Cambridge: Harvard University Press, 1958), no. 18 (Emily Dickinson to Abiah Root, South Hadley, 6 November 1847); see also Habegger, *My Wars Are Laid Away in Books*, 182.
3. Lavinia Norcross Dickinson (1833–1899), Diary, autograph manuscript, 1 January–31 December 1851, Dickinson family papers, 1757–1934, MS Am 1118.95 (226), Houghton Library, Harvard University, https://iiif.lib.harvard.edu/manifests/view/drs:47289000$1i.
4. Richard Benson Sewall, *The Life of Emily Dickinson* (New York: Farrar, Straus and Giroux, 1974), 54.
5. Johnson, *Letters*, no. 128 (Emily Dickinson to Austin Dickinson, 19 June 1853).
6. Johnson, *Letters*, no. 42 (Emily Dickinson to Austin Dickinson, 8 June 1851).
7. Habegger, *My Wars Are Laid Away in Books*, 256.
8. Wendy Martin, "The Soul Selects Her Own Society," in *An American Triptych: Anne Bradstreet, Emily Dickinson, Adrienne Rich* (Chapel Hill: University of North Carolina Press, 1984), 89.
9. Johnson, *Letters*, no. 77 (Emily Dickinson to Susan Gilbert, ca. February 1852); Habegger, *My Wars Are Laid Away in Books*, 256, quoted in Jay Leyda, *The Years and Hours of Emily Dickinson*, 2 vols. (New Haven: Yale University Press, 1960), 1:236, and dated by Leyda to "February 22?: Sunday morning."
10. *The Complete Poems of Emily Dickinson*, ed. Ralph W. Franklin (Cambridge: Harvard University Press, 1999), no. 236, "Some keep the Sabbath going to Church — " (1861).
11. "Mother needed me & like Emily, I feared displeasing father even after he was gone." Quoted in Leyda, *The Years and Hours of Emily Dickinson*, 2:231. In 1866 Dickinson would write to Thomas Wentworth Higginson that her father was "in the habit of me." Johnson, *Letters*, no. 316 (Emily Dickinson to Thomas Wentworth Higginson, early 1866).
12. George Frisbie Whicher, *This Was a Poet: A Critical Biography of Emily Dickinson* (New York: Charles Scribner's Sons, 1939), 32–33. Construction of The Evergreens was also financed in part by Susan's brothers. See *Open Me Carefully: Emily Dickinson's Intimate Letters to Susan Huntington Dickinson*, ed. Ellen Louise Hart and Martha Nell Smith (Ashfield, MA: Paris Press, 1998), 63.
13. Vivian R. Pollack and Marianne Noble, "Emily Dickinson (1830–1886): A Brief Biography," in *A Historical Guide to Emily Dickinson*, ed. Vivian R. Pollack (New York: Oxford University Press, 2004), 33.
14. "The standard categories of published parlor songs—love ballads, operatic arias, patriotic songs, laments, comic ditties, mother songs, and hymn-like tunes—suggests clearly that publishers were targeting women; the overarching themes of nostalgia and idealization of the home and the family likewise appealed to this niche." Katherine Preston, "Music in the McKissick Parlor," in *Emily's Songbook: Music in 1850s Albany*, ed. Mark Slobin et al., Recent Researches in the Oral Tradition of Music, no. 9. (Middletown, WI: A-R Editions, 2012), 14.
15. Leyda, *The Years and Hours of Emily Dickinson*, 1:104. The last digit of the handwritten date was trimmed off, likely during the binding process.
16. Johnson, *Letters*, no. 53 (Emily Dickinson to Austin Dickinson, 1 October 1851).
17. Johnson, *Letters*, no. 198 (Emily Dickinson to Susan Gilbert Dickinson, ca. 1858). This letter contains the poem "Sleep is supposed to be" (Franklin, *The Complete Poems*, no. 35, 1858). Elizabeth Barrett Browning's poem "Aurora Leigh" (1856) had an impact on Dickinson, who cites Browning and the poem in her letters. See Johnson, *Letters*, no. 234 (Emily Dickinson to Louise and Frances Norcross, 1861?).
18. For an overview of Edward Dickinson's time in Congress, see Millicent Todd Bingham, *Emily Dickinson's Home: Letters of Edward Dickinson and His Family* (New York: Harper and Brothers Publishers, 1955), 334–38.
19. Georgiana Strickland, "Emily Dickinson's Philadelphia," *Emily Dickinson Journal* 13, no. 2 (2004): 83–85.
20. Richard Wolfe, *Early American Music Engraving and Printing: A History of Music Publishing in America from 1787 to 1825 with Commentary on Earlier and Later Practices* (Urbana: University of Illinois Press, 1980), 44–45.
21. Strickland, "Emily Dickinson's Philadelphia," 100–101.
22. Harry Dichter and Elliott Shapiro, *Handbook of Early American Sheet Music, 1768–1889* (New York: Dover Publications, 1977), 211.
23. For information on circulating music libraries see Wolfe, *Early American Music Engraving and Printing*, 227–30.

24. Sewall, *The Life of Emily Dickinson*, 447.
25. Habegger, *My Wars Are Laid Away in Books*, 330.
26. "The Affection Waltz with Brilliant Variations by Czerny" (Philadelphia: E. Ferrett & Co., 1851). From the sheet music collections of the American Antiquarian Society.
27. Douglas W. Shadle, *Orchestrating the Nation: The Nineteenth-Century American Enterprise* (New York: Oxford University Press, 2016), 61–62.
28. Shadle, *Orchestrating the Nation*, 57.
29. Irving Lowens, *Music and Musicians in Early America: Aspects of the History of Music in Early America and the History of Early American Music* (New York: W. W. Norton, 1964), 217–18. For more background on Fry and the case for American music, see Richard Crawford, *America's Musical Life: A History* (New York: W. W. Norton, 2001), 320–29. See also Shadle, *Orchestrating the Nation*, 56–68.
30. *Dwight's Journal of Music*, which was published between 1852 and 1881, elevated music criticism to a major writing form. See Ora Frishberg Saloman, "John Sullivan Dwight," in *The New Grove Dictionary of Music and Musicians*, 2nd ed., 29 vols., ed. Stanley Sadie and John Tyrell (New York: Grove, 2001), 7:814.
31. Shadle, *Orchestrating the Nation*, 67–68.
32. Vera Brodsky Lawrence, *Strong on Music: The New York Music Scene in the Days of George Templeton Strong*, vol. 1, *Resonances, 1836–1849* (Chicago: University of Chicago Press, 1988), 110; Crawford, *America's Musical Life*, 301–3.
33. Michael Broyles, *Beethoven in America* (Bloomington: Indiana University Press, 2011), 293.
34. Andrew Lamb, "Joseph Labitzky," in Sadie and Tyrell, *The New Grove Dictionary of Music and Musicians*, 14:84.
35. See Johnson, *Letters*, no. 302 (Emily Dickinson to Louise Norcross, early 1865).
36. Harry Dichter and Elliott Shapiro, *Handbook of Early American Sheet Music*, 222–23.
37. Donald W. Krummel and Stanley Sadie, *Music Printing and Publishing*, Norton/Grove Handbooks in Music (New York: W. W. Norton & Co., 1990), 363; William Osborn, *Music in Ohio* (Kent, OH: Kent State University Press, 2004), 511.
38. Richard D. Wetzel, *Oh! Sing No More That Gentle Song: The Musical Life and Times of William Cumming Peters (1805–66)* (Warren, MI: Harmonie Park Press, 2000), 543–44.
39. Ben Casseday, *The History of Louisville: From Its First Settlement till the Year 1852* (Louisville: Hull and Brother, 1852), app., 35. See also Richard D. Wetzel, "The Search for William Cumming Peters," *American Music* 1, no. 4 (Winter 1983): 27–41.
40. Krummel and Sadie, *Music Printing and Publishing*, 363–64.
41. The *Musical Times* (1849–1852) was absorbed by the *Musical World* in 1852.
42. Frank J. Metcalf, *Stories of Hymn Tunes* (New York: Abingdon Press, 1928), 43–44; Hezekiah Butterworth and Theron Brown, *The Story of the Hymns and Tunes* (New York: George H. Doran Company, 1906), 466–68.
43. For a listing of periodicals to which the Dickinsons subscribed that contained music content, see Carlton Lowenberg, *Musicians Wrestle Everywhere: Emily Dickinson and Music* (Berkeley: Fallen Leaf Press, 1992), 128.
44. Henry Augustin Beers, *Nathaniel Parker Willis* (Boston: Houghton Mifflin, 1885), 9–10, 14.
45. Beers, *Nathaniel Parker Willis*, 170, 264; Nathaniel Parker Willis, *Pencillings By the Way: Written During Some Years of Residence and Travel in Europe* (New York: C. Scribner, 1852).
46. Russell does not provide a date for the visit, but he does mention that it occurred "not very long after the publication of 'A Life on the Ocean Wave,'" one of his most popular compositions, set to a poem by Epes Sargent (ca. 1838). Henry Russell, *Cheer Boys Cheer: Memories of Men and Music* (London: John Macqueen, 1895), 136–37.
47. Nathaniel Parker Willis, *Letters from Under a Bridge* (London: G. Virtue, 1840). Today that bridge is the Talcott Street Bridge in the village of Owego. See "The Family Willis and Friend," http://www.owegopennysaver.com/PS/2015/09/25/the-family-willis-and-friend/; Beers, *Nathaniel Parker Willis*, 222–31, 276, 287, 326–27.
48. *Home Journal*, published by Morris and Willis, New York (1846–1901), continues as *Town and Country*, published by the Hearst Corporation since 1901. Copies are held by The New York Public Library, call number *ZAN 2293 (microfilm) (1847–2002).
49. George Kingsley, *The Social Choir: Designed for A Class Book, And the Social Circle*, vol. 3 (Boston: Crocker and Brewster, 1847), 62–63.
50. Habegger, *My Wars Are Laid Away in Books*, 318.

51. See Johnson, *Letters*, no. 75 (Emily Dickinson to Austin Dickinson, ca. February 1852); Marty Rhodes Figley, "'Brown Kisses' and 'Shaggy Feet': How Carlo Illuminates Dickinson for Children," *Emily Dickinson Journal* 14, no. 2 (2005): 120–27.
52. Russell, *Cheer Boys Cheer*, 175–77. See "'The New Foundland Dog.' Descriptive Ballad Sung with enthusiastic applause by Mr. H. Russell. The Words by F. W. N. Bailey, Esqr. The Music Composed by Henry Russell" (New York: Firth & Hall, 1843). The illustration shows the dog jumping ship after a baby goes overboard. A distraught woman on the upper deck points toward the water, while next to her a seaman shines a searchlight on the dog. Men on the upper and lower decks are preparing a lifeboat to be lowered. NYPL/LPA, call number AM2-V, Russell, Henry. The New Foundland Dog.
53. "Shaggy Ally": Johnson, *Letters*, no. 280 (Emily Dickinson to T. W. Higginson, February 1863); "Goblins kidnap me": Johnson, *Letters*, no. 271 (Emily Dickinson to T. W. Higginson, August 1862).
54. Sol Papadopoulos, *My Letter to the World: A Look at the Life and Work of Arguably America's Greatest Poet, Emily Dickinson* (Hurricane Films, 2017); Marta McDowell, *Emily Dickinson's Gardening Life: The Plants and Places That Inspired the Iconic Poet* (Portland, OR: Timber Press, 2019), 45–47.
55. "Cousin John [Graves] has made us an Aeolian Harp, which plays beautifully, alone, whenever there is a breeze." Johnson, *Letters*, no. 115 (Emily Dickinson to Austin Dickinson, 12 April 1853); from Dickinson's music book, "Taylor, Richard B. Æolian Waltz. Composed for the Piano Forte." The final section of this piece (Andantino) is marked "Piano & Aeolian."
56. Judith Farr, *The Gardens of Emily Dickinson* (Cambridge: Harvard University Press, 2004), 11.
57. For a list of some of the groundskeepers and others who worked for the Dickinsons, see Aife Murray, *Maid as Muse: How Servants Changed Emily Dickinson's Life and Language* (Durham: University of New Hampshire Press, 2009), 18.
58. For a description of the Dickinson grounds and gardens, see McDowell, *Emily Dickinson's Gardening Life*, 15–18.
59. "Nature's buff message—left for you in Amherst. She had not time to call." Johnson, *Letters*, no. 812 (Emily Dickinson to Mrs. Jonathan L. Jenkins, date unknown), quoted in MacGregor Jenkins, *Emily Dickinson, Friend and Neighbor* (Boston: Little, Brown, 1939), 120–21.
60. "The Tulip," in *Poems of Emily Dickinson*, 3rd ser., ed. Mabel Loomis Todd (Boston: Roberts Brothers, 1896), 102.
61. Martha Dickinson Bianchi, *Emily Dickinson Face to Face: Unpublished Letters with Notes and Reminiscences* (Boston: Houghton Mifflin, 1932), 39.
62. Johnson, *Letters*, no. 823 (Emily Dickinson to Mrs. J. Howard Sweetser, early May 1883), quoted in Farr, *The Gardens of Emily Dickinson*, 192.
63. Farr, *The Gardens of Emily Dickinson*, 11.
64. "Eden": Johnson, *Letters*, no. 59 (Emily Dickinson to Austin Dickinson, 25 October 1851); conservatory: Farr, *The Gardens of Emily Dickinson*, 4.
65. Marta McDowell, email correspondence with the author, 2 February 2019. See also McDowell, *Emily Dickinson's Gardening Life*, 206.
66. Marta McDowell, email correspondence with the author, 30 January 2019. For the visit to Mount Auburn Cemetery, see Johnson, *Letters*, no. 13 (Emily Dickinson to Abiah Root, Boston, 8 September 1846).
67. Johnson, *Letters*, no. 85 (Emily Dickinson to Susan Gilbert, 5 April 1852).
68. Johnson, *Letters*, no. 830 (Emily Dickinson to Maria Whitney, late June 1883), quoted in Farr, *The Gardens of Emily Dickinson*, 11.
69. Farr, *The Gardens of Emily Dickinson*, 295.
70. Marta McDowell, email correspondence with the author, 30 January 2019.
71. Johnson, *Letters*, no. 315 (Emily Dickinson to Mrs. J. G. Holland, early March 1866). Dickinson may have been referring to Maluku, which was part of the Spice Islands, the eastern Indonesian archipelago. It's also possible that she was punning on the homonym "aisle" in describing a specific location in her conservatory.
72. Richard Wolfe, *Secular Music in America, 1801–1825: A Bibliography*, vol. 2 (New York: The New York Public Library, 1964), nos. 6127–34. Wolfe cites fifteen editions or reissues.
73. For additional biographical information on Moran, see *Anthology of Early American Keyboard Music: 1787–1830*, ed. Bunker J. Clark (Middleton, WI: A-R Editions, 1977), x–xi; Wolfe, *Secular Music in America*, 592–93. For information on the "Swiss Waltz" and "Kinloch of Kinloch," see online Appendix B.

74. Krystyn Moon, *Yellow Face: Creating the Chinese in American Popular Music and Performance* (New Brunswick, NJ: Rutgers University Press, 2006), 22-24
75. Claire McGlinchee, *The First Decade of the Boston Museum* (Boston: Bruce Humphries, 1940), 147.
76. Comer provided music for many other Boston Museum spectacles including *The Christmas Gift, or The Golden Axe* (1843–44) and *The Enchanted Beauty, or a Dream of 100 Years* (1850). See McGlinchee, *The First Decade of the Boston Museum*, 133, 140. Comer composed and arranged music for various publications including *The Boston Musical Institute's Collection of Church Music* (1841). In 1847 he founded the Musical Fund Society in Boston. Silas Steele's *Exhibition Dialogues*, published in 1882, was recently reprinted. The cover lithography of the sheet music to *Aladdin; or, the Wonderful Lamp* is attributed to John Henry Bufford (1810–1870).
77. Olios were the middle section of the three-part minstrel show containing stump speeches, comic dialogues, and other novelties. See Eric Lott, *Love and Theft: Blackface Minstrelsy and the American Working Class* (New York: Oxford University Press, 1993), 6; Robert B. Winans, "Inside the Minstrel Show Music, 1843–1852," in *Inside the Minstrel Mask: Readings in Nineteenth-Century Blackface Minstrelsy*, ed. Annemarie Bean, James V. Hatch, and Brooks McNamara (Hanover, NH: Wesleyan University Press, 1996), 144.
78. McGlinchee, *The First Decade of the Boston Museum*, 147. Andrea Stulman Dennett, *Weird and Wonderful: The Dime Museum in America* (New York: New York University Press, 1997), 87–90.
79. See Leyda, *The Years and Hours of Emily Dickinson*, 1:86–87. Just as her father had instructed her to see "interesting places" on her earlier visit to Boston and Worcester in 1844, the same holds true for this trip regarding her visits to the State House, Bunker Hill, and the Chinese Museum.
80. Johnson, *Letters*, no. 13 (Emily Dickinson to Abiah Root, 8 September 1846). Emily was taken to the Chinese Museum by the Norcross family during the first week of her visit.
81. Amanda Porterfield, *Mary Lyon and the Mount Holyoke Missionaries* (New York: Oxford University Press, 1997), 21, 85.
82. From the *Boston Daily Atlas*, 1 September 1846: "This Large and Splendid Collection, consisting of upwards of 60 figures as large as life, more than 400 paintings by Chinese Artists, numerous models of Temples, Houses, Vessels, &c. specimens of manufactures, musical instruments, exquisite carvings, curious and splendid lanterns, &c. &c. together with occasional playing on Chinese instruments and singing by one of the Chinese attached to the Museum, is exhibiting every day from 9 A. M. till 10 P. M. Admittance 25 cents; Season tickets, $1."
83. For a detailed article on the Chinese Museum, see Ronald J. Zboray and Mary Saracino Zboray, "Between 'Crockery-Dom' and Barnum: Boston's Chinese Museum, 1845–47," *American Quarterly* 56, no. 2 (June 2004): 271–307.
84. Johnson, *Letters*, no. 13 (Emily Dickinson to Abiah Root, Boston, 8 September 1846).
85. Hiroko Uno, "Emily Dickinson's Encounter with the East: Chinese Museum in Boston," *Emily Dickinson Journal* 17, no. 1 (2008): 61.
86. *Boston Daily Atlas*, 1 September 1846.
87. Leyda, *The Years and Hours of Emily Dickinson*, 1:112.
88. Johnson, *Letters*, no. 13 (Emily Dickinson to Abiah Root, 8 September 1846). "Long, Long Ago," with words and music by Thomas Bayly (1833), was not collected by Dickinson but was widely known. The published sheet music is held by many libraries. There is a theme and variations set on "Auld Lang Syne" in the Dickinson bound music book (see online Appendix B, no. 9).

Chapter 4: The Age of the Virtuosi

1. Daniel Cavicchi, *Listening and Longing: Music Lovers in the Age of Barnum* (Middletown: Wesleyan University Press, 2011), 3.
2. See the "Entertainment" section of the local newspaper card file index at the Jones Library, Amherst.
3. The Dickinsons had multiple opportunities to hear the Dodworth band during commencement week in Amherst in 1850 and 1855, and later Patrick Gilmore's band in 1864. See the "Entertainment" section of the local newspaper card file index at the Jones Library, Amherst.
4. Ralph T. Dudgeon, *The Keyed Bugle*, 2nd ed. (Lanham, MD: Scarecrow Press, 2004), 57.

5. For background on the Amherst Cattle Show, see Millicent Todd Bingham, *Emily Dickinson's Home: Letters of Edward Dickinson and His Family* (New York: Harper and Brothers, 1955), 192.
6. Martha Dickinson Bianchi, *The Life and Letters of Emily Dickinson* (Boston: Houghton Mifflin, 1924), 40–41.
7. For an overview of the Kendall, Dodworth, and other bands, see Margaret Hindle Hazen and Robert Hazen, *The Music Men: An Illustrated History of Brass Bands in America, 1800–1920* (Washington, DC: Smithsonian Institution Press, 1987).
8. *Springfield Republican*, 10 August 1849. See also Jay Leyda, *The Years and Hours of Emily Dickinson*, 2 vols. (New Haven: Yale University Press, 1960), 1:157.
9. *Springfield Republican*, 5 January 1849. For a citation for pianist Jason Collier, see W. Robert Pierce, *Pierce Piano Atlas* (Long Beach, CA: Bob Pierce, 1982), 91.
10. *The Letters of Emily Dickinson*, ed. Thomas H. Johnson and Theodora Ward (hereafter Johnson, *Letters*), 3 vols. (Cambridge: Harvard University Press, 1958), no. 7 (Emily Dickinson to Abiah Root, 3 August 1845). See *Springfield Republican*, 13 June 1845, for a description of Eastcott's 13 June concert. On the program was Thomas Comer's choral ode "Friendship, Love and Truth," dedicated to the Independent Order of Oddfellows. The work was published in Boston by George P. Reed, 1843. See Comer's "Aladdin Quick Step" in Dickinson's music book.
11. See *Springfield Republican*, 1 April 1845, for a notice advertising Eastcott's services; for piano sales, see the *Republican* for 7 June 1845.
12. Johnson, *Letters*, no. 9 (Emily Dickinson to Abiah Root, 12 January 1846). See *Springfield Republican*, 1 July 1845, for a description of the Eastcott 2 July concert.
13. Kurt Gänzl, *Victorian Vocalists* (Abingdon, England: Routledge, 2018), 219–23.
14. Lavinia Norcross Dickinson (1833–1899), Diary, entry for 15 May 1851. Dickinson, Lavinia Norcross, 1833–1899, Diary: autograph manuscript, 1851 January 1 through December 31, Dickinson Family Papers, 1757–1934, MS Am 1118.95 (226), Houghton Library, Harvard University, https://nrs.harvard.edu/urn-3:FHCL.HOUGH:11350672. William Howland (1822–1880) was a tutor at Amherst College and worked in Edward Dickinson's law office. For a time he may have been a love interest of Lavinia's. See Leyda, *The Years and Hours of Emily Dickinson*, 1:liv. From 1848 until about 1860, Emily Dickinson often used the spelling, and was referred to as, "Emilie." See Richard Benson Sewall, *The Life of Emily Dickinson* (New York: Farrar, Straus and Giroux, 1974), 380, n. 5; Alfred Habegger, *My Wars Are Laid Away in Books: The Life of Emily Dickinson* (New York: Random House, 2001), 211–12.
15. Quoted in Leyda, *The Years and Hours of Emily Dickinson*, 1:198. George F. Hayter was a pianist and arranger. In 1848 he succeeded his father, Aaron Upjohn Hayter (1799–1873), as organist of the Handel and Haydn Society, Boston. See "The Late A. U. Hayter," *Folio* 9, no. 4 (October 1873): 101. Hayter's arrangements include a piano transcription of Rossini's *Stabat Mater*, op. 12, which was one of his signature arrangements. See Vera Brodsky Lawrence, *Strong on Music: The New York Music Scene in the Days of George Templeton Strong*, 3 vols., vol. 2, *Reverberations, 1850–1856* (Chicago: University of Chicago Press, 1995), 748. Joseph Proctor (1816–1897) was best known for his association with Louis Medina's anti-Indian melodrama *Nick of the Woods* (1839). See Jeffrey H. Richards and Heather S. Nathans, eds., *The Oxford Handbook of American Drama* (New York: Oxford University Press, 2014), 152–53. The *Hampshire and Franklin Express* was published weekly "each Friday morning in Amherst." See Bingham, *Emily Dickinson's Home*, 121.
16. A similar performance billed as a "Grand Vocal and Instrumental Concert" was presented in Hampden Hall in Springfield on Tuesday evening, 10 March 1846, as advertised in the *Springfield Republican* on 6, 9, and 10 March. The concert was repeated in Cabotville on Thursday evening, 12 March. For information about "Mr. Wood," see chapter 5.
17. Hans Nathan, *Dan Emmett and the Rise of Early Negro Minstrelsy* (Norman: University of Oklahoma Press, 1962), 112.
18. Dudgeon, *The Keyed Bugle*, 83, 87.
19. On 7 May 1856 the *Springfield Republican* advertised performances by the Spaulding and Rogers New Railroad Circus.
20. Dudgeon, *The Keyed Bugle*, 83–84.
21. Dickinson's copy of "Wood Up" was published in 1834 by Charles Bradlee; see Carlton Lowenberg, *Musicians Wrestle Everywhere: Emily Dickinson and Music* (Berkeley: Fallen Leaf Press, 1992), 126.
22. "Favorite Melodies from the Grand Chinese Spectacle of Aladdin or the Wonderful Lamp

Produced at the Boston Museum," by Thomas Comer and Silas Steele, from Dickinson's music book.
23. *Springfield Republican*, 5 and 7 August 1850.
24. Lawrence, *Strong on Music*, 2:425.
25. Lawrence, *Strong on Music*, 1:105–6.
26. Corinne Robinson Alsop Cole papers, call number MS Am 1785.8 (578), ser. 7, Pamphlets and Fliers, and Edith Kermit Carow Roosevelt, "In Memory of Corinne Roosevelt Robinson"; this collection is part of the Theodore Roosevelt Collection, Houghton Library, Harvard University: "Then the family went abroad, and when they returned came the dancing class, the happiness of many New York children of those years; and the last scene is of two little girls dancing the minuet all alone on the wide dancing floor, the only two who satisfied our difficult and critical teacher, Mr. Dodworth—one child the valiant lady of today, and before you stands the other."
27. "The Celebrated Spanish Retreat" includes an attractive lithographed cover containing a caption title, "Shoulder Arms." The illustration was the product of Benjamin W. Thayer's printing house in Boston. See the online Appendix B for information on De Anguera.
28. See Katherine K. Preston, *Opera on the Road: Traveling Opera Troupes in the United States, 1825–60* (Urbana: Illinois University Press, 1993), 253–54; and R. Allen Lott, *From Paris to Peoria: How European Piano Virtuosos Brought Classical Music to the American Heartland* (New York: Oxford University Press, 2003), 3–8. Both Preston and Lott have written extensively on the European virtuosi and ensembles who were introduced to American audiences during the first half of the nineteenth century.
29. Carleton Sprague Smith, introduction to Richard Wolfe, *Secular Music in America, 1801–1825: A Bibliography*, 3 vols. (New York: The New York Public Library, 1964), 1:x. Carleton Sprague Smith (1905–1994) was Chief of the Music Division of The New York Public Library from 1931 to 1959.
30. Lott, *From Paris to Peoria*, 25.
31. Henry Russell, *Cheer Boys Cheer: Memories of Men and Music* (London: John Macqueen, 1895), 175.
32. Nathan, *Dan Emmett*, 158; Lawrence, *Strong on Music*, 1:55; Dale Cockrell, *Demons of Disorder: Early Blackface Minstrels and Their World* (New York: Cambridge University Press, 1997), 151–53. In the 1840s and 1850s, Amherst residents could also have seen other singing groups such as the Baker Family, the Hoffer Family, the Wright Family, and the Hadley Quartette Club. See the "Entertainment" section of the local newspaper card file index at the Jones Library, Amherst.
33. On 25 June 1849 Strakosch performed in the Springfield Town Hall with Madame Casini, "the celebrated Prima Donna Assoluta, from the Grand Opera in New Orleans," who sang selections from Italian and French opera. *Springfield Republican*, 25 June 1849.
34. For instance, during Emily Dickinson's year at the Mount Holyoke Female Seminary, the Mount Holyoke journal letter reported on 4 July 1848, "Last eve. We had a serenade, from the So. Hadley band, good, though somewhat thrown in the shade by one we had a few nights since by the Baker family." Mount Holyoke Journal Letter 14, September 1847–3 August 1848, 100. The Baker Family performed at Hampden Hall in Springfield on 4 July. See the review in the *Springfield Republican*, 6 July 1848.
35. Richard Wolfe, *Secular Music in America, 1801–1825: A Bibliography*, vol. 2, 494–97. Wolfe cites forty extant published editions, reissues, and states of the "Battle of Prague." The manuscript is dated 1788 and may have been published earlier than the accepted date of 1789. The first published US edition is dated 1802. See also H. C. Colles, ed., *Grove's Dictionary of Music and Musicians*, 3rd ed., 6 vols. (New York: Macmillan, 1939), 3:46.
36. See Lott, *From Paris to Peoria*, 295–301. Herz, de Meyer, and Sigismund Thalberg all gave concerts in Springfield in the 1840s and 1850s. We do not know if the Dickinsons attended any of those concerts, although Herz's "Celebrated Henrietta Waltz" is in Emily Dickinson's music book.
37. Cavicchi, *Listening and Longing*, 74.
38. Cristanne Miller, *Reading in Time: Emily Dickinson in the Nineteenth Century* (Amherst: University of Massachusetts Press, 2012), 2.
39. Johnson, *Letters*, no. 46 (Emily Dickinson to Austin Dickinson, 6 July 1851).
40. *Springfield Republican*, 12 November 1849.
41. Ernest Albert Spångberg, *The Life of Jenny Lind, Oct. 6, 1820–Nov. 2, 1887: A Compilation from Various Sources, in Commemoration of the Centenary of Her Birth* (Minneapolis, MN, 1920),

53. According to an 1850 Oliver Ditson catalog, some of the music composed in honor of Lind's visit included the "Jenny Lind Waltz" by Bellak; Jenny Lind waltzes by Strauss; and "Jenny Lind's Welcome to America" by J. G. Jones. None of this music is in the Dickinson bound music book, although Dickinson did collect the "Coolidge Quickstep" composed by bandmaster Jones. See the Catalog of Sheet Music and Music Books Published by Oliver Ditson, American Antiquarian Society, call number Book Dealers Cats. Dits., Bib ID 40111. Jenny Lind's 1850 Castle Garden program states that "the Orchestra will consist of Sixty Performers, including the first Instrumental talent in the country." The violin section included from the Philharmonic Society of New York, concertmaster, violinist Joseph Noll and violinist George Bristow. The name Eastcott also appears in the program as a member of the violin section. See the Jenny Lind program fil NYPL/LPA call number *MBD (Uncat), Lind, folder 3.

42. *Springfield Republican*, 2 July 1851.
43. William Porter Ware and Thaddeus C. Lockhard Jr., *P. T. Barnum Presents Jenny Lind: The American Tour of the Swedish Nightingale* (New Orleans: Louisiana State University Press, 1980), 110. The ticket prices for the Northampton concert Dickinson attended were $2, $3, and $4 each. *Springfield Republican*, 4 July 1851.
44. Sewall, *Life of Emily Dickinson*, xx; Habegger, *My Wars Are Laid Away in Books*, 271. For Jenny Lind's concert schedule, see https://www.setlist.fm/setlists/jenny-lind-3bc6f068.html.
45. Johnson, *Letters*, no. 43 (Emily Dickinson to Austin Dickinson, 15 June 1851). The Boston visit was rescheduled for July, but on July 13 Emily wrote to her brother that now health reasons prevented the family from making the trip. See Johnson, *Letters*, no. 47 (Emily Dickinson to Austin Dickinson, 13 July 1851).
46. Johnson, *Letters*, no. 44 (Emily Dickinson to Austin Dickinson, 22 June 1851).
47. Johnson, *Letters*, no. 46 (Emily Dickinson to Austin Dickinson, 6 July 1851). Dickinson consistently spells Jenny Lind as "Jennie." Speculation suggests that the misspelling of Lind's name and the persistent, repetitive use of the words "how we . . ." as Dickinson almost breathlessly describes the events of the evening and the concert, offer an ironic casting of Dickinson's own "calumnious whisper" regarding her critique of Lind's voice and the heightened anticipation that accompanied Lind's performances.
48. Judith Pascoe, "'The House Encore Me So': Emily Dickinson and Jenny Lind," *Emily Dickinson Journal* 1, no. 1 (Spring 1992): 7. Distractions in church often found their way into Dickinson's letters and poems. See Johnson, *Letters*, no. 88 (Emily Dickinson to Susan Gilbert, late April 1852).
49. Lyndall Gordon, *Lives Like Loaded Guns: Emily Dickinson and Her Family's Feuds* (New York: Penguin Books, 2010), 48. Dickinson had an interest in the actress Fanny Kemble (1809–1893). Her father, however, saw Kemble differently. "Do you still attend Fanny Kemble?" Emily asked her cousin Louisa Norcross. "'Aaron Burr' and Father think her an 'animal,' but I fear zoology has few such instances." Johnson, *Letters*, no. 199 (Emily Dickinson to Louise Norcross, 4 January 1859). Dickinson probably refers to the retired Amherst College professor Aaron Warner. See Habegger, *My Wars Are Laid Away in Books*, 388.
50. Lawrence, *Strong on Music*, 2:37–38.
51. Johnson, *Letters*, no. 46 (Emily Dickinson to Austin Dickinson, 6 July 1851).
52. Wilhelm Taubert (1811–1891), music, and C. C. Rosenberg, lyrics, "Jenny Lind's Celebrated Bird Song" (New York: S. C. Jollie, 1850). The "Bird Song" was a staple at Lind's concerts, as was Jacob Niclas Ahlström's "Echo Song" (New York: Schuberth and Co., 1851). These are not in Dickinson's music book. The song "Home, Sweet Home" is in Dickinson's music book, as is an instrumental variation set on the song "The Last Rose of Summer."
53. *Springfield Republican*, 4 July 1851.
54. The bel canto style of singing had its origins in the eighteenth century and into the early nineteenth. In Dickinson's day it was generally describes as "a style of singing that emphasized beauty of tone in the delivery of highly florid music." Owen Jander, "Bel canto," rev. Ellen T. Harris, in *The New Grove Dictionary of Music and Musicians*, 2nd ed., 29 vols., ed. Stanley Sadie and John Tyrell (New York: Grove, 2001), 3:161–62.
55. Johnson, *Letters*, no. 46 (Emily Dickinson to Austin Dickinson, 6 July 1851). Dickinson's mention of the amount of money paid to Lind is evidence that Lind's market value was top of mind for the readers of local newspapers. The following day, the *Springfield Republican* (4 July 1851) observed that "the best of musical performances in this region rarely draw over 300

or 400 people at 25 cents a ticket. But in this case, the merited name and fame of one young woman crowds our most spacious edifices with thousands of admiring listeners, freely paying 2, 3 and $4 for the opportunity of drinking in her soul-inspiring music." As to the size of the crowd, the paper noted that at the Northampton concert, "sixteen to seventeen hundred pairs of eyes beamed a welcome to the Swedish songstress, and she warbled back her richest tones. . . . The receipts of the Northampton Concert vary but a trifle, if anything, from those of the Concert here [in Springfield]." Perhaps Dickinson was trying to ascertain from the numbers in the paper how much money Lind took in on the basis of ticket prices and the estimated crowd size.

56. *The Complete Poems of Emily Dickinson*, ed. Ralph W. Franklin (Cambridge: Harvard University Press, 1999), no. 1270, "The Show is not the Show" (1872).
57. Franklin, *The Complete Poems*, no. 256, "The Robin's my Criterion for Tune — " / Because I grow — where Robins do — " (1861). "The nightingale is England's bird for 'high art'": Helen Vendler, *Dickinson: Selected Poems and Commentaries* (Cambridge: Belknap Press of Harvard University Press, 2010), 86.
58. Jennifer Lynn Stoever, *The Sonic Color Line: Race and the Cultural Politics of Listening* (New York: New York University Press, 2016), 90.
59. Lawrence, *Strong on Music*, 2:60–63. "Transpositions": see "Comin thro' the Rye" in online Appendix C.
60. Over a decade had elapsed since singers such as Anna Bishop and Mr. and Mrs. Wood had helped to popularize the Italian operas of Bellini and others in the United States. See Stoever, *The Sonic Color Line*, 102.
61. Lawrence, *Strong on Music*, 2:151.
62. For a discussion of these influences on Dickinson, see Aífe Murray, *Maid as Muse: How Servants Changed Emily Dickinson's Life and Language* (Durham: University of New Hampshire Press, 2009), 82, 120–28. On 7 June 1851, Austin left for Boston. The next day Emily wrote to him using a quote from the Scotch-Irish song "Comin' thro' the Rye." Although not in her music book, this song was "in the air" (and in her listening ear) just weeks before Emily saw Jenny Lind perform: "Whether a certain passenger in a certain yesterday's stage has any somber effect on our once merry household, or the reverse 'I dinna choose to tell.'" Johnson, *Letters*, no. 42 (Emily Dickinson to Austin Dickinson, 8 June 1851). See online Appendix C.
63. Johnson, *Letters*, no. 46 (Emily Dickinson to Austin Dickinson, 6 July 1851).
64. "Swan of Erin," see Lawrence, *Strong on Music*, 2:205–7.
65. Basil Walsh, *Catherine Hayes, 1818–1861: The Hibernian Prima Donna* (Dublin: Irish Academic Press, 2000), 197.
66. Bingham, *Emily Dickinson's Home*, 187–89. Austin states in this draft letter that he saw Catherine Hayes "last Sunday." Hayes's first Boston concert was at the Tremont Temple on Tuesday, 14 October. The only Sunday concert in Boston occurred on 26 October. See Walsh, *Catherine Hayes*, 192.
67. "Girls — write often — letters are meat and drink . . . am very well — going to hear Sontag." Dickinson Family Papers, Houghton Library, Harvard University, 1 Austin Dickinson Papers, A. Austin Dickinson Correspondence, 1842–1896, box 1, To Emily, [Cambridge?], undated [6 December 1853?]. Date assigned by and quoted in Leyda, *The Years and Hours of Emily Dickinson*, 1:288. For a listing of Sontag's Boston concerts with the Germania Musical Society, see Nancy Newman, *Good Music for a Free People* (Rochester: University of Rochester Press, 2010), 238.
68. Franklin, *The Complete Poems*, no. 2, "Sic transit gloria mundi" (1852).
69. Franklin, *The Complete Poems*, no. 4, "I have a Bird in spring" (1854). See Johnson, *Letters*, no. 173 (Emily Dickinson to Susan Gilbert, ca. 1854).
70. Amherst College Digital Collections, Archives and Special Collections, Emily Dickinson Collection, Amherst Manuscript no. 602, box 7, folder 49. This excerpt about the Germanians was first published in *Letters of Emily Dickinson*, ed. Mabel Loomis Todd (Boston: Roberts Brothers, 1894), 122. The second publication, *Letters of Emily Dickinson*, ed. Mabel Loomis Todd (Boston: Roberts Brothers, 1931), 120, alters the line to "I never heard [such] *sounds* before." In her 1955 book *Emily Dickinson's Home* (280–81), Millicent Todd Bingham publishes the complete letter and retains this alteration. In Thomas Johnson and Theodora Ward's 1958 publication of the complete letters, no. 118 they follow the convention set by Todd in 1931 and continued by Bingham in 1955. For the date of the exhibition, see the

notes in Johnson, *Letters*, no. 118 (Emily Dickinson to Austin Dickinson, 21 April 1853). For a history of the Germania Musical Society, see Newman, *Good Music for a Free People*.

71. Franklin, *The Complete Poems*, no. 4, "I have a Bird in spring" (1854). This poem was included in a letter sent to Dickinson's future sister-in-law Susan Gilbert. See Johnson, *Letters*, no. 173 (Emily Dickinson to Susan Gilbert, ca. 1854). Although this early poem does carry interpretive metaphorical descriptors regarding music that can be applied to Dickinson's concert-going experiences around this time, it is important to note that in her letter to Austin, Emily's words regarding "Susie" and her "consent" may hold significance beyond missing an important concert. The announcement that Susan and Austin would marry had been made about three weeks earlier on 23 March (Sewall, *Life of Emily Dickinson*, xxi). Dickinson scholars have shown that Sue and Emily were very close, and Martha Nell Smith provides some important context to Emily and Susan's relationship and to this particular letter of 1854. See Martha Nell Smith, *Rowing in Eden: Rereading Emily Dickinson* (Austin: University of Texas Press, 1982), 163–64. See also *Open Me Carefully: Emily Dickinson's Intimate Letters to Susan Huntington Dickinson*, ed. Ellen Louise Hart and Martha Nell Smith (Ashfield, MA: Paris Press, 1998), 63–69.
72. See Johnson, *Letters*, no. 118 (Emily Dickinson to Austin Dickinson, 21 April 1853). See also Bingham, *Emily Dickinson's Home* (1955), 280–81.
73. Franklin, *The Complete Poems*, no. 819, "The Luxury to apprehend" (1864).
74. John Sullivan Dwight in *The Harbinger*, 28 October 1848, quoted in Newman, *Good Music for a Free People*, 41.
75. Lawrence, *Strong on Music*, 1:110–11.
76. Michael Broyles, "Music and Class Structure in Antebellum Boston," *Journal of the American Musicological Society* 44, no. 3 (1991): 451–52.
77. Douglas W. Shadle, *Orchestrating the Nation: The Nineteenth-Century American Enterprise* (New York: Oxford University Press, 2016), 116. See also John S. Dwight, "Music a Means of Culture," *Atlantic Monthly* 26, no. 155 (September 1870): 321–25, in *Music in the USA: A Documentary Companion*, ed. Judith Tick with Paul Beaudoin (New York: Oxford University Press, 2008), 166–69.
78. In January 1844 the English composer/vocalist Henry Russell was touring the United States. In New Orleans he crossed paths with the touring Norwegian violinist Ole Bull, who had just endured a rude concert audience. When he mentioned it to Russell, the composer observed that "until the beginning of this century, musical culture was a thing practically unknown outside such towns as New York, Philadelphia, and Boston. It is only now the denizens of the smaller towns are beginning to take an interest in things musical." Russell, *Cheer Boys Cheer*, 147. See also Andrew Lamb, *A Life on the Ocean Wave: The Story of Henry Russell* (Croydon, UK: Fullers Wood Press, 2007), 338. As to the smaller towns eagerly welcoming performances by the less polished opera companies, see Preston, *Opera on the Road*, 253–54.
79. Broyles, "Music and Class Structure in Antebellum Boston," 489.
80. Dickinson's niece Martha Dickinson Bianchi (an accomplished singer and pianist) is a much more reliable source, offering clear evidence not of Emily's musical taste but rather of the contrast to the music that had become available since the time of her aunt Emily: "Then when [Susan Dickinson's] own little girl began to take piano lessons, how their excitement increased from the first piece of 'sheet-music' to the first movement from a Beethoven sonata, and how Emily characterized the difference from the book of 'Selections' set before her own childish fingers!" See Martha Dickinson Bianchi, *Emily Dickinson Face to Face: Unpublished Letters with Notes and Reminiscences* (Boston: Houghton Mifflin, 1932), 159.

Chapter 5: Home Music-Making

1. Daniel Cavicchi, *Listening and Longing: Music Lovers in the Age of Barnum* (Middletown: Wesleyan University Press, 2011), 74.
2. Millicent Todd Bingham, *Emily Dickinson's Home: Letters of Edward Dickinson and His Family* (New York: Harper and Brothers Publishers, 1955), 153.
3. Lavinia Dickinson to Austin Dickinson, 10 July 1853, Emily Dickinson Collection, box 7, folder 60, letter 612c, Amherst College Archives and Special Collections, Amherst College Library. Published in Bingham, *Emily Dickinson's Home*, 308.
4. Lavinia Dickinson to Austin Dickinson, Thursday, 25 March 1852, Emily Dickinson

Collection, box 7, folder 39, letter 592f, Amherst College Archives and Special Collections. Published in Bingham, *Emily Dickinson's Home*, 234.
5. Andrea Stulman Dennett, *Weird and Wonderful: The Dime Museum in America* (New York: New York University Press, 1997), 89.
6. Christine Merrick Ayars, *Contributions to the Art of Music in America by the Music Industries of Boston, 1640–1936* (New York: W. H. Wilson, 1937), 11–12.
7. Ralph T. Dudgeon, *The Keyed Bugle*, 2nd ed. (Lanham, MD: Scarecrow Press, 2004), 291–92.
8. *Springfield Republican*, 29 January 1848, 12 March 1850.
9. Lavinia Dickinson to Austin Dickinson, 10 October 1852, Emily Dickinson Collection, ser. 4, box 7, folder 25, letter 582b, Amherst College Archives and Special Collections; published in Bingham, *Emily Dickinson's Home*, 210–11.
10. "'Oh the Merry Days When We Were Young,' A favorite Ballad. Sung with unbounded Applause by Mrs. Wood. Arranged with an accompaniment for the Piano Forte" (New York: Atwill, 1840). This song is not in Emily Dickinson's music book. NYPL/LPA, call number AM2-V Anon. "Oh the Merry Days When We Were Young." An edition of this song published by Frederick D. Benteen of Baltimore in 1843 notes on the first page of music, "The Air [is] altered from the English copy and rearranged for the Piano Forte." Copies of the Atwill and Benteen publications, and the Loder composition of the same name, are part of the sheet music holdings of the American Antiquarian Society: "'Oh! the Merry Days When We Were Young' Sung by Mr. Leffler. Music by Loder" (Boston: Keith's Music Publishing House, [1845]), plate number 381, 3.
11. Vera Brodsky Lawrence, *Strong on Music: The New York Music Scene in the Days of George Templeton Strong*, vol. 1, *Resonances, 1836–1849* (Chicago: University of Chicago Press, 1988), 87, 101–2.
12. Olivia Coleman died of tuberculosis at home in Princeton, New Jersey, on 26 September 1847. See Jay Leyda, *The Years and Hours of Emily Dickinson*, 2 vols. (New Haven: Yale University Press, 1960), 1:121.
13. *The Letters of Emily Dickinson*, ed. Thomas H. Johnson and Theodora Ward (hereafter Johnson, *Letters*), 3 vols. (Cambridge: Harvard University Press, 1958), no. 76 (Emily Dickinson to Austin Dickinson, 18 February 1852); Lavinia Dickinson to Austin Dickinson, "Wed. morn., Feb. 18, 1852," Emily Dickinson Collection, box 7, folder 28, letter 585c, Amherst College Archives and Special Collections, quoted in Bingham, *Emily Dickinson's Home*, 221.
14. Susan Key, "'Forever in Our Ears': Nature, Voice, and Sentiment in Stephen Foster's Parlor Style," *American Music* 30, no. 3 (Fall 2012): 292.
15. Nicholas E. Tawa, *Sweet Songs for Gentle Americans: The Parlor Song in America, 1790–1860* (Bowling Green, OH: Bowling Green Popular Press, 1980), 113. The song associated with Mrs. Wood (which is without authorship) was published in New York by Atwill in 1840; the Loder composition was first published under the imprint of Edward Riley in the *New York Mirror: A Weekly Gazette of Literature and the Fine Arts* 19, no. 42 (Saturday, 16 October 1841): 336. The copy of the Loder composition originally sent home by Austin was probably the edition published in Boston by Keith in 1845. The chronology of these three publications points to the Woods' return trip to the United States in 1840, Leffler's New York debut in late 1840, and Leffler's return to the States in 1845. The publishers were promoting Leffler's association with the Woods and his subsequent success by marketing a new song with the same title.
16. See Katherine K. Preston, *Opera on the Road: Traveling Opera Troupes in the United States, 1825–1860* (Urbana: University of Illinois Press, 1993), 113–14.
17. Lawrence, *Strong on Music*, 1:217.
18. See Katherine K. Preston, *Opera on the Road*, 19, 382, n. 42.
19. On 17 and 18 July 1845 the *Springfield Republican* listed a concert performance at Town Hall scheduled to take place on 18 July. On the program was the duet "Take Them I Implore Thee," performed by Mrs. Andrews and Mrs. Maeder, who before her marriage to James Gaspard Maeder (1809–1876) performed as Miss Clara Fisher (1811–1898). In 1827 and 1828 Fisher had success with the song "Hey the Bonnie Breast Knots." See the song "The Bonnie Clay Flag," which is discussed in chapter 7. See also the online Appendix B. For information on James Maeder, see Lawrence, *Strong on Music*, 1:41. For an entry on Clara Fisher Maeder, see *Notable American Women, 1607–1950: A Biographical Dictionary* ed. Edward T. James, Janet Wilson James, and Paul S. Boyer (Cambridge: Belknap Press of Harvard University Press, 1971), 622.
20. Thomas Hood, "'You And Me.' Song. Words by the late Thomas Hood. Composed & Dedicated with Esteem to 'Cally.' Arranged with Symphonies & Accompaniments for the Piano Forte" (Albany: Boardman & Gray, 186 N. Pearl St.; New York: Firth, Pond & Co., [1847]), NYPL/LPA, call number AM2-V, Hood. See also online Appendix C.

21. Lavinia Dickinson to Austin Dickinson, 10 October 1852, Emily Dickinson Collection, ser. 4, box 28, folder 23, letter 572b, Amherst College Archives and Special Collections; published in Bingham, *Emily Dickinson's Home*, 184–86.
22. Draft letter from Austin Dickinson to Susan Gilbert, 11 October 1851, Dickinson Collection, Houghton Library, Harvard University, call number MS Am 1118.95 Series: IB (31), Austin Dickinson letters to Susan Huntington Dickinson, 1851 [11] October; quoted in Leyda, *The Years and Hours of Emily Dickinson*, 1:218. For additional information on Austin Dickinson's correspondence with the Gilbert sisters, see Bingham, *Emily Dickinson's Home*, 186–89.
23. *Open Me Carefully: Emily Dickinson's Intimate Letters to Susan Huntington Dickinson*, ed. Ellen Louise Hart and Martha Nell Smith (Ashfield, MA: Paris Press, 1998), xi.
24. Alfred Habegger, *My Wars Are Laid Away in Books: The Life of Emily Dickinson* (New York: Random House, 2001), 271.
25. Cobb & Smith opened in 1847. In 1849 Cobb withdrew and Solomon Smith joined his brother as the J. W. Smith Dry Goods Company, located at 40–42 Seneca Street. The store closed its doors in 1977, "one of the country's oldest continuously operating department stores." *Images of America: Geneva* (Charleston: Arcadia Publishing, © 2003 Geneva Historical Society), 17. See also Joel H. Monroe, *A Century and a Quarter of History: Geneva from Seventeen Hundred and Eighty-seven to Nineteen Hundred and Twelve* (Geneva, NY, 1912), 158.
26. Leyda, *The Years and Hours of Emily Dickinson*, 1:302, 314. Ebenezer White Arms, a Yale graduate, had a successful law practice in Aurora, New York. Habegger, *My Wars Are Laid Away in Books*, 265.
27. *Open Me Carefully*, 148.
28. *Open Me Carefully*, 4, 47. For references to music between Emily and Susan, see Johnson, *Letters*, no. 107 (Emily Dickinson to Susan Gilbert, 12 March 1853). In this letter Dickinson references the lullaby "Rock a bye Baby" from *Mother Goose's Melody*, possibly an oblique reference to Susan and Austin's pending engagement, which took place eleven days later, on 23 March. Johnson, *Letters*, no. 134 (Emily Dickinson to Susan Gilbert, October 1853). Susan was visiting relatives in New York State when Emily sent her a sketch consisting of musical scales ascending into the clouds, a "little air" Dickinson titled "Music of the Spheres." Johnson, *Letters*, no. 154 (Emily Dickinson to Susan Gilbert, 15 January 1854). Susan was away visiting her sister-in-law's family, the Bartletts, in Manchester, New Hampshire. Emily, "just [in] from meeting," recounts an episode with the church choir in which "the singing reminded me of the Legend of 'Jack and *Gill*,' allowing the Bass Viol to be typified by *Gill*, who literally tumbled after, while Jack—i e the choir, galloped insanely on, 'nor recked, nor heeded' him." The parish acquired the double bass viol in 1839, and it was still in use early in 1854, nearly four years after the parish had allotted funds to purchase an organ. See Leyda, *The Years and Hours of Emily Dickinson*, 1:54, 171. For the date of Susan and Austin's engagement, see Richard Benson Sewall, *The Life of Emily Dickinson* (New York: Farrar, Straus and Giroux, 1974), xxi.
29. "And music—though she herself did not play as well as Emily—what would Susan not commit or leave uncommitted for the sake of it!" Martha Dickinson Bianchi, *Emily Dickinson Face to Face: Unpublished Letters with Notes and Reminiscences* (Boston: Houghton Mifflin, 1932), 159.
30. Moses Mears Bagg, *Memorial History of Utica, N.Y.: From Its Settlement to the Present Time* (Syracuse: D. Mason & Co., 1892), 240.
31. "'Any Thing: Composed and Respectfully Dedicated to Any Body' by J. Finley Smith. Auburn [NY]: Published by H. Ivison Jr. [n.d.], With: Andante for Piano Forte and Flute," NYPL/LPA, call number Am2-I Smith, John. Any Thing.
32. See *Alpha Delta Phi, 1832–1882 Semi-Centennial Catalog* ([Boston:] Rockwell and Church, 1882), 8, NYPL/GRD, call number SSY Alpha Delta Phi Fraternity.
33. Melvin Gilbert Dodge, *Fifty Years Ago: The Half-Century Annalists' Letters to Hamilton College Alumni Association, 1865–1900* (Kirkland, NY: Hamilton College, 1900), 210. The opening of this tribute reads: "In 1839 the vacancy in the chair of Latin and Greek was filled by the promotion of Tutor John Finley Smith, of the class of 1834. He was the only son of Rev. John Smith of Cooperstown, and had been graduated from Auburn Seminary in 1838. He gave instruction for a single term in French."
34. *Comfort for Christian Mourners: A Sermon Delivered with Reference to the Death of Prof. John Finley Smith on the Lord's Day, Oct. 15, 1843; In the Chapel of Hamilton College by the Rev. H. Mandeville; Professor of Moral Science, and Belles-Lettres, in Hamilton College, N. Y. Published at the Request of the Faculty and Students* (Utica: Press of Bennett, Backus, & Hawley, 1843), call number PAM EI HAM.47; *The*

Uses of Music. An Address Delivered at the First Public Rehearsal of the Utica Musical Academy, February 5, 1858. By Professor Edward North of Hamilton College with an Appendix, containing A Historical Sketch of the Academy, its Constitution, Names of Officers, and Catalogue of Members (Utica: T. R. McQuade, Printer, 47 Genesee and 7 Broad Street. 1858), from the collections of the Oneida County History Center, Utica, NY, call number PAM UT UMA.1.

35. *Circular and Catalog of the Utica Female Academy from 1871–72* (Utica: Curtiss & Childs, printers, 1872), from the collections of the American Antiquarian Society. An example of the publications issued by Henry Ivison's firm is *The Church Hymnbook; With Tunes for the Worship of God* (New York: Ivison, Blakeman, Taylor, 1873).
36. William Lewis Montague, ed., *Biographical Record of the Non-Graduate Members of Amherst College* (Belchertown, MA: Press of John L. Montague, 1881), 51.
37. "Student petition for a band and proposed constitution, March 1836," Amherst College Early History Manuscripts and Pamphlets Collection, 1820–1843, box 1, folder 52, Amherst College Archives and Special Collections, call number MA.00217, Amherst College Digital Collections.
38. Published records show a Robie Harris Loomis of Syracuse, New York, born 1822. See Elias Loomis, *The Descendants of Joseph Loomis* (New Haven: Tuttle, Morehouse and Taylor, 1875), 118. Robie Harris was the child of Harvey Loomis of Syracuse. She married John J. Peck (b. 1820) of Syracuse. This dating would have put Fowler's student at about twenty-five years of age at the time the "Syracuse Polka" was first published in 1847. In some seminaries it was not uncommon to have students as old as thirty. At Mount Holyoke, Mary Lyon preferred mature women, who were more likely to succeed at both the challenging course work of the senior class and the difficult missionary work that many undertook after graduation. See Jewel A. Smith, *Transforming Women's Education: Liberal Arts and Music in Female Seminaries*, Music in American Life (Urbana: University of Illinois Press, 2019), 66.
39. "[Mr. Fowler's] compositions first became popular as recreations for his scholars." See "Cherry Valley Female Academy," *Musical World. A Journal for "Heavenly Music's Earthly Friends* 12 no. 40, ed. Richard Storrs Willis (24 March 1855): 141. The article is quoting from the catalog of Fowler's New York publisher William Hall and Son.
40. Polkas originated in Bohemia (today a region of the Czech Republic) around 1830 and circulated quickly to all corners, "causing a veritable 'polkamania' that lasted until the end of the century." See the entry on "Polka" in Willi Apel, *Harvard Dictionary of Music*, 2nd ed., rev. and enlarged (Cambridge: Belknap Press of Harvard University Press, 1973), 685.
41. Habegger, *My Wars Are Laid Away in Books*, 146.
42. Johnson, *Letters*, no. 15 (Emily Dickinson to Abiah Root, 14 March 1847).
43. Johnson, *Letters*, no. 87 (Emily Dickinson to Austin Dickinson, 21 April 1852).

Chapter 6: Edward Dickinson

1. Richard Benson Sewall, *The Life of Emily Dickinson* (New York: Farrar, Straus and Giroux, 1974), 54.
2. Edward Wilton Carpenter and Charles Frederick Morehouse, *The History of the Town of Amherst, Massachusetts, 1731–1896* (Amherst: Press of Carpenter and Morehouse, 1896), 313.
3. *The Letters of Emily Dickinson*, ed. Thomas H. Johnson and Theodora Ward (hereafter Johnson, *Letters*), 3 vols. (Cambridge: Harvard University Press, 1958), no. 45 (Emily Dickinson to Austin Dickinson, 29 June 1851).
4. See Carpenter and Morehouse, *History of the Town of Amherst*, 315.
5. Millicent Todd Bingham, *Emily Dickinson's Home: Letters of Edward Dickinson and His Family* (New York: Harper and Brothers Publishers, 1955), 216–19. Bingham notes that "Logtown, the point at which construction of the Amherst & Belchertown Rail Road began . . . was the local name for Dwight's, a hamlet in the valley known also as North Belchertown." Notice of the commencement of construction appeared in the *Hampshire and Franklin Express*, 6 February 1852. See also Alfred Habegger, *My Wars Are Laid Away in Books: The Life of Emily Dickinson* (New York: Random House, 2001), 289. For Emily's news about the railroad, see Johnson, *Letters*, no. 72 (Emily Dickinson to Austin Dickinson, 6 February 1852).
6. *Poems by Emily Dickinson*, 2nd ser., ed. T. W. Higginson and Mabel Loomis Todd (Boston: Roberts Brothers, 1891), 39.

7. Johnson, *Letters*, no. 123 (Emily Dickinson to Austin Dickinson, 16 May 1853).
8. *The Journals and Miscellaneous Notebooks of Ralph Waldo Emerson*, ed. A. W. Plumstead et al., 16 vols. (Cambridge: Harvard University Press, 1969), 7:482, quoted in Jill Lepore, *These Truths: A History of the United States* (New York: W. W. Norton, 2018), 229.
9. Mark M. Smith, *Listening to Nineteenth-Century America* (Chapel Hill: University of North Carolina Press, 2001), 129–30.
10. Johnson, *Letters*, no. 127 (Emily Dickinson to Austin Dickinson, 13 June 1853). See also Bingham, *Emily Dickinson's Home*, 294.
11. Johnson, *Letters*, no. 128 (Emily Dickinson to Austin Dickinson, 19 June 1853).
12. See Jay Leyda, *The Years and Hours of Emily Dickinson*, 2 vols. (New Haven: Yale University Press, 1960), 2:71.
13. See Richard F. Palmer, "Looking Back at a Railroad 175 Years after Its First Ride," *The Auburn Citizen*, 6 January 2013, https://auburnpub.com/news/local/looking-back-on-a-railroad-years-after-the-first-ride/article_abef6b91-e97a-5855-a31c-9537d872294d.html. See also City of Auburn, https://www.auburnny.gov/mayor/pages/city-auburn-mayors.
14. Kate Clifford Larson, *Bound for the Promise Land: Harriet Tubman, Portrait of an American Hero* (New York: One World/Random House, 2005), 163–64.
15. Habegger, *My Wars Are Laid Away in Books*, 22. Edward Dickinson was a member of the Third Regiment of Infantry in the First Brigade and Fourth Division of the Massachusetts militia. See Vivian Pollack, *A Poet's Parents: The Courtship Letters of Emily Norcross and Edward Dickinson* (Chapel Hill: University of North Carolina Press, 1988), 35.
16. Nancy L. Todd, *New York's Historic Armories: An Illustrated History* (Albany: State University of New York Press, 2006), 20.
17. Johnson, *Letters*, no. 339 (Emily Dickinson to Louise and Frances Norcross, early spring 1870).
18. Sewall, *Life of Emily Dickinson*, 52. For dating of the music, see online Appendix B.
19. *Springfield Republican*, 25 August 1845.
20. Arthur James Weise, *The History of the City of Albany, New York: From the Discovery of the Great River in 1524 by Verrazano to the Present Time* (Albany: E. H. Bender, 1884), 487. "Bayeaux's Quick Step" was published in 1842 by Boardman and Gray, 4 N. Pearl Street, Albany. Boardman and Gray also manufactured pianos. See Arthur Loesser, *Men, Women & Pianos: A Social History* (New York: Simon and Schuster, 1954), 510. Dickinson's copy was published in Boston by Charles H. Keith in 1844, the year of Captain Thomas Bayeaux's death. Dickinson's copy lacks the splendid illustrated cover of the editions published by Gray (NYPL/LPA). See online Appendix B.
21. Todd, *New York's Historic Armories*, 26.
22. *Springfield Republican*, 24 June 1843.
23. As sourced from the *Rochester Daily Democrat*, 3 March 1848. See the online Rochester newspaper index in the Rochester Public Library.
24. William Farley Peck, *A Semi-centennial History of the City of Rochester* (Syracuse: D. Mason, 1884), 433; *Rochester Daily American Directory of the City of Rochester for 1847–48* (Rochester: Jerome & Brother), 51, 132. The *Rochester Daily Democrat* reported on 25 March 1847 that the Grays received an "acknowledgement from the Albany Burgesses Corps for courtesy extended to them while in Rochester." The *Rochester Daily Advertiser* reported on 24 September 1847 that the Union Grays "paraded under the command of Major Swan, accompanied by Adams Brass Band." Adams was also a composer; on 30 April 1847 the *Advertiser* reported that Captain Adams had composed his "Adams Athenaeum March." See the online Rochester newspaper index in the Rochester Public Library.
25. A notice in the *Rochester Daily Democrat* on 19 June 1846 reads, "Rev. addresses large audience [of the Independent Order of Oddfellows]. Dinner and music by Adams Brass Band." See the Newspaper Index of the Rochester Public Library, https://roccitylibrary.org/rochester-newspaper-index/.
26. On 4 August 1848 Edward Dickinson was elected president of the (Zachary) Taylor Club of Amherst. See Leyda, *The Years and Hours of Emily Dickinson*, 1:86, 150.
27. Genevieve Taggard, *The Life and Mind of Emily Dickinson* (New York: Alfred A. Knopf, 1930), 48.
28. Ralph W. Franklin, "Emily Dickinson to Abiah Root: Ten Reconstructed Letters," *Emily Dickinson Journal* 4, no. 1 (Spring 1995): 31. See also Johnson, *Letters*, no. 69 (Emily Dickinson to Abiah Root, January 1852). Jay Leyda dates this letter to mid-January 1852. See Leyda, *The Years and Hours of Emily Dickinson*, 1:229.

29. Dickinson's 17 January 1848 letter to Abiah Root recounts the activities of Thanksgiving night, 25 November 1847. Johnson, *Letters*, no. 20 (Emily Dickinson to Abiah Root, South Hadley, 17 January 1848). Here Dickinson references the song "Ten O'clock! or, Remember Love Remember," which is not in the Dickinson music book. See online Appendix C. Dickinson's mention of this song was brought to my attention by R. H. Winnick, who is working on a study of unrecognized, unidentified, and misidentified allusions and echoes in Dickinson's correspondence.
30. James Parakilas, "A History of Lessons and Practicing," in *Piano Roles: Three Hundred Years of Life with the Piano*, ed. James Parakilas (New Haven: Yale University Press, 1999), 150.
31. My thanks to pianist and composer Kit Young for her speculations (with which I am in complete agreement) regarding the influence of Edward Dickinson on the content of Emily's music book. Kit Young, conversation with the author, 6 September 2019.
32. Habegger, *My Wars Are Laid Away in Books*, 22.
33. Johnson, *Letters*, no. 65 (Emily Dickinson to Austin Dickinson, 15 December 1851).
34. Sewall, *Life of Emily Dickinson*, 429, n. 1.
35. Sewall, *Life of Emily Dickinson*, 227, 240. According to Alfred Habegger, "posing" was a major Dickinson theme, espoused by Dickinson biographer Richard Sewall. See Habegger, *My Wars Are Laid Away in Books*, 456, n. 2.

Chapter 7: Music-Making and the Dickinson Family Correspondence

1. *The Letters of Emily Dickinson*, ed. Thomas H. Johnson and Theodora Ward (hereafter Johnson, *Letters*), 3 vols. (Cambridge: Harvard University Press, 1958), no. 42 (Emily Dickinson to Austin Dickinson, 8 June 1851).
2. Johnson, *Letters*, no. 20 (Emily Dickinson to Abiah Root, South Hadley, 17 January 1848); Johnson, *Letters*, no. 42 (Emily Dickinson to Austin Dickinson, 8 June 1851).
3. Susan Key, "'Forever in Our Ears': Nature, Voice, and Sentiment in Stephen Foster's Parlor Style," *American Music* 30, no. 3 (Fall 2012): 291.
4. *The Complete Poems of Emily Dickinson*, ed. Ralph W. Franklin (Cambridge: Harvard University Press, 1999), no. 1577, "The Bible is an antique Volume — " (1882). Victoria Morgan writes: "The word 'warbling' here is significant in that it suggests the bird imagery which Dickinson often invokes when writing about worship. . . . It also carries with it connotations of the female singer." Victoria N. Morgan, *Emily Dickinson and Hymn Culture: Tradition and Experience* (Farnham, England: Ashgate Press, 2010), 115–16.
5. For "spoof of established [biblical] doctrine," see Judith Farr, *The Passion of Emily Dickinson* (Cambridge: Harvard University Press, 1992), 64–65. "Slant' lines" also noted by Judith Farr, refers to Dickinson's poem "Tell all the truth but tell it slant — ." Franklin, *The Complete Poems*, no. 1263 (1872). In his analysis of "The Bible is an antique Volume — ," Michael Manson argues that "Dickinson establishes an analogy between [the poem's] biblical subjects and romance novels." See Michael L. Manson, "'The Thews of Hymn': Dickinson's Metrical Grammar," *A Companion to Emily Dickinson*, ed. Martha Nell Smith and Mary Loeffelholz (Malden, MA: Wiley-Blackwell, 2014), 376.
6. Richard Benson Sewall, *The Life of Emily Dickinson* (New York: Farrar, Straus and Giroux, 1974), 227. According to Alfred Habegger, "posing" was a major Dickinson theme espoused by biographer Richard Sewall. See Alfred Habegger, *My Wars Are Laid Away in Books: The Life of Emily Dickinson* (New York: Random House, 2001), 456, n. 2.
7. See Johnson, *Letters*, no. 12 (Emily Dickinson to Abiah Root, 26 June 1846) and his annotations.
8. "Are We Almost There? A Touching Ballad Written and Composed by Florence Vane" (Boston: Oliver Ditson, c1845), NYPL/LPA, call number AM2-V Vane.
9. Susan Key, "'Forever in Our Ears': Nature, Voice, and Sentiment in Stephen Foster's Parlor Style," *American Music* 30, no. 3 (Fall 2012), 293–94.
10. Martha Dickinson Bianchi, *The Life and Letters of Emily Dickinson* (Boston: Houghton Mifflin, 1924), 37–38.
11. Regarding the degree of difficulty in some of the music in Dickinson's music book, see Carolyn Lindley Cooley, *The Music of Emily Dickinson's Poems and Letters: A Study of Imagery and Form* (London: McFarland and Company, 2003), 12–18.

12. Johnson, *Letters*, no. 65 (Emily Dickinson to Austin Dickinson, 15 December 1851). The popularity of the song "Charity," words by Charles Jefferys and music by Stephen Glover, is supported by Dickinson's reference to it, and the large number of editions at NYPL/LPA, call number AM 2-V Glover. While the song "Charity" is not in Dickinson's music book, her bound volume does contain a waltz arrangement of the song "A Home That I Love" (Library of Congress, loc.gov) with words by, but not attributed to, Charles Jefferys and music by Stephen Glover (1843). Dickinson's bound volume also contains the popular song "The Rose of Allandale," words by Charles Jefferys and music by Sydney Nelson. See online Appendix B.
13. Johnson, *Letters*, no. 71 (Emily Dickinson to Austin Dickinson, 28 January 1852). See also Millicent Todd Bingham, *Emily Dickinson's Home: Letters of Edward Dickinson and His Family* (New York: Harper and Brothers, 1955), 211–14. Both Johnson and Bingham identify this part of the letter as being "on a separate slip of paper." While Johnson dates the two letters 15 December 1851 and 28 January 1852, Bingham dates them 12 and 28 January. Bingham's dating would have given Lavinia approximately sixteen days to learn her part of the duet as opposed to the nearly six weeks afforded by the Johnson dating.
14. The fingerings found in Dickinson's music book follow the convention used by Henri Bertini (whose method book Dickinson used) and others, in which the letter X refers to the thumb and the number 4 to the pinky. Thanks to pianist/composer Kit Young for our discussion regarding the fingerings in Dickinson's music book.
15. Martha Dickinson Bianchi, *Emily Dickinson Face to Face: Unpublished Letters with Notes and Reminiscences* (Boston: Houghton Mifflin, 1932), 34.
16. The catalog record for the piano at the Houghton Library reads: "Renaissance revival square piano; floral and scroll carved legs and apron. Hallet, Davis & Co., Boston, Massachusetts. Brazilian rosewood, Brazilian rosewood veneer, spruce, ivory, iron; height 93.9 cm., width 207.0 cm., depth 99.0 cm." In the absence of a serial number, the bridge contains the stamp "Patent suspension bridge[.] Patented September 23rd[,] 1851[.] Manufactured by Hallet, Davis & Co.[,] No 409 Washington Street, Boston, Mass." Thanks to Leslie Morris, the Houghton Library's Gore Vidal Curator of Modern Manuscripts, and Andrea Cawelti, Ward Music Cataloger, for sharing this information with me.
17. Cynthia Adams Hoover and Edwin M. Good, "Piano," in *The Grove Dictionary of American Music*, 2nd ed., ed. Charles Hiroshi Garrett, vol. 6 (New York: Oxford University Press, 2013), 484–87; Arthur Loesser, *Men, Women, & Pianos: A Social History* (New York: Simon and Schuster, 1954), 476–77.
18. Beethoven's sonata was originally dedicated to Charles Polgreen Bridgetower, an Afro-Polish violinist. Thanks to musicologist Katie Callam for this information.
19. Edward J. Dent, *The Rise of Romantic Opera* (New York: Cambridge University Press, 1979), 55–60.
20. "A Tale of Poland" was reprinted from *The Knickerbocker* or *New York Monthly Magazine*, 7 April 1836, 378–84. See *Republican and Journal* (Springfield, MA), 11 June 1836.
21. Thomas Christensen, "Public Music in Private Spaces: Piano-Vocal Scores and the Domestication of Opera," in *Music and the Cultures of Print*, ed. Kate van Orden, with afterword by Roger Chartier (New York: Garland Publishing, 2000), 79.
22. Richard Wolfe, *Secular Music in America, 1801–1825: A Bibliography*, vol. 2 (New York: The New York Public Library, 1964), nos. 5172–5177A. Published editions for two hands can be located in the sheet music holdings of the American Antiquarian Society and The New York Public Library for the Performing Arts.
23. Donald W. Krummel, *Guide for Dating Early Published Music: A Manual for Bibliographic Practices* (Hackensack, NJ: Joseph Boonin; Kassel: Barenreiter Verlag, 1974), 32.
24. Musicologist Dale Cockrell, conversation with the author, 1 March 2018.
25. Christensen, "Public Music in Private Spaces," 71.
26. "In Germany of the later eighteenth century, and for three or four generations thereafter, music, especially wordless instrumental music, was a more serious concern to more people than it has ever been anywhere before or since." This "attitude toward music as an art" emigrated with the Germans to the United States, and Americans responded to it. Arthur Loesser, (New York: Simon and Schuster, 1954), 89, 490–91.
27. A copy of "Aria alla Scozzese" published by Benteen of Baltimore (1844?) identifies this as "a Scotch Air." See the sheet music collections of the American Antiquarian Society. For information on "Believe Me If All Those Endearing Young Charms," or "My Lodging Is

on the Cold Ground," see Andrew Kuntz, "Fiddler's Companion: A Descriptive Index of North American, British Isles and Irish Music for the Folk Violin and Other Instruments," http://www.ibiblio.org/fiddlers/BE_BELI.htm.

28. Wolfe, *Secular Music in America*, 2:920.
29. "Ode Sung at the Second Centennial Celebration" (Boston: Parker & Ditson, undated). See James J. Fuld, *The Book of World-Famous Music: Classical, Popular, and Folk* (New York: Dover Publications, 2000), 138–39. See also Harry Dichter and Elliott Shapiro, *Handbook of Early American Sheet Music, 1768–1889* (New York: Dover Publications, 1977), 220.
30. See the annotation for Johnson, *Letters*, no. 22 (Emily Dickinson to Austin Dickinson, 17 February 1848).
31. "Believe Me If All Those Endearing Young Charms": Johnson. *Letters*, no. 22 (Emily Dickinson to Austin Dickinson, 17 February 1848); "The Last Rose of Summer": *Letters*, no. 337 (Emily Dickinson to Louise Norcross, late 1869) and no. 669 (Emily Dickinson to Louise and Frances Norcross, 1880?); "Bonnie Doon": see Franklin, *The Complete Poems*, no. 2, "Sic transit gloria mundi" (1852). See also Carlton Lowenberg, "A Concordance of Musical Terms in the Poems and Letters," in *Musicians Wrestle Everywhere: Emily Dickinson and Music* (Berkeley: Fallen Leaf Press, 1992), 109–18.
32. Olivia Coleman to Emily Fowler, [8 May 1846], Emily Fowler Ford Papers, General Correspondence, box 1, folder 3, Manuscripts and Archives Division, The New York Public Library, call number Mss Col 1038.
33. See Jay Leyda, *The Years and Hours of Emily Dickinson*, vol. 1 (New Haven: Yale University Press, 1960), xxxiv–v: "[Rev.] Coleman's next schools [after Amherst] were in Princeton, N.J. ([arrival date] 27 Feb.–13 March '46) and in Philadelphia (21 Sept. '48)." My thanks to Dickinson scholar Georgiana Strickland for guiding me to this information.
34. Johnson, *Letters*, no. 30 (Emily Dickinson to Jane Humphrey, 23 January 1850). See Lewis F. Thomas, Esq., with William R. Dempster, "'I'm Alone All Alone,' Dedicated to Miss Abby Ball of Boston" (Boston: Oliver Ditson, 115 Washington St., 1846), plate no. 1097, NYPL/LPA, call number AM 2-V Dempster.
35. On Dudley's being an Amherst College graduate, see *The Semi-Centennial Catalog of Amherst College: Including the Officers of Government and Instruction, the Alumni, and all others who have received honorary degrees* (Amherst: Clark W. Bryan & Company, 1872), 61.
36. Johnson, *Letters*, no. 225 (Emily Dickinson to Louise and Frances Norcross, mid-September 1860); see also Johnson's annotations, 368. Dickinson biographer Alfred Habegger has established the name of Dickinson's cousin as Louisa, not Louise, as given by Johnson. See Alfred Habegger, *My Wars Are Laid Away in Books*, 394, n. 1. See also Cristanne Miller, "Emily Dickinson's Letters: A Preview," *Emily Dickinson Journal* 30, no. 1 (2021): 31.
37. Polly Longsworth, "'Was Mr. Dudley Dear?': Emily Dickinson and John Langdon Dudley," *Massachusetts Review* 26, nos. 2–3 (Summer–Autumn 1985): 365.
38. Johnson, *Letters*, no. 302 (Emily Dickinson to Louise Norcross, early 1865).
39. Johnson, *Letters*, no. 99 (Emily Dickinson to Emily Fowler [Ford], early 1853?). The lock of hair resides in the Amherst College Special Collections, and the letter is part of the Emily Fowler Ford Papers in the Manuscripts and Archives Division of The New York Public Library. See online Appendix C for a citation of the song "John Anderson My Jo."
40. Johnson, *Letters*, no. 110 (Emily Dickinson to Austin Dickinson, 27 March 1853).
41. Habegger, *My Wars Are Laid Away in Books*, 30. According to Leyda, *The Years and Hours of Emily Dickinson*, Edward Dickinson and Susan Gilbert were admitted to the First Church of Christ on 11 August 1850 (1:178); Lavinia was admitted to the First Church of Christ on 3 November 1850 (1:182); and Austin Dickinson was admitted on 6 January 1856 (1:339).
42. Bingham, *Emily Dickinson's Home*, 486.
43. Lavinia Dickinson, letter no. 615b, Amherst College, Special Collections. Published in Bingham, *Emily Dickinson's Home*, 315.
44. As to the bond between Edward and Austin, see Johnson, *Letters*, no. 108 (Emily Dickinson to Austin Dickinson, 18 March 1853).
45. Johnson, *Letters*, no. 141 (Emily Dickinson to Austin Dickinson, 14 November 1853).
46. "'There's a Good Time Coming.' Ballad Composed & Sung by the Hutchinson Family. The Symphonies & Accompaniments by E[dward] L. White. Written by Charles Mackay" (Boston: Oliver Ditson, 1846).
47. Franklin, *The Complete Poems*, no. 259, "A Clock stopped — " (1861).

Chapter 8: The American Political Struggle

1. *Springfield Republican*, 27 March 1844. Following the "Whig Nominations" on page one, column one, is this notice: "We have resolved to try the experiment of a daily paper in Springfield. . . . After continuing the publication six months, or a year, if we find in it too much of a loss, we shall stop. . . . We find that towns much smaller than ours, and of much less business have supported one or more daily papers several years."
2. *The Letters of Emily Dickinson*, ed. Thomas H. Johnson and Theodora Ward (hereafter Johnson, *Letters*), 3 vols. (Cambridge: Harvard University Press, 1958), no. 133 (Emily Dickinson to Dr. and Mrs. J. G. Holland, autumn 1853). Jay Leyda dates this letter to "late September?" 1853. See Jay Leyda, *The Years and Hours of Emily Dickinson*, vol. 1 (New Haven: Yale University Press, 1960), 283–84.
3. *Springfield Republican*, 20 September 1844.
4. The music for "The Bonnie Clay Flag" was deposited for copyright in the Library of Congress on 6 January 1844; see loc.gov. Thanks to traditional Irish performer and historian Don Meade for alerting me to the fact that the tune for "The Bonnie Clay Flag" was sourced from "Hey the Bonnie Breast Knots." "Hey the Bonnie Breast Knots" saw publication in many songsters and song collections, including *The American Minstrel: A Choice Collection of the Most Popular Songs, Glees, Duets, Choruses, &c. Many of which are Original. With Select Music* (Cincinnati: Stereotyped and Published by J. A. James and Co., 1837), 28. "Hey the Bonnie Breast Knots" was made popular by "Miss George," also known as Mrs. Oldmixon (d. 1835). See Donald W. Krummel, "The Displaced Prima Donna: Mrs. Oldmixon in America," *The Musical Times* 108, no. 1487 (January 1967): 25, 27–28. "Hey the Bonnie Breast Knots" was also associated with the "celebrated" singer Miss Clara Fisher (1811–1898), who in 1827 and 1828 performed the song widely to great success. The melody became part of the published traditional tune repertoire. See online Appendix B.
5. "NEW SONG—Keith, 67 and 69 Court street, has just published 'The Bonnie Clay Flag,' written by John H. Warland, Esq., and dedicated to the 'Boston Clay Club, No. 1.' It is written to John Sinclair's popular music 'the bonnie breast knots.'" *The Daily Atlas* (Boston), Saturday, 20 January 1844. Brainard's Music Store in Cleveland advertised this and other Whig songs. *Cleveland Herald*, 14 May 1844.
6. Martha Ackmann, *These Fevered Days: Ten Pivotal Moments in the Making of Emily Dickinson* (New York: W. W. Norton, 2020), 106–7.
7. Johnson, *Letters*, no. 5 (Emily Dickinson to Abiah Root, 23 February 1845).
8. *The National Clay Melodist: a collection of popular and patriotic songs*, ed. John H. Warland (Boston: B. Adams, 1844). See the promotional advertisement for this songster in the *Springfield Republican*, 3 April 1844. The lines quoted here are quoted in the promotional piece.
9. *The National Clay Melodist*, 29–30. The *Melodist* was first published in Boston in 1842 as *The Harry Clay Melodist*. See also "'Old Kentucky' as Sung by the Henry Clay Clubs adapted to the Air 'Old Dan Tucker'" (New York: Published by Firth & Hall and J. L. Hewitt, [1844–45]), NYPL/LPA, call number AM 2-V Emmitt, Old Dan Tucker, tune, Old Kentucky.
10. Also to the tune of "Old Dan Tucker": "'Clay and Frelinghuysen' written by J. Greiner, of Dayton, Ohio, for the Philadelphia Clay Minstrels, and sung by them with unbounded applause, at the Great Ratification Convention in Baltimore." The lyrics were published in the *Raleigh Register*, Friday, 24 May 1844. Another piece of contrafacta, "The Little Red Fox," was published in the *Milwaukee Sentinel* on 6 April 1844. For more on appropriations of "Old Dan Tucker," see online Appendix B.
11. Van Wyck Brooks, *The Flowering of New England, 1815–1865* (New York: E. P. Dutton, 1936), 114; Millicent Todd Bingham, *Emily Dickinson's Home: Letters of Edward Dickinson and His Family* (New York: Harper and Brothers Publishers, 1955), 261.
12. Bingham, *Emily Dickinson's Home*, 333.
13. Austin Dickinson to Susan Gilbert (1850), quoted in Richard Benson Sewall, *The Life of Emily Dickinson* (New York: Farrar, Straus and Giroux, 1974), 99.
14. Regarding Austin Dickinson as a Know Nothing sympathizer, and the family's views on Irish immigrants, see Aífe Murray, *Maid as Muse: How Servants Changed Emily Dickinson's Life and Language* (Durham: University of New Hampshire Press, 2009), 141–44.
15. Johnson, *Letters*, no. 43 (Emily Dickinson to Austin Dickinson, 15 June 1851).
16. Karin Pendle, *Women and Music: A History* (Bloomington: Indiana University Press, 2001), 210.

"The Blue Juniata," or "The Indian Girl, Bright Alfarata," also referred to as "Alfarata, The Maid of Juniata," was "said to have been inspired by a canal-boat journey through the Juniata Valley between Harrisburg and Pittsburgh." Henry W. Shoemaker, ed., *North Pennsylvania Minstrelsy* (Altoona: Altoona Tribune Company, 1919), 135–36. The tune is mentioned in Laura Ingalls Wilder's book *Little House on the Prairie* in the chapter titled "The Tall Indian." See Dale Cockrell, ed., *The Ingalls Wilder Songbook*, Music of the United States of America 22, Recent Researches in American Music 71 (Middleton, WI: Published for the American Musicological Society by A-R Editions, 2011), 237–38, 387. The Ingallses were homesteaders in Kansas, encroaching on Native American territory.

17. For a discussion of the concept of the "noble savage," see Alden T. Vaughn, "From White Man to Red Skin: Changing Anglo-American Perceptions of the American Indian," *American Historical Review* 87, no. 4 (October 1982): 950–53.
18. Helen Hunt Jackson, *A Century of Dishonor: A Sketch of the United States Government's Dealings with Some of the Indian Tribes* (New York: Harper Brothers, 1881), 82–83.
19. Jackson, *A Century of Dishonor*, 291.
20. Amy Kaplan, "Manifest Domesticity," in *Anarchy of Empire in the Making of U.S. Culture* (Cambridge: Harvard University Press, 2003), 34.
21. Philip J. Deloria, *Playing Indian* (New Haven: Yale University Press, 1998), 5.
22. Sewall, *Life of Emily Dickinson*, 578–83. About a dozen of Dickinson's poems (some reprinted) saw anonymous publication in her lifetime. Helen Hunt Jackson was relentless in her efforts to get her to publish. Dickinson finally agreed to publish her poem "Success is counted sweetest," which appeared in the anonymous volume *A Masque of Poets* published by Roberts Brothers in 1878. Most readers at the time assumed the anonymous author of Dickinson's poem was Ralph Waldo Emerson.
23. See Carol Brink, *Harps in the Wind: The Story of the Singing Hutchinsons* (New York: Macmillan, 1947), 89; Dale Cockrell, *Excelsior: Journals of the Hutchinson Family Singers, 1842–1846* (New York: Pendragon Press, 1989), 263–66.
24. "The presence of the Hutchinson Family Singers in Dickinson's musical experience—that is, the likelihood that she heard them perform at Mount Holyoke while a student there and the presence of four Hutchinson Family songs in her sheet music collection—is particularly interesting because of the Hutchinsons' prominent place in the social reform movements of the time." Sandra Runzo, *"Theatricals of Day": Emily Dickinson and Nineteenth-Century American Popular Culture* (Amherst: University of Massachusetts Press, 2019), 50.
25. Amelia D. Jones, "Sunny Memories of Holyoke Life," *The Mount Holyoke* 12, no. 6 (February 1903): 290–91. The original typescripts are housed in the Mount Holyoke College Archive. See also Beth Bradford Gilchrist, *The Life of Mary Lyon* (Boston: Houghton Mifflin, 1910), 383–84. Jane T. Woodruff of Catskill, NY, is the only "Jane W." in any of the classes listed in the 1847–48 catalog. See the *Eleventh Annual Catalog of the Mount Holyoke Female Seminary, South Hadley, Mass., 1847–48* (Amherst: Press of J. S. & C. Adams, 1848), 6, Mount Holyoke College Archives and Special Collections: Catalogs, registers, and directories, identifier rg10s01–1847.
26. Richard Jackson, retired Curator of American music at The New York Public Library for the Performing Arts, in a conversation with the author, 1990.
27. Brink, *Harps in the Wind*, 89. See also Cockrell, *Excelsior*, 252–54. The Hutchinsons performed in Springfield on 28 February 1848. The *Springfield Republican* reported the next day, on the twenty-ninth, that "Hampden Hall was filled to overflowing." The concert included the song "There's a Good Time Coming," as reported in a pre-concert notice on 21 February.
28. Jesse Hutchinson, "'Get off the track!' A song for emancipation, sung by The Hutchinsons" (Boston: Published by the author, 1844), NYPL/LPA, call number AM 2-V Hutchinson, Jesse Jr.
29. Quoted in Charles Hamm, *Music in the New World* (New York: W. W. Norton, 1983), 193–94.
30. Charles Hamm, *Yesterdays: Popular Song in America* (New York: W. W. Norton, 1979), 154. Kansas achieved statehood in 1861 as a free state.
31. Johnson, *Letters*, no. 182 (Emily Dickinson to Mrs. J. G. Holland, ca. 20 January 1856).
32. Amy Kaplan, "Manifest Domesticity," *American Literature* 70, no. 3 (September 1998): 585.
33. Kaplan, "Manifest Domesticity," in *Anarchy of Empire in the Making of U.S. Culture*, 28.
34. Dale Cockrell, *Demons of Disorder: Early Blackface Minstrels and Their World* (New York: Cambridge University Press, 1997), 153.
35. Helen Hunt Jackson, *Ramona: A Story* (Boston: Roberts Brothers, 1885).
36. Johnson, *Letters*, no. 266 (Emily Dickinson to Samuel Bowles, early summer 1862).
37. See the entry on Sydney Nelson in *Musical Scotland Past and Present: Being a Dictionary of Scottish*

Musicians from about 1400 till the Present Time, comp. and ed. David Baptie (Edinburgh: John Menzies and Co.; London: Houlston and Sons, 1894), 207.

38. Sara E. Quay, *Westward Expansion* (Westport, CT: Greenwood Press, 2002), 170–72.
39. "If ever I git off this warpath / And the Indians they don't find me / I'll go right back to see that gal / The gal I left behind me." See *Publications of the Folklore Society of Texas*, no. 1, ed. Stith Thompson (Austin: Folklore Society of Texas, 1916), 29. For "Brighton Camp," see Andrew Kuntz, "Fiddler's Companion: A Descriptive Index of North American, British Isles and Irish Music for the Folk Violin and Other Instruments," http://www.ibiblio.org/fiddlers/FCfiles.html. For "The Girl I Left Behind Me," see *American Ballads and Folk Songs*, ed. John A. Lomax and Alan Lomax (New York: Macmillan, 1935), 280–81.
40. Others include "Home, Sweet Home," "Juniata," "All Quiet Along the Potomac To-Night," "Annie Laurie," and "Just Before the Battle Mother." See Richard B. Harwell, *Confederate Music* (Chapel Hill: University of North Carolina Press, 1950), 6; Christian McWhirter, *Battle Hymns: The Power and Popularity of Music in the Civil War* (Chapel Hill: University of North Carolina Press, 2012), 102.
41. Shira Wolosky, *Emily Dickinson: A Voice of War* (New Haven: Yale University Press, 1984), 37. Recent scholarship by John Shoptaw, Cody Mars, and especially Shira Wolosky has expanded a view into Dickinson "as a witness of and a commentator on the great struggles of her times." Quoted in Sandra Runzo, *"Theatricals of Day,"* 184.
42. "A Day! Help! Help!" in *The Complete Poems of Emily Dickinson*, ed. Ralph W. Franklin (Cambridge: Harvard University Press, 1999), no. 58 (1859). Even in 1858, when this poem was written, "the rhetoric of war and the conflict of issues were already making themselves felt in the national consciousness." Wolosky, *Emily Dickinson: A Voice of War*, 40.
43. Edward Dickinson also had a hand in raising money for uniforms and organizing an additional regiment. See Wolosky, *Emily Dickinson: A Voice of War*, 53.
44. On 14 October 1862 the *Springfield Republican* reprinted a piece from the *New York Evening Post*, a parody of "Yankee Doodle" whose first verse reads: "The rebs have trampled down our fields, / Destroyed our walls and ditches, / But Abe can build the fence again, / And Andy mend the breaches. / Lincoln is the man we need; / Johnson, too, is handy; / Yankee Doodle, boys hurrah for Uncle Abe and Andy!"
45. For "Drunken Sailor," see Kuntz, "Fiddler's Companion." "Believe Me If All Those Endearing Young Charms" as "My Lodging Is in the Cold Ground," "Hail to the Chief," and "The Girl I Left Behind Me" can be found in George B. Bruce and Daniel Decatur Emmett, *The Drummer's and Fifer's Guide or Self-instructor: Containing a Plain and Easy Introduction of the Rudimental Principles for the Drum and Fife* (New York: Wm. Hall, 1862), nos. 45, 52, 62.
46. *Philadelphia Press*, 17 January 1861, quoted in McWhirter, *Battle Hymns*, 34; see also 188.
47. John Stevens Cabot Abbott, *The History of the Civil War in America: Comprising a Full and Impartial Account of the Origin and Progress of the Rebellion . . .* , vol. 1 (New York: Ledyard Bill, 1863), 89, 207, 230.
48. Jan Swafford, *Charles Ives: A Life with Music* (New York: W. W. Norton, 1996), 25.
49. For an example of a Civil War regimental band book, see [Hosea Ripley], "Manuscript collection of dances, marches and other music for band. J. W. Perkins, 17th U.S. Regt. Band, Dec. 27, 1862," and, added in a different hand, "Hosea Ripley's book, Bethel, Me., no. 328 'Sweet Home,'" NYPL/LPA, call number Mus. Res. Amer. *MV.
50. The Twenty-first Regiment had a roster of about forty musicians led by Reuben K. Waters and Warren B. Johnson, both of Webster, Massachusetts. See Charles Folsom Walcott, *History of the 21st Regiment Massachusetts Volunteers* (Boston: Houghton Mifflin, 1882), 438.
51. McWhirter, *Battle Hymns*, 127–29.
52. Austin was drafted on 13 May 1864. See Sewall, *Life of Emily Dickinson*, xxiv.
53. Frazar Stearns had enlisted in the Twenty-first Regiment of Massachusetts Volunteers and was a member of Company I. An account of the battle at New Bern and Stearns's death appeared in the *Springfield Republican* on 19 and 22 March 1862. See also Walcott, *History of the 21st Regiment Massachusetts Volunteers*, 61–65. That Stearns was "the first Amherst casualty," see Leyda, *The Years and Hours of Emily Dickinson*, 1:lxxi. William Stearns succeeded Edward Hitchcock as president of Amherst College in 1854, serving until 1876.
54. Ackmann, *These Fevered Days*, 118. According to the Reverend Stearns's published tribute to his son, Frazar "was composing music," and "though he had been subjected to the drill of exercises, and had his favorite pieces, he generally preferred, whether in social circles or

in private, to improvise his music. When the inspiration was upon him, he would express in subdued or stirring chords, the mood of the hour. One might learn from the sweet, sad sounds of his piano, or its semitonic intervals, or from its jubilant notes, or its slow and solemn measures the otherwise hidden emotions of his heart." William A. Stearns, *Adjutant Stearns* (Boston: Sabbath School Society, 1862), 28, 149–50. See also Barton Levi St. Armand, *Emily Dickinson and Her Culture: The Soul's Society* (New York: Cambridge University Press, 1984), 112.

55. Johnson, *Letters*, no. 255 (Emily Dickinson to Frances and Louise Norcross, late March 1862). A report on the funeral "from the Village Church" appeared in the *Springfield Republican* on 24 March 1862.

56. *The Poems of Emily Dickinson*, ed. Thomas H. Johnson (Cambridge: Belknap Press of Harvard University Press, 1955), no. 335, 'Tis not that Dying hurts us so — " (1862). This poem of consolation was sent by Dickinson to her Norcross cousins on the death of their father, Loring Norcross. See Johnson, *Letters*, no. 278 (Emily Dickinson to Louise and Frances Norcross, late January 1863). For a discussion of Dickinson and her poems as gifts, see Daniel Manheim, "'And row my blossoms o'er!': Gift-Giving and Emily Dickinson's Poetic Vocation," *Emily Dickinson Journal* 20, no. 2 (2011): 1–32.

Chapter 9: Fiddle Tunes, Minstrel Music, and Musical Borrowing

1. The vernacular music represented in Dickinson's bound volume includes fifteen tunes associated with the Irish/English/Scottish and American fiddle repertoire. Additional music of this type can be found in the variation sets. See "Kinlock of Kinlock" and "Speed the Plough"; from the march section, see "Bonaparte's March Crossing the Rhine"; from the quickstep section, see the "Lucy Neal Quick Step"; and from the waltz section, "Linden Waltz." (For more information on these pieces, see the online Appendix B, the annotated bibliography.)
2. Charles Hamm, *Yesterdays: Popular Song in America* (New York: W. W. Norton, 1979), 99.
3. *The Complete Poems of Emily Dickinson*, ed. Ralph W. Franklin (Cambridge: Harvard University Press, 1999), no. 686, "It makes no difference abroad — " (1863).
4. According to Miller: "Dickinson does anthropomorphize an animal as a black man.... [T]he line 'No Black bird bates His Banjo — ' must allude to African Americans, since no bird plays a banjo and stereotyped black men do, as depicted on sheet music for minstrel tunes Dickinson owned ('It makes no difference abroad'; [Franklin, *The Complete Poems*, no. 686])." Cristanne Miller, *Reading in Time: Emily Dickinson in the Nineteenth Century* (Amherst: University of Massachusetts Press, 2012), 15–16. Helen Vendler argues that "the Banjo, sometimes associated with black musicians, or musicians in blackface, may be making the Black bird into an American Black Banjo-Player, the antithesis of the warbling English nightingale." Helen Vendler, *Dickinson: Selected Poems and Commentaries* (Cambridge: Belknap Press of Harvard University Press, 2010), 287.
5. Dale Cockrell, *Everybody's Doin' It: Sex, Music, and Dance in New York, 1840–1917* (New York: W. W. Norton, 2019), 17.
6. For "Ethiopian creations," see Vera Brodsky Lawrence, *Strong on Music: The New York Music Scene in the Days of George Templeton Strong*, vol. 1, *Resonances, 1836–1849* (Chicago: University of Chicago Press, 1988), 104. The origins of "Turkey in the Straw" are ambiguous, having been derived from two or more tunes such as "Natchez Under the Hill," as noted in Christopher J. Smith, "Blacks and Irish on the Riverine Frontiers: The Roots of American Popular Music," *Southern Culture* 17 (Spring 2011): 94. Referred to as a "floater," the tune was associated with several names and tune branches. See Andrew Kuntz, "Fiddler's Companion: A Descriptive Index of North American, British Isles and Irish Music for the Folk Violin and Other Instruments," http://www.ibiblio.org/fiddlers/FCfiles.html; Cockrell, *Everybody's Doin' It*, 14–15. For additional background on minstrelsy and the minstrel music in Dickinson's bound volume, see Sandra Runzo, "Popular Culture," in *Emily Dickinson in Context*, ed. Eliza Richards (New York: Cambridge University Press, 2013), 219–25.
7. See Christopher J. Smith, *The Creolization of American Culture: William Sydney Mount and the Roots of Blackface Minstrelsy* (Urbana: University of Illinois Press, 2013), 33; Eric Lott, *Love and Theft: Blackface Minstrelsy and the American Working Class* (New York: Oxford University Press, 1993), 48–49.

8. Lott, *Love and Theft*, 78.
9. Charles Mackay, *Extraordinary Popular Delusions and the Madness of Crowds* (New York: Barnes & Noble, 2002), 629. Originally published in 1841 as *Memoirs of Extraordinary Popular Delusions and the Madness of Crowds* by the Office of the National Illustrated Library, London. A second edition was published in 1852.
10. Davy Crockett made more than one trip to New York City, the last being in 1835. In 1842 Dickens came over from England to make a tour of the United States. In February he visited several subterranean dance halls in the Five Points district of New York City. See Cockrell, *Everybody's Doin' It*, 18–19, 27–29.
11. Chris Goertzen, *George P. Knauff's Virginia Reels and the History of American Fiddling* (Jackson: University Press of Mississippi, 2017), 20.
12. Dale Cockrell, *Demons of Disorder: Early Blackface Minstrels and Their World* (New York: Cambridge University Press, 1997), 155–57.
13. Smith, *The Creolization of American Culture*, 25.
14. Hamm, *Yesterdays*, 134.
15. *Springfield Republican*, 20 September 1850. As to the "veil of respectability," see Hans Nathan, *Dan Emmett and the Rise of Early Negro Minstrelsy* (Norman: University of Oklahoma Press, 1962), 216.
16. Dickinson, Lavinia Norcross, 1833–1899. Diary: autograph manuscript, 1851 January 1 through December 31, Dickinson Family Papers, 1757–1934, MS Am 1118.95 (226), Houghton Library, Harvard University, https://iiif.lib.harvard.edu/manifests/view/drs:47289000$107i; see the entry for 17 September 1851. On 9 September, Lavinia also noted in her diary that she had "heard Othello at Museum." Edward le Roy Rice, *Monarchs of Minstrelsy, from "Daddy" Rice to Date* (New York: Kenny Publishing Co., 1911), 62, reports that "P. S. Gilmore, who organized and led for many years the famous band bearing his name, was a member of Ordway's Aeolians in Boston, 1851, where he sat on the end and played the tambourine. June 24, 1851, he began an engagement in Hartford, Con., with the above company."
17. Smith, *The Creolization of American Culture*, 76.
18. Sandra Runzo, *"Theatricals of Day": Emily Dickinson and Nineteenth-Century American Popular Culture* (Amherst: University of Massachusetts Press, 2019), 63–64, 99.
19. *The Letters of Emily Dickinson*, ed. Thomas H. Johnson and Theodora Ward (hereafter Johnson, *Letters*), 3 vols. (Cambridge: Harvard University Press, 1958), no. 223 (Emily Dickinson to Samuel Bowles, early August 1860). See also Runzo, *"Theatricals of Day,"* 94–96; Jay Leyda, *The Years and Hours of Emily Dickinson*, 2 vols. (New Haven: Yale University Press, 1960), 2:12. Leyda dates this to Sunday night, 5 August 1860.
20. For "staging [of] racial categories, boundaries, and types," see Lott, *Love and Theft*, 37. For interpretations of this letter from Dickinson to Bowles, see Runzo, *"Theatricals of Day,"* 94–95. See also Wesley King "The White Symbolic of Emily Dickinson," *Emily Dickinson Journal* 18, no. 1 (2009): 60.
21. Johnson, *Letters*, no. 34 (Emily Dickinson to George H. Gould, February 1850); "Valentine," *The Indicator* 2, no. 7 (February 1850): 223–24. Thanks to musicologist Katie Callam for the observation on Dickinson employing a pseudo-Latin. For Dickinson's use of Latin grammatical models, see Wendy Martin, "Earth Is Heaven," in *An American Triptych: Anne Bradstreet, Emily Dickinson, Adrienne Rich* (Chapel Hill: University of North Carolina Press, 1984), 141.
22. Johnson, *Letters*, no. 29 (Emily Dickinson to Joel Warren Norcross, 11 January 1850). Dickinson asks in this letter, "Have you found *Susannah* yet?" Sandra Runzo, *"Theatricals of Day,"* 198, n. 18, cites this as a reference to Stephen Foster's "Oh, Susannah!" Dickinson continues, "Roses will fade—time flies on—Lady of beauty." This is a reference to the song "Lady of Beauty," published in many collections, including *Diprose's Royal Songbook* (1845) and *The British Minstrel* (1848). The music is by William Knyvett (Boston: Oliver Ditson, [1849–1854]). NYPL/LPA, call number AM 2-V, Knyvett. Thanks to R. H. Winnick for bringing this song title to my attention.
23. Franklin, *The Complete Poems*, no. 381, "I cannot dance upon my Toes — " (1862).
24. Runzo, "Popular Culture," 221.
25. See the entry on "Glee" in Willi Apel, *Harvard Dictionary of Music*, 2nd ed., rev. and enlarged (Cambridge: Belknap Press of Harvard University Press, 1973), 348.
26. Gumbo Chaff [pseud. Elias Howe], *The Ethiopian Glee Book; a Collection of Popular Negro Melodies in four parts. Arranged for Quartette Clubs* (Boston: Published by Elias Howe, no. 9 Cornhill, 1848–50), NYPL/LPA, call number JNB 96-5.

27. Mary Elizabeth Kromer Bernhard, "Portrait of a Family: Emily Dickinson's Norcross Connection," *New England Quarterly* 60, no. 3 (September 1987): 375.
28. Lydia Maria Child, *The Frugal Housewife: Dedicated to Those Who Are Not Ashamed of Economy* (Boston: Carter, Hendee, & Babcock, 1831). A marked copy from the Dickinson library is in the Dickinson Collection in the Houghton Library, Harvard University. See Alfred Habegger, *My Wars Are Laid Away in Books: The Life of Emily Dickinson* (New York: Random House, 2001), 62–63. See also Aífe Murray, *Maid as Muse: How Servants Changed Emily Dickinson's Life and Language* (Durham: University of New Hampshire Press, 2009), 59–62.
29. Martha Dickinson Bianchi, *The Life and Letters of Emily Dickinson* (Boston: Houghton Mifflin, 1924), 13.
30. Johnson, *Letters*, no. 8 (Emily Dickinson to Abiah Root, 25 September 1845).
31. "She makes all the bread for her father only likes hers." Thomas Wentworth Higginson to his wife, 17 August 1870, in Leyda, *The Years and Hours of Emily Dickinson*, 2:152.
32. Murray, *Maid as Muse*, 10; for the names and dates of some of the first servants hired by the Dickinsons, see 243.
33. Murray, *Maid as Muse*, 18, 10.
34. For examples of Dickinson writing on scraps, see Emily Dickinson, *The Gorgeous Nothings*, ed. Marta L. Werner and Jen Bervin with a preface by Susan Howe (New York: New Directions, in association with Granary Books, 2013).
35. Franklin, *Poems*, no. 79, "New feet within my garden go — " (1859).
36. Johnson, *Letters*, no. 907 (Emily Dickinson to Frances and Louise Norcross, early August 1884).
37. See Murray, *Maid as Muse*, 166.
38. Franklin, *The Complete Poems*, no. 383, "I Like to see it lap the miles" (1862). This poem was titled "The Railway Train" by her first editors and published in *Poems by Emily Dickinson*, 2nd ser., ed. T. W. Higginson and Mabel Loomis Todd (Boston: Roberts Brothers, 1891), 39.
39. These artworks include James Henry Beard (1812–1893), *Western Raftsmen* (1846); William Sidney Mount (1807–1868), *Study for Dance of the Haymakers*; and George Caleb Bingham (1811–1879), *The Jolly Flatboatmen* (1846). See Smith, *Creolization of American Culture*, 4, 56–60.
40. Smith, "Blacks and Irish on the Riverine Frontiers," 75–102; Karol Mullaney-Dignam, "Sources for the Study of Music in the Irish Country House," paper presented at the International Association of Music Libraries conference, Dublin, 2011. According to Mullaney-Dignam, ledger books show that in the eighteenth and nineteenth centuries, local musicians were brought in to perform at the country house estates owned by the Irish Protestant nobility and gentry. See also Lenwood Sloan and Mick Maloney, "Two Roads Diverged: A Dialogue on Irish and Black Contributions to American Culture," presentations given at the Irish Arts Center, New York City, 18 September, 24 October, and 7 November 2012.
41. Johnson, *Letters*, no. 156 (Emily Dickinson to Austin Dickinson, 14 March 1854). In March 1854, the Holden family moved from Amherst to New Haven. See Murray, *Maid as Muse*, 244. Even in her eventual seclusion, Dickinson reached out to all classes. In an obituary for Emily Dickinson published in the *Springfield Republican*, Susan Dickinson wrote, "There are many houses among all classes into which treasures of fruit and flowers and ambrosial dishes for the sick and well were constantly sent, that will forever miss those evidences of her unselfish consideration, and mourn afresh that she screened herself from close acquaintance." *Springfield Republican*, 18 May 1886.
42. Johnson, *Letters*, no. 44 (Emily Dickinson to Austin Dickinson, 22 June 1851).
43. Millicent Todd Bingham, *Emily Dickinson's Home: Letters of Edward Dickinson and His Family* (New York: Harper and Brothers Publishers, 1955), 145, n. 1.
44. Susan Dickinson, "Society at Amherst Fifty Years Ago," autograph manuscripts and typescripts, [undated], Dickinson Family Papers, Am 1118.95, Houghton Library, Harvard University; quoted in Bianchi, *Life and Letters*, 39–40.
45. M. R. Dakin, "Desk Chair Detective: Around the World with Charles Thompson," in *The Consecrated Eminence*, Archives and Special Collections, Amherst College, https://consecrate-deminence.wordpress.com/2016/02/27/desk-chair-detective-around-the-world-with-charles-thompson/.
46. Murray, *Maid as Muse*, 126. For biographical information on Thompson, see James Avery Smith, *History of the Black Population of Amherst, Massachusetts, 1728–1870* (Boston: New England Historic Genealogical Society, 1999), 125.
47. Abigail Eloise (Stearns) Lee, *Professor Charley: A Sketch of Charles Thompson by A.E.L.* (Boston: D.

C. Heath, 1902), 8. Abigail Stearns had two brothers, William French Stearns (b. 1834) and Frazar Augustus Stearns (1840–1862), who was killed at the battle of New Bern. During the war, Charles Thompson was the servant of the assistant surgeon of the Twenty-first Regiment of Massachusetts Volunteers, in which Frazar Stearns served, and was present at Stearns's death. Frazar Stearns was quite musical. See Stearns, *Adjutant Stearns*, 141–42. The "brother" that Abigail Eloise Stearns Lee refers to who was being taught by Thompson would have been Frazar Stearns.

48. Lee, *Professor Charley*, 8.
49. Goertzen, *George P. Knauff's Virginia Reels*, 50–51. See also Kuntz, "Fiddler's Companion," http://www.ibiblio.org/fiddlers/MON.htm.
50. Franklin, *The Complete Poems*, no. 79, "New feet within my garden go —" (1859). See Aífe Murray, *Maid as Muse*, 156, 245. Murray notes the death of longtime Dickinson gardener Amos Newport in August 1859. For biographical information on Newport, see Smith, *History of the Black Population of Amherst, Massachusetts*, 102.
51. Elias Howe Jr., *Figures to the 18 Sets of Cotillions and Several of the Hornpipes & Contra Dances Contained in the Musician's Companion by a Professor of Dancing* (Providence: Published by Elias Howe, no. 98 Westminster Street, 1842), 22–23, from the collections of the American Antiquarian Society. This cotillion pamphlet contains "figures" (instructions) for dances to "Fishers Hornpipe" and "Durang's Hornpipe," the music for both of which was collected by Dickinson. Howe moved from Providence, settling permanently in Boston in 1843. See Paul F. Wells, "Elias Howe, William Bradbury Ryan, and Irish Music in Nineteenth-Century Boston," *Journal of the Society for American Music* 4, no. 4 (November 2010): 408.
52. For an example of one of these method books, see Elias Howe Jr., *Howe's School for the clarionett; containing new and complete instructions for the clarionett, with a large collection of favorite marches quick-steps, waltzes, hornpipes, contra dances, songs and six setts of cotillions, arranged with figures, containing over 150 pieces of music* (Boston: E. Howe Jr., [ca. 1843]).
53. Paul Wells, email correspondence with the author, 5 October 2019.
54. Goertzen, *George P. Knauff's Virginia Reels*, 72–73.
55. Johnson, *Letters*, no. 184 (Emily Dickinson to John Graves, late April 1856).
56. Gertrude M. Graves, "A Cousin's Memories of Emily Dickinson," *Boston Sunday Globe*, 12 January 1930, reprinted in *Dickinson in Her Own Time: A Biographical Chronicle of Her Life, Drawn from Recollections, Interviews, and Memoirs by Family, Friends, and Associates*, ed. Jane Donahue Eberwein, Stephanie Farrar, and Cristanne Miller (Iowa City: University of Iowa Press, 2015), 185. Jay Leyda situates this event at the end of March 1854, when Edward Dickinson and his family left for Washington, DC. See Leyda, *The Years and Hours of Emily Dickinson*, 1:301–2.
57. MacGregor Jenkins, *Emily Dickinson, Friend and Neighbor* (Boston: Little, Brown, 1930), 36.
58. After Emily's death, Susan Dickinson made a short list of her outstanding memories and traits of Emily Dickinson. On that list is Emily's performance at the piano of "The Devil." Martha Nell Smith, "Distance and Beloveds," Emily Dickinson International Society annual meeting, 1 August 2020.
59. Mrs. Kate Anthon to Mrs. Susan Dickinson, 6 September 1906, quoted in Leyda, *The Years and Hours of Emily Dickinson*, 1:366.
60. This quote refers to a social evening at The Evergreens in either late February or mid-March 1859. Mrs. Kate Anthon to Martha Bianchi, 8 October 1917, in Martha Dickinson Bianchi, *Emily Dickinson Face to Face: Unpublished Letters with Notes and Reminiscences* (Boston: Houghton Mifflin, 1932), 156–57. See also Johnson, *Letters*, no. 202 (Emily Dickinson to Mrs. J. G. Holland, ca. 20 February 1859). Johnson's note verifies Kate Anthon's visit. See also Johnson, *Letters*, no. 203 (Emily Dickinson to Catherine Scott Turner, ca. March 1859). When Anthon visited Dickinson in 1859 and heard her improvisations, they commemorated Anthon's visit with a daguerreotype, recently discovered, in which the two are supposedly pictured. See Runzo, *"Theatricals of Day,"* 151, 217, n. 6.
61. Clara Newman Turner, [Emily Dickinson: reminiscences]: MS. (unsigned, unidentified hand), [n.p., undated], 30s. (33p.) in 3 folders, MS Am 1118.7 (*54M-225 [2]), Houghton Library, Harvard University, https://iiif.lib.harvard.edu/manifests/view/drs:43771408$1i. Turner remembers the Dickinson piano incorrectly as a Chickering, not the 1851 Hallet & Davis piano that is in the Dickinson Room at the Houghton Library. In describing Emily Dickinson's improvisations, Millicent Todd Bingham paraphrases Turner: "One who heard her strange, limited repertoire said that before seating herself at the piano Emily covered the upper and

lower octaves so that the length of the keyboard might correspond to that of the old-fashioned instrument on which she had learned to play." Bingham, *Emily Dickinson's Home*, 153.
62. Alfred Habegger, *My Wars Are Laid Away in Books: The Life of Emily Dickinson* (New York: Random House, 2001), 282.
63. "Clara Newman Turner, Reminiscences, ca. 1896," in Eberwein, Farrar, and Miller, *Dickinson in Her Own Time, 144*; see also the introductory note on 137.
64. Turner, "Emily Dickinson: Reminiscences," 18.
65. Bianchi, *The Life and Letters of Emily Dickinson*, 64.
66. Dickinson uses the word "tunes" several times in her letters. See Johnson, *Letters*, no. 7 (Emily Dickinson to Abiah Root, 3 August 1845): "Aunt Selby says she shant let me have many tunes now"; no. 20 (Emily Dickinson to Abiah Root, 17 January 1848): "After our return, Father wishing to hear the Piano, I like an obedient daughter, played & sang a few tunes, much to his apparent gratification"; no. 184 (Emily Dickinson to John Graves, late April 1856): "I play the old, odd tunes"; no. 255 (Emily Dickinson to Frances and Louise Norcross, late March 1862): "We will play his tunes—maybe he can hear them." Here Dickinson refers to Frazar Stearns's compositions and his improvisations at the piano.
67. "And the lounge polka a little": Johnson, *Letters*, no. 204 (Emily Dickinson to Mrs. G. J. Holland, 2 March 1859); "Auld Lang Syne" and "Long, Long Ago": no. 13 (Emily Dickinson to Abiah Root, 8 September 1846). The references to "Bonnie Doon" and the jigs can be found in Franklin, *The Complete Poems*, no. 2, "Sic transit gloria mundi" (1852), and no. 45, "I counted till they danced so" (1858), respectively.

Chapter 10: The Poetry Takes Hold

1. Dickinson's first poems were written in 1850 (one), 1852 (one), 1853 (one), 1854 (one), 1858 (forty-three), 1859 (eighty-two), 1860 (fifty-four), 1861 (eighty-eight), 1862 (227), and so on. See Aífe Murray, *Maid as Muse: How Servants Changed Emily Dickinson's Life and Language* (Durham: University of New Hampshire Press, 2009), 79.
2. *The Complete Poems of Emily Dickinson*, ed. Ralph W. Franklin (Cambridge: Harvard University Press, 1999), no. 1, a Valentine (1850); no. 2, "Sic transit gloria mundi" (1852). The line "How doth the busy bee" is sourced from Isaac Watts, "How doth the little busy bee," see *Divine Songs for the Use of Children* (New Haven: J. Babcock, 1824), 19–20. See also Franklin, *The Complete Poems*, no. 1779, "To make a prairie it takes a clover and one bee" (undated).
3. Victoria N. Morgan, *Emily Dickinson and Hymn Culture: Tradition and Experience* (Farnham, England: Ashgate Press, 2010), 21, 162.
4. Franklin, *The Complete Poems*, no. 4, "I have a Bird in spring" (1854). See chapter 4 for additional musical context for this early poem.
5. Julie Dobrow, *After Emily: Two Remarkable Women and the Legacy of America's Greatest Poet* (New York: W. W. Norton, 2018), 127; Jane Donahue Eberwein, "Introducing a Religious Poet: The 1890 Poems of Emily Dickinson." *Christianity and Literature* 39, no. 3 (Spring 1990): 241.
6. *The Letters of Emily Dickinson*, ed. Thomas H. Johnson and Theodora Ward (hereafter Johnson, *Letters*), 3 vols. (Cambridge: Harvard University Press, 1958), no. 265 (Emily Dickinson to T. W. Higginson, 7 June 1862).
7. Dickinson scholar Paul Crumbley demonstrates that the letters exchanged between Dickinson and Higginson through the practice of nineteenth-century gift culture not only supported Dickinson's activities as a poet but also motivated "her to eclipse even further the limits of conventional poetic form in the pages of her manuscript books." See Paul Crumbley, "Dickinson's Correspondence and the Politics of Gift-Based Circulation," in *Reading Emily Dickinson's Letters: Critical Essays*, ed. Jane Donahue Eberwein and Cindy MacKenzie (Amherst: University of Massachusetts Press, 2009), 43–50.
8. Johnson, *Letters*, no. 265 (Emily Dickinson to T. W. Higginson, 7 June 1862).
9. Johnson, *Letters*, no. 261 (Emily Dickinson to Thomas Wentworth Higginson, 25 April 1862). See also Carolyn Lindley Cooley, *The Music of Emily Dickinson's Poems and Letters: A Study of Imagery and Form* (London: McFarland and Company, 2003), 20. Cooley argues that expressing these words to Higginson may have been an indicator of "Dickinson's growing awareness that the music of nature might, indeed, supersede that of the man-made, instrumental variety."

10. Franklin, *The Complete Poems*, no. 1020, "There is a Zone whose even Years / No Solstice interrupt — " (1865). For a discussion of Dickinson's "noon," see Richard Benson Sewall, *The Life of Emily Dickinson* (New York: Farrar, Straus and Giroux, 1974), 680–81.
11. Franklin, *The Complete Poems*, no. 378, "Better — than Music!" (1862).
12. Judith Farr, *The Passion of Emily Dickinson* (Cambridge: Harvard University Press, 1992), 297; *The Complete Poems of Emily Dickinson*, ed. Thomas H. Johnson (Boston: Little Brown and Company, 1960), no. 797, "By my Window have I for Scenery" (ca. 1863).
13. Franklin, *The Complete Poems*, no. 402, "To hear an Oriole sing" (1862).
14. Farr, *The Passion of Emily Dickinson*, 254.
15. Franklin, *The Complete Poems*, no. 873, "It is a lonesome Glee — " (1864). At Mount Holyoke, Dickinson used *The Vocalist: Consisting of Short and Easy Glees, or Songs in parts: Arranged for Soprano, Alto, Tenor, and Bass Voices* (Boston: Wilkins, Carter, 1844). See Carlton Lowenberg, *Emily Dickinson's Textbooks* (Lafayette, CA: C. Lowenberg, 1986), 72.
16. Franklin, *The Complete Poems*, no. 873, "It is a lonesome Glee — " (1864); Jed Deppman, "Dickinson and Philosophy," in *Trying to Think with Emily Dickinson* (Amherst: University of Massachusetts Press, 2008), 107.
17. Christina Pugh, "'Criterion for Tune': Dickinson and Sound," in *The New Emily Dickinson Studies*, ed. Michelle Kohler (Cambridge: Cambridge University Press, 2019), 70–71.
18. Franklin, *The Complete Poems*, no. 347, "I dreaded that first Robin, so" (1862).
19. Franklin, *The Complete Poems*, no. 1042, "When they come back — if Blossoms do — " (1865).
20. Johnson, *Letters*, no. 190 (Emily Dickinson to Joseph A. Sweetser, early summer 1858), Amherst, July(?), Friday night, as noted by Jay Leyda, *The Years and Hours of Emily Dickinson*, 2 vols. (New Haven: Yale University Press, 1960), 1:356.
21. Sewall, *Life of Emily Dickinson*, 464.
22. "Long Time Ago," words attributed to George Pope Morris. A quartet arrangement of this tune, "On the Lake Where Drooped the Willow," titled "A Southern Melody," arranged by George Kingsley, is included in Kingsley's *Social Choir*, which was one of the required music books at Mount Holyoke. See George Kingsley, *The Social Choir: Designed for a Class Book, and the Social Circle*, vol. 3 (Boston: Crocker and Brewster, 1847), 160–61.
23. Franklin, *The Complete Poems*, no. 1042, "When they come back — if Blossoms do — " (1865).
24. Johnson, *Letters*, no. 261 (Emily Dickinson to Thomas Wentworth Higginson, 25 April 1862).
25. See James R. Guthrie, *Emily Dickinson's Vision: Illness and Identity in Her Poetry* (Gainesville: University of Florida Press, 1998).
26. Sewall, *Life of Emily Dickinson*, 204; Alfred Habegger, *My Wars Are Laid Away in Books: The Life of Emily Dickinson* (New York: Random House, 2001), 436–37; "Loss of her muse would overwhelm her": Thomas H. Johnson, *Emily Dickinson: An Interpretive Biography* (Cambridge: Belknap Press of Harvard University Press, 1955), 84; Civil War: Genevieve Taggard, *The Life and Mind of Emily Dickinson* (New York: Alfred A. Knopf, 1930), 6–10; see also Connie Ann Kirk, *Emily Dickinson: A Biography* (Westport, CT: Greenwood Press, 2004), 79–80.
27. Dickinson's use of "a fuller tune" appears in her 1861 poem "I shall kéep singing!" Franklin, *The Complete Poems*, no. 270.
28. Clara Bellinger Green, "The Sketch Book: A Reminiscence of Emily Dickinson," *The Bookman: A Review of Books and Life* 60, no. 3 (November 1924): 291–93, reprinted in *Dickinson in Her Own Time: A Biographical Chronicle of Her Life, Drawn from Recollections, Interviews, and Memoirs by Family, Friends, and Associates*, ed. Jane Donahue Eberwein, Stephanie Farrar, and Cristanne Miller (Iowa City: University of Iowa Press, 2015), 180. This anecdote is quoted in Sewall, *Life of Emily Dickinson*, 409, n. 6; and in Cooley, *The Music of Emily Dickinson's Poems and Letters*, 20. Josephine Pollitt, in discussing Dickinson's piano playing, wrote, "It is said that she had despaired of acquiring perfection in the art after having heard Rubinstein play in Boston." Josephine Pollitt, *Emily Dickinson: The Human Background of Her Poetry* (New York: Harper and Brothers, 1930), 309.
29. Judy Jo Small, *Positive as Sound: Emily Dickinson's Rhyme* (Athens: University of Georgia Press, 1990), 51.
30. Sewall, *Life of Emily Dickinson*, 407.
31. Petra Meyer-Frazier, "American Women's Roles in Domestic Music Making as Revealed in Parlor Song Collections: 1820–1870" (PhD diss., University of Colorado, 1999), 29.
32. R. Allen Lott, *From Paris to Peoria: How European Piano Virtuosos Brought Classical Music to the American Heartland* (New York: Oxford University Press, 2003), 171.

33. "Rubinstein Concert Haynes Opera House," *Springfield Republican*, 15 October 1872; "Among the Arrivals at the Haynes House Yesterday," *Springfield Republican*, 22 October 1872; "Rubinstein Farewell Grand Concert," *Springfield Republican*, 5 May 1873. For an overview of Rubinstein's American tour, see R. Allen Lott, "Anton Rubinstein in America (1872–1873)," *American Music* 21, no. 3 (Autumn 2003): 291–318.
34. Franklin, *The Complete Poems*, no. 1270, "The Show is not the Show" (1872). See also *Emily Dickinson's Poems: As She Preserved Them*, ed. Cristanne Miller (Cambridge: Belknap Press of Harvard University Press, 2016), 565–66. Dickinson's manuscript interchanges the lines "Fair Glee" and "Fair Play."
35. See Sandra Runzo, *"Theatricals of Day": Emily Dickinson and Nineteenth-Century American Popular Culture* (Amherst: University of Massachusetts Press, 2019), 195, n. 4. Copies of Rubinstein's published piano compositions are in the Martha Dickinson Bianchi Papers in the John Hay Library, Brown University. These include his *Serenade Russe* and *Kamennoi-Ostrow*.
36. Johnson, *Letters*, no. 370 (Emily Dickinson to Mrs. J. G. Holland, ca. 1872). Jay Leyda dates this letter to mid-October. Leyda, *The Years and Hours of Emily Dickinson*, 2:191.
37. Johnson, *Letters*, no. 381 (Emily Dickinson to Thomas Wentworth Higginson, late 1872); Leyda, *The Years and Hours of Emily Dickinson*, 2:196. Leyda assigns this letter to December 1872. Higginson had paid his first visit to Amherst to see Dickinson in "mighty summer," August 1870.
38. Franklin, *The Complete Poems*, no. 1511, "The fascinating chill that Music leaves" (1879); Cooley, *The Music of Emily Dickinson's Poems and Letters*, 20; Johnson, *Poems of Emily Dickinson*, no. 1480, "The fascinating chill that music leaves" (ca. 1879).
39. Sewall, *Life of Emily Dickinson*, 407–9.
40. See Johnson, *Letters*, no. 190 (Emily Dickinson to Joseph A. Sweetser, early summer 1858).
41. Johnson, *Letters*, no. 390 (Emily Dickinson to Frances Norcross, late May 1873).
42. *Springfield Republican*, 12 May 1873. See also Chauncy Loomis, "Charles Francis Hall (1821–1871)," *Arctic* 35, no. 3 (September 1982): 443.
43. Lott, *From Paris to Peoria*, 166.
44. Johnson, *Letters*, no. 665 (Emily Dickinson to Mrs. Elizabeth Carmichael, ca. 1880).
45. "Noise in the Pool, at Noon": Johnson, *Letters*, no. 261 (Emily Dickinson to T. W. Higginson, 25 April 1862); "Experiment": Franklin, *The Complete Poems*, no. 1042, "When they come back — if Blossoms do — " (1865); "If fame belonged to me," and "on the chase — ": Johnson, *Letters*, no. 265 (Emily Dickinson to Thomas Wentworth Higginson, 7 June 1862).

Chapter 11: Hymns and Ballads: More Musical Borrowings

1. *The Letters of Emily Dickinson*, ed. Thomas H. Johnson and Theodora Ward (hereafter Johnson, *Letters*), 3 vols. (Cambridge: Harvard University Press, 1958), no. 39 (Emily Dickinson to Abiah Root, late 1850); Ralph W. Franklin, "Emily Dickinson to Abiah Root: Ten Reconstructed Letters," *Emily Dickinson Journal* 4, no. 1 (Spring 1995): 27, 29. For a discussion of the revival of 1850, see Roger Lundin, *Emily Dickinson and the Art of Belief* (Grand Rapids: William B. Eerdmans Publishing, 2004), 50–56.
2. Richard Benson Sewall, *The Life of Emily Dickinson* (New York: Farrar, Straus and Giroux, 1974), 24.
3. Johnson, *Letters*, no. 750 (Emily Dickinson to Otis P. Lord, 30 April 1882).
4. *The Complete Poems of Emily Dickinson*, ed. Ralph W. Franklin (Cambridge: Harvard University Press, 1999), no. 365, "I know that He exists" (1862), and no. 128, "Going to Heaven!" (1859).
5. Emma Duncan, "Defamiliarizing Faith: Emily Dickinson's Use of Hymn Meter, Scripture, and Metaphor," paper delivered at the Emily Dickinson International Society conference, Asilomar, CA, 2019. Cited with permission of the presenter. For "If I'm lost — now — ," see Franklin, *The Complete Poems*, no. 316 (1862).
6. Johnson, *Letters*, no. 8 (Emily Dickinson to Abiah Root, 25 September 1845). The scripture reference is from James 2:17.
7. The tune "Evening Shade," words by John Leland (1792), music by Stephen Jenks (1805), is sung today, and is a staple of the shape note repertoire, most notably sung from *The Sacred Harp* (1991), which was first published in 1844 (hymn no. 209). In the same letter, Dickinson

immediately continues, noting the approach of autumn's "sere and yellow leaf," referencing act 5, scene 3 of Shakespeare's *Macbeth*. See Páraic Finnerty, *Emily Dickinson's Shakespeare* (Amherst: University of Massachusetts Press, 2006), 127.

8. Johnson, *Letters*, no. 278 (Emily Dickinson to Louise and Frances Norcross, late January 1863).
9. Here "scalding" refers to the poem "I shall know why — when Time is over — ." See also Cristanne Miller, *Emily Dickinson: A Poet's Grammar* (Cambridge: Harvard University Press, 1987), 168.
10. "The cordiality of the Sacrament extremely interested me when a Child, and when the Clergyman invited 'all who loved the Lord Jesus Christ, to remain,' I could scarcely refrain from rising and thanking him for the to me unexpected courtesy, though I now think had it been to all who loved Santa Claus, my transports would have been even more untimely.'" Johnson, *Letters*, no. 926 (Emily Dickinson to Mrs. Clara Newman Turner, late 1884). Here Dickinson refers to a childhood experience dating to about age seven (January 1838). See Johnson's annotations; also quoted in Jay Leyda, *The Years and Hours of Emily Dickinson*, 2 vols. (New Haven: Yale University Press, 1960), 1:39.
11. Thomas H. Johnson, *Emily Dickinson: An Interpretive Biography* (Cambridge: Belknap Press of Harvard University Press, 1955), 85. Christine Ross refutes Johnson's metrics claim, saying that in Dickinson's day, metrics were integrated into the study of grammar as part of a "basic education." Christine Ross, "Uncommon Measures: Emily Dickinson's Subversive Prosody," *Emily Dickinson Journal* 10, no. 1 (2001): 70.
12. See Carlton Lowenberg, "Music and Books on Music in the Dickinson Library," in *Musicians Wrestle Everywhere: Emily Dickinson and Music* (Berkeley: Fallen Leaf Press, 1992), appendix 2, 125–28.
13. Johnson, *Emily Dickinson: An Interpretive Biography*, 84–86. Johnson discusses Dickinson's use of hymn meter: most often Dickinson employs common meter (alternating eight and six syllables per line), and similarly ballad meter, followed by common particular meter (8-8-6/8-8-6), and a few in short meter (6-6-8-6). See also Miller, *Emily Dickinson: A Poet's Grammar*, 141–43.
14. See the foreword by Richard B. Sewall in Carlton Lowenberg, *Musicians Wrestle Everywhere*, x.
15. Richard Benson Sewall, *The Life of Emily Dickinson* (New York: Farrar, Straus and Giroux, 1974), 389.
16. Wendy Martin, "The Soul Selects Her Own Society," in *An American Triptych: Anne Bradstreet, Emily Dickinson, Adrienne Rich* (Chapel Hill: University of North Carolina Press, 1984), 94.
17. Johnson, *Letters*, no. 30 (Emily Dickinson to Jane Humphrey, 23 January 1850).
18. Franklin, *Poems*, no. 398, "The Morning after Wo — " (1862). Reading from different clefs was a skill that Dickinson would have been familiar with. In the front matter to Webb and Mason's *Odeon* which Dickinson used at Mount Holyoke, only the treble and bass clefs are explained and used in the text; the authors advise, however, that "it is sufficient that all the pupils are taught to sing from both [clefs]." G. J. Webb and Lowell Mason, *The Odeon, A Collection of Secular Melodies Arranged and Harmonized for Four Voices* (Boston: J. H. Wilkins and R. B. Carter, 1843), ix. For more on this poem, see Lundin, *Emily Dickinson and the Art of Belief*, 158–59. See also Carolyn Lindley Cooley, *The Music of Emily Dickinson's Poems and Letters: A Study of Imagery and Form* (London: McFarland and Company, 2003), 44. Contrapuntal, as in counterpoint, is defined as two or more individual melodies or lines of music sounding simultaneously. A homophonic texture consists of a vocal line (e.g., hymn tune) supported underneath by voices moving in the same or similar rhythm. See Willi Apel, *Harvard Dictionary of Music*, 2nd ed., rev. and enlarged (Cambridge: Belknap Press of Harvard University Press, 1973), 208, 390.
19. Victoria N. Morgan, *Emily Dickinson and Hymn Culture: Tradition and Experience* (Farnham, England: Ashgate Press, 2010), 118. See "Dear Sister, Brother has visited, and the night is falling, so I must close with a little hymn." Johnson, *Letters*, no. 307 (Emily Dickinson to Louise Norcross, March 1865). Dickinson enclosed the poem "This was in the White of the Year" (Franklin, *The Complete Poems*, no. 1014).
20. Johnson, *Letters*, no. 269 (Emily Dickinson to Dr. and Mrs. J. G. Holland, summer 1862?). Dickinson is actually referring here to birdsong and is applauding the bird's otherwise "unnoticed hymn" because it is the bird's business to sing; but the urgency of the metaphor for Dickinson herself to sing as a poet is palpable, and it is often remarked as such. See Judy Jo Small, *Positive as Sound: Emily Dickinson's Rhyme* (Athens: University of Georgia Press, 1990), 30. See also Elizabeth Phillips, *Emily Dickinson: Personae and Performance* (University Park: Pennsylvania State University Press, 1988), 115; Sewall, *Life of Emily Dickinson*, 556–57.
21. Morgan, *Emily Dickinson and Hymn Culture*, 112.

22. For a contemporary biographical source on Phoebe Hinsdale Brown and Eliza Lee Follen, see John Julian, *Dictionary of Hymnology* (New York: Charles Scribner's Sons, 1892), 185, 380. For their relationship to Emily Dickinson, see Morgan, *Emily Dickinson and Hymn Culture*, 119–49. Julia Ward Howe's "Battle Hymn of the Republic" was set to the tune of "John Brown's Body." The lyrics were printed by Samuel Bowles in the *Springfield Republican*, 16 January 1862, one of the first newspapers to publish it. See Wayne E. Phaneuf and Joseph Carvalho III, *A Not So Civil War: Western Massachusetts at Home and in Battle*, vol. 1, *April 1861–June 1863* ([Battle Ground, WA:]: Pediment Publishing, 2015–16), 56. The cover of the sheet music to "Battle Hymn of the Republic" attributes the words to "Mrs. Dr. S. G. Howe" and states that the song was "written for the *Atlantic Monthly*." The sheet music, published by Oliver Ditson, was registered for copyright on 9 April 1862. Library of Congress, loc.gov.
23. "I Love to Steal Awhile Away," titled "Evening twilight," hymn 285, is attributed to "B," and published in Asahel Nettleton, *Village Hymns for Social Worship, Selected and Original. Designed as a supplement to the Psalms and Hymns of Dr. Watts* (New York: Printed for the Publishers and sold by Elisha Sands, 1826). The Dickinson copy dates from 1838, p. 233. The hymn, along with three others by Brown, first appeared in Nettleton in 1824. On Brown and Lyon as friends, see Lowenberg, *Musicians Wrestle Everywhere*, 133. See also George Thomas Kurian and Mark A. Lamport, eds., *Encyclopedia of Christianity in the United States*, vol. 5 (Lanham, MD: Rowman & Littlefield, 2016), 342–43.
24. Morgan, *Emily Dickinson and Hymn Culture*, 125. See also Isaac Watts, *Psalms carefully suited to the Christian Worship in the United States of America: Being an improvement of the old version of the Psalms of David* (New York: Williams and Whiting, 1810); EDR 7 in the Dickinson Collection, Houghton Library, Harvard University.
25. Alfred Habegger, *My Wars Are Laid Away in Books: The Life of Emily Dickinson* (New York: Random House, 2001), 30–31.
26. Martha Winburn England, "Emily Dickinson and Isaac Watts: Puritan Hymnodists," *New York Public Library Bulletin* 69, no. 2 (2 February 1965): 88.
27. See the foreword by Sewall in Lowenberg, *Musicians Wrestle Everywhere*, x.
28. Morgan, *Emily Dickinson and Hymn Culture*, 30, 87–94.
29. Morgan, *Emily Dickinson and Hymn Culture*, 133.
30. Franklin, *The Complete Poems*, no. 236, "Some keep the Sabbath going to Church — " (1861).
31. Lowell Mason and David Greene, *Church Psalmody: a collection of psalms and hymns, adapted to public worship. Selected from Dr. Watts and other authors* (Boston: Perkins and Marvin, 1831), 159.
32. Morgan, *Emily Dickinson and Hymn Culture*, 83. See also chapter 4.
33. On the Puritan "plain style" as speaking from personal knowledge, see Miller, *Emily Dickinson: A Poet's Grammar*, 143–44. See also Wendy Martin, "Earth Is Heaven," in *An American Triptych*, 137.
34. Franklin, *The Complete Poems*, no. 489, "My Faith is larger than the Hills — " (1862); *Emily Dickinson's Poems: As She Preserved Them*, ed. Cristanne Miller (Cambridge: Belknap Press of Harvard University Press, 2016), 243. Miller dates this poem to late 1862.
35. "When purples come on Pelham, in the afternoon we say 'Mr. Bowles's colors.'" Johnson, *Letters*, no. 536 (Emily Dickinson to Mrs. Samuel Bowles, early 1878). For Dickinson's poetic reference to her "Scientist of Faith," see Franklin, *The Complete Poems*, no. 1261, "The Lilac is an ancient shrub (1872). For a discussion on Dickinson's "Scientist of Faith," see James R. Guthrie, *Emily Dickinson's Vision: Illness and Identity in Her Poetry* (Gainesville: University Press of Florida, 1998), 54–55.
36. Isaac Watts, *The Psalms, Hymns, and Spiritual Songs, of the Rev. Isaac Watts, D.D., to which are added Select Hymns from other authors; and Directions for Musical Expression by Samuel Worcester, D D., Late Pastor of the Tabernacle Church, Salem, Mass.* (Boston: Samuel T. Armstrong, 1827), 186. Dickinson uses a similar Watts image of the passing years in the line "Grand go the Years, / In the Crescent above them — " from her poem "Safe in their Alabaster Chambers — " (Franklin, *The Complete Poems*, no. 124), written in 1859.
37. Johnson, *Letters*, no. 381 (Emily Dickinson to Thomas Wentworth Higginson, late 1872).
38. "Oh God Our Help in Ages Past," text by Isaac Watts (1770), melody, "St. Anne" (1708), by William Croft (1678–1727).
39. Franklin, *The Complete Poems*, no. 519, "This is my letter to the World" (1863); Miller, *Emily Dickinson's Poems: as She Preserved Them*, 254 (1863).
40. Cristanne Miller, *Reading in Time: Emily Dickinson in the Nineteenth Century* (Amherst: University of Massachusetts Press, 2012), 49.

41. Franklin, *The Complete Poems*, no. 1614, "Blossoms will run away — " (1883).
42. Henry Russell, "The Old Arm Chair" (Boston: Geo. P. Reed, 1840), NYPL/LPA, call number AM 2-V Russell.
43. "'The Rose of Allandale,' written by Charles Jeffery[s]. The Music by S[ydney]. Nelson" (Boston: Keith & Moore, [1839–1842?]). See online Appendix B.
44. On Dickinson and the ballad form, see Miller, *Reading in Time*, 49–81.
45. Franklin, *The Complete Poems*, no. 12, "I had a guinea golden — " (1858).
46. Franklin, *The Complete Poems*, no. 409, "The Soul selects her own Society — " (1862); Domhnall Mitchell, *Emily Dickinson: Monarch of Perception* (Amherst: University of Massachusetts Press, 2000), 8.

Chapter 12: The White Dress

1. As to when Dickinson may have begun to wear the white dress, see Elizabeth Phillips, *Emily Dickinson: Personae and Performance* (University Park: Pennsylvania State University Press, 1988), 71; Richard B. Sewall, *The Lyman Letters: New Light on Emily Dickinson and Her Family* (Amherst: University of Massachusetts Press, 1965), 68–69.
2. See the description of Lind's dress written on a copy of Jenny Lind's program in New York's Metropolitan Hall (also called Tripler's Hall) for Tuesday, 18 May 1852, in the Jenny Lind program files in the Music and Recorded Sound Division of the New York Public Library for the Performing Arts, call number *MBD (Uncat.), Lind, Jenny. See also "Tripler's Hall, or Metropolitan Hall, 1854. (From an old print in the collection of George P Elder, Esq.)," Picture Collection, New York Public Library, Digital Collections, nypl.org.
3. Aífe Murray, *Maid as Muse: How Servants Changed Emily Dickinson's Life and Language* (Durham: University of New Hampshire Press, 2009), 115.
4. Elizabeth Phillips, *Emily Dickinson: Personae and Performance*, 2.
5. *Springfield Daily Republican*, 26 September 1850; Daniel Cavicchi, *Listening and Longing: Music Lovers in the Age of Barnum* (Middletown: Wesleyan University Press, 2011), 14–19, 38. See The New York Public Library for the Performing Arts, Music and Recorded Sound Division, Jenny Lind program file: "Jenny Lind Concert, Tremont Temple. Notice to Visitors. . . . That First Ticket. As the sum of six hundred and twenty-five dollars, PREMIUM, was paid for the first choice of a seat to this Concert, and as it is a higher one than was ever before paid upon any like occasion in the world, it is with pleasure that we announce the name of the purchaser to be OSSIAN E. DODGE, a vocalist and musical composer of much celebrity and worth. It is believed that he paid this sum in order to show respect to JENNY LIND, who is justly regarded as being at the head of the profession to which Mr. D. belongs.". That the auction event continued to be discussed long afterwards, Daniel Cavicchi argues that Dodge transformed America's musical life. "Dodge, the hustling 'Boston vocalist,' was part of a passing generation, but Dodge, the music loving ticket bidder, was a symbol of the future." Cavicchi, *Listening and Longing*, 39.
6. Judith Pascoe, "'The House Encore Me So': Emily Dickinson and Jenny Lind," *Emily Dickinson Journal* 1, no. 1 (Spring 1992): 8–10.
7. *Springfield Republican*, 19 January 1852.
8. See Cavicchi, *Listening and Longing*, 16.
9. Lavinia Dickinson to Austin Dickinson, 10 October 1852, Emily Dickinson Collection, ser. 4, box 7, folder 25, letter 582b, Amherst College Archives and Special Collections; published in Millicent Todd Bingham, *Emily Dickinson's Home: Letters of Edward Dickinson and His Family* (New York: Harper and Brothers Publishers, 1955), 210–11.
10. See Pascoe, "'The House Encore Me So,'" 13.
11. Páraic Finnerty, "'If fame belonged to me, I could not escape her': Dickinson and the Poetics of Celebrity," *Emily Dickinson Journal* 26, no. 2 (2017): 27.
12. Richard Benson Sewall, *The Life of Emily Dickinson* (New York: Farrar, Straus and Giroux, 1974), 226.
13. *Open Me Carefully: Emily Dickinson's Intimate Letters to Susan Huntington Dickinson*, ed. Ellen Louise Hart and Martha Nell Smith (Ashfield, MA: Paris Press, 1998), 204.
14. Polly Longsworth, *Austin and Mabel: The Amherst Affair of Austin Dickinson and Mabel Loomis Todd* (New York: Farrar, Straus and Giroux, 1984), 4.

15. Sewall, *Life of Emily Dickinson*, 216–17.
16. Sandra Runzo, *"Theatricals of Day": Emily Dickinson and Nineteenth-Century American Popular Culture* (Amherst: University of Massachusetts Press, 2019), 175.
17. *The Letters of Emily Dickinson*, ed. Thomas H. Johnson and Theodora Ward (hereafter Johnson, *Letters*), 3 vols. (Cambridge: Harvard University Press, 1958), no. 330 (Emily Dickinson to Thomas Wentworth Higginson, June 1869).
18. Adrienne Rich, "Vesuvius at Home," *Parnassus: Poetry in Review* 5, no. 1 (1976): 49–74, http://parnassusreview.com/archives/416.
19. Sewall, *Life of Emily Dickinson*, 565: "Vinnie's remark that Emily was always on the lookout for the rewarding person, by whom she meant someone who could listen without apparent bewilderment and respond approximately in kind, applied to a very few people."
20. See Murray, *Maid as Muse*, 24, 124–31.
21. Franklin, *The Complete Poems*, no. 927, "Each Second is the last" (1865), emphasis added.
22. Jane Donahue Eberwein, "New England Puritan Heritage," in *Emily Dickinson in Context*, ed. Eliza Richards (New York: Cambridge University Press, 2013), 53; Franklin, *The Complete Poems*, no. 411, "Mine — by the Right of the White Election!" (1862).
23. Johnson, *Letters*, no. 184 (Emily Dickinson to John Graves, late April 1856).

Postlude: "Musicians wrestle everywhere"

1. *The Complete Poems of Emily Dickinson*, ed. Ralph W. Franklin (Cambridge: Harvard University Press, 1999), no. 229, "Musicians wrestle everywhere — " (1861). Dickinson's use of "fuller tune" appears in her 1861 poem "I shall keep singing!" See Franklin, *The Complete Poems*, no. 270, "I shall keep singing!"
2. For the reference to the Germanians, see Richard Benson Sewall, *The Life of Emily Dickinson* (New York: Farrar, Straus and Giroux, 1974), 408. On 19 April 1853, Dickinson witnessed the touring instrumental ensemble the Germania Serenade Band in a performance that concluded the Spring Exhibition at Amherst College. See *The Letters of Emily Dickinson*, ed. Thomas H. Johnson and Theodora Ward (hereafter Johnson, *Letters*), 3 vols. (Cambridge: Harvard University Press, 1958), no. 118 (Emily Dickinson to Austin Dickinson, 21 April 1853). Dickinson's reference to the tambourine may be a visual allusion to the sheet music cover of the song "The Jolly Raftsman," which is in her bound music book: *Dan Emmit's Original Banjo Melodies* 2nd ser. (Boston: C. H. Keith, 1844). It's possible that Dickinson may be reaching further back to a lively "tambourin," an "old Provençal dance, originally accompanied by pipe and a medieval drum called a tambourin." See Willi Apel, ed., *Harvard Dictionary of Music*, 2nd ed., rev. and enlarged (Cambridge: Belknap Press of Harvard University Press, 1973), 833.
3. *Emily Dickinson's Poems: As She Preserved Them*, ed. Cristanne Miller (Cambridge: Belknap Press of Harvard University Press, 2016), 749, n. 94. Regarding Dickinson's words "The 'Morning Stars' the Treble led / On Time's first afternoon," Cristanne Miller cites from the book of Job 38:7. Miller also cites the hymn "Morning Star" (1830) as composed by Lowell Mason. To corroborate this musical attribution, the tune "Watchman! Tell us of the night" was sometimes referred to as "Morning Star," words by John Bowring (1792–1872), music attributed to Mason (1830). See *The Church Hymnbook; With Tunes for the Worship of God* (New York: Ivison, Blakeman, Taylor, 1873), 435. As a possible source for Dickinson's words, one might also consider verse three of the Isaac Watts hymn "Before the heavens were spread abroad": "Ere sin was born, or Satan fell, / He led the host of morning stars: / His generation who can tell, / Or count the number of his years?" This hymn by Watts was sourced by Lowell Mason for his compilation *Church Psalmody: A Collection of Psalms and Hymns adapted for public worship* (Boston: Perkins & Marvin, 1831), 291–92. "Watchman! Tell us of the night" is also included in this hymn collection (576), but under the hymn's first line, not under the title "Morning Star." This hymnbook was part of the Dickinson library.
4. Miller, *Emily Dickinson's Poems: As She Preserved Them*, 109–10.
5. Franklin, *The Complete Poems*, no. 764, "My Life had stood — a Loaded Gun — " (1863). According to Cristanne Miller, in this poem "the speaker is liberated from the stasis of her past and recounts moment by moment the successive activities of her new life." See Cristanne Miller, *Emily Dickinson: A Poet's Grammar* (Cambridge: Harvard University Press, 1987), 35.
6. "Because I see — New Englandly — ": Franklin, *The Complete Poems*, no. 256, "The Robin's my

Criterion for Tune — " (1856). See also Helen Vendler, *Dickinson: Selected Poems and Commentaries* (Cambridge: Belknap Press of Harvard University Press, 2010), 86–88.
7. Sewall, *Life of Emily Dickinson*, 681; Franklin, *The Complete Poems*, no. 690, "Forever — is composed of Nows — " (1863).
8. Stuart Feder, *Charles Ives, "My Father's Song": A Psychoanalytic Biography* (New Haven: Yale University Press, 1992), 254.
9. Oja notes that the American composer Henry Cowell "seized upon Ives to help construct a 'usable past,' to provide an ancestor for the ultra-modern group [of composers that Cowell] sought to build." Carol Oja, *Making Music Modern: New York in the 1920s* (New York: Oxford University Press, 2000), 195.
10. This ultra-modernist group included, in chronological order, Carl Ruggles (1876–1971), Edgard Varèse (1883–1965), Wallingford Riegger (1885–1961), John J. Becker (1886–1961), Leo Ornstein (1895–2002), Henry Cowell (1897–1965), Carlos Chávez (1899–1978), and Ruth Crawford (1901–1953).
11. As to a modernist style ascribed to Dickinson, see Wendy Martin, "Earth Is Heaven," in *An American Triptych: Anne Bradstreet, Emily Dickinson, Adrienne Rich* (Chapel Hill: University of North Carolina Press, 1984), 141.
12. *Emily Dickinson's Reception in the 1890s: A Documentary History*, ed. Willis J. Buckingham (Pittsburgh: University of Pittsburgh Press, 1989), xvi.
13. See Carlton Lowenberg, *Musicians Wrestle Everywhere: Emily Dickinson and Music* (Berkeley: Fallen Leaf Press, 1992). Since the publication of Lowenberg's compendium of Dickinson settings in 1992 (about 1,600 settings cited), the interest in setting Dickinson in music, theater, and the arts has not diminished. See Jonnie Guerra, "Dickinson Adaptations in the Arts and the Theatre," in *The Emily Dickinson Handbook*, ed. Gudrun Grabher, Roland Hagenbuchle, and Cristanne Miller (Amherst: University of Massachusetts Press, 1998), 400–403; Fred D. White, "Celebrating Emily Dickinson in Belles Lettres, Music and Art," in *Approaching Emily Dickinson: Critical Currents and Crosscurrents since 1960* (London: Boydell and Brewer, 2008), 176–86. See also Gerald Holmes, "'Invisible as Music — ': What the Earliest Musical Settings of Emily Dickinson's Poems, Including Two Previously Unknown, Tell Us about Dickinson's Musicality," *Emily Dickinson Journal* 28, no. 2 (2019): 73–105.
14. Oja, *Making Music Modern*, 4.
15. J. Peter Burkholder, *All Made of Tunes: Charles Ives and the Uses of Borrowing* (New Haven: Yale University Press, 1995), 37.
16. Cristanne Miller, *Reading in Time: Emily Dickinson in the Nineteenth Century* (Amherst: University of Massachusetts Press, 2012), 50.
17. Johnson, *Letters*, no. 381 (Emily Dickinson to Thomas Wentworth Higginson, late 1872).
18. Van Wyck Brooks, *The Flowering of New England, 1815–1865* (New York: E. P. Dutton, 1936), 530–31.
19. Charles Ives, *Essays Before a Sonata, The Majority, and Other Writings*, ed. Howard Boatwright (1961; repr., New York: W. W. Norton & Company, 1961), 47.
20. Charles Ives, *Second Pianoforte Sonata, Concord, Mass., 1840–1860*, 2nd ed. (New York: Arrow Music Press, 1947); Burkholder, *All Made of Tunes*, 199.
21. Richard Brantley, "Dickinson the Romantic," in *Transatlantic Trio: Empiricism, Evangelicalism, Romanticism; Essays and Reviews, 1974–2017* (Ames, IA: Culicidae Press, 2017), 332.
22. Sewall, *Life of Emily Dickinson*, 406–9. Dickinson's use of the "fuller tune" appears in her 1861 poem "I shall keep singing!" See Franklin, *The Complete Poems*, no. 270, "I shall keep singing!" (1861).
23. Brooks, *The Flowering of New England*, 506.
24. Charles Ives, *114 Songs*, no. 43, "The Things Our Fathers Loved" (New York: Peer International, for the National Institute of Arts and Letters, 1975), 91–92. See also Feder, *Charles Ives, "My Father's Song,"* 253.
25. Franklin, *The Complete Poems*, no. 374, "It will be Summer — eventually" (1862).
26. See Sewall, *Life of Emily Dickinson*, 407.
27. MacGregor Jenkins, *Emily Dickinson Friend and Neighbor* (Boston: Little, Brown, 1930), 36.
28. Franklin, *The Complete Poems*, no. 374, "It will be Summer — eventually" (1862).

Index

Emily Dickinson has been abbreviated as *ED* throughout the index, except where the name appears as a main heading. Page numbers referring to figures are italicized.

abolitionist movement, 118–19, 122–25
Ackmann, Martha, 129
Adams, Elizabeth C., 64, 92–93
Adams, Jesse C., and Adams Brass Band, 100, 177, 208nn24–25
The Adventures of Huckleberry Finn (Twain), 133
aeolian harp, 58, 198n55
"Æolian Waltz" (R. B. Taylor), 58, 180, 198n55
"Affection Waltz" (W. H. Fry), 50–51, 69, 179
African Americans, 132–34, 138, 165–66, 215n4, 217n39. *See also* abolitionist movement; minstrel music
Ahlström, Jacob Niclas, 76, 202n52. *See also* "Echo Song"
Aladdin; or the Wonderful Lamp ("Grand Chinese Spectacle"), 61–62, 64, 199n76
"Aladdin Quick Step" (Comer), 61, 64, 178
Albany Burgesses Corps, 93, 99–100, 208n24
Alcott family, 17, 172
"The Alcotts" (C. E. Ives), 171–72
"Amazing Grace" (hymn), 155
Amenia Seminary, 31–32
American band movement. *See* bands; *specific bands*
Amherst, Massachusetts, 20; aurora borealis seen, 48–49; Cattle Show, 66, 137; Civil War soldiers, 128, 129, 214nn52–53 (*see also* Stearns, Frazar); concerts and performances, 65, 66, 123, 201n32; railroad, 94–97, 207n5; religious revivals, 154; singing school, 20–21. *See also* Amherst Academy; Amherst College; Dickinson home
Amherst Academy, 13, 19, 22, 26–28, 44, 57, 64, 89, 92, 195n86. *See also* Coleman, Lyman
Amherst and Belchertown Rail Road Company, 95, 207n5
Amherst College: catalogs, 192n13; commencements, 47, 69; concerts, 69, 80, 225n2; founded, 19, 27, 94; J. A. Fowler at, 92; meetinghouse, 21; Thompson, 139; "tutors" from, 138–39. *See also* Hitchcock, Edward; Stearns, William Augustus
"Andre's Request to Washington" (N. P. Willis; Kingsley), 57
Andrews, Mrs., 205n19
Anthon, Catherine (Kate) Scott Turner, 89, 142–43, 218n60
"Any Thing" (J. F. Smith; waltz), 91, 180
"Araby's Daughter" (Moore; Kiallmark), 41, 182, 194n73
"Are We Almost There?" (Vane; poem/song), 105
"Aria alla Scozzese" (var. Valentine), 110, 175, 210n27

"L'Ariadne Waltz" (J. Flint), 179
Ashton, John, Jr., 85
Atlantic Monthly, 115, 145–46, 223n22
Auburn, New York, 97
"Auld Lang Syne" (song; variations), 64, 109, 140, 144, 176, 199n88
"Aurora Leigh" (E. Barrett Browning), 196n17
"Aurora Waltz" (Labitzky), 48–49, 52, 179
"Aurora Waltz" (Unger), 48–49, 179
Austen, Jane, 8, 187n34
Austin, Elizabeth, 87
"Awake ye muses mine, sing me a strain divine" (ED), 145

"Baden Baden Polka." *See* "The Celebrated Baden Baden Polka"
Bailey, Candace, 7–8
Baker Family (singing group), 71, 201n32, 201n34
Balfe, Michael William, 41, 50, 67, 69, 79, 181. *See also The Bohemian Girl*
ballads, 15–16, 156, 160, 166–67. *See also* songs
bands, 14, 15, 65–70, 98, 128–29. *See also* militias; *specific bands and individuals*
banjo, 132, 140, 215n4
Banks of the Mohawk (J. A. Fowler), 31
Barnum, Phineas T., 73, 75, 77, 78, 163. *See also* Lind, Jenny
"Basket Cotillion" (fiddle tune), 24, 25, 181
"The Battle Cry of Freedom" (song), 129
"Battle Hymn of the Republic" (J. W. Howe), 223n22
"Battle of Prague" (Kotzwara), 38, 72, 140, 177, 201n35
"Bayeaux's Quick Step" (Glynn), 93, 99–100, 177, 208n20
Bayly, Thomas. *See* "Long, Long Ago"
"Bay State Quick Step" (Glynn), 69, 100, 178
Beethoven, Ludwig van, 51, 81–82, 108–9, 172, 210n18; waltzes misattributed to, 51–52, 82–83, 110, 178–79

"Beethoven's Dream" (Weber), 52, 179
bel canto singing, 76, 77, 202n54. *See also* Lind, Jenny
Belchertown Brass Band, 66
beliefs of Dickinson: bird imagery used in writing of, 209n4 (*see also* bird imagery); church attendance, 47, 50, 158, 202n48, 206n28, 222n10; individual, personal, 158–59; M. Lyon, Mount Holyoke, and, 37–38; nature and the divine, 27, 154, 155, 159; poetry and, 156–59; simultaneous belief and disbelief, 154–55. *See also* hymns
"Believe Me If All Those Endearing Young Charms" (arr. Valentine), 38, 106, 110–11, 128, 176, 183
Bellini, Vincenzo, 41, 66, 68–69, 72, 87, 176–77, 203n60. *See also Norma*; *La Sonnambula*
"Bell Polka" (W. Buchheister), 80
Bertini, Henri, 22, 24, 30, 72, 188n45, 210n14
"Better — than Music!" (ED), 146–47, 149
Bianchi, Martha ("Mattie") Dickinson (niece of ED), 3, 59, 107, 204n80
"The Bible is an antique Volume — " (ED), 105
binder's volumes, 10. *See also* bound volumes of music; music book of Dickinson
Bingham, George Caleb, 217n39
Bingham, Millicent Todd, 5; ED's letters edited/transcribed, 81, 203–4n70, 210n13; on ED's music and musicality, 4, 83, 218–19n61; on Edward Dickinson's politics, 119; on Lavinia's singing, 84; on reading clubs, 139
bird imagery: in ED's correspondence, 80, 153, 169, 222n20; in ED's poetry, 77, 79, 80–81, 145–48, 161, 169, 215n4
"Bird Song" (Taubert), 75–76, 77, 202n52
"Bird Waltz" (Panormo), 50, 58, 179

INDEX [229]

Bishop, Anna, 71, 203n60
Bishop, Henry Rowley, 41, 71, 182. *See also* "Home, Sweet Home"
blackface performers, 132–34. *See also* minstrel music
Blockley, John J., 42, 109, 177, 194n76
"Blossoms will run away —" (ED), 160
"The Blue Juniata" (M. D. Sullivan), 70, 109, 120, *121*, 178, 188n42, 188n44, 213n16, 214n40. *See also* "The Juniata Quick Step"
The Bohemian Girl (Balfe), 50, 67, 69, 79, 134, 181, 188n44
Bohlman, Henri, 50, 180
"Bonaparte's March Crossing the Rhine" (tune), 141, 177, 215n1
"The Bonnie Blue Flag" (tune), 129
"The Bonnie Clay Flag" (Warland; Sinclair), 101, 115–18, *117*, 182, 212nn4–5
"Bonnie Doon" (song), 41, 111, 144, 176, 182
"The Bonny Boat" (song), 41, 182
book binders, 9. *See also* bound volumes of music
Boston: Brooks on provinciality of, 171; Bunker Hill Monument celebration, 100; concerts and concert scene, 64, 69–70, 74–75, 78–79, 82, 85, 149, 203n66; ED's visits to, 23, 62–64, 74, 134, 149, 190n23, 202n45; goods sent for from, 84–85; music publishers, 13, 85, 140; piano-making in, 190n26; Whig Party in, 101. *See also specific institutions and music publishers*
Boston Academy of Music, 34–35, 40, 64, 82
Boston Brigade Band, 69–70, 98–99
Boston Clay Club No. 1, 116. *See also* "The Bonnie Clay Flag"
Boston Daily Atlas, 63
Boston Daily Journal, 64
Boston Museum and Gallery of Fine Arts, 61–62, 85, 199n76
boundary crossing by Dickinson, 6, 134–36, 138, 161, 162, 167, 171,
217n41. *See also* performance persona of Dickinson
bound volumes of music (generally), 7–10, 109, 111, 187n34. *See also* music book of Dickinson
The Bouquet of Melody (anthology of songs), 31
Bowdoin, Emily, 42–43, 194–95n77
Bowles, Mary (wife of S. Bowles III), 115
Bowles, Samuel, II (1797–1851), 115
Bowles, Samuel, III (1826–1878), 46, 89–90, 115, 117–18, 223n22; ED's letters to, 127, 134. *See also Springfield Daily Republican*
Bowring, John, 34, 225n3
Bradbury, William, 34
Brantley, Richard, 172
bread-making, 136–37
Brontë, Charlotte, 57
Brooks, Van Wyck, 171, 172
Brown, Phoebe Hinsdale, 157–58, 223n23
Browne, Augusta, 41
Broyles, Michael, 52, 82
Buckingham, Willis J., 170
bugle (keyed bugle), 66
Bull, Ole, 70, 186n18, 204n78
Burditt, Benjamin Augustus, 69–70, 99, 178. *See also* "The Juniata Quick Step"
Burgmüller, Johann Friedrich Franz, 72, 180, 188n45
Burkholder, J. Peter, 171
"busy bee," 2, 145
"By my Window have I for Scenery" (ED), 147

"Caledonian Hunt" (fiddle tune), 24, 181
"Camp Barnum Quick Step" (Wilson), 93, 100, 177
"Canadian Boat Song" (Moore), 41, 182
"Can I My Love Resign" (from the opera *Cinderella*), 68
Carlo (dog), 57–58, 146
Carmichael, Elizabeth, 153

Carmina Sacra (Mason), 40, 194n66
Cashman, Dennis, 166
Cavicchi, Daniel, 73, 163, 224n5
"The Celebrated Baden Baden Polka" (arr. Musard), 50, 181
"Celebrated [Empress] Henrietta Waltz" (Herz), 70, 180, 201n36
"The Celebrated Polka Dance" (Offenbach), 62, 84–85, 181
"The Celebrated Spanish Retreat" (quickstep; arr. De Anguera), 70, 98–99, *99*, 177, 201n27
A Century of Dishonor (Jackson), 120–22
Chadwick, L. Thayer, 93, 97, 177–78
"Charity" (Glover), 88, 106, 210n12
Cherry Valley Female Academy, 29–31, 92, 192n17
China, Western interest in, 61–63
Chinese Museum (Boston), 45, 62–64, 199nn79–80, 199n82
Christensen, Thomas, 108–9
Christian Psalmody (Watts), 156
Church Psalmody (Mason), 21, 156, 158, 225n3
circuses, 68
Civil War, 129, 149, 169, 214nn41–43, 214nn52–53; music of, 15, 127–29, 214n40, 214n44
"Clare de Kitchen" (minstrel tune), 133
Clay, Henry, 101, 116. *See also* "The Bonnie Clay Flag"
"A Clock stopped — " (ED), 114
"The Coast of Mexico" (J. W. Turner), 43. *See also* "Lucy Neal"
Cockrell, Dale, 132
Coleman, Eliza, 49–50, 111–12
Coleman, Lyman, 44, 49, 111, 195n86, 211n33
Coleman, Olivia, 49, 86, 111, 205n12
"College Hornpipe" (fiddle tune), 24, 141, 181
Collier, Jason, 67
Comer, Thomas, 61, 69, 178, 199n76, 200n10
"Comin' thro' the Rye" (song), 78, 105, 203n62

common meter, 156, 158, 159, 171, 222n13. *See also* meter
composite volumes, 10. *See also* bound volumes of music; music book of Dickinson
concerts and concert scene. *See* bands; minstrel music; musical virtuosi; *specific cities, venues, performers, and groups*
Concord Sonata (C. E. Ives), 171–72
"Congress March" (J. Z. Hesser), 176
Conkey, Ithamar Frank (Francis), 95, 112
Cook, Eliza, 160, 181. *See also* "The Old Arm Chair"
Cooley, Carolyn Lindley, 4–5, 152, 219n9
"Coolidge Quickstep" (Jones), 178, 202n41
Cooper, James Fenimore, 54–55, 120
correspondence of Dickinson: bird imagery, 80, 153, 169, 222n20; first reference to music, 9, 20; on her father's anxieties, 47; informed by musical experiences, 4, 6; interest in music expressed, 4, 12, 24; literary quotes and references, 57, 90, 104, 222n7; musical references, 64, 73, 104, 111–12, 144, 148, 151–52 (*see also specific works, performers, and groups*); musical sentiment expressed, 48, 79; on "Wood Up," 68–69; word "tunes" used in, 219n66. *See also specific correspondents*
Cowell, Henry, 170
The Creation (Haydn), 64
Crockett, Davy, 133, 216n10
Crumbley, Paul, 219n7
Cushing, Caleb, 63
Cutler, William and Harriet Gilbert, 89
Czerny, Carl, 30, 50, 72, 106, 108–9, 175, 188n45

Daily Evening Traveller, 64
dancing, 38, 132, 133–34, 135, 138, 139, 218n51

INDEX [231]

"A Day! Help! Help!" (ED), 127, 214n42

De Anguera, José, 70, 177

Deloria, Philip J., 122

de Meyer, Leopold, 70, 201n36

Dennis, Cyrus C., 97, 177–78

Deppman, Jed, 147, 186n16

"The Devil" (improvisation; ED), 15, 142–43, 218n58

Dickens, Charles, 54, 133, 216n10

Dickinson, Austin (brother of ED): as Amherst College treasurer, 27; birth and death, 19; Civil War service avoided, 129, 214n52; concerts attended, 68, 71, 74–75, 78–79, 203n66; courtship and marriage, 89, 206n28 (*see also* Dickinson, Susan Huntington Gilbert); and ED's piano improvisations, 142; on ED's "posing," 81, 103; ED's relationship with, 20; education and graduation, 69, 189n6; expected to dinner, 112–14; familiarity with "Fair Harvard" tune, 110; father's correspondence with, 95; father's relationship with, 47; home, 47, 137, 196n12 (*see also* The Evergreens); Lavinia's correspondence with, 9–10, 14, 84–88, 113, 163, 185–86n11; law studies and career, 14, 110, 112, 120; minstrel show attended, 134; mistress, 164; Moore's *Lalla Rookh* owned, 194n73; politics, 119–20; religious beliefs, 112, 211n41; sheet music acquired for sisters, 14, 84–88, 106; teaching career, 14, 84, 119–20. *See also* Dickinson, Austin, ED's letters to; Dickinson family

Dickinson, Austin, ED's letters to: on aurora borealis, 48–49; on four-hand duet, 106, 109, 210n13; on the Germanians concert, 80–81, 204n71; on her father's demeanor, 103, 113; on his nonarrival for dinner, 113–14; on his teaching, 120; on Lavinia's singing and playing, 104–5; Lavinia's thanks conveyed, 86; on Lind, 74–76; from Mount Holyoke, 43, 111; on Pliny Dickinson's visit, 93; on the railroad, 95–97; requests for music, 14; on singing school, 20; song quoted, 203n62; on a stormy evening, 104; on their Reading Club, 138–39; on *Village Hymns*, 112; on visitors and houseguests, 96–97

Dickinson, Edward (father of ED), 94; as Amherst College treasurer, 27, 92, 94; anxiety over ED's absences, 47, 58; and aurora borealis, 48–49; birth and death, 19; book binder sought, 9; buildings sold to Kelley, 138; children's relationship with, 46–47, 103, 196n11; conservatory built, 59; correspondence, 21–22, 23, 28; dog given to ED, 57, 146; and domestic work, 136–37; and ED's piano playing, 14, 101–2; and ED's poetry writing, 156; and ED's visits to Boston, 62, 199n79; and education, 27–28; finances, 19–20, 23, 36, 94; homes, 19–20, 125 (*see also* Dickinson home); Lind concert attended, 74–77; and militias and military units, 94, 98, 128, 208n15; and minstrel music, 134; personality, 98, 102–3; piano purchased, 22–23; and politics, 14, 49, 94, 101, 112, 119–20, 208n26 (*see also* Whig Party); and railroads, 94–97; relationship to music, 14; religious beliefs, 211n41; sister, 143; views on women, 46, 75, 202n49

Dickinson, Emily: birth, 19; death and burial, 138, 166–67; enigmatic nature of, 18; health, 44–45, 47, 62, 149, 194–95n77, 195n86, 202n45; household duties, 46, 136–38; obituary, 217n41; piano improvisations, 141–44; "posing" (stretching the truth), 81, 103, 105, 209n6; spelling of given name, 200n14; "terror," 149, 152; white dress, 16, 78, 162–65; withdrawal from public life, 150–51, 161–63, 165, 225n19. *See also* beliefs

Dickinson, Emily (*continued*) of Dickinson; correspondence of Dickinson; Dickinson family; Dickinson home; education of Dickinson; musical education of Dickinson; musicality of Dickinson; musicality of Dickinson's poetry; music book of Dickinson; performance persona of Dickinson; poetry of Dickinson

Dickinson, Emily Norcross (mother of ED), 19, 113, 120, 136, 156–57. *See also* Dickinson family

Dickinson, Lavinia "Vinnie" (sister of ED): and Austin's teaching position, 120; birth and death, 19, 138; concerts attended, 67–68, 74–75, 79–80, 134, 216n16; correspondence with Austin, 9–10, 14, 84–88, 112–13, 163, 185–86n11; on departing houseguests, 46; on ED and the rewarding person, 225n19; ED lonely in absence of, 111; and Eliza C. Dudley, 112; on her bound volume of music, 9–10; "Home as a Waltz" inscribed by ED to, 48; interest in music, 4; musicality of, 15; news consumption, 115, 116; in Philadelphia, 49, 50; piano playing, 15, 104, 106–7; relationship with father, 47, 196n11; religious beliefs, 211n41; sheet music collected, 14, 84–88, 163; singing, 15, 71, 84, 104–6. *See also* Dickinson family

Dickinson, Martha (daughter of Austin Dickinson), 151

Dickinson, Nathan, 19–20

Dickinson, Ned (son of Austin Dickinson), 151

Dickinson, Pliny, 93

Dickinson, Samuel Fowler (grandfather of ED), 19, 27, 94

Dickinson, Susan Huntington Gilbert (wife of Austin Dickinson): Austin's correspondence with, 88–89, 119; birth, childhood, family, 89; concert not attended, 80; courtship and marriage, 89, 206n28 (*see also* Dickinson, Austin); ED's friendship and correspondence with, 49, 60, 89–90, 204n71, 204n71, 206n28; ED's obituary written, 217n41; and ED's piano playing, 141–42, 167, 218n58; education, 32; on E. Fowler, 139; home (*see* The Evergreens); and music, 90, 206n29; N. P. Willis poetry book owned, 57; religious beliefs, 211n41

Dickinson, Vinnie. *See* Dickinson, Lavinia

Dickinson, William (uncle of ED), 23

Dickinson, William Austin. *See* Dickinson, Austin

Dickinson family: concerts attended, 65, 68, 71–72, 74–77, 79–81, 199n3; disappointed by Austin's non-appearance, 112–14; ED's musicality recognized, 21–23; finances, 9, 19–20, 23; home's importance to, 13, 46; members, 19; music-making, and music's role, 1, 12, 13, 15, 101–3; pianos, 9, 22–23, 107, 143, 190n26, 210n16, 218n61 (*see also* piano); and politics, 112, 117; religious beliefs, 112, 206n28, 211n41; sheet music collected by, 9–10, 72, 84, 163; songs performed, 71. *See also* Dickinson family library; Dickinson home; servants of Dickinson family; *specific individuals*

Dickinson family library: hymnbooks, 13, 21, 156–58, 222n23, 225n3; music books, 5–6, 9–10, 34, 40–41, 194n66; N. P. Willis poetry collection, 57; periodicals read, 54, 115–16; sheet music collected, 9–10, 69, 72, 84, 163

Dickinson home: aeolian harp, 58, 198n55; ED on, 13; ED's homesickness, when away, 44; Edward Dickinson's desire to keep daughters at home, 46, 47; family finances and, 19–20, 23, 36; family's love of home, 13, 46; garden and conservatory, 13, 58–60; housework and cooking, 136–38; music's role in, 1, 12, 13, 101–3; visitors and houseguests, 46–47, 93, 96; West Street house, 20, 23. *See also* Dickinson family; Dickinson family library; Homestead; servants of Dickinson family

Ditson, Oliver. *See* Oliver Ditson & Co.

Divine and Moral Songs for Children (Watts), 145

"Dixie" (tune), 129, 133

Dodge, Ossian, 88, 163, *164*, 224n5

Dodworth, Allen, 69, 201n26

Dodworth, Thomas, Sr., and family, 69

Dodworth brass band, 65–66, 69, 199n3

dog (Carlo), 57–58

domesticity: Brown and, 158; ED's kitchen duties, 136–38; music as feminine domestic activity, 8, 14, 47–48, 102; and national expansion, 126

domestic servants. *See* servants of Dickinson family

"Drops of Brandy" (fiddle tune), 131, 181

"Drunken Sailor" (tune), 128, 141, 181

Dudley, John Langdon, 111–12

duets. *See* opera: four-hand overture

Duncan, Emma, 155

"Durang's Hornpipe" (fiddle tune), 24, 131, 141, 181, 188n42, 218n51

Dutton, George, 32–33, 90–91, 176

Dvořák, Antonín, 50–51

Dwight, John Sullivan, 51, 82

Dwight's Journal of Music, 51, 197n30

"Each Second is the last" (ED), 166

Eastcott, Richard, and his band, 67, 200n10, 202n41

"Echo Song" (Ahlström), 75–76, 202n52

education of Dickinson: Amherst Academy, 13, 22, 26–28, 44, 57, 195n86 (*see also* Amherst Academy); ED's music book and, 26; Mount Holyoke, 13, 28–29, 34, 36–43 (*see also* Mount Holyoke Female Seminary); nature studies, 27, 57; philosophy, 186n16; primary school, 26; textbooks, 27, 193n35. *See also* musical education of Dickinson

Edward Riley (publisher), 140, 205n15

"The Elfin Waltzes" (Labitzky), 52, 179

Emerson, Ralph Waldo, 17, 54, 96, 171, 213n22

Emily Dickinson and Her Culture: The Soul's Society (St. Armand), 97

Emily Dickinson and Hymn Culture (Morgan), 2

"Emily Dickinson and Isaac Watts" (England), 2

Emily Dickinson: An Interpretive Biography (Johnson), 2, 156

Emily Dickinson Museum, 19. *See also* Homestead

Emily Dickinson: Personae and Performance (Phillips), 163

Emily Dickinson's Home (M. T. Bingham), 4

Emily Dickinson's Poems: As She Preserved Them (ed. Miller), 169

Emmett, Daniel Decatur, 68, 133, 183. *See also* "Old Dan Tucker"; Virginia Minstrels

"L'Enfer Quadrille Diabolique" (Bohlman), 50, 180

England, Martha Winburn, 2, 158

The Ethiopian Glee Book (E. Howe), 136

Ethiopian Vocalists, 134

"Evening Shade" (Leland & S. Jenks; hymn), 155, 221n7

The Evergreens (Austin Dickinson home), 47, 137, 142, 165, 196n12

Extraordinary Popular Delusions and the Madness of Crowds (Mackay), 133

"Fair Harvard" (song), 110

Farr, Judith, 58, 147

"The fascinating chill that music leaves" (ED), 152

"Favorite Melodies from the Grand Chinese Spectacle of Aladdin." *See* "Aladdin Quick Step"

Feder, Stuart, 170
Fellow's Ethiopian Opera Troupe, 134
female seminaries and academies, 13, 28–29. *See also* Amherst Academy; Mount Holyoke Female Seminary; *other institutions*
fiddle tunes: as early pedagogical aids, 24, 191n29; in ED's music book, 9, 10, *11*, 12, 15, 24, 131, 136, 140–41, 181, 215n1; ED's piano improvisations and, 143–44; Thompson's fiddling, 139–40; tunebooks, 140–41, 218n51; tune etymologies, 17. *See also specific tunes*
Finnerty, Páraic, 164
Fisher, Clara, 205n19, 212n4
"Fisher's Hornpipe" (tune), 24, 131, 141, 181, 188n42, 218n51
Fitch, Susannah, 39–40
The Flowering of New England (Brooks), 171, 172
Follen, Eliza Lee, 157
foreign lands, ED's interest in, 13, 45, 60–64
"Forever — is composed of Nows — " (ED), 170
Fowler, Charles, 139
Fowler, Emily, 111, 112, 139
Fowler, Jonathan Amos, 29–31, 92, 181, 192n17, 207n38
"From Greenland's Icy Mountains" (Heber; Mason), 34
Fry, Joseph Reese, 50
Fry, William Henry, 50–51, 69, 179. *See also Leonora*

garden and gardening, 13, 58–60. *See also* nature; "New feet within my garden go — "
"Gems from *The Bohemian Girl*" (Balfe), 50, 181. *See also The Bohemian Girl*
Geneva, New York, 89–90
George E. Blake (publisher), 49, 140
George P. Reed (publisher), 85, 91, 110, 176, 179–82
George Willig & Co., 49
German classes, 44

Germania Musical Society, 71, 79–81, *80*, 169, 225n2
"Get Off the Track" (Hutchinson; adaptation), 118–19, *123*, 124–25
Gilbert, Martha, 32, 78, 89, 90
Gilbert, Susan Huntington. *See* Dickinson, Susan Huntington Gilbert
Gilman, Samuel, 110
Gilmore, Patrick, band of, 199n3, 216n16
"The Girl I Left Behind Me" (tune), 24, 25, 43–44, 115, 127–28, 181, 214n39
glees, 135–36, 147, 156–57
The Glenmary Waltzes (R. S. Willis), 54–57, *55*, *56*, 58, 178
Glover, Stephen, 88, 106, 210n12
Glynn, William Cooper, 99–100, 177, 178, 180. *See also* "Bayeaux's Quick Step"; "Bay State Quick Step"; "Rockaway Waltzes"
Goertzen, Chris, 141, 191n29
"Going to Heaven!" (ED), 155
Gordon, Lyndall, 18, 75
Gould, George H., 135
"Grand March in *Norma*" (Bellini), 140, 177. See also *Norma*
Grant, Lucy Evans, 67
Grant, Ulysses S., 128
Grant, Zilpah P., 35
"The Grave of Bonaparte" (L. Heath), 24, 185n11, 188n44
Graves, John, 15, 79, 141–42, 143, 167, 219n66
Green, Clara Bellinger, 149
Gung'l, Josef, 52, 71, 112, 176, 179

Habegger, Alfred, 46–47, 89, 98, 102–3, 112, 157, 209n6
Haile, Harriette C., 40
"Hail to the Chief" (tune), 140. *See also* "Roderick Dhu's March"
Hall, Charles F., 152–53
Hamm, Charles, 131–32
Hammond, William Gardiner, 38–39
Hampshire and Franklin Express, 9, 27, 68, 115, 200n15

INDEX [235]

Hancock Light Infantry, 98–99, 177
Handel, George Frideric, 78, 86
Handel and Haydn Society (Boston), 64, 68, 78, 200n15
Harmoneon Family (minstrel troupe), 71, 126, 136, 188n42
Harrison, William Henry, 101, 118
Hart, Ellen Louise, 90
Harvard University: Dickinson Collection (*see* Houghton Library); Law School, 110, 120 (*see also* Dickinson, Austin: law studies)
Harwood, Marion P., 38
Haskell, D. H. *See* "Prize Banner Quick Step"
Hastings, Thomas, 33–34, 92
Hawes, Harriet, 39, 194n62
Haydn, Franz Joseph, 64, 78
Hayes, Catherine, 71, 78–79, 203n66
Hayter, George F., 68, 200n15
Heber, Reginald, 34
"Henrietta Waltz." *See* "Celebrated [Empress] Henrietta Waltz"
Henry Prentiss (publisher), 85, 98, 177
"Herdsman's Song" (Ahlström). *See* "Echo Song"
"Herr Cline's Dance" (tune), 24, 181
Herz, Henri, 70, 72, 180, 201n36
"Hey the Bonnie Breast Knots" (Sinclair), 212nn4–5. *See also* "The Bonnie Clay Flag"
Higginson, Thomas Wentworth, 5, 96, 122, 136, 145–46; ED's correspondence with, 145–46, 150, 151–52, 165, 219n7, 219n9
Hitchcock, Edward, (pres., Amherst College), 22, 27, 57, 159, 192n13
Holden, Jeremiah (Jerry), 58, 137–38, 217n41
Holland, Elizabeth (Mrs. J. G. Holland), 116, 125–26, 151, 157, 222n20
Holland, Josiah Gilbert, 46, 115–16
Holloway, John, 68–69
home, and music (generally), 8, 14–15, 47–48, 102
"Home, Sweet Home" (H. R. Bishop): Civil War and, 128–29, 214n40; composer, 71; in ED's music book, 41, 48, 71, 76, 106, 115, 182, 202n52; "Home as a Waltz" (arrangement), 48, 180; referenced in ED's correspondence, 44, 76; in tunebooks, 140. *See also* Bishop, Henry Rowley
"Home as a Waltz," 48, 180. *See also* "Home, Sweet Home"
Home Journal, 56, 197n48
"Home Quick Step" (W. Smith), 31–32, 48, 178
Homestead: annual commencement reception at, 137; ED's retreat into, 16 (*see also* Dickinson, Emily); family finances and, 19–20, 23, 36; family's return to, 125–26; garden and conservatory, 58–60; music books in library, 5; ownership, 19–20, 125; servants employed, 137. *See also* Dickinson family library; Dickinson home; servants of Dickinson family
"A Home That I Love" (Glover), 210n12
"The Home That I Love" (song; waltz arr. by White), 48, 180
"Hope Again" (air and var.; Dutton), 32–33, 90, 176
Horne, Charles Edward, 41
Houghton, Ann Eliza, 22
Houghton Library (Harvard): Dickinson Collection, 1, 34, 69, 191n30 (*see also* Dickinson family library); Dickinson piano in, 107, 210n16, 218n61; Harvard Theatre Collection, 8
"How doth the little busy bee" (Watts), 2, 145, 219n2
Howe, Elias, 136, 140, 149, 218n51
Howe, Julia Ward, 157, 223n22
Howland, William, 68, 200n14
Humphrey, Jane, 111, 156
Hünten, Franz, 30, 72, 188n45
Hutchinson Family Singers, 3, 71, 113–14, 118–19, 122–25, 136, 182, 185–86n11, 213n24, 213n27
hymns, 153–61; ED's familiarity with New England hymnody, 1–2, 16,

hymns (*continued*)
21, 153, 155; female hymnists, 157; hymnbooks, 13, 16, 21, 33–34, 37, 112, 156, 225n3; influence on ED's poetry, 2, 16, 34, 153, 155–61, 168, 169, 171, 189n54; Watts's hymns popular, 21. *See also specific hymn writers, hymnbooks, hymns, and tunes*

Hyry, Tom, 189n60

"I dreaded that first Robin, so" (ED), 148

"I Dreamt I Dwelt in Marble Halls" (Balfe), 79, 188n44. See also *The Bohemian Girl*

"I dwell in Possibility — " (ED), 18

"If I'm lost — now — / That I was found — " (ED), 155

"I had a guinea golden" (ED), 161

"I have a Bird in spring" (ED), 79, 80–81, 145, 204n71

"I know that He exists" (ED), 155

"I know that my Redeemer liveth" (Handel), 74

"I Like to see it lap the miles" (ED), 95–96, 138, 217n38

"I Love to Steal Awhile Away" (Brown), 157–58, 223n23

"The Indian Girl, or Bright Alfarata" (M. D. Sullivan), 120, *121*, 213n16. See also "The Blue Juniata"

instrumental music: musical culture and, 109–10, 210n26; preferred by ED, 15, 106, 109. *See also* bands; banjo; piano; sheet music; *specific genres and works*

Ipswich Female Seminary, 35

Irish immigrants: and African Americans, 133, 138, 217n39; anti-Irish sentiment, 116–17, 119–20; Dickinson family servants, 78, 165–66 (*see also* servants of Dickinson family); laborers, 95, 138

"It is a lonesome Glee — " (ED), 147

"It will be Summer — eventually" (ED), 172–73

Ives, Charles E., 17, 128, 170–72

Ives, George Edward, 128, 170

Ivison, Henry, Jr., 91–92

Jackson, Helen Fiske Hunt, 120–22, 126, 192n13, 213n22

Jane Eyre (Brontë), 57

Japan, 60

"Japonica Waltz," 58, 60, 179

Jefferys, Charles, 88, 182, 210n12. *See also* "The Rose of Allandale"

Jenkins, MacGregor, 142, 151

"Jenny Lind's Celebrated Bird Song" (Taubert). *See* "Bird Song"

"Jerusalem, my happy home!" (hymn), 189n4

"Jim Along Josey" (minstrel tune), 133

"Jim Crow" (minstrel song), 133

"John Anderson My Jo" (song), 111, 112

John Ashton & Co., 85

Johnson, Thomas, 2, 81, 105, 156, 203–4n70, 210n13, 222n13

"The Jolly Raftsman" (minstrel song), 132, 133, 183, 188n42, 225n2

Jones, Amelia D., 36–37, 42–43, 194–95n77

J. S. & C. Adams Co., 191–92n13

"The Juniata Quick Step" ("The Blue Juniata"; arr. Burditt), 70, 109, 115, 120, *178*, 188n42, 188n44. *See also* "The Blue Juniata"

J. W. Smith Dry Goods Company (Geneva, NY), 89, 206n25

Kansas, 125

Kaplan, Amy, 122, 126

Kelley, Tom, 138, 166

Kellogg, William, 86, 88

Kemble, Fanny, 202n49

Kendall, Edward ("Ned"), 65, 66–69, 99

Kendall, Emily, 68

Kendall, James, 66–68

Kendall, Mary Jane, 68

Kimball, Moses, 62, 85

Kingsley, George, 41, 220n22

"Kinloch of Kinloch": tune, 181; variations (Moran), 61, 176, 215n1

knowing without telling, 148

Know Nothings, 119
Kosovsky, Robert, 10
Kotzwara, Franz, 72, 177. *See also* "Battle of Prague"
Kreutzer, Rodolphe, 38, 106–9, 175, 210n22. See also *Lodoïska*
Krummel, Donald, 109

Labitzky, Joseph, 48, 52, 71, 72, 179
"Lady of Beauty" (W. Knyvett), 216n22
"The Lament of the Alpine Shepherd Boy" (Brown), 68
"The Lament of the Irish Emigrant" (Mrs. P. Blackwood; W. R. Dempster), 181–82, 185n11, 188n44
"The Lancers Quick Step" (F. L. Raymond), 24
"The Last Rose of Summer": in concerts, 68, 77–78; piano variations (Miné), 38, 41, 109, 176, 202n52; referenced in ED's correspondence, 111
Lee, Abigail Eloise Stearns, 139–40, 218n47
Lee & Walker's Music Store & Circulating Library (Philadelphia), 50
Leffler, Adam, 85, 86, 87, 205n15
Le-Kaw hing, 63–64
Leland, John, 19, 23
Lenschow, Charles. *See* Germania Musical Society
Leonora (W. H. Fry), 50–51, 69, 134
Letters from Under a Bridge (N. P. Willis), 55, 197n47
"Letter to a Young Contributor" (Higginson), 146
Leyda, Jay, 5, 9, 48
The Life and Letters of Emily Dickinson (Bianchi), 3
The Life and Mind of Emily Dickinson (Taggard). *See* Taggard, Genevieve
The Life of Emily Dickinson (Sewall), 4
Lincoln, Abraham, 128
Lind, Jenny, 14, 73–79, 84, 88, 162–64, *164*, 201–2n41, 202n43, 202n47, 202n52, 202–3n55, 224n2, 224n5

"Linden Waltz" (Burgmüller), 58, 180, 215n1
Lines, Julia, 32
"The Little Maid" (Hutchinson), 183, 185n11
"Locomotive Quick Step" (Chadwick), 93, 177–78
Loder, Edward James, 86, 205n10, 205n15
Lodoïska (Kreutzer), 38, 106–9, 175, 210n22; four-hand piano overture, 9, 12, 15, 106–7, 175
"Long, Long Ago" (Bayly), 64, 144, 148, 188n44, 199n88
Longfellow, Henry Wadsworth, 54–55, 120
Lord, Otis, 46, 154
Lott, R. Allen, 70
"Louisville March and Quick Step" (Peters), 53–54, 140, 177
"Love Not" (Blockley), 42, 109, 177, 194n76
Lowenberg, Carlton, 5–6, 34
"Lucy Neal" (tune; quickstep arr.), 43, 68–69, 178, 188n42, 188n44, 215n1
Lyon, Lucy, 63
Lyon, Mary, 13, 28–29, 35, 37, 39–40, 63, 124, 157, 193n50, 207n38. *See also* Mount Holyoke Female Seminary

Mack, David, Jr., 20, 125
Mack, Rosina, 78, 137
Mackay, Charles, 113–14, 133, 182
"Magnum bonum" (ED/Emmett), 135, 143
Maher, Margaret (Maggie), 78, 138, 162
Maid as Muse (Murray), 137, 218n50
"Maiden Weep No More" (tune), 24, 191n30
Manifest Destiny, 122
"Manifest Domesticity" (Kaplan), 122, 126
"March and Quick Step in the Battle of Prague" (Kotzwara). *See* "Battle of Prague"

marches, in Dickinson's music book, 9, 10, *11*, 12, 66, 98, 102, 140, 176–77. *See also specific marches*
Marsh's Music Saloon (Springfield, MA), 85
Martin, Wendy, 47, 156
Mason, Lowell, 21, 34–36, 40–41, 156, 158, 191n30, 222n18, 225n3. *See also* "Morning Star"; *The Vocalist*
A Masque of Poets (anthology), 213n22
Mattfeld, Julius, 13, 188n44
Matthews, Richard (Dick), 138
McClellan, George, 46, 128
McDowell, Marta, 59, 60
Melodeon (Boston), 64
Melville, Herman, 54, 171
meter, 2, 16, 155–56, 158, 159, 171–72, 222n11, 222n13
Mexican-American War, 43–44, 195n79, 195n82
Meyer-Frazier, Petra, 7–8
militias, 93, 98, 208n15
Miller, Cristanne, 2, 73, 132, 160, 169, 171, 225n3, 225n5
Miné, Jacques Claude Adolphe, 72, 188n45
minstrel music, 3, 132–36; in ED's music book, 9, 10, 15, 132–33, 169, 183, 188n42; ED's piano improvisations and, 143–44; and ED's poetry, 132, 169, 215n4; olios, 199n77. *See also* Harmoneon Family; "Old Dan Tucker"; *specific songs*
missionaries, 37, 45, 63, 207n38
"Missionary Hymn" (Mason tune), 34
Mitchell, Donald Grant, 57
modernism, 17, 170–71, 226nn9–10
Mohawk Valley region, 90–93
"Money Musk" (fiddle tune), 139–40
Moon, Krystyn, 61
"The Moon Was Shining Silver Bright" (song), 118–19. *See also* "Old Dan Tucker"
Moore, Thomas, 41, 109, 110, 182–83, 194n73
Moran, Peter K., 60–61, 176
Morgan, Victoria, 2, 157, 158–59

"The Morning after Wo — " (ED), 156
"Morning Star" (Mason), 225n3
"Mountain Song" (from *The Vocalist*), 42
Mount Holyoke Female Seminary, 13, 28–29; annual journal letters, 41–42, 193n50, 193n52, 194n62, 194n75, 195n79, 201n34; catalogs, 191–92n13; ED at, 13, 28–29, 34, 36–45, 111, 157; entrance exams and course requirements, 28, 191n13; founder, 35; Hutchinson Family concert, 124, 213n24; and missionaries, 37, 45, 63, 207n38; music books and textbooks, 40–42, 57, 135, 220n22, 222n18; religious evangelism at, 37–38, 193n50, 193n52; vocal music instruction, 35–37, 39–42, 194n62, 195n77. *See also* Lyon, Mary
Moynihan, Dan, 166
Mozart, Wolfgang Amadeus, 41, 81, 146
"The Much Admired Waltz" (arr. Valentine), 110, 179
Mullaney-Dignam, Karol, 217n40
Murray, Aífe, 137, 162–63, 218n50
Musard, Philippe, 50, 181
music: Afro-Caribbean and Irish exchanges, 133, 138; community and local relationships commemorated through, 33; as feminine domestic activity, 8, 14, 47–48, 102; modernism, 17, 170–71, 226nn9–10; sentimentality in, 86, 105–6, 109, 160–61. *See also* concerts and concert scene; musical culture; musical education of Dickinson; music education; musicality of Dickinson; *specific genres, composers, performers, and groups*
musical culture: ED engaged with, 72–73, 82–83 (*see also* musicality of Dickinson); growth of, in America, 50–51, 65, 172, 186n18, 204n78; instrumental music and, 109–10, 210n26; modernism, 17, 170–72; music as part of genteel education, 23; novelty appreciated,

131–32; orchestral music and, 81–83; popular/vernacular music and, 3–4, 127, 131–32 (*see also* bands); virtuosi and, 72–73. *See also* concerts and concert scene; musical virtuosi; music education; popular music; singing schools; vernacular music; *specific composers, works, and performers*

musical education of Dickinson: at Amherst Academy, 27; ED's ambition for music, 22, 23–24, 190n27 (*see also under* musicality of Dickinson); at Mount Holyoke, 13, 37–43; piano method book, 22, 24; piano studies, 3, 12–13, 21–25; vocal instruction, 20–21, 40–42. *See also* piano

musicality of Dickinson: ambitions, 22, 23–24, 149–50, 167, 190n27; clef reading, 156, 222n18; earlier biographers on, 4–5; early interest and aptitude, 21–23; and her poetry (generally), 16, 144, 172–73; industrialization and, 96; influence of virtuosi, 70–72 (*see also* musical virtuosi); instrumental music preferred, 15, 106, 109; reaction to Lind's singing, 75–77 (*see also* Lind, Jenny); transition from music to poetry, 144, 145–50, 152–53, 168–69, 172. *See also* musical education of Dickinson; musicality of Dickinson's poetry; nature: music of; piano; *specific types of music*

musicality of Dickinson's poetry: compositional musicality, 5, 16–18, 170–71; Cooley on ED's musical studies and, 4–5; ED's responses to music and, 79–81, 83 (*see also specific performers and composers*); generally, 16, 18, 144, 172–73; meter, 2, 155–56, 158, 159, 171–72, 222n11, 222n13; modernism, 17, 170–71; Rubinstein concert and, 151–52; scholars and writers on, 2, 170–71 (*see also specific authors*); settings of ED's poetry, 5, 170–71, 226n13. *See also* poetry of Dickinson

musical virtuosi, 14, 70–83. *See also* American band movement; *specific individuals*

Musical World (journal), 30, 54

Musica Sacra (Oneida Musical Society), 33

music book of Dickinson, 1, 167; American social and political issues reflected, 43–44, 115–29; annotated bibliography (online), 17; band repertoire, 65–66, 68–70 (*see also* bands); binding of, 9–10, 144, 150; Civil War music, 15, 127–29, 214n40, 214n44; contents listed, 5–6, *11*, 175–83; current location, 1; dates of collection, 9, 12–13; digitization and access, 10; and ED's turn to poetry, 18, 149–50; female seminaries and, 28–43; front cover, 7; handwritten fingerings and markings, 24, 107, 210n14; home as musical subject, 48; index, handwritten, 10, *11*; New York State affiliations in, 90–93; popularity of pieces in, 12–13; prominent composers and pedagogues included, 72; publishers represented, 13, 50–51 (*see also* music publishers); The Red Skies Music Ensemble programs and, 6, 187n30; size, scope, and organization, 9–12, *11*, 107; as transformative link to ED as musician/poet, 16; travel and foreign lands evoked, 45, 60–62, 64. *See also* bound volumes of music; fiddle tunes; marches; minstrel music; opera; polkas; quadrille; quicksteps; sheet music; songs; variation sets; vernacular music; waltzes; *specific works*

music education (generally), 3, 13, 20–21, 27–35, 37–43. *See also* musical education of Dickinson; piano: pedagogy

"Musicians wrestle everywhere — " (ED), 16–17, 81, 168–72; "Before the heavens were spread abroad" (Watts), 225n3

Musicians Wrestle Everywhere (Lowenberg), 5–6
"Music in the Life and Poetry of Emily Dickinson" (Reglin), 4
The Music of Emily Dickinson's Poems and Letters: A Study of Imagery and Form (Cooley), 4–5
music publishers: Boston publishers, 13, 85; minstrel music popularized, 133; misleading marketing, 87; music of composer/teachers published, 26, 34; in New York City, 140; Peters, 53–54; in Philadelphia, 49–50; sheet music marketed, 8, 47; of tunebooks, 140; variety of music, 109; vernacular tunes available from, 12, 24; waltzes misattributed to Beethoven, 51–52 (*see also* Beethoven, Ludwig van). *See also* sheet music; *specific publishers*
music stores, 33, 50, 53, 85. *See also* music publishers
"My Faith is larger than the Hills — " (ED), 159
"My Life had Stood — a Loaded Gun — " (ED), 169, 225n5
"My Lodging Is on the Cold Ground" (song), 110. *See also* "Believe Me If All Those Endearing Young Charms"

Nash, Margaret A., 28
The National Clay Melodist (ed. Warland), 119, 212n9
Native Americans, 15, 120–22, *121*, 126–27, 214n39. *See also* "The Blue Juniata"
nature: and the divine, in ED's thought, 27, 154, 155, 159; ED's love of, 57, 58; music of, 145–48, 151–52, 219n9. *See also* garden and gardening
Ned Kendall's Boston Brass Band, 65–68. *See also* Kendall, Edward
"Nelly Bly" (S. Foster), 88
Nelson, Samuel, 41, 182. *See also* "The Rose of Allandale"
Nettleton, Asahel, 21, 37, 112, 155–57, 223n23. *See also Village Hymns*
New England, 16–17, 170–72. *See also* hymns; Ives, Charles E.; *specific locations*
"New feet within my garden go — " (ED), 137, 140
"The New Foundland Dog" (Russell), 57–58, 198n52
Newman, Clara, 143, 218n61
Newman, Mark Haskell, 34, 92, 143, 193n35
New Orleans Serenaders Opera Company, 134
Newport, Amos ("old Amos"), 138, 218n50
newspapers, Dickinson family and, 115–16. *See also specific publications*
New York (state), 90–93, 98. *See also locations and institutions*
New York City: concerts and concert scene, 61, 69, 73–74, 81–82, 86–87, 133; minstrel music in, 133; music publishers, 140
The New York Public Library for the Performing Arts, 8
"No Black bird bates His Banjo — " (ED), 132, 215n4
Noble, Marianne, 47
noon, 16, 146
Norcross, Betsey Fay (grandmother of ED), 157
Norcross, Emily (mother of ED). *See* Dickinson, Emily Norcross
Norcross, Emily Lavinia (cousin of ED), 36, 39–40
Norcross, Frances (cousin of ED), 111–12, 152, 219n66
Norcross, Joel (uncle of ED), 134, 135
Norcross, Lavinia (aunt of ED), 12–13, 21–23, 62, 117
Norcross, Louisa (cousin of ED), 111–12, 152, 202n49, 219n66
Norcross family, 21–22, 46, 62, 111–12, 129, 199n80, 215n54. *See also specific individuals*
Norma (Bellini), 68, 69, 76, 87–88, 106, 140, 176–77, 205n19
Northampton, Massachusetts: band concerts, 65–66; Edwards Church,

21 (*see also* Watts, Isaac); Hutchinson Family concerts, 123; Lind concert, 14, 73–78, 163, 202n43; "lunatic hospital," 94

O'Brien, Margaret, 78, 137
The Odeon (Webb & Mason), 40–41, 222n18
Offenbach, Jacques, 62, 84–85, 181
"Oft in the Stilly Night" (Moore; J. Stevenson), 41
"Oh, Susannah!" (S. Foster), 216n22
"Oh Give Me a Home If in Foreign Land" (M. S. Pike; L. V. H. Crosby), 115, 126–27, 183, 188n42
"Oh God Our Help in Ages Past" (Watts; W. Croft), 158–59, 171
"Oh the Merry Days When We Were Young" (anon.; sung by Mrs. Wood), 85–87, 185–86n11, 205n10, 205n15
"Oh the Merry Days When We Were Young" (Loder; sung by Leffler), 85–86, 87, 205n10, 205n15
Oja, Carol, 170, 171, 226n9
"The Old Arm Chair" (Cook; Russell), 71, 106, 160, 181
"Old Dan Tucker" (minstrel song; tune), 183; composer, 133; in ED's music book, 15, 115, 133, 188n42, 188n44; illustrated cover, 132; "Magnum bonum" based on, 135, 143; other lyrics set to, 118–19, 124, 212n10; Runzo on, 3, 134–35
"The Old Granite State" (Hutchinson), 182, 185n11, 188n44
"Old Zip Coon" (Rice; trad. tune), 132
olios, 199n77
Oliver Ditson & Co., 24, 56, 85, 105, 110, 176–80, 182–83, 195n81, 202n41, 223n22
opera: American interest in, 132; bel canto singing, 76–77, 202n54 (*see also* Lind, Jenny); blackface burlesques of, 134; four-hand overture (Kreutzer), 9, 12, 15, 106–7, 175 (see also *Lodoïska*); popularity in the United States, 77, 203n60; selections in ED's music book, 41, 50–51, 69, 72, 77, 79, 87–88, 106–7. *See also specific composers and works*
orchestras, 81–82. *See also* Germania Musical Society
Ordway's Aeolians, 134, 216n16
"Ossian's Serenade" (Dodge), 88, 163, 164
"Our Native Song" (Russell), 71, 182
Overture to *Lodoïska* (Kreutzer). See *Lodoïska*
Owego, New York, 54–55, 197n47

"Panharmonic March," 140, 181
Panormo, Francis (Francesco), 50, 179. *See also* "Bird Waltz"
Parker, Samuel H., 110. *See also* Oliver Ditson & Co.
parlor songs. *See* ballads; songs
Pascoe, Judith, 75, 163
Pelham, R. W. (Dick), 133. *See also* Virginia Minstrels
performance persona of Dickinson, 4, 6, 16, 161, 162–65. *See also* white dress
performers. *See* American band movement; musical virtuosi; *specific performers and ensembles*
Pestalozzi, Johann Heinrich, 34
Peters, William Cumming, 53–54, 72, 177, 180, 188n45
Philadelphia, 49–50
Philadelphia Courier, 125
Philadelphia Press, 128
Philharmonic Society of New York, 69, 81–82
Phillips, Elizabeth, 163
piano: beginner repertoire, 24; Dickinson family pianos, 9, 22–23, 107, 143, 190n26, 210n16, 218–19n61; eclipsed by nature, 16, 146–48; ED's early interest in, 21–22; ED's father and her piano playing, 14, 101–2; ED's skill, 15, 106–7; ED's studies, 3, 12–13, 21–25, 37–38 (*see also* musical education of Dickinson); improvisations by ED, 3, 15, 141–44, 147,

piano (*continued*)
218n58, 218n60, 218–19n61; "old, odd tunes" played, 167; pedagogy, 22, 30, 204n80 (*see also* Bertini, Henri); previous biographers on ED's playing, 3–5; Rubinstein concert and ED's playing, 149–53. *See also specific musical works*

poetry of Dickinson: belief and disbelief in, 154–55; bird imagery in, 77, 79, 80–81, 105, 145–48, 169, 209n4, 215n4; breathlessness of, 170; Civil War and, 127–29, 214nn41–42; editors (*see* Higginson, Thomas Wentworth; Todd, Mabel Loomis); first poems, 145, 219n1; hymns' influence on, 2, 16, 21, 34, 155–61, 168, 169, 171, 189n54; Irish and African American influences, 165–66; jotted during kitchen duties, 137; Lind and, 14, 79 (*see also* Lind, Jenny); meter, 2, 16, 155–56, 158, 159, 171–72, 222n11, 222n13; modernism, 17, 170–71; musical imagery and references in, 144–48, 160, 168–69, 172–73; musical settings of, 5, 170–71, 226n13; New England aesthetic, 16–17, 169–73; poetic performance persona, 6, 16, 161, 162–65; publication of, 146, 213n22; sacred vs. secular, 156–57; shaped by ED's engagement with music (generally), 16, 168–70; "slant" lines, 105, 209n5; songs and ballads and, 48, 160–61, 166–67, 171; transition from music to poetry, 144, 145–50, 152–53, 168–69, 172; unconventional nature of, 146. *See also* musicality of Dickinson's poetry; *specific poems*

politics: 1840s–50s, 114; abolitionist movement, 118–19, 122–25; Dickinson family and, 112, 117; Edward Dickinson and, 14, 49, 94, 101, 112, 119–20, 208n26; Mount Holyoke students isolated from, 43; political issues reflected in ED's music book, 115–29. *See also* Know Nothings; territorial expansion; Whig Party

Polk, James K., 116

"Polka Dance" (Offenbach). *See* "The Celebrated Polka Dance"

polkas: in ED's music book, 9, 10, *11*, 12, 62, 84–85, 92, 180–81; "lounge polka" referred to, 144; popularity and origin, 12, 207n40. *See also specific works*

Pollack, Vivian, 47

Pollitt, Josephine, 220n28

popular music: popular music culture (nineteenth century), 2–4, 70; popular pieces (1843–1844), 13, 188n44; sentimental songs, 86, 105–6, 109. *See also* bands; musical culture; musical virtuosi; songs; vernacular music; *specific composers, performers, and works*

Positive as Sound: Emily Dickinson's Rhyme (J. J. Small), 2

"Prize Banner Quick Step" (Haskell), 101, 115, 177

Proctor, Joseph, 68, 200n15

Progressive and Complete Method for the Piano-forte (Bertini), 22, 24, 30

Psalms, Hymns, and Spiritual Songs (Watts), 21, 37, 40, 156, 194n66

"Publication — is the Auction / Of the Mind of Man — " (ED), 163–64

Pugh, Christina, 147

pussy willow, 59

quadrille, in ED's music book, 9, 10, *11*, 12, 50, 180

quicksteps, in ED's music book, 9, 10, *11*, 12, 66, 93, 97–101, 102, 115, 177–78. *See also specific works*

quince (flowering quince), 60

railroads, 94–97, 138, 207n5. *See also* "I Like to see it lap the miles"

"The Railway Train" (ED), 95–96

Rainer Family, 71

Ramona (Jackson), 120, 126

Rassely, Charles W., 185n1

reading clubs, 138–39
Reading in Time: Emily Dickinson in the Nineteenth Century (Miller), 2
The Red Skies Music Ensemble, ix, xi, 6, 17–18, 187n30
Reglin, Louise W., 4
religion. *See* beliefs of Dickinson; Dickinson family: religious beliefs; hymns; missionaries; Transcendentalism
Religious Lectures on Peculiar Phenomena in the Four Seasons (Hitchcock), 27, 192n13
Reveries of a Bachelor (Mitchell), 57
Rice, Thomas Dartmouth ("Daddy"), 132
robins, 77, 80–81, 145, 148, 161, 169. *See also* bird imagery
"The Robin's my Criterion for Tune — " (ED), 77, 189n55
Rochester Union Grays, 93, 100, 177, 208n24
"Rockaway Waltzes" (Glynn), 100, 180
"Rock of Ages" (Hastings), 33
"Roderick Dhu's March," 94, 128, 177
Roosevelt, Theodore, and siblings, 69, 201n26
Root, Abiah, 67, 138
Root, Abiah, ED's letters to: on "Are We Almost There?" 104–5; on Boston entertainments, 62–64; on bread-making, 136; deletions made by Root, 190n10; on Eastcott, 67; on entering society, 46; on her beliefs, 38, 154, 155; on her education, 22; on her father's requests for music, 102, 209n29; on her health, 44; on her music lessons, 21, 23–25, 44, 219n66; on Miss Adams's departure, 92–93; on Mount Holyoke, 37, 191n13; Root's story requested, 118; on the seasons, 155, 222n7; on wishing she were someone else, 154, 173
"The Rose of Allandale" (Jefferys & Nelson), 106, 127, 160, 182, 210n12
Ross, Christine, 222n11

Rossini, Gioachino, 41, 66, 72, 106, 176, 200n15
Rubinstein, Anton, 149–53, 220n28
Runzo, Sandra, 2–3, 54, 134–35, 151, 165, 213n24
Russell, Henry, 54–55, 58, 70–71, 113, 160, 181–82, 186n18, 197n46, 204n78
"Russian March" (tune), 140, 177

sacred music, 33–34. *See also* hymns
"Safe in their Alabaster Chambers — " (ED), 146
Santa Anna, Antonio López de, 44, 195n82
Scanlon, Dennis, 166
Scotch-Irish music, 78. *See also specific pieces*
Scott, Winfield, 43
Selby, Ann Elizabeth Vaill ("Aunt"), 23–24, 190n26
A Selection of Irish Melodies, 110
sentimentality, in music, 86, 105–6, 109, 160–61
servants of Dickinson family: ED's interactions with, 137–40, 162–63, 165–67; music-making by, 15, 78, 138–40, 141; none before 1850, 136–37. *See also specific individuals*
settings of Dickinson's poetry, 5, 170–71, 226n13
Sewall, Richard, 4, 23, 28, 148–50, 156, 158, 170, 172, 209n6, 225n19
Seward, William H., 97
Shadle, Douglas, 82
sheet music: associated with New York State in ED's music book, 90–93; associated with the Woods, 85–88, 205n10, 205n15; bound volumes (generally), 7–9; collected by Dickinson family members, 9–10, 14, 69, 72, 84–88, 106, 163; ED's acquisition/consumption of, 9, 12–14, 47–48, 84–85; eighteenth- and nineteenth-century production and marketing of, 8; misleading marketing, 87; piano editions of fiddle or vernacular tunes, 140;

sheet music (*continued*)
protective wrappers, 109; women as consumers of, 7–9, 47, 196n14. *See also* music book of Dickinson; music publishers; music stores; *specific genres and works*

"The Show is not the Show" (ED), 77, 150

"Sic transit gloria mundi" (ED), 145

"The Silver Moon" (J. W. Turner), 42

Sinclair, John, 116, *117*, 182, 212nn4–5. *See also* "The Bonnie Clay Flag"

singing groups, 71–72. *See also specific groups*

singing schools, 3, 20–21, 33, 35

slavery. *See* abolitionist movement

"Sleep is supposed to be" (ED), 49

Small, Christopher, 21

Small, Judy Jo, 2, 149

Smith, Carleton Sprague, 70

Smith, Christopher, 134

Smith, Jewel, 41

Smith, John Finley, 91–92, 180, 206n33

Smith, John Williams, 89, 206n25

Smith, Martha Nell, 90, 142

Smith, William, 31–32, 178. *See also* "Home Quick Step"

Snyder, Rudolph, 33

The Social Choir (ed. Kingsley), 41, 57, 220n22

"Some keep the Sabbath going to Church — " (ED), 47, 158

"The Song of Blanche Alpen" (Jefferys & Glover), 88

songs: categories, 196n14; in ED's music book, 3, 9, 10–12, *11*, 40–41, 64, 71–72, 101, 106, 113–14, 181–83, 202n52, 210n12; influence on ED's poetry, 16, 156, 160 (*see also* hymns); Lavinia and, 15, 71, 85–88; sentimental songs, 86, 105–6, 109, 160–61. *See also* vocal music; *specific songs*

La Sonnambula (Bellini), 86, 87, 134

Sontag, Henriette, 71, 78–79, 203n67

sound, ED and, 80–81, 147–48. *See also* bird imagery; musicality of Dickinson; musicality of Dickinson's poetry

"Sounds From Home" (Gung'l), 45, 48, 52, 112, 179, 195n93

"Spanish Dance" (two tunes), 24, 181

"Spanish Retreat." *See* "The Celebrated Spanish Retreat"

Spaulding and Rogers North American Circus, 68

"Speed the Plough" (tune; var. Dutton), 32, 90, 106, 141, 176, 215n1

Spice Islands, 45, 60, 198n71

Springfield, Massachusetts: concerts, 65, 66–67, 69, 74, 108, 134, 150, 200n16, 201n36, 205n19; music stores, 85

Springfield Daily Republican, 115, 212n1; on the Albany Burgesses Corps, 100; Andrews and Maeder concert listed, 205n19; "Battle Hymn of the Republic" printed, 223n22; ED an avid reader of, 115–16; on the Hancock Light Infantry's visit, 99; on the Hutchinsons Family concert, 213n27; on Lind, 73–74, 76, 163, 202–3n55, 224n5; on the Mexican-American War, 43; minstrel groups advertised, 134; on Mount Holyoke exhibitions, 39; *The National Clay Melodist* reviewed, 119; obituary for ED, 217n41; on the *Polaris* expedition, 152–53; political leanings, 117–18; on the Prize Banner, 101; publishers, 46, 89–90; Rubinstein concert advertised, 150; "Tale of Poland" reprinted, 108; on the Westfield band, 66

Stace, Mary. *See* Willis, Mary Stace

"St. Anne" (Croft), 159, 171. *See also* "Oh God Our Help in Ages Past"

Stanton, Luke W., 31–32, 178

St. Armand, Barton Levi, 2

Stearns, Frazar, 129–30, 214n53, 214–15n54, 218n47, 219n66

Stearns, William Augustus, 106, 129, 139, 214–15n54

Steele, Silas, 61, 199n76

Steyermarkische Orchestra, 52, 71. *See also* Gung'l, Josef
Stibbins, Mr., 20
Stoever, Jennifer Lynn, 186n20
Strakosch, Maurice, 71, 201n33
Strauss, Johann, 52, 66, 202n41
Strickland, Georgiana, 49–50, 190n14, 193n35
"Success is counted sweetest" (ED), 213n22
Sullivan, Marion Dix, 109, 120. *See also* "The Blue Juniata"
Sullivan, Stephen, 166
Sweetser, Joseph, 148, 150
Sweetser, Luke, 88, 95, 106, 138
"Swiss Guards March" (tune), 181
"The Swiss Waltz" (tune; var. by Moran), 60–61, 140, 176
symphony orchestras, 81–82
Syracuse, New York, 92–93, 97
"Syracuse Polka" (J. A. Fowler), 29, 31, 92, 181, 207n38

Taggard, Genevieve, 3, 101–2
"Take Them, I Implore Thee" ("Deh conte"; Bellini), 87, 176, 205n19. *See also Norma*
tambourine, 168–69, 225n2
Tancredi (Rossini), 106, 176
Taubert, Wilhelm, 76, 202n52. *See also* "Bird Song"
Tawa, Nicholas, 87
Taylor, Jeremiah (teacher), 64
Taylor, Richard B. *See* "Aeolian Waltz"
"Tell all the truth but tell it slant — " (ED), 209n5
"Ten O'clock! or, Remember Love Remember" (song), 102, 209n29
territorial expansion, 120–22, 126
"That Pretty Little Gal" (tune), 127, 214n39. *See also* "The Girl I Left Behind Me"
"Theatricals of Day": Emily Dickinson and Nineteenth-Century American Popular Culture (Runzo), 2–3
"Then You'll Remember Me" (Balfe), 79, 188n44. *See also The Bohemian Girl*
"There's a Good Time Coming" (Russell; Hutchinsons & White), 113–14, 182, 185n11, 213n27
"This is my letter to the World" (ED), 159, 171
This Was a Poet: A Critical Biography of Emily Dickinson (Whicher). *See* Whicher, George Frisbie
"This was in the White of the Year" (ED), 222n19
Thompson, Charles, 139–40, 218n47
Thoreau, Henry David, 17, 171
"'Tis not that Dying hurts us so — " (ED), 130, 215n56
Todd, David Peck, 165
Todd, Mabel Loomis, 5, 81, 96, 146, 164–65, 203–4n70, 207n5
Tolman, Susan, 39, 41–42, 193n50, 193n52, 194n62, 195n79
Town and Country (magazine), 56, 197n48
Transcendentalism, 82, 123. *See also specific individuals*
travel, ED's interest in, 13, 45, 60–64
T'sow Chaoong, 63–64
Tubman, Harriet, 97
"The Tulip" (ED), 59
"Tulip Waltz," 58, 59, 179
"Turkey in the Straw" (fiddle tune), 132, 215n6
Turner, Clara Newman, 143, 218n61
Turner, Joseph W., 42–43, 178, 195n81
Twain, Mark, 133

umbrellas, 85
Underground Railroad, 97, 124
Unger, Ferdinand, 48, 179
Uno, Hiroko, 64
Utica Female Academy, 32–33, 89, 92, 192n31
Utica Musical Academy, 33, 90–91

"Valentine" (ED), 135
Valentine, Thomas, 72, 110, 176, 188n45

Vane, Florence, 105
variation sets, in ED's music book, *11*, 83, 87–88, 106, 110, 175–76. *See also specific works*
Variety Music Cavalcade (Mattfeld), 13
Vendler, Helen, 215n4
vernacular music: in ED's music book, *11*, 12, 15, 24–25, 61, 131–32, 136, 140–41, 181–83, 215n1; ED's piano improvisations and, 143–44; servants' music-making, 15, 78, 138–40; tunebooks, 140–41, 218n51. *See also* fiddle tunes; minstrel music; songs; *specific pieces*
Village Hymns (Nettleton), 21, 37, 40, 112, 155–57, 194n66, 223n23
Virginia Minstrels, 133, 136, 183
Virginia Serenaders, 134
The Vocalist: Consisting of Short and Easy Glees (Mason & Webb), 40, 41–42, 135–36, 191n30, 194n66, 194n74
vocal music: bel canto singing and repertoire, 76, 77, 202n54; collections published by M. H. Newman, 34; in ED's music book, 3, 8–9, 10, *11*, 40–41, 64, 71–72, 77, 101, 106, 113–14, 181–83, 202n54; instruction at Mount Holyoke, 35–37, 39–42, 194n62, 195n77; secular music books, 40–41; sentimentality in, 86, 105–6; singing groups, 71–72 (*see also specific groups*); singing schools, 3, 20–21, 33, 35. *See also* hymns; opera; songs; *specific composers and performers*
"Von Weber's Last Waltz" (Weber), 52, 179

Wadsworth, Charles, 50
waltzes: in ED's music book, 9, 10, *11*, 12–14, 48, 50–61, *55*, *56*, 69–70, 82–83, 178–80, 195n93, 210n12; in honor of Lind, 202n41; misattributed to Beethoven, 51–52, 82–83, 110, 178–79; popularity of, 12
"warbling Teller," 105, 209n4
Ward, Pat, 166

Ward, Theodora, 81, 203–4n70
Warland, John Henry, 116–18, *117*, 182, 212n5. *See also* "The Bonnie Clay Flag"
"Watchman! Tell us of the night" (Bowring; Mason), 34, 225n3
Watson, Henry Coad, 77
Watts, Isaac, 17; ED's familiarity with, 21, 156; influence on ED's poetry, 2, 145, 156–58, 171, 225n3; *Psalms, Hymns, and Spiritual Songs*, 21, 37, 40, 156, 194n66
Webb, George James, 34, 40–41, 191n30, 222n18. *See also The Vocalist*
Weber, Carl Maria von, 41, 52, 71, 179
Webster, Noah, 27, 100
Wells, Paul, 140
Westfield band, 66
West Street home, 20, 23. *See also* Dickinson home
Wetzel, Richard, 53
"When the Swallows Homeward Fly" (F. Abt), 84
"When they come back — if Blossoms do — " (ED), 148, 161
Whicher, George Frisbie, 3–4, 83, 186n16
Whig Party, 14–15, 101, 116–19, 177. *See also* politics
White, Edward Little, 72, 113, 176, 180, 182, 183, 188n45
white dress, 16, 78, 162–65
Whitlock, William (Billy), 133. *See also* Virginia Minstrels; "Who's That Knocking at the Door"
Whitney, Maria, 60
"Who's That Knocking at the Door" (Whitlock; minstrel song), 132, 133, 183, 188n42
Wilder, Laura Ingalls, 213n16
Willard, Emma, 28
William H. Weed (music store, Springfield), 85
Williams, Trudy, ix, xi, 6, 18, 187n30
Willis, Imogen, 56–57, 178
Willis, Mary Stace (Mrs. N. P. Willis), 54, 56, 57

Willis, Nathaniel, Sr., 54
Willis, Nathaniel Parker, 54–55, 57
Willis, Richard (bandmaster), 66
Willis, Richard Storrs (composer/critic), 30, 51, 54, 55, 56–57, 77–78, 178
Willis, Sara Payson, 54
"Willow Waltz," 58, 59–60, 179
Wilson, Charles, 100, 177. *See also* "Camp Barnum Quick Step"
women: as consumers of sheet music, 7–9, 47, 196n14; education of, 27–29 (*see also* female seminaries and academies); female hymnists, 157; music as feminine domestic activity, 8, 14, 47–48, 102. *See also specific individuals*

Wood, Mary Anne Paton, 71, 85–88, 203n60
Woodman, Mr., 20–21
"Wood Up" (Holloway), 24, 68–69, 200n21
Wright, William Carey, 192n31

"Yankee Doodle" (tune; variations), 44, 70, 115, 128, 176
The Years and Hours of Emily Dickinson (Leyda), 5
Yellow Face: Creating the Chinese in American Popular Music and Performance (Moon), 61
"You And Me" (ballad), 88
Young, Kit, 17
Youth's Companion, 54

GEORGE BOZIWICK holds degrees from SUNY Oneonta (BA), Hunter College (MA, music composition), and Columbia University (MLS, library service). He is retired as chief of the Music Division of The New York Public Library for the Performing Arts. As a composer, his Magnificat is published by C. F. Peters, and his music is recorded on the Opus One label. He is currently writing an opera on Emily Dickinson and music. Boziwick is co-founder with Trudy Williams of The Red Skies Music Ensemble. They have co-created and co-presented several live musical and theatrical programs on Dickinson and music. He has contributed articles on Emily Dickinson and music to the *Journal of the Society for American Music* and the *Emily Dickinson Journal*. He currently serves on the board of the Emily Dickinson International Society. Boziwick's other interest and expertise is on the history of the song "Take Me Out to the Ball Game" and its connections to the suffrage movement of the early twentieth century. His article on the song was published in the scholarly journal, *Base Ball: A Journal of the Early Game* (2012). He has presented on the song at the Chautauqua Institution, and the National Baseball Hall of Fame and Museum in Cooperstown, New York.